WHITE ANGELS

WHITE ANGELS

John Carlin

BLOOMSBURY

First published in Great Britain 2004
This paperback edition published 2005

Copyright © Enobarbus S.L. 2004, 2005

The right of John Carlin to be identified as the author of this work has been asserted
by him in accordance with the Copyright, Designs and Patents Act 1988

All photographs copyright © Getty Images, Inc.

Bloomsbury Publishing Plc, 36 Soho Square, London W1D 3QY

A CIP catalogue record for this book is available from the British Library

ISBN 0 7475 7348 4
9780747573487

10 9 8 7 6 5 4 3 2 1

All papers used by Bloomsbury Publishing are natural,
recyclable products made from wood grown in well-managed forests.
The manufacturing processes conform to the regulations of the country of origin.

Typeset by Palimpsest Book Production Limited, Polmont, Stirlingshire

Printed in Great Britain by
Clays Ltd, St Ives plc

www.bloomsbury.com/johncarlin

For Sue and James

Contents

Introduction

I went to Africa to write about the AIDS epidemic but all that people kept wanting to talk about was David Beckham and Real Madrid. I shouldn't have been surprised. Barely a week had passed since what would turn out to be – with the arguable exception of the outbreak of war in Iraq – the news story with the greatest global impact of 2003: the transfer of the world's most glamorous footballer to the world's most glamorous club. But what did take me aback, what did leave me open-mouthed in astonishment as my minibus rattled and bumped through Nairobi's biggest slum, the AIDS-plagued labyrinth of Majengo, was the depth of knowledge of my travelling companions; the sheer detail with which the dozen other people in the vehicle debated not just David Beckham's transfer from Manchester United but the other great issue of the day, why Real Madrid's president had sacked the team coach.

'Does anybody – anybody at all – understand why Florentino Pérez got rid of del Bosque?' asked a man seated up at the front, next to the driver. 'I mean,' he said, twisting his body around to address the assembled passengers, 'I don't see the logic in it.' The speaker, as I would later establish, was a young Kenyan doctor. The other people in the minibus, English speakers all, were mostly medical staff headed, as I was, to a clinic in the centre of Majengo where they were conducting tests on a group of prostitutes who appeared to be immune to AIDS; who had failed to become HIV-positive despite years of sadly reckless efforts to succumb to the dreaded disease. But no one in the minibus had a clue who I was, no one knew that the tall, hairy white man jammed into the back right-hand corner of the vehicle had not only flown in from Spain the day before but also happened to be a very keen follower indeed of the beautiful game, especially as practised these days by Real Madrid Club de Fútbol. Which of course made it all the more remarkable to me that the subject had come up in the first place; that the man in the minibus had raised the names of Florentino Pérez and Vicente del Bosque in the clear expectation that everybody would immediately know who they were.

Dumb-founded, I shut up and listened.

'I know,' said a man sitting behind the one at the front who had initiated the discussion. 'It's not exactly as if anyone could accuse Real of having a bad season.'

'Right,' said the man at the front. 'They won the Spanish league and made it to the semi-final of the Champions League. So why then go and fire the coach?' 'Especially,' rejoined the second speaker, 'after the 6–5 win against Man United in the quarter-finals, *and* playing the best football anyone in the world can remember anywhere.' To which the assembled company responded with solemn murmurs and nods all round, and a smile or two of warm reminiscence. Until a man sitting next to me at the back piped up, 'Yes, but you don't understand. The thing about Real Madrid is that they have different standards from other teams. Second or third best is no good. Not acceptable. And especially now with this guy Pérez in charge. Look who he's bought since taking over the club a couple of years ago: Figo, Ronaldo, Zidane. Now Beckham.'

'Plus Roberto Carlos and Raúl are already there,' a voice somewhere in the bus reminded him.

'Yes, plus Roberto Carlos and Raúl. The best players in the world! So,' the wise one at my side continued, 'with that unbelievable collection of superstars you have to win the lot, otherwise the coach gets fired. That's just the way it is.'

The man at the front grimaced, shook his head and looked out of the window. He wasn't totally convinced. Or maybe he had come somehow to share in the sympathy the Spanish man in the street felt for Vicente del Bosque, a good soul whose portly bearing, lugubrious dress-sense and 1950s moustache were heroically at odds with the film-star fashionable footballers he had until three or four days ago coached; del Bosque, far from looking like a man who had himself played in midfield for Real Madrid in his day, evoked images of a kind but world-weary baker leading a life of honest toil in a small town deep in the Castillian meseta. 'I think Pérez had it in for him, for some reason,' said del Bosque's Kenyan defender. 'I read somewhere that Pérez just didn't like the look of him. Bad chemistry.

'No, you are mistaken' said someone else, a couple of rows up from me. 'Pérez is too cool a customer to let his feelings get in the way of a big decision like that . . .'

And so the conversation proceeded, moving from one end of the bus to the other, with me realising very quickly that – on the subject of Real Madrid at least – I had nothing whatsoever to offer these people. Outside our minibus window little children played naked in pools of viscous water, one out of every four adults we saw milling about Majengo's maze of rusty tin shacks had HIV, but their compatriots inside my bus – and I have no doubt a good number of them outside it – were as up to date on developments at Real Madrid as any of my friends back home in Spain. I could have introduced them to Angel the taxi-driver, with whom I go and watch games live on TV at a bar that's wall to wall with framed photographs of Real Madrid teams going back to the glorious Fifties, when the legendary Puskas, Gento and Di Stefano bestrode Europe like colossi. I could have introduced them to Pedro the tropical diseases doctor, whose joy should he succeed in his life's quest to find a cure for malaria would be forever tempered if he failed in his other great mission – to get tickets to watch what he calls this 'unrepeatable' Real Madrid side. I could have introduced them to Sebastián, who's been going through a tough marital separation and does not know how he would have made it without the consolation of a season ticket at Real's hallowed stadium, the Bernabéu. I could have introduced my fellow travellers on that minibus in Majengo to any number of home-grown Real Madrid fanatics and within seconds they would have fallen into conversation as if they had known each other all their lives.

Even if they did not understand each other's languages, football is so universal a medium of communication that what with the odd grunt, hand gesture and mention of evocative names – Ronaldo, Beckham, Florentino – they'd soon be getting on famously, nodding in furious agreement with each other. And then I reflected, sitting on that bus, that the discussion I was hearing was in all certainty being replicated not only in every corner of Spain, not only elsewhere in Kenya and Africa, but all over the world – in France, Germany, Japan, Russia, China. (How could they not be having this conversation in China when on 29 July 2003 in the city of Kunming, 20,000 fans paid between twenty and a hundred dollars each to watch a practice match between Real Madrid's first team and reserves?) They were probably even talking about the Pérez–del Bosque polemic somewhere in the United States, that last pagan bastion where the world's one great unifying religion – the only one to cut across all creeds, races, ideologies, flags – has yet fully to take hold.

The thing about Real Madrid, about that Real Madrid, the one that Florentino built, was that within one team you had the religion's most venerated deities – the holy trinity of David Beckham, Zinedine Zidane and Ronaldo – and in Raúl, Luis Figo and Roberto Carlos three others who, in the summer of 2003, would have made it into the dream eleven of practically every serious football coach in the world. Seven out of the last eight FIFA World Players of the Year played in this Real Madrid team. (The time they missed out, when Rivaldo won in 1999, Beckham came second; in 2001 Figo, Beckham and Raúl were first, second and third.) Even more remarkably, even more utterly without precedent, this team contained the captains of not one, two or three but five of the major footballing nations: England, Brazil, France, Spain and Portugal. Never in the one hundred and fifty year history of the game had such a prime collection of the planet's available talent been concentrated at one club. Football is played in every country in the world. Millions, from the Amazon jungle to the mountains of Tibet, kick a ball around every day. Millions of those millions dream one day of becoming professional footballers. And of all those innumerable souls, six of the best of them emerged from three continents and ended up distilled – pure gold – at Real Madrid. 'Los Galácticos' they call Real's magnificent six in Spain, as if they were cartoon superheroes. And just that, as players who are larger than life, as stars from another galaxy, was how football's vast planetary fraternity saw them. It was on the devotion their genius inspired, more even than the humdrum matter of whether they won or lost, that Real Madrid's global appeal rested. It was the reason why if football were Christianity (though it is much bigger than that – it has far more adepts), Real Madrid would have been the Catholic church – the biggest, most lavish denomination there was.

The devotion can be measured in numbers. Big businesses every-where were offering big money to link their names with Real Madrid's. Apart from large increases in income from stadium atten-dances, TV fees and shirt sales, the club has been making more and more money from companies like Audi and Siemens eager to asso-ciate themselves in the minds of their potential clients with the increasingly powerful brand name 'Real Madrid' – two words that put side by side have become powerfully evocative, bringing to mind notions of elegance, style and class that in the hands of clever marketing people are tools that can be deployed to very profitable effect. All of these reasons and more explain why at the end of the 2002/2003 European football season, even before the Beckham move, Real Madrid had for the first time outstripped Manchester United, according to *World Soccer* magazine, as the world's most profitable club.

Everything suggested that Real Madrid, boosted by Beckham Inc., would consolidate their ascendancy in the coming years. Everything suggested that the Florentino Pérez business model would continue to flourish. It was a revolutionary way to operate in football. Pérez's big idea, right from the start of his presidency in the year 2000, was that if you bought the best players, the very best, you always won out in the end, because they paid their own way. It is the same logic followed by Hollwood producers when they decide to pay vast sums of money to persuade the top box-office actors to appear in their films. 'We're content providers, like a film studio,' explained José Angel Sánchez, Real Madrid's exuberant director of marketing, in an inter-view with the *Economist*. 'Having a team with Zidane in it is like having a movie with Tom Cruise.' Such is the drawing power of the game's most charismatic players that by their very presence they will, at a minimum, cover their own costs. So while Pérez broke the world transfer record to bring Figo in 2000, destroyed it once again to bring Zidane in 2001 and then paid another fortune for Ronaldo in 2002, each year the club's profits grew.

But there was another side to the Pérez revolution. An enormously successful businessman in his own right, president of the third biggest construction company in Europe, he wasn't just changing football's business practices; he was smashing long-standing orthodoxies, altering the whole conception of the game. Every time he bought another superstar, but especially when he bought the golden boy Beckham, the high priests of the game – coaches, former coaches, former players and football writers – muttered that he was making a big mistake; that, sure Beckham passed the ball well, but the priorities lay elsewhere, that the team lacked 'balance'; that a new centre half was urgently needed, a defensive midfielder – strong, rough men to add ballast to the already overly refined Madrid mix. Pérez – and it really is he who decides things at the club – didn't believe a word of it. He went ahead and bet all his money, and all his prestige, on talent. Pure football talent. '*Los mejores*,' he says, '*Quiero a los mejores*.' The best, I want the best. Let the other teams get centre halves and defensive midfielders: against us they're going to need them!

Fabulously irresponsible. Some would have said – especially in Italy where they see football as a more complex version of chess – that the man was suicidal. And it was true that in terms of football's received wisdom this was no way to run a serious football club. Pérez's Real Madrid – sometimes known in Spain as *el Florenteam* – was the sort of fantasy football side that might have been picked in a computer game by a tactically unsophisticated ten-year-old boy. Pérez was of the view that, if truth be told, the ten-year-old boy knows as much about the game as the high priests. Though, in fairness to the high priests, Pérez's brash new philosophy rested on a premise that they themselves had never even considered. That winning was not the game's paramount objective. You had got to compete, of course. You had to play at the highest level, meaning the European Champions League – a competition that offered a far more reliable index of quality than the World Cup. You had to be perceived always to be a credible candidate to win everything. But whether you actually won everything or not, whether in the case of Real Madrid you perpetuated the grand tradition of lifting more European Cups by far than anybody else, that was not the be-all and end-all. The chief purpose – Madrid's wonderfully lucid sports director Jorge Valdano called it 'a social obligation' – was to provide what at Madrid they always refer to as *espectáculo*: spectacle. To put on the best show on earth. To thrill. More than the transient felicity of victory, what Real Madrid aspired to do was convey something of the enduring quality of art, something that moves all people everywhere, always.

All you needed to do was go and watch a Real Madrid game, any game, and keep your eyes firmly fixed on Zidane. Watch him spin and glide, all six foot two of him, with the ball at his feet and you saw what Beckham meant when he described him as 'a ballerina'; you saw the overwhelming reason why the world's most famous Englishman wanted to play at Real Madrid was for the privilege, the sheer fun of performing in the same dazzlingly talented troupe as his hero – because he was everybody's hero – Zidane.

Beckham's most extravagant football fantasies were made flesh in an early league game against Valladolid. The best passer in the game said later that maybe he had never made a better pass – but that most definitely no one had ever scored a more beautiful goal from a ball he had delivered. If you haven't seen it, do what you can to get hold of the video clip. Watch Beckham's fifty-yard pass, observe the grace of his movement and the purity of the ball's trajectory as it rises and drops, like a dead thing, in Zidane's path; then marvel at the magical way that – on the run, in one flowing movement – the Frenchman picks the ball out of the air with his left foot and cracks it across the goalkeeper into the right-hand corner of the net.

Zidane's football is art. Art that people will be admiring 500 years from now. And it has the great merit that it is not art reserved for the initiated, for the art historian, the classical music buff, the reader of Shakespeare and Cervantes. It is the one truly globalised art form, accessible to a more ample span of humanity than art has ever been before. Zidane's magnificent brushstrokes have a wonderfully democratic quality to them. They evoke exactly the same responses – the same admiration, the same delight – in the subsistence farmer in Rwanda as in the banker in the City of London. And like all art, what they do is embellish the human condition, enrich life. They offer inspiration, they offer joy, they offer – whether it be my well-off friend Sebastián going through his marital separation or the hungry millions in Africa – consolation for life's sorrows.

Joseph Conrad might spin in his grave but his definition of art as something that speaks to 'the solidarity . . . which binds men to each other, which binds together all humanity – the dead to the living and the living to the unborn': this definition can apply with as much validity to football as to music, literature or painting when the game is played with the flourish and genius displayed by the men in white of Real Madrid.

There were other fine teams, other great players around that summer of 2003. Van Nistelrooy at Manchester United, Henry at Arsenal, Totti at Roma, Kaká at Milan, Ballack at Bayern Munich were all individuals capable of elevating the game to a higher plane. It was just that – setting aside tribal considerations and examining what was available with dispassionate eyes – the players assembled at Real did so more often, more beautifully, on a more elevated plane. That was why that conversation I overheard in the Majengo minibus should have come as no surprise to me, obvious as it was that people were having the very same discussion in minibuses the length and breadth of planet earth.

On my return from Majengo to Nairobi, having spent a couple of hours talking to two of those AIDS-immune prostitutes at the clinic, I went for lunch to the city's main teaching hospital with a young doctor who was part of the team involved in researching why these women had managed against all odds to avoid infection. The reason I was there in the first place was to write a newspaper story about a vaccine these Kenyan doctors were trying to develop to combat AIDS on the basis of the prostitutes' remarkable natural defences. Eminent professors I had talked to at Oxford University had said this was the most cutting-edge project of its kind in the world. And, while hardly being one to judge the scientific merits of what was going on, I was mightily impressed by the brightness and dedication of people like the young doctor I was lunching with. Especially as I had been led to understand that a scientist as capable as he, just twenty-seven years old, could be making a lot more money if he were to sell his skills abroad. 'Ah, yes,' he explained, 'but for me it is such a big privilege to form part of this fantastic team of researchers doing such important work for the world. I would not change that for anything. Me joining this team, I feel the way Beckham must be feeling on joining Real Madrid.'

This time I did not react with open-mouthed astonishment, prepared as I had been by the ride to Majengo for out-of-the-blue footballing allusions. It was the doctor, not me, who raised the subject of Real Madrid first. I was there dutifully, solemnly talking about AIDS. But what really did surprise me was what happened next. Something that I shall always recall as a quite unbelievable coincidence. Within five seconds, no more, of my friend the doctor mentioning Real Madrid my mobile phone rang. I picked it up and José Angel Sánchez, the Real Madrid marketing chief – Florentino Pérez's right-hand man and alter ego, the second most powerful man in the club – announced himself. It was like a voice from another planet, so far removed was the opulence and glitz of the world he inhabited from the spare, grey, concrete vastness of the hospital I was in and the sordid squalor I had seen that morning at Majengo.

Sánchez wanted to know if I could make it over to Madrid the following week to interview Beckham for Real Madrid Television. It was going to be a world 'exclusive' to be broadcast in a hundred countries on the day of his official presentation as a Real Madrid player. Today was Thursday, the interview would be on the following Tuesday or Wednesday. What did I say?

This was madness. Here I was in Africa reporting on AIDS and the whole day had been a series of references to Real Madrid and Beckham. And now I was being summoned to Madrid to interview the man himself. Was there some mighty planetary realignment underway, with Real Madrid and David Beckham at the fulcrum? Even in deepest Africa you couldn't get away from them. Not for one minute.

Yet the answer to Sánchez's question was not immediately obvious to me. I had just flown in to Kenya, the first leg of a four-country, two-week reporting tour of Africa that I had spent more than a month diligently organising. Was I going to chuck all that work away, oblige myself to start once again the patient task of setting up appointments in Rwanda, South Africa, Angola all over again? And there was another thing. I had come to Africa on a weighty mission. To write about AIDS, nature's terrorist, the killer every single day, without cease, of twice as many people as died in the World Trade Center on September 11th, 2001. I was also going to write about war and poverty and hunger: about the plight, in short, of the most abandoned, most desperate people in he world. Was I going to ditch this momentous enterprise to go and interview David Beckham? Would my conscience ever let me forget it? Having spent twenty years of my life as a journalist covering wars, denouncing human-rights abuses, standing up, in so far as I could, for the wretched of the earth, would I be accused now of a trite and irresponsible dere-liction of duty?

I told Sánchez this was all too much for me to deal with right now and I would call him back. Then I turned to the doctor – this African hero, the noble opposite of the frivolous gadfly I was one step away from becoming – and, embarrassed, I explained my predica-ment. His first, and rather perplexed response was, 'Why you?' Unsurprisingly, he had imagined me to be a foreign correspondent rather than a sports journalist. I said yes, that's quite rights. Wandering about slums in poor countries and talking to people like him had always been much more my line of business. But in recent years my passion for football had been converging with my professional duties.

I am half-British and half-Spanish and, having spent seven years of my childhood in Buenos Aires (where they are arguably crazier about football than anywhere else on planet earth) it was my destiny to be a lifelong football fanatic. The other country where I grew up was England, where they invented the game. Much later, when I moved to Spain, I was taken by the passion and art of Spanish foot-ball, soon coming to the conclusion – shared by most football connoisseurs, I think – that the Spanish league was the world's best. And so it was that I began writing more and more about football.

Inevitably it was Real Madrid that my British editors wanted to hear about. One reason why I had received this remarkable phone call was that in the course of this new writing about football, I had interviewed Pérez and Sánchez at Real Madrid and we had got on well. Being bilingual helped. But the long and the short of it, the main reason why I figured Real Madrid wanted me for this interview, was that I neatly crossed the British and Spanish football worlds, spoke English – and might therefore be expected to put Beckham more at ease than a local Spanish journalist in Beckham's first big interview for his new team on Spanish soil.

But enough of all this autobiography. What I needed now, and urgently, was advice. 'You're a doctor,' I said. 'I trust doctors. I have this big choice to make. So tell me: what should I do?'

He smiled the smile of the good, the wise, the man of crystal-clear principles. 'My friend,' he said, his smile widening into a broad, beaming grin, 'when the train comes, you must take it.'

He was right. I knew he was right. I phoned Sánchez and told him I was catching the train. That I'd be in Madrid on Monday night.

Before that I made a brief stop in Rwanda, spent the Sunday before my return deep in the countryside of this tiny little country in the geographic heart of Africa, interviewing the most traumatised people in the world: the victims and killers of the worst atrocity the world has seen since the Second World War, the genocide that began in April 1994 in which Rwanda's majority Hutu population rose up against their Tutsi compatriots, killing one million in a hundred days – almost all of them hacked to pieces with machetes. That night I went for a drink with a Rwandan general, a Tutsi who had lost most of his extended family in the genocide, who had himself been shot through the face and had the scar to show it, and had been part of the rebel force that liberated the country and brought an end to the killing in June 1994. But I'd had it with harrowing tales. And so had he. We talked about football. About – what else? – Real Madrid and the Beckham transfer. How on earth did Manchester United let him go for so little money? What was the United coach, Alex Ferguson, thinking? What position was Beckham going to play in? Did he not run the risk of failing horribly alongside such fantastically talented players? And Ronaldo: he was back to his sensational best, but weren't people worried that he might suffer a recurrence of that terrible knee injury of his? And Roberto Carlos, and Zidane, and Figo, and Raúl: weren't they all just absolutely great? And, by the way, how come Pérez got rid of his winning coach, del Bosque?

Twenty-four hours later I was in a five-star hotel in Madrid preparing my interview with Beckham. It went fine. A month later, after I had been and gone to Africa one more time, this time finishing my work, I got a call from James, an American friend who works for the UN. He had just been in Sweden with a couple of boys aged eight and twelve, the sons of a good friend who had recently died cruelly young of an illness. Hoping to cheer the two boys up a little and turn their minds to other things, James mentioned that he had a friend who had interviewed Beckham. 'Their jaws dropped,' said James. 'They just stood there stunned, mute, in awe and admiration that I — poor, miserable me — should have a friend who had actually sat and talked with David Beckham.' It was at this moment, or very soon after, that James understood that I had to write a book about Beckham and Real Madrid. He called to tell me and I knew immediately he was right. Here it is.

John Carlin

1: Matadors and Bulls

A Brazilian journalist once said that the one-twos between Pelé and Tostão offered convincing proof of the existence of God. The most hardened agnostic might have been tempted to a similar conclusion at the Bernabéu on the night of 8 April 2003 after watching Zidane and Raúl stroke the ball around the congested edge of the Manchester United penalty area, as graceful and unrushed as if they were playing alone in a park.

Sitting in the press box at half-time during the first leg of the Champions League quarter-final between Real Madrid and United at the Bernabéu I remember the reaction of the British football writers. World-weary, weather-beaten journalists, veterans of a thousand games, they were agog at what they had just seen. I recall one journalist in particular, from one of the bigger-selling London tabloids, rising from his seat in a state of elation, as if he had just lived an intense religious experience. 'I don't think anyone's played football like that in 30 years,' he exclaimed. He might have been right. The men in white had scaled peaks rarely reached, if ever, on a football pitch since the great Brazil of 1970: the World Cup-winning team that had always served until then as the benchmark for the sublime. The appraisal needed updating. Players were not as fit or as fast, spaces were not as compressed, in the days of Pelé, Tostão, Rivelino, Gérson and Jairzinho. Three decades later the Real Madrid of Zidane and Raúl and Figo, Roberto Carlos and Ronaldo offered us the wonderfully reassuring reminder that it could still be done, that perfection, or something very much like it, was still possible. That never mind all the money in the sport, the disputes over satellite TV rights, the building of brand names, football – the game

itself as originally conceived by some inventively playful Englishmen
150 years ago – was bigger than all of that. Madrid that night at
the Bernabéu had the freshness, *élan*, and sense of adventure of that
1970 Brazil side. Johan Cruyff's Ajax in the Seventies and the Milan
of Ruud Gullit, Frank Rikjaard and Marco van Basten were both
in their different ways brilliant, but in a more methodical, rigorous,
solemnly professional sort of way. This lot gave the impression that
– tactics be damned – they played chiefly for fun.

The impression was deceptive. They were artists but they were
tough guys too, focused competitors who had worked hard at their
game. Otherwise they would never have made it through the merci-
less obstacle course that separates a twelve-year-old boy with a talent
for ball-juggling from a twenty-five-year-old professional playing regularly in a major European league. For Zidane, disciplined perseverance was what had allowed his genius to soar, taking him to the
summit of the world game. The previous season, 2001/2002, he had
scored one of the most memorable goals in the history of the game,
one that he himself would describe a couple of years later as 'the
goal of my life'. Receiving an awkward cross above waist height from
Roberto Carlos on the edge of the penalty area, he twisted and
turned and powered the ball, with his weaker left foot, into the roof
of the net. If he had done that in training his teammates would have
raised their hands to their heads in disbelief. But he did it in the
European Cup final against Bayer Leverkusen, before a live worldwide TV audience of 1,100 million, at a point in the game when
the Germans were clearly playing with more force and composure.
It was the winning goal, probably the greatest ever scored in a
European Cup final. Cometh the hour, cometh Zidane. He delivered when his team most needed it. Just as it had been when he
won the World Cup for France in 1998, scoring two of the three
French goals in the final against Brazil, demonstrating the true champion's capacity to rise to the big occasion, when the expectations
are highest and the pressure is most intense.

The Champions League quarter-final against Manchester United
was another big occasion, what English footballers like to describe
as 'a massive game'. More massive, in a way, than that 2002 final

against Bayer Leverkusen. The feeling all across Europe was that whoever won this clash of titans would win the European Cup; that the match was the final in all but name. Real Madrid were the reigning champions and clearly possessed the tournament's best players; and United looked a formidably impressive unit, conquerors of Juventus 3-0 away in the previous round of the competition.

Ronaldo, who seemed to thrive on big games more than anyone, couldn't wait. 'The whole of Europe – the whole world – is dying to see these games against Manchester,' he said. 'It is the King of Duels.'

Alex Ferguson, the Manchester United manager, had a try at spoiling the majesty of the occasion, striking a graceless note in comments he made to the press the week before the big game. It had to do with the rumours that had been surfacing in the press over the previous month concerning David Beckham's possible move to Real Madrid. 'You have to wonder why the stories about Beckham came out at this time, don't you?' he said, implying the idea had been to undermine United's team morale. 'We have to think there's some mischief.'

Maybe, but the stories might never have arisen in the first place had the Scot not dealt a blow of his own to United team morale a few weeks earlier. Had it not been for 'the Flying Boot Incident', the newspapers would have had a lot more trouble convincing the public that the rumours of Beckham's transfer were credible. The date was 17 February – six weeks before the big quarter-final at the Bernabéu. Manchester United had just lost 2-0 to Arsenal in the FA Cup and, in the presence of all the other players, Ferguson chose to pin all the blame for the defeat on Beckham. To which Beckham replied by doing the unthinkable in the strict boarding-school environment of the Manchester United dressing room. He snarled back. Initially stunned and amazed, then red with fury, Ferguson took a step towards his player and from the other side of the room, a distance of maybe eight yards, kicked a boot at him. It struck Beckham above the left eye, drawing blood. For Beckham it was the final straw. Over the previous months Ferguson had continually been singling him out for punishment, blaming him when the team played badly, keeping him on the bench for important games. The *Financial Times* even compared these 'mind games' Ferguson practised on Beckham with 'the ritual humiliation practised by Maoists during the Cultural Revolution'. The measure of how bitter Beckham's accumulated sense of injustice had become was that he leapt to his feet and, out of control with rage, charged at his boss. Luckily they were not alone in the dressing room. Ryan Giggs, Gary Neville and Ruud van Nistelrooy had to grab Beckham just in time to stop things getting violently out of hand.

Despite the rearguard efforts of a Manchester United spokesman ('Whatever happens in the dressing room remains private'), the story quickly got out. Beckham himself made no effort to conceal what had happened, pointedly displaying the bandage over his small wound to his ever-alert retinue of paparazzis. The story of 'Fergie's Flying Boot' made it around the world. Everybody quoted Ferguson's excuse for an apology. It had been 'a freak act of nature', he said, and it would never happen again. (Marcello Lippi, the Juventus manager, wryly remarked that he had tried fifty times in his career to do what Ferguson had done and failed. 'It's a question of technique, and the Scots must have a better technique,' Lippi said.) Inevitably the story made big headlines in the Spanish sports dailies. Equally inevitably, the rumours started to circulate in the Spanish and British press that Beckham was on his way out of United and that Spain might be his chosen destination.

Agents talked to journalists, journalists talked to club officials, who spoke to agents and, with newspapers unable to resist some embellishing of their own, the story grew and grew. This time clearly linking Beckham with Madrid. What did it, what made the story too irresistible for the papers to ignore, was that quarter-final draw pitting United against Real. Ferguson, a man once described by the *Daily Telegraph* as capable of starting a fight in an empty house, was enraged, convinced that Real mischief-makers lay behind the rumours. This time, though, he might have been partially right.

When Roberto Carlos said the week before the game at the Bernabéu that not only was Beckham a great player whom he would be proud to mark but that 'we [the Real players] have told the club president he ought to sign him', the Brazilian would have been aware of the destabilising impact his words would have had on the United dressing room. Whether Ferguson was actually aware at the time that Florentino Pérez would need no prompting from the players to sign Beckham, the fact is that the Scot knew all about playing mind games with the opposition, being a keen proponent of the art himself. So he would not have been too far off the mark in imagining that the people at Real had cheerfully seized on the uncertainty surrounding Beckham to alter the delicately taut mental balance that in top-flight football teams can mark the difference between victory and defeat.

Not that Real Madrid really needed much of a hand playing mind games. Going into that first leg at the Bernabéu the psychological advantage was entirely with them. Much the same United team had been defeated by a weaker Real team two years earlier in the same stage of the Champions League, losing 3-2 at Old Trafford after a 0–0 draw in Madrid. Moreover, everybody at United – like everybody else in the football world – was in awe of Real Madrid. 'I think Real have the strongest squad I've ever seen in terms of names,' said Ferguson – a powerful statement coming from a man who had been intimately involved with the football business for nearly half a century. And then Ferguson added, with more candour than his own players might have liked, 'You can see teams being unnerved at the Bernabéu just because of the names they are up against.'

To try and calm nerves, Ferguson's number two, the Portuguese assistant coach Carlos Queiroz, showed the United players some videos the evening before the game. Not videos of Real Madrid, as that would have served only to undermine morale, but highlights of United at their best. The idea was to turn thoughts away from their rivals' strengths and convince them that they had it in them to beat anybody. It was the kind of motivational technique that the cerebral Queiroz, admired by Ferguson as a 'modern' coach, had brought to United – and that he would soon be taking to Real Madrid.

Beckham's move to Real was not the only development that would in hindsight shed ironic light on that Champions League quarter-final. For Queiroz moved to Real too, taking over as coach after the surprise sacking of Vicente del Bosque in the summer.

Recalling that Madrid v United game nine months after the event, speaking in his office at the Real training complex, Queiroz told me he had sought through those videos to convey to his players at United that they too were great players and had nothing to fear. Whether the plan had the intended results, or whether it backfired from the strain of trying too hard to deny the United players' obvious technical inferiority, we do not know. What we do know, at least from what Queiroz said, was that United went into the tie feeling they had a fifty-fifty chance of winning – but that fifty-fifty depended on Real not playing at their best level. 'Real Madrid played wonderfully well, with players who could make things happen on their own. But they had their ups and downs. The question was which Real Madrid team would appear on the day.'

That was always the question. Player for player they were the best in the business but sometimes individuals failed, or the team did not gel, or both. But, football being the most unpredictable of all sports, they were capable of losing to teams whose entire wage bill was lower than Zidane's salary. At that very moment Real were second in the Spanish league behind just such a team, Real Sociedad, who had beaten them 4–2 at home. They had lost in the league already to minnows, barely known outside their own towns let alone Spain, like Racing Santander and Osasuna. Beneath the genius there was a fragility, or a failure to sustain the necessary intensity in game after game, a tendency to lose concentration. The bad news for Queiroz on the eve of that game at the Bernabéu was that if ever these great players were going to be at the top of their game it was going to be against Manchester United in the Champions League. At their best no one could live with Real. Queiroz knew that. But he also knew that for all the superlatives hurled their way the Galácticos were as prey to human weakness, and to the twists and turns of outrageous fortune, as anyone. Like any football team, they could be beaten.

Del Bosque, more keenly aware of his team's Jekyll and Hyde frailties than anyone, was far from complacent. Never mind those poor results in the domestic league, they had struggled far more than they should have done to make it to the Champions League quarter-finals, squeaking through against Belgium's Genk and Lokomotiv Moscow. I met del Bosque in a hotel cafeteria in Madrid one morning nine months after the game, seven months after Real Madrid had sacked him. Cheerful, philosophical, a man who would tell people that his life has been immeasurably enriched by the love of his second son, who had Down's syndrome, he spoke of his lifelong respect for '*el gran* Manchester'. A former Real player himself, del Bosque played in a team that lost 4-0 to United at Old Trafford in an exhibition game staged in August 1978 to celebrate the Manchester club's centenary. He enjoyed sweet revenge twenty-two years later when, with him as coach, Real beat United 3-2 on aggregate in the very same quarter-finals stage of the Champions League in 2000. He knew that game could, in truth, have gone either way and he knew more than enough about the United players to understand the damage they could cause his team. 'Paul Scholes we saw as the key to the midfield and Beckham, well, Beckham is an excellent player that I had been following closely since the time he was eighteen years old,' del Bosque told me, exuding the enthusiasm for the game that you see in all these old football pros. 'I saw him in an under-20 tournament in France playing for England and he was the best player in the whole competition. Our thoughts, though, were focused most on stopping Ryan Giggs. We were afraid of Giggs, who all the players saw as an extremely dangerous winger.'

United kicked off and instantly Roy Keane sent a high speculative pass sailing in the general direction of the feared Giggs. But his marker, the right back Michel Salgado, was quicker to the ball, heading it back with assurance into the arms of his goalkeeper, Iker Casillas. Casillas then rolled the ball out to Roberto Carlos, who dinked it over Beckham's head to Zidane, who rolled his boot over the ball – as if to say, no hurry, we own this, we're in charge – before slipping it out wide to one of his defenders. For fifty-five seconds United did not get a sniff of the ball. Before Real eventually lost possession on the front edge of the United penalty area they had made twenty-one passes involving ten of their players. Up in the Bernabéu press box we were mesmerised right from the start, gaping open-mouthed at the sheer class of these players.

The tone of the game was set there, in that first minute of play: United doing the good old-fashioned British thing, hoicking the ball upfield and charging after it; Real treating the ball like Brazilians do: as if it were an object of love, caressing it, jealously refusing to share it. It would be too much of a caricature to say that was the way the rest of the game unfolded. United were not quite so rustically direct over the ninety minutes; nor were Real so consistently smooth. But it did remain, all in all, poetry versus prose.

Vicente del Bosque did not look like a poet. With his slow, heavy manner, it was hard on the surface to imagine a man with a personality more at odds with the glamour of the club that employed him and the players he coached. Originally he had been appointed as a stop-gap, to provide cover after the abrupt departure of the Welshman John Toshack at the end of 1999. But del Bosque's understated, avuncular style seemed to work, not least as it seemed to keep in check the mighty egos of the Real dressing room. The players grew to respect him because they saw that, having spent all his life at Real either as a player or as a member of the coaching staff, he had as canny a knowledge of the game as anybody. Most important of all, he had absorbed and made his own the club's philosophy that winning is not all. Spend an hour talking with del Bosque about football and, sure, he would talk tactics. But the word that recurred – for in truth he was much more of a poet than he appeared to be – would be *espectáculo*: spectacle, performance, show.

It is the ethic of the bullfight. There's a lot more to it than killing the bull, than getting a result. It's the manner of the killing that counts. The bravery. The artistry. The flourish. Images of the *corrida de toros* were what came to mind during that quarter-final at the Bernabéu. This Manchester United was no ordinary bull. There was pedigree there. There was fight. And yet, especially during that magical first half, the faint-hearted neutral spectator must have longed for it to be all over, for the brave beast to be put out of its misery.

Twisted and turned this way and that, the United players were wrong-footed, dizzied, confused until at a certain point it seemed that, like the rest of us, all they could do was stand and stare, restraining what might have been the urge to nod their heads in appreciative wonder and break into applause. They looked so befuddled that for stretches it seemed as if they had given up on the one great defining quality with which Ferguson had famously imbued them: the desire to stand up and fight.

The gap in class was at times almost embarrassing. It was a pub band against a symphony orchestra. Real played such beautiful music because each had such perfect command of his instrument, such pure skill. No team possessed more players blessed with such an impeccable first touch. No one alive received the ball with such exquisite cushioning, standing still or on the run, as Zidane or the Portuguese maestro Luis Figo. Yet rarely did the Real players have to push their masterful control to the limit because the weight and pace and direction of the passes they received from each and every one of their teammates was so consistently fine. They had the time to look up and ponder their next option, keeping their opponents guessing, always one step behind.

Several passages of play illustrated the point, most of them occurring on the left side of midfield, where Zidane bestrode the stage, within a space not much bigger than half a tennis court on the periphery of the United penalty area. The players attempting to police these tight confines would be Roy Keane, David Beckham, Gary Neville and Rio Ferdinand – established internationals all, with big reputations in the game – assisted, as the situation became increasingly unmanageable, by Wes Brown and Nicky Butt. The assailants would be Zidane, Raúl and Roberto Carlos, dancing around them in tight little circles, threading and weaving the ball between and around their legs – until Figo would come cantering over from the right wing, like a little boy eager not to be left out of the action. Whereupon the space would open up, the level of danger would suddenly increase and circus would give way to palpable threat. It took Real just twelve minutes to score their first goal. Figo – delivering what Spanish commentators described as a '*centro-shoot*' – curled the ball with his right foot from the left-hand edge of the penalty area over the head of the United goalkeeper Fabien Barthez, shaving the angle between post and bar before spinning into the top right-hand corner of the net.

The difference between the two sides was a difference in the sense of time. All great players in all sports appear to have more time to do what they do than the ordinarily talented. Zidane always has more time than anyone else, meaning that he requires fewer milliseconds than any other player alive to get the ball – either when he is controlling it or passing it – to do exactly what he wants it to do. That is why against Manchester United he gave the impression at times, with that imperious manner of putting boot to ball that he has, of treating his opponents with contempt. It was not that. He is not the contemptuous type. He regarded the likes of Giggs and Beckham with respect. It is just that the game is much easier for him than it is for them.

Consider this statistic, courtesy of the Spanish sports daily *AS*. Zidane made seventy-five passes in that game, only eight of which failed to find their target. Beckham made forty-six, sixteen of which went astray.

But a great team cannot live by Zidane alone. Raúl, who scored twice, played one of the games of his life. Ferguson remarked after the game that for him – never mind Real's expensive purchases – the home-grown Raúl was the best player in the world. It was not an eccentric view. Zidane was on record as having said the same thing. Figo had this to say about him: 'I have played with a lot of good players, but Raúl is from another planet. I have never seen such a good player in my whole life.' If not everyone would have ageed, every big name in the game did consider him to be one of the greats of his generation, and certainly the greatest Spain had ever produced. His statistics, certainly, were remarkable. He was twenty-five and he had won three European Cups and three Spanish league cups and he was the top scorer by far in the history of the Champions League. And yet, for all that, if you did not know who he was and what he had achieved and you saw him for the first time alongside the likes of Zidane, Figo and Ronaldo you might scratch your head and wonder how on earth he had managed to insinuate himself into such princely company. Fernando Redondo, a former Argentine international and a teammate at Real when Raúl made his debut in October

1994, once remarked on how underwhelmed he had been by his first impression: 'He didn't look like a footballer. He didn't look like he would make it. That is the sensation I had on the day they put him in the first team.' A decade later he still did not look like he was up to much. Compare him to the other players with whom he had been competing in recent years for the European and World Footballer of the Year prizes and you would find that, by any conventional criteria, he fell way short. Beckham had an amazing right foot, Rivaldo an amazing left one, Michael Owen had lightning pace, Figo was a fantastic dribbler of the ball, Ronaldo blended grace and power, Zidane had it all . . . Summing up Raúl's genius was a far more elusive matter. He didn't ooze talent in any obvious sort of way, he had a weak right foot, he was not fast, he was a not a good header of the ball. His run was ungainly. He was not a dribbler. In possession, Raúl appeared to slouch over the ball. Far from imperious, in that head-raised, master-of-all-he-surveyed manner that Zidane had, Raúl was a hustler. If he were an animal, he would be a terrier, or a rabbit – or a fox.

The key to his success, more than any other contemporary great, was more what went on in his mind than what he could do with his feet. It was his rock-hard single-mindedness that set him apart, what Jorge Valdano called his 'insolent self-belief'. 'He possesses a superior intelligence,' Valdano said of Raúl, 'but what sets him apart is his extraordinary power of concentration. He has the self-control of someone who has lived three lives. Just watching him in training is chilling. He is so serious, so grave that nothing else in the world seems to exist. And when he is playing he lives every one of the ninety minutes as if his life depended on it.'

Raúl considered Valdano his footballing father. Valdano was Real's coach back in 1994. The Argentine was the man who had the faith and the vision to give him his league début when he was barely seventeen. Already identified as the boy wonder of Spanish football, the weight of expectation on his début, against Zaragoza, was immense. Yet the Zaragoza game failed miserably to follow the appointed script. Not only did the great Iberian hope fail to score, he missed three howling sitters. And yet each time, as one newspaper report at the time put it, 'his pulse did not alter'. The scrawny kid with the bandy legs seemed absolutely bloodless. And then in his next game in the big derby against Atlético Madrid, he scored a screamer from the edge of the penalty area, went down for a penalty and set up one of his teammates for the winner with an impeccable cross. The rest is history, but one thing that did not change and never would was that chilling self-control Valdano spoke of.

Strikers respond to missing open goals in different ways. Reactions range from a grimace and a shake of the head from the understated types like the Norwegian Ole Gunnar Solskjaer; to raging at the gods, Christian Vieri-style; to the hands-on-hips, head tilted, glancing skyward in search of an answer to the baffling philosophical question – this would be the Thierry Henry school – 'how can one rationally explain that a guy as cool and talented as me could possibly have missed a chance like that?' And then there was Raúl, who betrayed no emotion at all. He'd miss a chance in the eighty-ninth minute that would have won his team the game and he would just trot back into position as if the ball had gone for a throw-in. He never allowed himself even one millisecond of histrionic self-indulgence. There was serious business to attend to, no time to waste. Never should he reveal to his teammates or to his opponents the slightest sign of weakness; never should he let on that he was in anything less than complete control of himself and his environment.

There was something almost sinister about this on-pitch persona of his. If you looked at his eyes when the teams lined up before a game they were dark, cold and hard, with just a hint of disdain. There was no kindness there at all. He was humourless, pitiless, calcu-lating, ferociously single-minded. Think Al Pacino in *The Godfather*.

As for that intelligence Valdano spoke of, Raúl's greatest attribute lay in his ability to deploy the talents he had to maximum effect. Listen to Josep Guardiola, who spent most of his career as Raúl's rival at Barcelona, but played often with him in the Spanish national side. The thing about Raúl, Guardiola said, was that he always made the right choices. 'He is always in the right place, he always knows the right thing to do in each part of the pitch. If he is in midfield he will play just the one touch, if he is on the edge of the penalty box he will go for goal or slide a dangerous ball to a player who is better positioned. He holds the ball when he has to, he releases it when he has to, he does a one-two when a one-two is on. If I were a spectator I'd see him as the perfect player, because nothing is more irritating than footballers who dribble when they should pass, who pass when they should dribble, who hold the ball when they should pass it. Raúl teaches us how the game should be played.'

Never did he give a masterclass like the one in that first leg quarter-final at the Bernabéu against Manchester United. What was more, he knew it. 'I felt well in every possible sense that night,' he told me in a conversation we had at the Real training complex some months later. 'Physically, mentally, the connections with my team-mates, especially Zidane and Roberto Carlos out on the left – the one-twos we kept pulling of. It was a game in which everything worked out the way you wanted it to. The way you dream it will.'

Raúl had a reputation among journalists as a distant, wary, charmless individual. The Raúl I saw bore little resemblance either to the off-field caricature or to the cold-eyed assassin who had spent ten years terrorising defenders the length and breadth of Europe. Maybe it was that I happened to strike the right chord, that I could not possibly have hit upon a subject of conversation dearer to his heart. Whatever it was, he smiled and smiled as he spoke, he was enthusiastic, he was even at times self-effacing. 'That second goal against Manchester, the shot of mine from outside the penalty area, that showed how much confidence I had that day, because for me to shoot from that far out – well – it's not exactly known as my greatest strength. For others, yes. That's normal for them. Me, I wouldn't normally have even thought of trying it, but I was in such a state of grace that I did and – even more amazing – it worked.'

That night, and especially in the first half, everything worked for Real Madrid. 'We had so much possession,' Raúl recalled, 'but more than that there was the way we were moving the ball around, playing one-touch football, at most two touches. What a night! We all had the time of our lives, the players and the fans. I returned home that night feeling as satisfied as a player can be, with that great sensation that you really have done your job well.'

Del Bosque vividly recalled Raúl's performance in that chat we had nine months later over a coffee in a Madrid hotel. 'He murdered Manchester,' he said. 'They were simply incapable of controlling him.' His positioning, his intelligence on the ball, his devilish eye for goal, his work rate in attack as well as defence, plus the sheer lust to win that he transmitted to the rest of the players: all those qualities and more were on display that night, leaving Alex Ferguson with no option but to conclude in his post-match press conference that Raúl was the best in the business. But then you had two tough ball-playing centre halves in Fernando Hierro and Ivan Helguera both of whom had started off life as midfielders. And Claude Makelele, the work-horse who covered every inch of the pitch, who did what was needed to allow Zidane even more time and space to do his stuff and Roberto Carlos to abandon his left back duties and go join the fun up front.

Makelele started the move that led to Madrid's third goal. Demonstrating that they can play in all registers, not just the clever rococo stuff in midfield, it came from a swift counter-attack, the forwards charging upfield and fanning out like a fast advancing wave. Makelele robbed the ball on the front edge of the Madrid penalty area and did what he always did – passed it, from memory, to his fellow Frenchman Zidane. Zidane took a couple of strides upfield and passed it to Raúl who, just inside his own half, swept it wide to Figo on the right. Figo ran forward, checked himself, cut inside and passed it to Raúl on the edge of the United box, who controlled it, cut left and smacked it past a flying Barthez into the back of the next.

Poor Gary Neville, who missed more than half the passes he attempted that night, said afterwards that playing Real Madrid had been like playing the Harlem Globetrotters – by which he conveyed the perhaps unintended idea that United acted the part of the doltish stooges, gamely making up the numbers. And yet it was not, in truth, quite so simple. Analyse it all you like, football remains one of nature's unfathomable mysteries. Because, while that game shall for ever be remembered for the exhibition Madrid gave, and while the bare statistic shows that Real won 3-1, with a bit more luck United could have drawn, or at least salvaged a more respectable 3-2 scoreline.

But no one questioned the justice of the result. The British press were in raptures at Real's performance – 'Fantasy football!' said *The Times*; 'They belong in an art gallery', the *Telegraph* enthused – but so were the United players. Gary Neville had a nightmare trying to patrol that left side of Real's attack but had the class to salute his rivals' 'wonderful football'. 'It was breathtaking in the first half and sometimes – what can you do? – you just have to admire it,' Neville said. Beckham, similarly resigned, said, 'Madrid did with us as they pleased.' And he went further, recognising that for all Ferguson's fighting talk beforehand, and Queiroz's attempts to pep them up with motivational videos, United had gone into the game feeling inferior. 'We went out on to the pitch with too much respect for our rivals, intimidated,' Beckham told reporters after the game. Was the truth, though, that he was brimming over with admiration for the team he had played that night, tingling at the thought that one day he might be forming part of this fantastic team? As a man of enormous ambition – much steelier than his gentle personality would suggest – and as a devotee of what the Brazilians describe as 'the beautiful game', no challenge could be greater and no prospect more mouth-watering than to play week after week alongside Zidane, Ronaldo and the rest of the Real galaxy. Later, in his autobiography, he would offer a clue as to what his secret thoughts had been that night at the Bernabéu when he offered Real the highest compliment any professional footballer could ever give a rival team. 'They played football,' Beckham said, 'like I'd never seen it played before.'

Ferguson put it more bluntly. 'They drove us mad,' he said.

As for del Bosque, his considered view was this: 'Real Madrid played football in a manner that was faithful to the club's history.' The remark was simple but richly eloquent. The great achievement of Raúl, Zidane and company that April night at the Bernabéu was to have lived up to, and therefore embellished, the club's legend – a legend bigger than the individual players in the team. It is something Silvio Berlusconi understands. A larger-than-life figure himself who, after becoming the richest man in Italy, became its prime minister, Berlusconi was president of AC Milan during the Italian club's gloriously successful late Eighties, when they swept all before

them, including Real Madrid, who they met in the semi-finals of
the Champions League in 1989. On one of the most painful nights
in the Spanish club's history, Milan beat Real 5–0. After the game
was over Berlusconi went down to the Madrid dressing room to
console the shattered players. Ever theatrical, Berlusconi asked them
all to hold hands before delivering this ovation: 'Do not worry. We
are proud of having beaten Real Madrid because it is the best football club in the world. You have a good fortune which we do not
have and that is – that whether we win the European Cup or not
– we shall never, ever be like you.'

So what was it? What made Real so special? Why was it that
when football writers in England talked about Manchester United's
longing for global glory, or nouveau riche Chelsea's desire under
their billionaire Russian owner Roman Abramovich to become the
greatest club in world football, they reflexively wrote of United's or
Chelsea's aspiration to become 'England's Real Madrid'? Why not
England's Milan or Juventus or Bayern Munich? How had the idea
of Real Madrid as the paragon of footballing achievement become
so deeply rooted?

It certainly had nothing to do with the club's beginnings. That
was just the usual old story: British cultural imperialism doing its
stuff, bringing the most successful export in the history of globalisation to the Spanish capital just as it had done to other cities, towns,
villages, beaches, mountains and valleys around the world. Football
is Britain's great enduring gift to the world, and the one that has
been most gratefully received. So, sure enough, 'Madrid Football
Club' (English spelling preserved) was founded in 1902 – by a Catalan
from Barcelona, as fate would have it – and the team's first coach
was a Brit called Arthur Johnson. The all-white kit was chosen in
deliberately reverent imitation of the one worn by the Corinthians
Casuals, a London football club who were themselves to become
legendary as the emblem – the synonym – of fair play and the
amateur spirit in the game. Other than that, nothing much happened
over the next fifty years that did not happen at Barcelona FC, or
River Plate in Buenos Aires, or the Strongest in Bolivia or – for that
matter – Corinthians in Brazil. Except that in 1920 King Alfonso

XIII did the club the honour of awarding it the title of 'Real', meaning Royal, changing the name to the present one.

Real Madrid made their leap into greatness during the era of Alfredo Di Stefano, Ferenc Puskas and Francisco Gento. The Argentine, the Hungarian and the Spaniard were the standard-bearers of the team that won the first five European Cups in a row, culminating in the 1960 final at Glasgow's Hampden Park, a game described at the time as 'the Game of the Century'. Real's rivals were Eintracht Frankfurt and the final score, in a game preserved for posterity in grainy black and white, was Real 7 Eintracht 3. It was another Harlem Globetrotters extravaganza. Alex Ferguson, then a young professional scoring goals in the Scottish league for Queen's Park, was among the 127,000 people at the stadium dazzled and dumbstruck by the Real players' sustained trickery, speed and inventiveness, and by the finishing of Puskas, who scored four times, and Di Stefano, who scored three. The glow of that game continued to illuminate successive football generations. It is on that memory, on the unforgettable talent and brio of those players, and on what they achieved in the second half of the Fifties, that in the year 2000 FIFA officially declared Real Madrid the Best Club of the Twentieth Century.

It would not have occurred to anyone at FIFA, or anywhere else, to choose any other club. The only debate might have centred on who came second and third. The glory of a club rests on its trophies and the greatness of its players. It is remarkable how enduring that glory can be, how resistant to failure. Manchester United never lost their lustre despite going twenty-six years without winning an English league. Why? Partly it was the European Cup they had won in 1968, the first by an English club, but, more than that, it was the memory of the three great players in that team, the best England, Ireland and Scotland has ever produced: Bobby Charlton, George Best and Denis Law. In the same way, despite going thirty-two years without winning a European Cup (they won their sixth in 1966 and their seventh in 1998) Real Madrid's reputation rested on the unassailable and quite possibly unrepeatable achievement of winning those five successive trophies, and doing so with the best and most famous players of their era.

Di Stefano is always on everybody's list of the top four players of all time, usually – depending on the age or nationality of the person making the list – behind Pelé, Maradona and Cruyff. An absolute original who combined extraordinary stamina with electric speed, he was an all-terrain player who wore the number nine shirt but performed with equal gusto and efficiency as a defender, midfielder and goal-scoring centre forward. Explosive in and around the penalty area, he had a famously regal quality about him in midfield – shoulders back like a soldier on parade, head up, smoothly directing play, master of all he surveyed. Phenomenally, he scored at least one goal in each of the five European Cup finals in which he played. Born in Argentina, he arrived in Madrid aged twenty-seven and played there for ten years. He was later club coach. Florentino Pérez, who when he was a child watched Di Stefano play at the Bernabéu, named him honorary life president in 2000.

Puskas, whose name in Hungarian means 'rifle', had what all those who saw him described as the most lethal left foot they had ever seen. Di Stefano recalled years later how when he passed the ball to him in front of goal, he would not even bother to see what happened next. Instead he would turn towards the crowd to enjoy their response to the goal that Puskas would unfailingly proceed to rocket into the back of the net. There is a story about a goal the great Hungarian scored from a free kick on the edge of the penalty area in 1961 against Atlético Madrid. The referee told him he was sorry but the goal had to be disallowed because he had not blown his whistle. He had to take it again. Puskas shrugged, placed the ball on exactly the same spot where he had placed it the first time, kicked it with his same left foot, with exactly the same power, along the very same trajectory, past the despairing goalkeeper's same flailing dive into the same top left-hand corner of the net. A hero of the celebrated Hungarian team that demolished England 6–3 at Wembley in 1953 (the first time England were ever beaten on home soil), he went into exile after the Soviet invasion of Hungary in 1956 and turned up at Real, aged thirty-one, in 1957. As with Ronaldo four decades later, Puskas was often accused of being lazy and overweight. As with Ronaldo, Puskas was Spain's most prolific scorer season after season.

Di Stefano said of him: 'He controls the ball better with his left foot than I do with my hand.'

Gento, the greatest player Spain had produced until Raúl, is the only member of Real or any other team to have won six European Cups, his career spanning an amazing eighteen years, between 1953 and 1971. A left winger who could have been an Olympic sprinter, once he picked up speed with the ball at his feet there was, as they used to say about him in Madrid, 'no god that could stop him'. He was not only fast, he had that ability of the truly great player to stop dead in his tracks, to apply the handbrake when moving at top speed, then to turn and leave defenders sprawling in his wake. He also had tremendous stamina. He was a sprinter with the energy reserves of a marathon runner. Which came in handy in the third European Cup final Real Madrid played, this time against Milan. At the end of the ninety minutes the score was 2-2. It had been a wonderful game but the Madrid players were now exhausted. In the break before extra time Di Stefano went up to Gento and said, 'Look, the rest of us are finished. But they – they're still breathing. You're the only one of us that still looks fresh. So either you win it for us, or we don't bring the cup home.' Gento was a young lad next to the veteran Argentine. Inspired by the confidence placed in him by the great man, he did as he was told. He scored the winning goal. The final result was 3-2 to Real Madrid.

Magnificent as Real Madrid's players and achievements were in those days, the memories they left behind added up to more than the sum of those parts. That was how the legend came about. Maybe that is how all legends – be it saints, soldiers, or sports teams – are created. People need legends, they crave models of exemplary human behaviour. So what people do, by some subtly natural process seen in all places at all times, is fix on what they consider to be the most admirable quality in the saint, soldier or sports team and transform it into the flesh and blood expression of an ideal. The ideal the football world saw expressed in Real Madrid was the one people have always chosen to see in their favourite military heroes, the British with Lord Nelson, the Spanish with el Cid: the ideal of the champion who triumphs not just with courage but with panache. The

Real Madrid legend was that they didn't just win, they won beautifully. Danny Blanchflower, a contemporary player at Tottenham and huge admirer of Di Stefano's Real, was a philosopher of the game whose core belief was that there was much more to football than mere trophies. 'The game,' Blanchflower said, 'is about glory. It is about doing things with style.' And that remained the enduring ethos at Real Madrid. As Jorge Valdano, Real's polished director of sport, put it to me once, in those three decades without winning the European Cup, the tradition never died. 'The club never lost its grandeza, its greatness,' said Valdano, a pretty impressive figure himself, having won the World Cup with Argentina, having played for and coached Real Madrid, having written three clever books on the game. 'It is the same thing with Manchester United, who might have gone down to the second division but never lost that greatness either. The years passed and Real Madrid won the European Cup again eventually, then we assembled the finest collection of players maybe ever assembled in one team and now, look, it's a Rolls-Royce: a Rolls-Royce that's been in the garage for thirty years but has been dusted down, polished, oiled and now there it is, out on the road again, purring along, the greatest car in the world.'

They didn't always win, the team of Zidane and Ronaldo. But when the top players were on their top form, when they clicked as a team, Real would be providing the world with the most exquisite football there was.

As they did that night of 8 April 2003 at the Bernabéu. David Miller, the veteran of veterans among English football writers, remembered the Fifties Real team vividly and, with del Bosque, saw its spirit faithfully preserved in the twenty-first-century version. 'Real's most precious gift,' Miller wrote after watching Real win that quarter-final first leg against Manchester United, 'is to give us the embodiment of what football can and should be.' *L'Equipe*, the venerable French sports newspaper, described that game as 'the football summit of which we all dreamed', impatiently adding, 'Let the second leg begin!'

2: Performing Seals

Beyond the summit there was another summit. The second leg at Old Trafford turned out to be an even greater game, one to be placed right up there with that Real 7 Eintracht 3 game in 1960 – a treasure for those who were not old enough to have been in Glasgow then, or who had not even been born, to cling to through life as a golden memory of their own. Logic suggested that United did not have a prayer, but logic is always falling on its face in football and, as the wilder United optimists pointed out, Real's defence had looked shaky in the first game, van Nistelrooy was a formidable goal-scorer, Beckham could have one of those nights in which he delivers one 'half-goal' cross after another. Ferguson's United were nothing if not fighters and no one at Real Madrid was under any illusions that they would get an easy run. Still, United's fighter-in-chief, their captain and former boxer Roy Keane, did get the measure of the task ahead when he said that beating Real Madrid by a sufficient margin to make it to the Champions League semi-finals was the biggest challenge his team would ever face. Ferguson tried his best to convince himself and his players that it could be done. After watching the video of the Bernabéu game, he told the press, he had come away with some comforting lessons. 'Zidane does all these fancy tricks without really hurting you,' he said. 'He plays across you all the time.' More than a footballer, said the world's grouchiest coach of the world's greatest player, he was 'a performing seal'. Ferguson also trotted out the old Anglo-Saxon chestnut about continental teams not liking it 'up at them', that Real would not enjoy the battle that lay ahead at Old Trafford, that United would expose their 'soft centre'. Del Bosque, responding like a boxer to his rival's pre-fight taunts, warned United that Real 'were not a team of girls' and that if they needed to play hard, play hard they would.

Carlos Queiroz, more judicious and restrained than his then boss, observed that United's one goal at the Bernabéu could turn the tie their way. With away goals counting double in the event of a draw in the aggregate score, a 2-0 win would be enough for United. 'United had nothing to lose and Real Madrid had all to lose,' Queiroz said. 'The key for us was not to let Madrid score.'

In retrospect it sounds mad but United did have reason to believe they might silence Madrid's guns. Not least because the sharpshooter who had been most effective against them in the first leg would not be at Old Trafford. Ferguson had joked in the press conference immediately following the Bernabéu game that he hoped fate would intervene and prevent Raúl from playing at Old Trafford. 'I hope he doesn't like travelling,' Ferguson said, 'or failing that, that they won't let him into the country.' His wish came implausibly true. On the Monday before the Wednesday night of the game Raúl was rushed to hospital for an emergency appendix operation. These things do not happen to top-flight sportsmen. Training injuries, sure. Maybe even a bad cold. But appendicitis? God in his His mercy seemed to have decided to tilt the odds, just a little, in favour of the English underdogs.

Mercy was not a word, however, on Ronaldo's mind on that 23 April, the day of Saint George – warrior knight and patron saint of England – as the hour approached for the resumption of hostilities. His hunting partner was gone but now he'd show the world he was the man for the big occasion, just as he had done at the World Cup final the previous summer in Japan, when he scored the two goals that beat Germany. Half the world would be watching and the atmosphere at Old Trafford was the special one they reserve for what they call there the 'Big European Nights'. Nothing brings the United fans to life like the Champions League, especially against the most formidable rival of them all; the one they would most like to emulate. An hour before the game the singing was already relentless, the noise overwhelming, the 67,000 souls packed into Old Trafford grateful at the gift destiny had showered on them, the chance to be here on this night of all nights when, even if their team lost, they would be able to tell their children and their grandchildren they had been there to watch the Real Madrid of Ronaldo, Figo, Roberto Carlos and Zidane.

But when the team sheet was released, there was a big surprise. One which neither del Bosque nor any of the Real Madrid players could possibly have anticipated. Beckham would not be starting the game. Ferguson had left him on the bench. 'It was baffling,' del Bosque told me, his memory as fresh when we spoke about that game nine months later as if it had happened the day before. 'It was as if we had decided not to play Figo. Inconceivable. The only explanation I could think of was that there was a personal problem between the manager and the player, otherwise it was impossible to understand.'

Del Bosque was quite right, of course. Being left out of the starting line-up for that game of all games hurt Beckham a lot more than the flying boot had done. And Ferguson evidently wanted to hurt him. Yes, an argument of sorts could be made for not playing him. He had not done well at the Bernabéu. But neither had Giggs and, as for Keane, he had been by his own admission terrible, turned to stone by the Real magicians. But just as it was inconceivable in a game like this to leave out a player of Keane's class and experience, the same could be said of Beckham, England captain, veteran of a thousand battles, the hero – by Ferguson's own estimation – of United's European Cup triumph at the Camp Nou in Barcelona in 1999. All the more extraordinary was Ferguson's decision to play Juan Verón in his place. The Argentine had not only failed entirely to convince during the two years since United had broken the British transfer record to buy him, he had been out injured for a month and had to be lacking in the match fitness and mental tension required on such a night.

So there it was, the 'personal problem' between Ferguson and Beckham, between two of the biggest names in the game, drama-tised live on TV, for all the world to see. Beckham sat on the bench trying hard to look calm knowing that the cameras would be trained on his face from start to finish of the game. He tried to look impassive, he forced the odd smile, as if seeking to convince the watching world that he was taking the greatest setback, the greatest insult, of his footballing life with philosophy, that he was one of the boys and, sure, it was only natural that every now and again you would have to spend time on the bench, right? He wasn't kidding anybody. The hundreds of millions watching the game live around the world knew that he was badly hurt and seething with indignation, burning for a chance to get on the pitch and show everyone the blunder Ferguson had made in not putting him on from the start.

Not that, once the news of the Scot's extraordinary decision had been digested, it made any difference to the Real players. Their and their coach's attitude to the game was quite simple. Go out and play your natural game. In other words, attack and have fun. An Italian team, and probably a German and British and a French one too – and most other Spanish teams, for that matter – would have gone on to the pitch determined at all costs to salvage their lead, to bring down the portcullis and stop the other team from playing, never mind scoring. Real began the game as if it were they who were 3-1 down on aggregate, as if it were they who were desperate to score. It was an extraordinary sight. It was something that seemed new, but in truth harked back to a more innocent age. To the age of Di Stefano when Real Madrid conquered all, playing with devil-may-care fresh-ness, going all out not just to win but to seduce the world with their talent. After forty or fifty years in which the game had become increasingly stifled by the tacticians, by constipated coaches whose chief purpose in life was not to get their teams to play but to stop their rivals from playing: after all this, Real stormed into the game like revolutionaries – or rather counter-revolutionaries, bent on restoring the glorious ancient disorder.

Such thoughts were going through the mind more of Florentino Pérez, the architect of the counter-revolution, than of the players themselves. Ronaldo, Zidane and the rest of them just went out there to do what came naturally. Dressed in their black away strip, execu-tioner black, they strode on to the Old Trafford pitch resolved to put United to the sword.

Raúl, who had just been put to the knife, watched the game from home in Madrid. 'I was a lot more nervous than my teammates at Old Trafford were,' he told me. 'For starters, I had just got out of hospital that morning and I was worried that the tension of watching the game on TV was going to make my stitches burst!' As it turned out, the game started off as a bit of a breeze for Real. 'I was amazed,' Raúl said. 'Manchester had all the pressure on them to come at us and score and yet in the opening ten minutes we had all the possession, as if this were merely a continuation of game one.'

By the twelfth minute United's dreams lay in tatters. Guti, on for Raúl, slipped a beautifully guided ball through to Ronaldo who ran on to it like a hungry panther on the edge of the penalty area and whipped it into the back of the net past the left hand of the badly positioned Barthez, who had guessed wrongly that Ronaldo would send the ball to his right. But the response of the United players, driven on by the crowd, was a wonder to behold. Whether they really thought they could still win the tie, or were driven by the Dunkirk spirit of heroism in defeat, the fact was that they refused to lie down and die. What made their persistence all the more admirable was that during the rest of that first half, never mind Ferguson's pre-match boasts about going for the throats of the lily-livered Latins, the Real players were not only more skilful, they looked more commanding, stronger, bigger. Yet the United terriers kept coming, until in the forty-third minute van Nistelrooy seized on a loose ball in the penalty area and equalised. The crowd went crazy and the conviction spread around the stadium that United could still pull off the miracle. It was not an idea shared by the hundreds of millions around the world watching the game on TV. Outside the Old Trafford frenzy the sense was still that Real had plenty more ammunition than United; that there was no way the game would slip out of their control.

Yet del Bosque went into the dressing room at half-time a worried man. 'With Manchester United, more than any other team, you always know the game is not over till it's over,' he told me. 'It's something in their tradition but it's also the memory of that amazing European Cup final victory against Bayern in the Camp Nou, when they were 1-0 down on ninety minutes and won the game scoring twice in the three minutes of injury time. This was basically the same team and I needed no reminder that if they could have done that then, they could do it again now. At no stage of the game, right up until the final whistle, was I even remotely complacent.'

Queiroz's recollection of his feelings at half-time were different. Perhaps partly because he was talking to me six months into the Real job and his memory of that night had been confusingly tinged now with his loyalty for his new team. At any rate, he was exultant at the night's memories. 'Again, as at the Bernabéu, Real Madrid showed beautiful skills, fantastic individual performances. But above all in that game Ronaldo became Ronaldo again, and what happened was that he had the effect of a contamination, like a virus that spread to all the players on both teams and defined the spirit of the game. Both teams decided to play football; to play for playing's sake!'

Within five minutes of the restart Ronaldo had scored again. In terms of individual skill, it was the least spectacular of the goals that he was to score that night but the most magnificent goal of the game overall, and one of the best a team – a whole team – has ever scored. Rarely has a defence been opened up and dissected more clinically, more conclusively and with greater art.

It began deep in Real Madrid's half, with Roberto Carlos winning the ball by his left-hand corner flag. Four first-time passes out of defence and suddenly Zidane was free, running like an arrow down the middle of the pitch, across the centre circle, bound straight for goal. Shrugging off an attempted tackle by Giggs, who had run back as if his life depended on it, Zidane powered gracefully on. Approaching the D of the United penalty area he passed the ball, without breaking stride, to Figo out on the left. Figo ran into the penalty area, made as if to run down to the line and cross, checked himself, made as if to cross with his right, checked again, sending his defender this way and that, before turning left again and, catching the now massed United defence totally by surprise, he sought to replicate his goal in the Bernabéu, this time with his left foot. The ball sailed over Barthez, dipped and bounced off the top of the crossbar and back into play. But Real kept possession. The ball went out to Michel Salgado, a right back regarded as one of the least accomplished members of the team, but a born-again Garrincha compared to Gary Neville. Salgado played the ball back to Zidane, still there, the field marshal, on the edge of the D. He had a wall of red shirts before him. Nine United players were behind the ball. The chance to score had surely passed. You don't get through a defensive line like that. Zidane, the most comfortable player on earth with the ball at his feet and a defender on his back, had time to look around, ponder his next move. Out to Figo again, who passed it to Guti, who beat a man and gave it back to Zidane. The atmosphere in the stadium was as pulsating as it was bewildering, the crowd responding with the same gathering roar of excitement they would generate when their own team was on the attack.

There was something mesmeric about what Real were doing. They were buzzing around the United rearguard with the ball under complete control but the players were moving, and thinking – you could actually see Zidane weighing up his options – at lightning speed. With the sense building and building that a climax was coming, Roberto Carlos, *el hombre bala* – the bullet man – entered the stage. Zidane saw him over his left shoulder and slipped him the ball. Roberto Carlos passed it back to Zidane and darted – exploded – into the penalty area. Hypnotised, as if uncertain whether they were still actors in the game or had been reduced to spectators, the United defenders did not follow him.

They just watched him go. At precisely the right moment, not a fraction of a second too soon or too late, Zidane released a perfectly weighted pass back into Roberto Carlos's path. The Brazilian was free, inside the penalty area, behind the defence, but onside. He controlled the ball, looked up and slid it across Barthez, parallel to the goal line, to Ronaldo who alone, four yards out, prodded the ball into an empty net with his left foot. The whole move lasted forty seconds, seven players were involved, fifteen passes were made and not one United player got even a hint of a touch of the ball. People talk about the perfect drive in golf, the perfect ball in cricket, the perfect storm at sea. This was the perfect goal.

'So many touches of the ball!' said Raúl, remembering the goal as if it had been scored the night before. 'So many players involved!

It seemed as if the move was never going to end.' For del Bosque it was his most vivid memory of the game. 'What a move! What power and beauty! Everything: the whole build up, Figo's nearly remarkable goal, Roberto Carlos's run, Zidane's pass. Everything. Extraordinary. One of the great, great goals.'

But still United kept coming. Real were 2-1 up on the night, 5–2 up overall. To win the tie United had to score four goals in forty minutes and stop Real from scoring one. Sure enough, two minutes later Helguera, in his own penalty area, was hustled into putting the ball into his own net. 2-2. It was still hopeless. Still a lost cause. But the crowd roared United on, chanting their old war songs in a kind of kamikaze delirium, because they had to know that the more United ventured forward the greater the chances of Real scoring again. What was just as mad – madder – was that Real refused to do what every other team on earth would have done. Sit back, hold tight, defend.

It was the Ronaldo virus. The joyful Brazilian spirit of the game. Roberto Carlos, instead of doing what God intended left backs to do and defend, kept charging forward, hungry for a goal of his own. But Ronaldo, the natural-born predator, was hungrier still. With an unstoppable top-spin blaster from the edge of the box he rounded off his hat-trick. It was the fifty-ninth minute and Real were 3-2 up. There could be no coming back now. But Ferguson tried a last throw of the dice. The one remaining option. Painful as it was to him to admit his error to the watching world, but knowing that he would be viewed for ever as an ever greater fool if he did not do what his head – if not his heart – counselled him to do, he took off Verón and, with less than half an hour to go, brought on Beckham, who ran on to the pitch like a man on a mission from God.

'I got a bit of a fright when Beckham came on,' Raúl admitted. 'It was a hell of a surprise that a player of his talent and experience had not come on from the beginning but what I noticed in him that alarmed me was that he was so revved up, so full of that winner's rage that we all knew he had.'

A couple of minutes later Ronaldo, who had strained a muscle, went off. 'The entire stadium rose to salute him,' del Bosque recalled.

'I'd never seen anything like it. Unbelievable.' It was a spine-tingling moment. In a gesture of unbeatable nobility not one fan, not ten, not a hundred but all 60,000-plus United fans rose as if one to applaud off the pitch the man who had put their team to the sword, who had destroyed their dream of watching their heroes in a European Cup final scheduled to take place this year here, right here, in their very own stadium. Florentino Pérez told me some weeks later that this had been one of the greatest moments of his football life. 'I saw not only the entire stadium but also the chairman, Martin Edwards, and his board of directors, applauding Ronaldo off the pitch,' Pérez said. 'In the same way that Ronaldo said afterwards he would never forget it, I won't either.'

And then, as if there had not been enough drama for one night – for a hundred nights – Beckham scored. As fate had ordained that he should, as the sheer mad lust of his to show that he was the star of this team, that he was the captain of England, that if anyone was going to win this game, Sir Alex, it would be he. He scored ten minutes after coming on, from a free kick on the edge of the penalty area. His speciality but, as he would tell me afterwards, the cleanest, purest goal of its kind he had ever struck. 3-3 now in the seventy-first minute. Beckham did not so much jump for joy as let out a loud snarl. No time to savour the moment, he rushed back to the centre circle to restart the game. Just three more goals and United were home: suddenly nothing seemed impossible on this night. And still Real remained faithful to what del Bosque called the history of the club, Roberto Carlos juggling with the ball on the penalty spot, but in his own penalty area; Zidane and Figo charging forward, creating the second simplest chance of the night for Ronaldo's substitute, the young Javier Portillo, who missed. Beckham wasn't giving up. Abandoning all notion of tactical positioning, hurling himself at the enemy guns wherever they happened to be, he was one minute deep in defence, the next inside the Real penalty area. In the eighty-forth minute Beckham scrambled the ball over the line as if he were a born striker, as if he were van Nistelrooy, so mad was his desire, so desperate was he to get in on the action, prove a point, pull off the impossible dream. 4-3 to United. Just two more goals would do it. Injury time included, there were nearly ten minutes still to go. If they could do what they had done at the Camp Nou, they could do this. Del Bosque was in no doubt it was possible. Every Real Madrid fan watching at home was filled with the deepest dread, Raúl not excluded. When I asked him whether at any point he had felt the game was in the bag, his reply was instantaneous. 'No. This was Manchester United. We all remembered that European Cup final in 1999. That memory was in the back of my mind all the time during that game.' Only the neutrals believed lightning couldn't strike twice, only those without a passionate stake in the outcome believed it couldn't be done – though some were beginning to wonder what further dementia might yet lie ahead. The crowd sang on. The Old Trafford roar filled the night sky. Beckham was flying. In the ninety-first minute, another shot at glory, another free kick on the edge of the Real box, another Beckham free kick. Raúl was beside himself. 'I really did think my stitches were going to burst this time. If Beckham scored I knew that in the remaining three or four minutes of injury time anything could happen. Anything at all. I remember thinking, "Oh, my God! Oh, my God! Oh, my God!"'

But God decided He had been kind enough to Beckham for one night. The ball went sailing over the bar. And that was it. That was the end of the United resistance.

That was the final score. 4–3 to Manchester United, 6–5 to Real on aggregate. Zidane and Beckham exchanged shirts, Ferguson shook hands with del Bosque and the epic was over. The most charismatic fixture in world football had yielded eleven goals in two games. *L'Equipe* expressed the sentiment of the entire football world when it clamoured on its front page, 'We want more!' A good friend of mine, an eminent Spanish medical researcher and Real Madrid supporter called Pedro Alonso made it back home from a United Nations conference in Geneva just in time to catch the game on TV. After the game was over, elated and emotionally wrecked at the same time, he told me that his overwhelming feeling was one of relief that his plane had not gone down on the flight home from Geneva. 'Imagine,' he burbled, 'I would not have lived to see this game!'

Pierluigi Collina, the world's best referee and the man quite rightly appointed to officiate at this game of games, said afterwards that it was the best game he had ever seen. 'It was the best,' he said, 'for pace, for quality of passing, for combativeness and for fair play.' Bobby Charlton, the United legend and World Cup-winner with England in 1966, was at Old Trafford that night and he too said he could not recall a greater game of football.

Del Bosque, chatting in that hotel cafeteria in Madrid nine months later, still to find new employment after his sacking, shone like a little boy at Christmas reliving the images of that game. There was no regret, just a sense of gratitude that life had offered him a chance to participate the way he had done. 'That was the best advertisment you could ever come up with for the game' he said. 'The best example of how the game of football should be played. The atmosphere, the spectacle, the talent, the desire. The complete absence of anything dimly resembling defensive cynicism. It was the living expression of the great football ideal.'

Real were the better team but United could have gone through. It would not have been the first time in the history of football that pluck triumphed over talent. Del Bosque recalled in particular a header that flashed just wide of the post near the end by Solksjaer, from a perfect Beckham cross. And Beckham? 'God knows what might have happened if he had played from the start,' said del Bosque. 'He was so inspired, so wired up. Extraordinary that Ferguson left him on the bench, or did not bring him on earlier. Had a Spanish coach done that in a game of that magnitude he'd have been fired. No doubt about it.'

José Angel Sánchez, the first member of the Real Madrid staff to get to know Beckham (in his autobiography Beckham describes him as his 'friend José'), told me in a conversation some months later that this Manchester United v Real Madrid game had been decisive in terms of convincing the Englishman it was time to seek pastures new. 'Partly, of course, because of the way he was treated by the coach,' Sánchez said, 'but also because watching us play the way we did shaped his dreams and his ambition. There, and of course in the first game at the Bernabéu too, he glimpsed football of a quality he had not seen before. Let's face it, we deserved to win that first game 5-0; and as for the second one, the score was deceptive, because we were always the better team and David and the rest of them knew it. Still, I have to confess that as a Madrid fan, I felt fear run through my veins when David came on.'

Queiroz, who admired Ferguson and would always be loyal to him, refused to be drawn on the perplexing decision his old boss had made, a decision for which he was lashed by some sectors of the British press. 'The most important thing,' Queiroz said, 'is the memories that those two games left. Both games were magnificent, the best two of the last decade in my opinion. And I say that only because ten years is the time I have been involved in the world game. But probably it is the best in much more than ten years. Certainly I believe that if that second game in particular had been the European Cup final, as it deserved to be, it would have gone down as the greatest game ever. I mean, United scored five goals overall and still lost!

'In the end, it was a tribute to the game. A national anthem to football. And I must say very particularly that, independent of me being the coach of Real Madrid now and of Manchester United then, that I wish to pay my respects to all those fans in Old Trafford who, despite their team losing, supported their team in such an amazing way and applauded Ronaldo off the pitch and stayed in the stadium applauding – every single one of them, I am sure of it – until the last player had left the pitch at the end. Amazing! I will never, ever forget that. Those fans who through their pain recognised the glory of that game, showed such love for the game itself, recognised the quality and commitment not just of their own players but of Real Madrid's. Amazing . . .' Queiroz's voice trailed off, his eyes fixed on a distant place. 'Really, truly amazing . . .'

Del Bosque and Queiroz and Pérez, and pretty much everyone else involved with that game who was not English, agreed that such a response could only be found in the land that invented the game. England have the most notorious hooligans; at one international tournament after another, the ugliest bunch of fans. But there is also a sense of ownership of the game, as well as surviving flashes of the

British sense of 'fair play' and respect for a worthy oppon
foreign football fans who visit England remark upon. It is a heritage
and responsibility so strong that the English are capable, when a game
comes along that defines that footballing ideal of cutting through
the narrow tribal loyalties that week in, week out keep the not-
always-so-beautiful game going.

For in most respects to be a football fan is to be condemned to
a life of frustration. Waiting and hoping for a beautiful piece of play,
for an individual to do something thrillingly out of the ordinary, for
a team to string together three or four one-touch passes culminating
in something close to a goal. It happens so rarely. You have to be so
long-suffering, so madly optimistic. As in life, the moments of pure
joy are few and far between. Usually in football we are obliged to
feed on crumbs.

And that was why Real Madrid's display in those two games
against their great English rivals were so magically unforgettable. We
had waited not weeks, not months, but years – decades – to see
fantasy football like this and finally our patience had been rewarded.
Everything came together: the biggest game between the two biggest
teams in the world's best football competition, provided the stage for
the world's finest players to perform at the pinnacle of their ability.
Mario Zagallo, the coach of Pelé's Brazil 1970 side, was so thrilled
by Real's game that he confessed that here at last he had seen a team
fit to be called the true heirs of that magical side he had had the
privilege to lead. Comparing the Galácticos with Gérson, Rivelino,
Tostão, Jairzinho and Pelé, the grand old man of the beautiful Brazilian
game said, 'The Brazil 1970 team is Real Madrid today.'

Why or how it should all have come together on those two unforgettable nights at the Bernabéu and Old Trafford, nobody knows.
Del Bosque summed it up with typically elegant self-effacement in
comments he made to the press immediately after the game. 'To
those who say that there's no merit whatsoever in coaching this team,
my reply,' del Bosque said, 'is this: "You're absolutely right!" There is
nothing – nothing at all – that I can say to contradict you.'

3: The Biggest Sports Story of the Year

Peanuts. That was the word that sprung to mind as the knowledge struck that José Angel Sánchez, Director of Marketing at Real Madrid, had just pulled off the coup of his life; that he had clinched the purchase of David Beckham for a shockingly low sum of money. For peanuts. No word in his own language, Spanish, expressed with more biting economy his stupefaction at Manchester United's decision so lamely to surrender their most precious jewel.

Sánchez could not believe his ears when Peter Kenyon, Manchester United's chief executive, named his price. It was as if United had failed to realise what they, as the pioneers of merchandising and global sponsorship in the modern game, ought to have understood better than anybody. As if they had calculated Beckham's worth in terms merely of the market rate for a footballer of his abilities, failing entirely to add into the mix his value as the most resounding brand name in world sport. Never mind that football was humanity's great unifying religion. Never mind that Beckham was one of the idols of the world game. Beyond that, beyond everything, he had become very possibly the most famous man alive. Who else was there? The Pope? Maybe, though John Paul II cut less of a figure than Beckham in the Muslim world. The president of the United States? Perhaps, but his identity would have been less well known in large swathes of the Third World and his popularity significantly lower everywhere outside the United States. As for pop stars – Britney Spears, Michael Jackson, Madonna – or Hollywood actors – Julia Roberts, Brad Pitt, Tom Cruise – none reached an audience as deep and as wide. Household names they might have been in London, Paris or New York, but Beckham played on a bigger stage and his fame had spread – with the possible exception of parts of the US – to every corner of the planet. What couldn't you sell, with Beckham on your team?

Sánchez, a big man bursting with entrepreneurial ideas, wanted to shout for joy. But he could not. It was important now that he restrain his natural exuberance. Kenyon was sitting across a table from him, over lunch at a restaurant in Sardinia. They had chosen the quiet Mediterranean island as the venue for the negotiations in the hope that they would be able to elude the world's press, by now frantic to get their hands on a long-running story that seemed finally to be reaching its crescendo. (A photographer from the ever-intrepid *Sun* caught them at it though, sparking an inevitable frenzy of speculation, which this time turned out to be correct.) Sánchez had flown to Sardinia that morning from Madrid in the expectation of a long, hard slog; a tough day's bargaining. The surprise at the way things turned out only heightened his euphoria. But he had to keep himself in check. Deliciously aware that he was savouring a marketing man's equivalent of scoring the winning goal in the last minute of a European Cup final, Sánchez had to try and preserve a poker player's composure. He couldn't blurt out, 'Yes! Yes! I'll take him! Yes! Thank you. Thank you!' Besides, he hadn't spoken to his boss yet, to Madrid's formidable president, Florentino Pérez. He wasn't authorised to agree the deal on his own. Pérez had the last word.

So, with a heroic effort of will, Sánchez merely nodded in acknowledgement of Kenyon's proposal, battling to ignore the fireworks that were going off inside his head. Then, cool as could be, he began to argue some of the finer points of a potential deal. How much money would Real pay up front? How much would be contingent on Real winning trophies with Beckham in the side? Kenyon proposed a thirty million/five million euro breakdown. Sánchez said how about a bit less up front? After an hour Kenyon – to Sánchez's further surprise – relented, settling for 25 million down and ten million more if Real and Beckham won every trophy under the sun together. It was now four o'clock in the afternoon. Sánchez got up, left the table and phoned Pérez. 'Peanuts, they're asking peanuts!' he cried, this time translating the word into the Spanish *cacahuetes*, in case *el presidente* missed the point. But *el presidente* did miss the point. Or feigned to do so. 'Is that what you went to Sardinia for? You've got to be kidding!' he said. 'What?' replied Sánchez. 'I mean push them lower,' Pérez said. For the one and only time since he'd worked for Pérez, Sánchez lost his temper with his boss. He liked and admired the man everyone in Spain knew as Florentino. Sánchez was ever so slightly in awe of him. But the effort to contain his emotions these last few euphoric minutes had been too great and now he let go. 'What are you talking about, "push them lower"? Don't you see what we've got here, for Christ's sake?'

Pérez did see. He understood better than anybody the value of the Beckham brand. Buying Beckham had been his idea. As it had been to buy Luis Figo, Zinedine Zidane and Ronaldo. Florentino was a Spanish Medici, a lavish patron of the football arts resolved to assemble at the Bernabéu a contemporary collection to rival in their way the old masterpieces on display a couple of kilometres down the Paseo de la Castellana at Madrid's Prado Museum. But as well as patron, fan and president of Real Madrid he was a businessman, a tycoon who had made a fortune in the construction business, and his instinct, now that he smelt blood, was to keep squeezing. He would have responded the same way had Sánchez informed him that United had agreed to let him go for 20 million, for ten.

This time, though, Sánchez felt that Pérez was letting instinct get the better of his judgement. OK, so maybe they'd knock Manchester United down a million euros if they kept at it; but maybe too they'd lose their man. And that was a prospect too ghastly to contemplate. Having invested so much mental and emotional energy in an enterprise which had become in recent months the consuming obsession of Sánchez's life, which Pérez himself had identified as crucial to his strategic vision for Real Madrid, it would be sheer madness to risk scuppering everything now for a few euros more. Beckham was on offer for less money than Pérez had paid for the other three superstars – the so-called 'Galácticos' – that he had acquired since being elected club president in the summer of 2000. A lot less money. Figo had cost 60 million euros from Barcelona. Zidane had cost 75 million from Juventus. Ronaldo had cost 45 million from Inter Milan. And now here was Sánchez telling him that Manchester United were letting Beckham go for a fixed price of 25 million plus 10 million more conditional on how many trophies Real Madrid won with him on the team. The final amount that Madrid would have to pay out, Sánchez estimated, would be around 32 million. Which, in purely football terms, might have been a fair reflection of his worth compared to Zidane, Figo and Ronaldo, winners between them of six of the previous seven FIFA World Footballer of the Year awards; but if you factored in what Beckham would do for Real Madrid's bank balance, the income he would bring in from sponsorships – with or without a ball at his feet – it was the football bargain of all time. Mind-bogglingly, the price Manchester United were asking placed the sale of the global icon outside the top fifteen most expensive transfers in the world up to that point.

'OK,' Pérez told Sánchez. 'So how much is Beckham worth to you?' 'Five hundred million euros,' Sánchez shot back. Pérez pondered that for a moment. A ratio of one to fifteen. A 1,500 per cent return on his investment. Sánchez might have been exaggerating; but maybe he wasn't. Beckham, as Sánchez would say, was an industry.

Beckham, the richest footballer alive (Zidane and Ronaldo were the second and third richest), was a one-man global brand whose full money-making potential had yet to be fully tapped. Especially in the great booming market of the world, Asia, which was in the grip of football mania, especially Beckham-mania.

Five hundred million, thought Pérez, might not be all that wildly off the mark. Not at all. So what was that again? 25 million euros plus a maximum more of ten? That's right, said Sánchez, calming down. He and Sánchez had calculated, before Sánchez set off for Sardinia, that they might, if they were lucky, get away with paying 40 million euros for Beckham. They were prepared to pay 50 million if absolutely necessary. And if it really came to it, more. So it really wasn't a difficult decision to decide to go for Manchester United's offer. Sánchez knew, once he had got over his momentary panic, that his president would come around. But it was still with relief that he heard Pérez say at the other end of the phone line the sweet, magic words, 'All right, then. We'll have to take that.'

★   ★   ★

And that, almost, was that. The date was Friday 13 June 2003. What remained was to deal with the player and the player's agent. But Pérez and Sánchez had established lines of communication with them already and they were confident they'd wrap things up fairly briskly. What was certain, at any rate, was that the hard part was over. Manchester United had been persuaded, like Shakespeare's Othello, to throw away a pearl richer than all their tribe. And more easily and for much less than Pérez would have imagined possible when he first formed the idea, nearly a year earlier, of adding Beckham to his collection of superstars. Which was why a couple of hours after that heated conversation with Sánchez, Pérez surprised his trusted right-hand man by calling him on his mobile telephone, catching him as he was about to board his private plane back to Madrid. He did not say hello. He did not introduce himself. He just said two words, 'Congratulations, sunshine!'

So why had it all been so easy? Why so much cheaper than Figo, Zidane and Ronaldo? Six months after Beckham had joined I put those questions separately to four of the top Real Madrid executives. Their first response was, in each case, to shrug. They hadn't believed it at the time. They couldn't quite fully believe it now. But once they began examining the possible factors involved all roads led to one conclusion: that while the first three Galácticos had had to be prised away from their clubs in operations requiring all Pérez's tenacity and accumulated business cunning, as well as lots of cash, Beckham had been almost given away. Manchester United's position had been, 'Here, take him! We don't want him any more.' It had not been Peter Kenyon's position. Through little fault of his own, he found himself in a predicament where he had little choice but to hand over Beckham for a song, or at least for much less than he himself had originally estimated the selling price would be. Kenyon, while nominally chief executive, was not the real power at United. Someone else had the power to trump his initiatives, exercising almost godlike authority over the club's affairs. Someone else who was Real Madrid's secret weapon in the Beckham transfer, their unwitting ally. Without whom Manchester United had no intention whatsoever of letting Beckham go. In the late summer of 2002, when Beckham's last season at Manchester United began, neither the United fans, nor the players nor the directors of what was then the world's richest club had any inkling that the England captain would ever leave them. They would have reacted to the suggestion with protective rage. All, that is, except Pérez's ally, the most powerful individual in Manchester United's history, the club's manager, living legend and knight of the British realm, Sir Alex Ferguson.

Let us rewind two and a half years to the autumn of 2000. Ferguson had just published a book, *The Unique Treble*, a lovingly detailed, game-by-game account packed with pictures and diagrams of United's extraordinary 1998/99 season, when they became the first team ever to win the English league, the FA Cup and the European Cup. I flew to Manchester to interview him. We met in the airy reception area of the main building at United's training facility in Carrington in the Cheshire countryside, twenty minutes' drive from Old Trafford. It was a long, low, sleek building of clean metallic lines and glass-tinged turquoise blue, of a piece, in other words, with the modern, multinational, multimedia, megamerchandising operation that Manchester United plc had become in the Ferguson era.

We talked, among other things, about Beckham and the celebrity factor in the modern game. The rise of the multi-millionaire football player was a phenomenon he said he'd had the misfortune to live to see, but for now Beckham, he said, had posed him no problems whatsoever. On the contrary. 'Maybe thirty-five per cent' of United's goals came from Beckham and the 'thrust and penetration' he provided with his famous crosses simply had no price. 'He's been fantastic for us. Fantastic,' Ferguson said. 'He's concentrated for so long on that part of his game, worked on his technique with such application, that his range in his crosses is marvellous. Unbelievable. His width. His ability to use the ball so intelligently from out there, his crossfield passes, his short passes, his chips. Unbelievable.'

Ferguson did fear, though, that with time Beckham's celebrity might undercut the quality of his game. In the recent past, players as talented as any he had at United had succumbed disastrously to the siren songs of money and fame. Paul Gascoigne had been the most technically gifted English player in forty years, if not more, yet his celebrity had consumed him, destroyed a career in mid-flow. 'Aye, aye,' said Ferguson, wearily. 'How a player's image has changed since, say, the Sixties. And how aware they are that they have this image to keep up, an image completely outside football. Which is why some will get a fancy car, some will wear an earring. So you have to say to yourself, at what point do I lose my control? At what point do I say, right, enough's enough? I am forever keeping an eye on this side of things, judging to see if it gets too much.' And when did it get too much? 'When it starts interfering with their performance.' But how, I asked him, did he know when to relate one thing to the other? His reply shed a lot of light on the way things would eventually turn out between him and Beckham.

'If you see them change dramatically as an individual, as a person,' he said. 'Because the last thing I want is to see them change. I want to see them keep their feet on the ground. I want to see that they appreciate where they're coming from, and I want to see them go back to their parents and their wives the same person. I don't want to see a lot of bigheads running about the place.'

Change with Beckham was one thing he did see, and plenty of it. In 2000 he was big in England. By 2002, when the World Cup in Japan came around, he was a global superstar. The whole world, outside North America at any rate, appeared to have succumbed to his charms. Football was only part of the story. The more established Beckham became in the world of showbiz, the more difficult it became for his manager to keep him in his controlling sphere. Ferguson was more comfortable with the withdrawn young lad that he had nursed through the United youth teams, a boy so awkward, inarticulate and shy – so dependent on Ferguson to hold his hand when success on the pitch obliged him to make public appearances – that he would never have imagined one day ending up as the biggest thing since The Beatles. But over time that transformation in his personality did occur, much of it to do with the confidence he acquired from marrying his initially more famous pop star wife Victoria Adams, Posh of the Spice Girls. Ferguson never liked Victoria, nor she him. He was an old-fashioned Scot who had clear ideas as to what a woman's place in life ought to be. She was a driven young woman determined to make a success of her marriage, her family and her career all at the same time. Ferguson churned away inside, only making his feelings about her clear after Beckham had left United. 'He was blessed with great stamina, the best of all the players I've had here,' he told America's *Sports Illustrated* magazine a matter of days after Beckham had gone. 'After training, he'd always be practising, practising, practising. But his life changed when he met his wife. She's in pop and David got another image. He's developed this "fashion thing". I saw his transition to a different person.'

That much was quite true. If anything, Ferguson had fallen short. Beckham had undergone not so much a transition as a metamorphosis. Princess Diana's death had orphaned a large part of the British public. Beckham, the son of a gas-fitter, filled her role. He was the individual on whom the mantle fell of nourishing the popular appetite for vicarious drama. The tabloids, the nation's great arbiters of taste, anointed 'Posh and Becks' as England's favourite real-life soap opera couple, wheeling them on as substitutes for Diana and Charles. If Beckham was seen talking to another woman at a public place, if he and Victoria emerged from a restaurant looking as if they might have had a row, if baby Brooklyn vomited over mum's dress, if Beckham bought himself a fashionable new suit, or a new car, or even a new leather bag, the event would be recorded by the tabloid photographers, written up in breathless prose. Not that Beckham deserved any great sympathy for enduring such indignities. Much as Diana did, he and his wife-to-be appeared right from the beginning to love the intrusions of the press at least as much as they occasionally claimed to dislike them. Neither appeared to be in any hurry to flee the celebrity bubble.

Ferguson might have taken the changes in Beckham in a lighter mood. Noting that he was actually playing as well as he ever had, that love and celebrity had not dimmed his passion or commitment for the game, the manager might have good-humouredly teased him, as his teammates at United never ceased doing. Ryan Giggs nearer the time of Beckham's move to Real Madrid, said, 'Becks hasn't changed since I've known him – he's always been a flash Cockney git.' But Ferguson could not joke about Beckham the celebrity. He seemed to pose too much of a challenge to Ferguson the man. It was as if there were an Oedipal edge to the relationship. It was always Beckham who described Ferguson as a father figure but of the two it was Ferguson who seemed to suffer more, and as time went by to exhibit increasingly negative feelings towards his adopted football son. The Flying Boot incident was the dramatic flashpoint, the central Oedipal moment when the father explodes with rage and the son tries to kill him. But the seeds for the break had been sown earlier.

It was a visit to the Queen in November 2002 that first did it. Ferguson's reaction to Beckham's royal encounter revealed just how irrational the player's success had made him. Beckham tells the story in his autobiography *My Side*. He was off injured at the time with a cracked rib but had received an invitation to meet the Queen in his capacity as captain of the England team. Ferguson appeared to think that a visit to Buckingham Palace would in some way delay Beckham's recovery from injury. Whatever his reasoning it was, to say the least, perplexing for him to have told Beckham the next time they met, 'When I saw you turn up there, I questioned your loyalty to Manchester United.' Beckham's comment in the book is, 'That stung. I couldn't believe I was hearing it, to be honest. I'd been at the club for thirteen years.' And then he said to Ferguson, 'I love United. I want to be here. But if you don't want me to be, you should tell me.'

Ferguson did not tell him. He said nothing. And for Beckham it was a silence that spoke louder than words. Clearly Ferguson had judged that Old Trafford was not big enough for the both of them. And he showed it in the following weeks, continually niggling away at Beckham, reprimanding him for the smallest things, snubbing him and – the cruellest punishment in his power to inflict – dropping him from the team. Beckham says this was the worst period of his thirteen years at Manchester United. Jaap Stam, an excellent Dutch centre half who Ferguson had fallen out with and ditched a year earlier, knew exactly how he felt. 'Once Ferguson decides you are no longer part of his plans for whatever reasons, there is no turning back,' Stam told a British Sunday newspaper. 'You are like an unwanted piece of baggage and you have to weigh up whether it's worth hanging around when there is no chance of playing. I think you are just expected to accept it, there is no plan in place if you decide you're not going to other than the fact you will probably be left to rot in the reserves.'

As Stam had done, Beckham got the message loud and clear.

Florentino Pérez had it very clear in his mind well before then that Beckham had to be his next Galáctico signing. He had known, to be precise, since 2 September 2002, as the ink was still running dry on the contract he had signed with his previous superstar acquisition, Ronaldo. It had been a tough business, extracting the great Brazilian from Inter Milan, but no sooner had Pérez put pen to paper on the deal than his restless mind began fixing on who his next big buy would be. It took him about a second to make up his mind. 'Beckham had talent and global repercussion: I was never more sure about a player than David Beckham,' he would tell me much later.

Pérez had this hard-and-fast policy of making one stellar signing every summer. The season after he had signed Beckham it was more of a struggle to make up his mind. There were four players in his sights: Thierry Henry and Patrick Vieira of Arsenal, Francesco Totti of Roma and Ruud van Nistelrooy of Manchester United. For a while there was even a fourth pretender to the title of 'best player in the world who does not play at Real Madrid', Michael Owen of Liverpool. But with Beckham there had never been any doubt. The captain of Brazil was in the bag, the captain of England had to be Pérez's next prey. So how did he set about capturing Beckham? How did he get his man? At first, by doing nothing. Like a hunter in the forest, an image he himself liked, he hid in the undergrowth and lay in wait – eyes peeled, ears alert – believing that sooner or later, if he showed enough perseverance and patience, opportunity would come his way. He suspected from the start that his best chance of landing Beckham would come from what he wryly described as the looming *ruptura familiar* – family bust-up – between Beckham and Alex Ferguson. But it was not until February and the Flying Boot incident that Pérez became aware of how favourably things were turning out for him. It was not just that the family bust-up was clearly becoming irreconcilable, Pérez also knew that the more badly, and more visibly, United wanted to let go of Beckham, the lower the price would be. A seller who makes no secret of his desire to sell is every buyer's dream.

The newspapers were not slow on the scent. Two stories make up the staple diet of football journalism: games and transfer news. You do the preview of a game on the day it is played; you do the match report the day after; if the game was important enough you might even do an analysis of the game the day after that. Given that at most you have two days a week when games are played you are left with at least two, usually three, days out of seven in which you still have sports pages to fill. Transfers – more often than not transfer speculation – are what fills the void. How do the transfer speculation stories make it into the press? Sometimes people make the stories up. But usually there is not much need to be inventive. Agents talk unofficially to clubs; both talk off the record to journalists. Sometimes it suits agents or clubs to plant a transfer rumour in a newspaper – in order to test the interest of one of the relevant parties, perhaps, or to raise or lower a player's price. Sometimes it is simply a matter of a journalist being friends with an agent who is tuned in to the latest secret communications and, having picked up the crackle of a good story, does a favour to his pal. (In due course the agent will expect the journalist to reciprocate the favour, of course, and so the world goes round.)

And thus it came about, as day follows night, that after the Flying Boot incident the newspapers began to fill with stories about a) Beckham's imminent departure from Manchester United and b) his likely destination being Real Madrid. The second half of February and the first half of March saw a daily drip-drip of denials, half-denials, veiled hints and nudged semi-confirmations from sources, named and unnamed, related in some way with Beckham, Manchester United or Real Madrid. The drip-drip became a flood after Real Madrid were drawn to play Manchester United in the Champions League quarter-finals. Especially after the cat was let out of the bag, in the most unwitting way, on the night of 7 April, twenty-four hours before the big game at the Bernabéu. On a Spanish television programme called 'The Day After', Ricardo, Manchester United's Spanish reserve goalkeeper, let slip the following little nugget, captured as he was being filmed driving through the streets of Manchester: 'A couple of days ago when I asked him [Beckham] if he was going to move to Real Madrid this summer he started asking me questions about the quality of primary schools in Madrid. I told him that the schools there were the best in the world.' The remark was so obviously uncalculated, uttered in the course of what had clearly been a long and leisurely chat with the reporter in the car, that it had to be true.

The critical development in the transfer drama came in mid-April, between the first and second legs of that Champions League quarterfinal. Beckham's agent, Tony Stephens, and another father figure for him, contacted Real Madrid. Not directly, but in the discreet, circuitous way that is customary in the football world when a player wants to sniff out a club's interest in him. Agents talk to agents who talk to connections they have at the clubs. It is not the way things are supposed to happen. According to the strict letter of the law clubs are not allowed to sound out the availability of players under contract at other clubs. But it happens all the time. This is the way the network of football agents and clubs operates in Europe. The communications are constant. The lines never stop buzzing.

Why did Beckham make the first move? Common sense alone tells you that given the appalling deterioriation of relations with Ferguson at the end of 2002, he must have wondered at least as early as then whether his situation at Manchester United would soon become untenable, and whether he would be forced to join another club. Come April, Beckham knew that he had better start devoting urgent attention to where he was going to be playing his football the following season. Aged twenty-seven, with maybe his best five footballing years ahead of him, he had to do the responsible thing by his family but most of all, money not being likely to be too much of a problem in his life, by himself. Beckham might have been the world's biggest celebrity, a one-man global industry, but he loved football as much as he did when he arrived at Manchester United as a shy little fifteen-year-old boy. Professional players often take much less of an interest in the game, when they are off the pitch, than the average fan. Beckham is a football nut. Given how cruelly short a player's professional life is he was not going to resign himself to spending his few remaining years in misery, cringing in the shadow of the bully who had made him great. Obviously what to do next was the main subject of conversation at the time with Tony Stephens. (The Manchester United boss could never stand the sight of Stephens – a grave, soft-spoken man utterly different in style from Ferguson – of whose relationship with Beckham he was wary and jealous.) Real Madrid would have been the club that Stephens' business brain would have judged to be best suited to enhance the Beckham brand. It was crystal clear what Stephens had to do: get in touch, via the agents' bush telegraph, with Real Madrid.

So what did the message from the Beckham camp to the Bernabéu say? Quite simply this: might Real Madrid be interested at some point in signing David Beckham? By the same path as the message had arrived, back came the unequivocal reply: Yes.

Pérez, lying in wait in his Bernabéu lair, quietly thrilled to the news. After learning that the Beckham–Ferguson marriage was in trouble, this had been the message he had been hoping to hear. The ice had been broken, the final chapter of Beckham's career at Manchester United had begun to be written and, if things went according to past form, Pérez would once again get his man. The two big transfers of the previous two years had also been initiated by the players themselves. Zidane and Ronaldo, again through the agents' network, had been the ones to make the first move. That is the way Real Madrid likes it. For reasons, in the first place, of dignity and pride; but also because it makes good business sense. The more a player wants to come to your club, and your club alone, the lower the price you're going to have to pay for him.

Pérez understood this better than anybody. He is a proud Spaniard and a prouder Real Madrid fan. He venerates the club over which he presides, like a cardinal his cathedral. That is why it is important to him that prospective players show the club its due respect, why they should – in an attitude of proper deference – make the first contact. But he is dreamy only up to a point. He possesses, in abundance, what Saul Bellow describes as 'the cheating imagination of the successful businessman'. He schemes, he plots and, as his amazing record both at Real Madrid and in the construction business indicates, he is invariably several moves ahead of his rivals. There were still a couple of months to go but he already had the endgame in mind.

The first contact between Real and United on the Beckham affair came six days after their game at Old Trafford. Pérez and the United chief executive Peter Kenyon, as well as other directors of both clubs, were gathered at a general assembly of the G14 in Brussels. The G14 is an organisation where Europe's most powerful clubs seek to come up with collective strategies aimed at ensuring that the game rewards them with the income they feel their power and fame deserve. Inevitably when the United and Real people met the subject of Beckham came up. Neither side had broached the matter until now, but given the media frenzy, and that here they were face to face, it would have been ridiculous to pretend the issue wasn't there. Besides Kenyon was glad of the opportunity to make his position clear. Beckham was staying at United, he maintained, and that was that.

Kenyon knew Beckham was worth more to the club in marketing terms than all the rest of the Manchester United players combined. Kenyon did not want him to leave. In his heart of hearts, he would rather have let Ferguson go than Beckham. Kenyon was privately of the opinion that Ferguson had got far too big for his boots, that he had come to see himself as bigger not just than the players but than the club itself. But the successes of the previous decade had made Ferguson's position unassailable among the fans, especially the hard-core who went every other weekend to watch the team at Old Trafford. It was on that base, resting as it did on the prospect of mass mutiny by the fans were he to be forced by the directors to leave, that Ferguson's power resided.

Kenyon, being aware of Ferguson's feelings towards Beckham, knew the odds on the player remaining at Old Trafford were not much better than 50-50. His chief purpose in stating to Real his refusal to let him go was to park all discussion of the matter until after the season was over. For United were still in a neck-and-neck battle for the English championship with Arsenal and one thing no one at the club would have wanted to do was destabilise the team. So Kenyon let it be known to Real Madrid at that G14 meeting that he would appreciate them saying something to help put a stop to the speculation. This Real Madrid did not mind doing. Stopping a deal with Beckham: that would be a huge problem. Stopping the speculation, or being seen to be trying to: there was no harm in that. The very night of that G14 meeting, 29 April, Real Madrid issued an official statement on their website.

> *Surrounding the speculation regarding the supposed interest from Real Madrid in signing David Beckham, the club wishes to state that:*
> 1. *No contact has existed between Real Madrid and Manchester United on this issue.*
> 2. *Neither directly nor indirectly has there been any contact between Real Madrid and Mr Beckham.*
> 3. *Despite the speculation surrounding this issue, Madrid has no intention of negotiating the transfer of Mr Beckham.*
> 4. *Against the general policy of the club which never uses official sources to reject rumours, this press release has been issued with the objective of putting an end to the growing speculation which has circulated without any foundation linking Mr Beckham with Real Madrid.*
> 5. *On top of the recent rumours, the unconditional friendly relationship between both clubs and the respect due for Mr Beckham still remains.*

Apart from point 5, it was all rubbish, of course. Just as Pérez's remarks to a radio reporter had been on the same day that the statement was issued. 'Never, never, never!' was his reply to a BBC radio reporter who asked him whether he was going to sign David Beckham. So Real Madrid were not interested, then? the radio reporter persisted. 'No. Not now. Never.' So he would never sign Beckham? 'Never, never!'

It wasn't the Real Madrid president's finest hour. He liked to think of himself as a man of honour. All Spaniards do – it's the defining national aspiration. But there was no denying that this was a raging, bare-faced lie. Why did Real issue so categorical a statement denying their interest in Beckham? What possessed Pérez to say what he did into a reporter's microphone? Why was he so trenchant? How did these lies square with Real's idea of itself as a noble institution and Pérez's own notions of personal integrity?

Quite simple, really. When it comes to the busines of buying and selling top football players, the truth is that everybody lies. Real Madrid's director general of sport Jorge Valdano, asked some months later in an interview with the Spanish sports newspaper *Marca* if he ever lied, casually – unhesitatingly – replied: 'Only when I am involved in negotiations over a player, because the other parties also read the newspapers and you can't let them have an advantage. You can't tell the whole truth.'

All's fair in love, war and football transfers. Everybody speaks rubbish. But it is strategic rubbish. A means to an end. All the big clubs get up to all manner of skullduggery once their minds have been made up to buy or sell a player.

Florentino Pérez told his lies about his intentions regarding David Beckham in the service, therefore, of a higher virtue. He had to ensure that Beckham played next season in the Real Madrid colours. Enraging Manchester United – and putting Beckham, for that matter, in a very awkward position – was not the way to achieve his objective.

Pérez could thus more than salvage his conscience, he could actually reinforce his sense of himself as a man of honour, in the knowledge that by saying what he did he had acted in the noblest spirit of self-sacrifice.

Of course, Kenyon would not have been taken in by Pérez's denials. He understood the game as well as anybody. Pérez told me later that it had been a moment of playful banter, no more; that he and Kenyon had a good laugh about it later that night. It was in a similar spirit of nudge-nudge mutual understanding that Kenyon issued a little statement of his own after Pérez had done him the favour of saying what he did. 'I am delighted Mr Pérez has confirmed this in such an emphatic manner but, anyway, we at Manchester United never had any intention of selling him.' That was also, if not quite a lie, a pious half-truth.

If you wanted to know what was really going on at this delicate stage in the game you had to look elsewhere. Once again, far more genuinely revealing than anything said by the drama's leading players was something that happened off-stage. In the United States, to be precise, and that very same 29 April when the big men were making all their denials, David Beckham's wife, Victoria, all but gave the whole elaborate game away. A guest of *Vogue* magazine for a fashion launch in New York, she was tracked down by Britain's GMTV, who asked her whether she was 'intending to move to Italy or Spain'. 'I can't possibly answer that . . .' she replied. But then, as the answer hung in the air, she delivered in full view of the camera the most emphatic of nods and the broadest of mischievous smiles.

The *Daily Mirror* was in no doubt as to where the truth lay. 'Whatever country they come from,' the paper wrote, 'soccer chairmen speak the same language. So when the boss of Real Madrid says that Beckham will never, never, never go to his club, it means only one thing. He will be there by the start of next season.' The prospect moved *Mirror* columnist Tony Parsons to shed bitter tears. 'It will be a national disaster if Beckham leaves,' Parsons wailed. 'He is more than the biggest celebrity since we buried Princess Diana. He is more than a world-class athlete, loving father, devoted husband, cultural icon and role model. In a land increasingly full of fame pygmies, Beckham is the real thing.' And then there was this from the octogenarian William Rees-Mogg in his column in *The Times*, whose pages he once edited with venerable distinction: 'Only a very academic mother would not wish her son to grow up like Beckham, straightforward, good looking, English and able to do with a football what Muralitharan can do with a cricket ball . . . Apart from Princess Diana herself, there has been no greater celebrity in England since Charlie Chaplin was a young man, nor before Chaplin since Nelson.'

And there was this from the *Guardian*, summing up the mood of the nation in its issue of 1 May. 'It was a busy news week,' the *Guardian* said, 'by anyone's standards: the US announced its pullout from Saudi Arabia, Israel suffered another suicide bombing and Argentina went to the polls in the hope of electing an economic saviour. But one question and one question alone exercised the hearts and minds of Britain and its press: would David Beckham really leave Manchester United for Real Madrid?'

On 4 May Manchester United won the English league championship and four days later Florentino Pérez confided in a meeting at his office that, now that the crunch was coming, he was beginning to feel really optimistic about clinching the Beckham deal. Everything, he said, was in place. 'Ferguson wants him to go, Beckham wants to go, we would like to have him and so, therefore, let's make everybody happy.' José Angel Sánchez, his eyes glowing, told me that same day why landing Beckham was, from his point of view, an absolute must. 'Today Real Madrid and Manchester United represent the South and the North, the Latin and the Anglo-Saxon,' Sánchez said. 'To get Beckham would allow us to cross over to the North, to get the Anglo-Saxons too. Real Madrid would be the United Nations.'

On 11 May Manchester United put an end, once and for all, to the farce. The team rounded off their successful domestic season with a 2-1 victory at Everton, in which Beckham scored, and that same evening Kenyon came clean, finally revealing all. Acknowledging that offers were being made, he said that something in the region of 50 million euros would have to be considered. 'It would be remiss not to,' Kenyon said. 'The success of Manchester United is about the team. David Beckham is an essential part of our team. But ultimately players retire, there is a life span and there will reach a time when we have to replace him.'

On 19 May there was another meeting of the G14 clubs. This time the venue happened to be Manchester. Sánchez went in representation of Real Madrid. The purpose of the meeting was to shape a common policy on television rights. Sánchez's purpose was to talk to Kenyon about Beckham. So the Spaniard took the Englishman to one side and asked him to clarify what the situation was. In truth Beckham was all but out of the door but Kenyon wanted to try and keep a few cards close to his chest. 'There is still some debate within the club, but yes, there's movement,' Kenyon said. Sánchez said, 'OK. Can we do one thing? Can I have your permission to talk to Beckham's agent?' Kenyon thought about it for a moment, then said yes. That was the green light Sánchez had been waiting for. The final act in the drama had begun. Sánchez travelled to Nice, where Tony Stephens was with the Beckham family, and met with Stephens. Sánchez's purpose was to establish whether Beckham did indeed wish to come to Real Madrid; whether there was any doubt in his mind that if he left Manchester United, Real Madrid was the club where he would most want to go. Stephens told him just what he wanted to hear. That, yes, no doubt about it. After Manchester United the only possible club for Beckham had to be Real Madrid. Anything else would be a come-down.

Then Sánchez put the basic outlines of a financial offer on the table. Before going any further there were two things Beckham should know, Sánchez said. The salary he would receive at Real Madrid would be non-negotiable. He would be paid no more, no less than the other four Galácticos, Ronaldo, Zidane, Figo and Raúl – which was 5.5 million euros a year. And, like the other Galácticos, he would have to cede fifty per cent of his image rights – meaning money he made from endorsing brand names like Pepsi-Cola and Adidas – to the club.

It was a delicate moment for Sánchez. Scary. He knew perfectly well that this was an awful lot to ask of a one-man multinational like Beckham. The whole deal could have fallen apart on that one point. And Sánchez, a man of business, would have understood Beckham's position if he had said no. Kenyon had in fact warned him in a private chat they'd had that there was no way Beckham would accept such a deal. But whatever Beckham said, Real Madrid were not going to make an exception for him; they were not going to risk the whole Galáctico edifice coming down for one man. To Sánchez's boundless relief and surprise, Stephens told him not to worry. These two contractual stipulations of Real Madrid's were not insuperable. 'In the end David's decision will not be based on economics; it will be made with the heart,' said Stephens. Another, more hard-nosed reason that Stephens did not mention was that while half Beckham's image rights was an awfully big slice of the pie, the pie itself would be likely to be bigger with Real Madrid, whose appeal to the multinationals was now greater than United's and growing fast. Besides, Real Madrid was the only club in the world that would assuredly enhance the Beckham brand; whereas joining any other team might risk diminishing it. All the same, Stephens, remembering he was an agent after all, did mention to Sánchez that the field was not all clear for Real yet; that there was still interest from other teams, one Spanish and two Italian – meaning Barcelona, Inter and AC Milan.

Real Madrid's bargaining position had not yet reached that optimal point of advantage that Pérez sought. But the time had come for him to emerge once and for all from his lair and openly pursue his prey. Real Madrid began formal talks with Manchester United. Beckham left them all to get on with it. He flew to South Africa with the England team; met his hero – he said that he had no greater hero – Nelson Mandela; played against South Africa and then rushed back home and on to the United States for a three-week holiday with his family. In his absence, things began to unravel. The pundits all started venturing opinions on which of the continental giants Beckham should go to; everyone started openly throwing their hats into the ring: Barcelona, Milan, even the veteran Roma coach Fabio Capello, who said he would be thrilled to have Beckham on his team. On 7 June Manchester United issued a statement confirming that clubs from Italy and Spain had expressed an interest in signing Beckham. The statement confirmed that SFX were also in contact with the interested clubs and all parties were in regular and close communication. That was not entirely true. What was happening at this time was that Manchester United were in very close contact indeed with Barcelona and neither SFX nor Beckham were being told much about it.

Or rather, United were in touch with Joan Laporta, a candidate to the Barcelona presidency. Whether he did become president or not would be decided in an election involving the club's 100,000 members later in the month. As furious speculation grew during the first week of June that a deal with Laporta was imminent, Pérez stayed cool, sat tight, waited to make his move. The time was not quite right to put money on the table – a bidding war with Barcelona or anyone else was precisely what he did not have in mind. He wanted the field clear all to himself.

Good news suddenly arrived from Italy. Good news for Pérez and, indeed, for the actively negotiating Laporta. The Italians had pulled out. Inter just fizzled out of the picture and Milan, following lots of noises from the club's vice-president Adriano Galliani suggesting they would fight to the bitter end to get Beckham, unambiguously withdrew. 'There are many better ways of spending money, earned with such sacrifice,' said the club president Silvio Berlusconi, 'than signing Mr Beckham.' And that was the end of that.

Then, suddenly, quite out of the blue, calamity struck for Pérez. On 9 June, Manchester United plc issued a statement saying they had accepted an offer of 45 million euros from Joan Laporta. In the event of him winning the Barcelona presidency that coming weekend, 15 June, Beckham would be sold to the big Catalan club. At Real Madrid they did not know how to take the news. Had everybody been lying to them, even in the private conversations that had taken place? Had both Manchester United and Beckham been leading them up the garden path? No. Only Manchester United had. Neither Beckham nor Stephens had even been consulted.

It was an extraordinary way of behaving for a club of the stature of Manchester United. Quite apart from the sheer oddness of negotiating with a man who at that point seemed no more likely than any of the other five candidates to become Barcelona president, they were behaving towards Beckham – a loyal servant of the club for thirteen years, whatever Ferguson might think – with a quite brutal lack of respect. George Best, United's great player of the Sixties and Seventies, attacked United for the 'dismal' way in which they had treated Beckham. Gordon Taylor, chief executive of England's Professional Footballers' Association, was similarly indignant. 'You wouldn't want to sell your second-hand car in such a way,' he said, 'never mind one of your finest assets.'

Beckham, in California, received the news with dismay. He felt angry and betrayed. He was genuinely hurt.

Pérez saw that his big chance had come. Via Sánchez and Stephens he let Beckham know that now at last was the time for him to put his cards on the table. Beckham needed little encouragement. He spoke to Stephens who immediately issued a statement through SFX expressing the player's 'disappointment and surprise' at being 'used as a political pawn in the Barcelona presidential elections'. The last line of Beckham's short statement from California – 'David's advisors have no plans to meet Mr Laporta or his representatives' – was a polite way of saying, 'Barça, get lost!'

If Manchester United had made public the deal, as some British newspaper commentators suggested, in order to flush out Real Madrid and raise the stakes in negotiations with them, the plan had spectacularly backfired. Barcelona were out of the running. If Beckham didn't want to go there that was that. The moment Pérez had been patiently waiting for since that moment of blinding clarity ten months earlier following his capture of Ronaldo, had finally arrived. Manchester United openly wanted to sell, Beckham wanted to come to Real Madrid and, best of all, no other club remained in the running.

The decisive meeting between Real Madrid and Manchester United had taken place on Friday 13 June in Sardinia, over that long lunch in which Peter Kenyon gave Beckham away to José Angel Sánchez for 'peanuts'. But two things remained to be done before the deal was sealed. Beckham had to talk to Pérez personally and give him his 'password'; and then Sánchez and Stephens had to sit down to hammer out the details of Beckham's personal terms. The password was Pérez's term for what others might have described as the kissing of the papal ring. Pérez had a thing about hearing the players' themselves issue a pledge of allegiance to the club. He had insisted Zidane and Ronaldo do it, and now he wanted Beckham to do the same: hear him say that, above all other football clubs, it was his heart's desire to join Real Madrid. Sánchez made sure the message got through to Beckham. Beckham did as he was told.

The telephone conversation took place on Sunday 15 June, the day of the Barcelona elections, which Laporta won, thanks – as was widely said – to 'the Beckham effect', to the greater ambition he had shown than his rivals in seriously contemplating the purchase of the world's most celebrated football player. That night Real Madrid played Atlético Madrid at Atlético's stadium, the Vicente Calderón. It was the penultimate game of the season. Real Madrid had to win if they were going to win the championship the following weekend. As is customary before these Madrid derbies, the directors of Real and Atlético got together at a restaurant for lunch. Halfway through the meal Sánchez, mobile in hand, came running over to Pérez in a state of intense excitement. He had David Beckham on the line. Pérez got up and scanned the restaurant for a quiet place to talk. Nothing. He went outside, but the area around the entrance to the restaurant was also milling with people. Pérez was a man of steady nerves, but he was beginning to lose his cool. He had David Beckham at the end of the line, waiting – no doubt in growing confusion and anxiety – to have one of the most important conversations of either men's lives and there he was, the president of Real Madrid, scrambling around for a place where he could sit down and talk. He tried the kitchen: hopeless. He tried the corridor outside the toilets: no good either. The gents' toilet: it too was teeming. There was only one possibility left. The ladies' toilet. He dived in. There was nobody there. Peace at last! Popping his head out, he instructed his bodyguard to stand at the door, and not to let anyone in, however desperate the emergency.

Beckham, evidently well prepared by Sánchez, did not deviate from the expected script. 'My dream,' he told Pérez, 'is to play for Real Madrid.' 'I am delighted to hear it,' replied Pérez. 'You will never regret it. We are a family. We will look after you well here. You are a great player. Here we will make you an even better player.' Beckham thanked Perez for those kind words and then promised him that he would be watching the Atlético–Real game that night. He wished his soon-to-be new team good luck.

Pérez in turn thanked Beckham, said goodbye, then emerged – not without a little circumspection – from the ladies' toilet, went over to Sánchez and gave him instructions to meet with Tony Stephens the next day to finalise arrangements. Beckham, who was back home in Hertfordshire having a barbecue with his family, had a conversation with his wife at the end of which they both agreed once and for all that, yes indeed, Real Madrid it would be. And then he sat down to watch the game. Real Madrid were 3-0 up within half an hour. They won 4-0 in the end.

After the game Beckham phoned Stephens and asked him to go and wrap things up with Real Madrid. The negotiations between Stephens and Sánchez and Madrid's lawyers began the next day, a Monday, and ended on the Tuesday afternoon. Money was never discussed. Stephens had not been kidding when he told Sánchez that Beckham was letting his heart be his guide. There were no discussions about Beckham's salary or about him ceding fifty per cent of his image rights to the club. Neither was the length of the contract, four years, an issue. Discussion centred on small points, chiefly relating to the not unimportant question of the Beckham family having as soft a landing in Madrid as possible: things like provisions for Beckham's accommodation during the early days of his stay, help finding him a house, a school for his children, a trustworthy house-keeper.

On the evening of Tuesday 17 June, with a deal done between player and club, all that remained was to notify Manchester United and exchange the necessary faxes to confirm the purchase and sale. But there was still one twist left to the tale. Not that either Real or United were now going to renege in any way on the Sardinia deal. The time for bluffing and deceit was over. All the cards were finally on the table. The problems that remained were purely technical. Agreeing on the right contractual language for the papers that needed to be faxed between the two institutions; agreeing also the wording of the press statements each club would be issuing, putting the world out of its misery once and for all on a saga that had been spinning on for more than three months. A further, and unexpected, compli-cation would concern the actual busines of transmitting the faxes between Madrid and Manchester.

The reason it all got so difficult was that that very night Pérez, Sánchez and two other Real Madrid officials had a long-standing dinner arrangement with a very important man in the business world: the president of Audi-Volkswagen, a tall and imposing German by the name of Dr Bernd Pischetsrieder. He was accompanied by three other senior executives of the company, one of them being the head man in Spain, Jesús Gasanz, from whom I heard the story of what happened in a meeting I had with him at his office in Barcelona six months later.

Real Madrid had been negotiating a sponsorship deal with Audi in recent weeks and this dinner was a chance for the top men in each organisation to meet prior to ratifying the deal formally. The venue was the Audi Forum in Madrid, the focal point of the company's Spanish operations. The time set for the dinner was 9.30. For an event of this kind of importance no one ever arrives late, especially not Pérez who is a stickler for punctuality. The Real Madrid delegation were late. Ten minutes passed, twenty, thirty. No sign of them. Dr Pischetsrieder, a man unaccustomed to being treated with such disrespect, was not disguising his growing irritation. But then, to the vast relief of Audi's increasingly embarrassed Spanish contingent, they appeared. Shortly after ten they bundled in through the door, flustered, their minds clearly elsewhere, Pérez's and Sánchez's ears each to a mobile phone. 'What extraordinarily bad manners!' Gasanz recalls the Audi executives muttering. Pérez understood he was being rude. Interrupting his call, he shook hands briefly with the four men, assured them that when he explained they would understand, then he put the phone back to his ear and proceeded with his call.

It wasn't until 10.30 that they managed to sit down and reveal to their increasingly bemused guests what was going on. 'We're in the process of completing the signing of David Beckham,' Pérez explained. 'Cadena Ser – our biggest radio station here in Spain – has already broken the news, saying that the deal is done. But it isn't. We haven't quite finalised all the details but we have to do so now because the media are all over us and Beckham is at Heathrow airport about to board a plane to Japan and we want to get the whole thing done and dusted before he takes off.' The mood of the Audi bosses changed abruptly. On the one hand they were thrilled to be present at what Dr Pischetsrieder described as 'a historical moment'; more important, the truth quickly dawned on them that, at no extra cost than the one they had already negotiated with Real Madrid, they were going to get Beckham thrown into the sponsorship package.

'We thought, "Great, if there had been any doubt remaining over the validity of the deal we were making with Real Madrid, this piece of news emphatically dispelled it,"' Gasanz told me. 'We were thrilled. If the deal with Real Madrid without Beckham was worth 100; now it was worth 150. We had improved on our deal by fifty per cent right there that night without lifting a finger, without offering a penny more. Amazing! The phone calls – to Manchester United, from the press – just kept coming now we had ceased to be confused spectators; we had become active participants in the drama, as anxious as the Real Madrid people suddenly that the deal should go through. We now had a very big vested interest in this thing coming off!'

The calls kept pouring in. The Audi men hung on every word, sitting in breathless silence when it became evident that the call was an important one. 'We discovered suddenly,' Gasanz recalled, 'that José Angel's big worry was that there might not be anybody in his office at the Bernabéu to receive the key fax, confirming the sale, from Manchester United. It was with more relief than joy that we finally overheard José Angel confirming, at eleven at night, that the decisive letter from Manchester United had finally come through.'

There was hardly time to raise a celebratory toast before the phones started ringing again. The whole world wanted to know what was going on. Pérez once more apologised to Dr Pischestsrieder. 'This is going to go down as the dinner that never was,' he said. The response of the Audi-Volkswagen superpresident could not have been more benign. 'Don't worry,' he replied. 'If the dinner had unfolded normally we might perhaps have forgotten about it very quickly, or recalled it vaguely as one more protocol evening. As it is, we will never forget this night!'

The news was ratified minutes later by simultaneous announcements on the official websites of Real Madrid and Manchester United. 'The summer soap opera has ended,' Cadena Ser informed the waiting world. 'David Beckham, the most charismatic player in world football, has signed for Florentino Pérez's Real Madrid for the next four seasons.'

The news shot around the globe like an electric current. Gasanz told me, 'Our people all over the world reported to us in huge excitement next morning that news programmes absolutely everywhere had been interrupted to break the news of Beckham's transfer, even in the United States.' Six months later, in December, the Associated Press conducted a worldwide poll to choose the number one sports event of 2003. Never mind Lance Armstrong equalling the record of five Tour de France wins in a row; Michael Schumacher setting even more records in crowning himself Formula One champion once again; or England becoming the first nation from the northern hemisphere to win the rugby World Cup. Beckham's move to Real Madrid, a transaction which involved no sporting activity whatsoever, was the international sports event of the year. By far.

Beckham and his wife heard the news on the phone from Tony Stephens at Heathrow airport, minutes before they boarded their plane to Tokyo. Smiling and holding his wife's hand, off he flew, not into the sunset but towards a new dawn, happy and serene in the knowledge that, after all the pain and uncertainty of the previous six months, he had finally found refuge in a safe, magical place, a football heaven where they played football like angels, and everybody wore white.

4: Men in White

'What happened during those thirty-six hours that David Beckham was in Madrid to sign for Real Madrid will go down as a unique case study in the history of advertising. The international exposure our company received in that brief period was so immense that our three-year investment in the club was repaid – and several times over – right there.'

Jesús Gasanz is a measured, courtly Spaniard but when he recalled the events of 1 and 2 July 2003, and their significance for his company, he struggled to contain himself. It began – Gasanz, the president of Audi in Spain, recalled – with Real Madrid asking Audi if they would supply them with three cars for Beckham and his retinue during his short stay in the Spanish capital. Audi had just struck a deal to become Real's official car supplier. Pérez and the head of Audi-Volkswagen international had shaken hands on it at that 'dinner-that-never-was' two weeks earlier, on the night Beckham's transfer was announced. But the deal had not actually been signed yet and no cars had officially been handed over. 'Just as well we did not hesitate to respond to their request,' Gasanz said. 'Such was the international media clamour for pictures of David Beckham at that time, and so busy was he going from one appointment to another – to his medical check-up, to sign his contract with Florentino, to that amazing official presentation of his with half the world's press there – that the Audi he travelled in was continually on TV and in newspaper photographs everywhere. It turned out to be the greatest news coverage in the world, in history I am sure, in which one company was visibly associated with the brand it sponsored.'

I asked Gasanz if he might be able put a value on that 'free' advertising Audi had enjoyed? 'Put it this way,' he said. 'If Audi had tried to carry off an equivalent ad campaign – one in which we received so much exposure on prime time TV and on front pages of newspapers in virtually every country in the world – it would have been, quite simply, unpayable. In order to pay for that quality of advertising we would have had to sell the company first! I repeat, what we got during those thirty-six hours was unpayable. Unpayable! And it was not just one but three of our cars that were in that convoy Beckham travelled in! Never has a coup like it been seen in the history of marketing, I am convinced of it.' Could he imagine ever improving on that coup? 'The only comparable set of images – and I am being frivolously hypothetical here – might be if Osama Bin Laden were arrested and then driven off in an Audi. Neither the Pope nor the president of the United States nor anyone else I can think of could give us publicity like that.'

Audi were not alone among Real's corporate sponsors in their inability to believe their luck. I spoke to the sportswear firm Adidas – patrons not only of the club as a whole but individually of Beckham, Zidane and Raúl – and to the vast German multinational Siemens, whose mobile phones logo blazed across the front of the official Real shirt. I talked to their top people on the marketing and sponsorship side of things and found them to be in the same state of barely suppressed euphoria as Gasanz.

Adidas's Jan Runau, head of corporate communications and global PR, and Gunter Weigl, head of football, said that what was so exciting for them, as a multinational with markets everywhere, was that Real Madrid was what they called 'a world team – the world team'. 'Beckham and Ronaldo are the two most famous players in the world, maybe even the most famous people,' said Runau. 'And Zidane,' cut in Weigl, 'is the world's best player!' 'What more,' they both said in happy unison, 'could you possibly want?' And when they heard that Beckham – Adidas's man for ten years – had joined Real – their club since 1998 – how did they respond? The two men laughed, or rather giggled, as if found out. What did they do? Did the whole Adidas building explode as if they had scored the winner in a cup final? Did they dance around the office? 'Yes,' confessed a slightly sheepish Runau. 'We danced around the office.'

Adidas's association with Beckham and Real was a natural fit, an obvious thing to do. Not so obvious was the idea of linking Siemens with a Spanish football club. The man who came up with the idea is now regarded within the company, and beyond, as something of a genius. Rolf Beisswanger, Siemens's head of global sponsorship, is besieged by business people all over the world begging him to come and address their marketing conferences. 'You have no idea how many requests I turn down,' Beisswanger told me. 'I could make conference speech-making a full-time job.' The story they want to hear is how he managed so swiftly and audaciously to transform his company's public image. Siemens, Beisswanger told me, was the third or fourth biggest multinational in the world, with 420,000 employees, operating in 200 countries. The company had made its name in the field of mechanical engineering. This turned out to be a problem when the decision was taken six or seven years ago to go into the mobile phones business. The company's brand image – respectable, conservative, stolidly German – did not fit the new product. And, since Siemens barely operated in the retail market, the company name was not well known. 'What our high-profile link-up with Real Madrid did,' Beisswanger said, 'was to resolve these two problems for us in one stroke. We became, almost overnight, a sexy firm with global appeal.'

The wonder of it all is how a football club from Spain, a country whose global brand is not especially resonant, should serve as such a lethally effective marketing tool, should operate with such insidious power on the hearts and minds of people in a far away land like, say, China – which happened to be precisely the country whose market Siemens and Audi chiefly had in mind when they signed up with Real Madrid. Because the funny thing is that, viewed from Spain, Real Madrid conjures up such specifically national associations. I asked a Madrid-based journalist I know to define what Real meant for his compatriots and he replied '*Españolidad*' – Spanishness. And what, I asked, was that? The journalist began by explaining what it was not. According to various polls, he said, there were only three cities in the whole of Spain where at least half the population did not support Real. These were Barcelona, naturally, and the two big

Basque cities, Bilbao and San Sebastián. Outside these places most people bought into the idealised notions of Spanishness which Real Madrid had come to represent. (According to an internal survey the club did there were more Real Madrid supporters in Sevilla than there were supporters of the city's two big first division teams – Sevilla and Betis – combined.) 'A sense of being naturally aristocratic is part of it,' my friend said. 'Don't forget that since Spain ruled the waves in the sixteenth century, since the time of Philip II, Real is the biggest thing Spain has produced in terms of international reach. What Real does for the Spanish is feed a nostalgic longing somehow to recover those imperial glories. These are aristocratic, elitist notions but the curious thing is that they are shared by Spaniards independent of their social station. The vast majority of the fans – right down to the ones inhabiting the remotest mountain village – seem to possess these aristocratic longings, seem to crave that smattering of nobility in their lives that they feel the association with Real Madrid brings.'

But what about the fact that the team was full of foreigners, I asked. 'Not a problem,' my friend replied. 'First of all, as any student of Spanish history knows, Philip II expanded his empire on the back of foreign soldiers and foreign money. Second, Real Madrid exploded on the world scene in the Fifties, when Spain was politically isolated by Franquismo and was a very poor country (poorer than Iraq in those days) whose inhabitants went abroad in droves in search of work. Having a football team to which the best players in the world emigrated, and which in turn became the best in the world, served to soothe Spaniards' wounded national pride. Today Spain is democratic and rich but the hang-ups have not entirely gone away. So now that you have Real Madrid conquering the world again, the fans – meaning more or less half of Spain – are absolutely thrilled. They almost don't care whether the team wins or not, their vanity having been so thoroughly nourished by the admiration and acclaim that has been pouring in.'

One of Real Madrid's more illustrious contemporary fans was Inocencio Arias, Spain's ambassador to the United Nations and a former director general of Real Madrid. He too was keen on making connections between Philip II, Spain's great sixteenth-century imperial king, and the foreign soldiers in the Real Madrid armada. Arias remarked in the course of a series of lectures at a Madrid university in the summer of 2003 that Beckham was going to achieve for Spain what King Philip had tried and failed to do: extend Spanish rule to every corner of the globe. 'We are going to observe a paradox,' Arias said. 'The goal Philip II was unable to achieve because of the British, namely that the sun should never set over his empire, is now going to be achieved by Real Madrid – thanks to a British man.' The evidence, Arias said, was already in. 'Look what Beckham has done for us. If Real Madrid was already famous in three-fourths of the world, now it will be famous across the whole planet.' Spain's UN ambassador agreed that the Beckham phenomenon 'bordered on the messianic' and was 'a kind of madness' but, he concluded, 'it provides a cocktail of money and popularity for Real Madrid and we must take advantage of it'.

So potent was the cocktail, indeed, that the Spanish prime minister (*presidente de gobierno*) at the time, José María Aznar, was prompted to observe that Real was proving to be an extremely effective instrument in the effort to open up new markets for Spain in parts of the world like Asia where the word 'Spain' traditionally meant very little. So in awe was Aznar of the '*Florenteam*' that one day when he was talking to Pérez at a social event and someone came up to him and addressed him as '*Señor Presidente*', Aznar turned to the person and asked, 'Which one of the two of us do you mean? Because I am not at all sure which one of us is the more significant "*presidente*" here?'

Nor was it very clear which of the two was more ambitious. Pérez always spoke of his desire to 'universalise' the Real Madrid name. Once – revealing the religious dimension of his football fanaticism, conjuring echoes of Philip II's Catholic conquistadors – he even went so far as to use the word '*evangelise*' to describe his global mission. More than once he defined his purpose to me as generating '*ilusión colectiva global*'. *Ilusión* is a wonderful Spanish word, much more layered and subtle and cheerful than 'illusion' in English, which conveys the idea of self-deception, or false hopes. *Ilusión* is a combination of things – enthusiasm, hope, expectation, thrill – but at the heart of the world is the idea of a dream, an optimistic, childlike waking dream. Nothing expresses more succinctly the relationship the football fan has with the game. Pérez understood this instinctively. He saw that football was the world's great dream machine and he wanted Real Madrid to provide the biggest, brightest, most vivid dreams of all.

For José Angel Sánchez, his director of marketing, the connection with Hollywood was self-evident. To a large extent it defined the Pérez revolution's new vision of what football was about. 'We're like a big blockbuster movie,' he told me. 'Like *Men in Black* – or, in our case, Men in White. We have a great story to tell, a great production and the biggest box-office stars. Think about it, Real Madrid is a company that provides content, like Universal Studios. We could produce the same movie with cheap, little-known actors, if we chose. But the point about the expensive big name actors is that with them box-office success is assured. What we deliver audiences worldwide, therefore, is high-class high drama. Through the drama of a game – and games are an elemental human activity, for young and old – you behold all the primary values and passions of Man: beauty and talent, yes, but also courage, sacrifice, cunning, perseverance – as well as the eternal Hollywood storyline of heroes overcoming odds to triumph.'

As in all drama, there is a strong element of make-believe in football. The fans, up to a point, have to suspend their disbelief. Football is fairy stories for adults as well as children, with its larger than life heroes and the fantasy always implicit in the minds of the fans that their teams are armies, that the players are soldiers, waging war. Hence the special affection fans feel for the conspicuously brave players – Roy Keane at Manchester United would be the classic contemporary example – even if they know there are other team members who are more skilful.

The difference with Hollywood is that football, like all spectator sports, is live theatre. The denouement is not predetermined as it is in a film and so the emotions it elicits are both more enduring and more intense. Nor is it a one-off phenomenon; it is an endlessly recyclable drama in which *ilusión* never dies, in which no matter how badly the results might have gone one week, or over one season, there is always the next week or the next season to make it better. No matter how disastrous things might seem, redemption – or the hope of redemption – is never far away. That is why Sánchez says that football is resistant to failure. 'Football is a cyclical reality,' he told me, 'and what those of us involved in the running of a club are charged, among other things, with doing is keeping those dreams and expectations bubbling along. That is why we think it is important here at Real Madrid at the end of every season to regenerate the team, and the "*ilusión*", by buying great new players. The annual football drama lasts ten months. The drama is usually resolved in the last couple of weeks. If the drama has not been resolved in a way that is satisfactory to your team, if you have failed, then you've got the two months of the summer to rebuild your hopes.'

You actually have more than two months. The most compelling proof that football really does exist in the orbit of dreams, that the football fan is only partially concerned with the here and now – that what he or she is really thinking about is some unattainable nirvana in the future – comes midway through the season when the press start speculating about which players will move to which clubs the following summer. The underlying fantasy behind all the chatter is the *ilusión* that your team will achieve perfection, that your intimate association with the team will make you gloriously invincible.

So much excitement does all the speculation about the possible arrival of new heroes generate, so much talk among football people everywhere, that you sometimes wonder whether the transfers are the sub-plot of a larger drama, or the plot itself.

'The thing is to generate excitement on a permanent basis,' Sánchez said, positing the chief article of faith of the new football model his boss Pérez had envisioned. 'And we generate special excitement at Real Madrid in this global sport of transfer guessing because we have fixed in people's minds that the players we are going to be interested in will be the best, the ones people most like to talk about. That's where the Florentino model comes up trumps again. Those who think they are the clever buggers of the game, the ones privy to the game's inner truths, say, for example, that you've got to buy a centre half instead of Ronaldo. These are the same kind of people, the game's messiahs, who think it is shrewd to leave Beckham on the bench for a quarter-final Champions League game against Real Madrid. Ask yourself, what do people want? The solemn, serious football as understood by people who are prepared to sell players like Beckham – the guy who strikes the ball better than anybody else in the world – or the frivolous game propagated by people like myself and Florentino who bet on talent and fantasy and the best players in the world.'

Sánchez is not only thoughtful and bright, he thinks big. Before Pérez took over as Real president he was director general of southern Europe for the Japanese firm Sega, the major international producer of video games for children. Pérez had to battle to prise him away from Sega. Not because Sánchez did not want to go – a Real Madrid fan all his life, he was longing to take up the challenge of milking the hitherto untapped marketing potential of the club of his dreams. But Sega valued him immensely and fought hard to keep him. In the end – for much the same reason that after Manchester United there was no real question of Beckham going anywhere other than Real Madrid – Sánchez signed for Real. Pérez came to value him so much that he described him to me once as his 'Galáctico in a jacket and tie'. Mid-thirties, tall, handsome, with curly black hair, he was an expansive fellow. The first time I met him at his office at the Bernabéu I was struck by his robust, cheerful energy. People who knew him better viewed him in the same light. 'He is always spilling over with good humour,' Valdano enthused. 'In everything he sees an opportunity. He is the most optimistic man in the world, a guy who transforms what others see as catastrophe into a reason for celebration. Maybe the toughest blow we've had to endure in the Pérez years was losing the Spanish Cup final at the Bernabéu to Deportivo la Coruña on the very day of the club's 100th anniversary. At the end of the game José Angel, who was sitting next to me, said, "Bah! This lot have won today but they remain Deportivo la Coruña. Hell, we are Real Madrid! Give us a couple of years and we'll have won it all. They'll only have this to show for themselves."'

He was right enough. A couple of months later Real Madrid won the European Cup. The season after that they won the Spanish league.

Compared to those two achievements the Spanish Cup is, by common consent, small potatoes. But even if he had been wrong, even if Deportivo had outdone them in terms of trophies won, they were still, as he said, Real Madrid: a huge brand name with huge fan loyalty. And here was another factor that not only Real Madrid but all football clubs had in their favour. The unswerving loyalty of the football fan. 'Movies come and go,' Sánchez said. 'So do the products of lots of other big companies when they are susceptible to fads. Look at Levi jeans, how they faded from a position of seeming invincibility; or Pioneer in televisions, who were once very strong. We in the football world, by contrast, enjoy almost total fidelity. In the mature football world – and I should draw a distinction here with Asia where many people are more loyal to players than clubs – fans are the most loyal people in the world. I mean we have scientifically established, through surveys, that people are more likely to change spouse, religion – or even sex – than change football clubs!'

The advantage Real Madrid had over almost all other clubs is that the fidelity phenomenon extended beyond its own set of fans to the whole football world. Real Madrid was to football as Ferrari was to motor racing. Ferrari might have gone two decades without winning the Formula One championship but there was a magic about the name that made you feel, whether you knew much about motor racing or not, that they were the best. And this was because Ferrari, like Real Madrid, had succeeded in acquiring what people in the marketing world describe as the holy grail of an enduringly resonant 'brand mythology'. 'The resistance of our model at Real Madrid is such that it has distanced itself from the tyranny of results,' Sánchez said. 'The resistance comes first from the power of our brand name, but also from Florentino Pérez's policy of buying only the world's greatest players, the ones the world most wants to see. If on top of that we win, so much the better. Winning helps build the mystique.'

Rolf Beisswanger of Siemens is a great fan of José Angel Sánchez's. 'You wouldn't know it from being with him,' said Beisswanger, 'that he lives under huge and permanent pressure. How could he not be as the marketing head of the biggest sports brand in the world?'

Beisswanger did not know that Real was the biggest sports brand in the world, though he did suspect it, when he joined Siemens as head of global sponsorship in March 2002, having worked previously for the clothes firm Hugo Boss. The reason Siemens hired him was to fire up their image. 'There was a problem,' Beisswanger told me. 'Siemens mobile phones advertising slogan was "Be Inspired" but the brand was not inspiring enough. We had to do something to make the slogan and the brand a better fit. I looked around and saw that we had sponsorship agreements with lots of football clubs in Europe [Bayern Munich and Chelsea, among them] but the conclusion was that it was not good enough to have partners scattered about, aimed at specific markets in specific countries. We needed something new, something to unify our message and project our brand more widely and powerfully.'

Beisswanger's thoughts naturally turned to football. 'First because it is the great unifying international language; second because the World Cup was being held in Japan and South Korea that summer of 2002.' He thought and thought until one day in April it hit him, out of the blue and with great force. 'Shit, I thought! It must − it has to be − Real Madrid! We must get Real Madrid!' The idea came to him in his office late in the day and he was so excited, and so convinced it was the right thing to do, while at the same time aghast at the difficulty he knew he would have in persuading the Siemens board to splash out the money to make it come true, that he sat at his desk until late into the night, typing away at his computer, setting out the arguments for putting his vision into practice. 'I made a list of ten arguments in favour. That was easy. The list of arguments against was more difficult. Obviously we would have to pay a lot of money but in terms of the pure marketing value of signing with Real Madrid I could not think of one reason not to do it.'

The good news, as Beisswanger confirmed the next day, was that Real had no shirt sponsor yet. The less encouraging news was that, while the Siemens board were intrigued, they wanted more information. So Beisswanger contacted the London office of the American firm Landor, the world leaders in brand and design consultancy. He hired them to find out where Real Madrid stood in the international constellation of sports brands. 'When they came back to me with their report it was to say that Real Madrid was by far – but by far – the biggest sports brand in the world. Far ahead of the only possible rival in the football world, Manchester United; far ahead of Ferrari; far ahead of the LA Lakers and the New York Yankees. And this was BEFORE Ronaldo and Beckham had arrived. Before! So you can imagine what has happened since! The gap has, to say the least, widened appreciably.'

I contacted Landor who showed me part of their report. They had done a convincingly exhaustive job. The survey behind the rankings consisted of 11,000 interviews conducted during the first quarter of 2002 in ten countries. In Europe, the 'big five' footballing countries – England, France, Germany, Italy and Spain. In the Americas, the three largest footballing countries – Argentina, Brazil and Mexico – together with the US. In Asia Landor surveyed Japan.

'Regardless of how it is attained,' the report said, 'a successful brand is one that generates an "unfair share" of customer loyalty and affection because it provides a level of belief, belonging, quality, trust, convenience, assurance and allure for which customers are willing to pay a premium . . . If one thinks of the core promise behind a football brand – victory and/or a good show, and not necessarily in this order – Real Madrid has more consistently delivered that promise.' While one could see how Real Madrid had managed that 'unfair share' trick, had done what all great brands do which is to stand out amidst the vast sea of choices the global market offers, it was still a surprise to discover among the detail of Landor's findings that Real was considered the world's number one football club in Italy, where fans tend not only to be insular but rather smug about the merits of *Serie A*. More interesting still, Landor's scientific methods yielded the same subversive conclusion that Pérez and Sánchez had reached at Real Madrid. Subversive in the sense that it violated the game's dominant orthodoxy – especially dominant in Italy – namely that winning was paramount. 'A good show', or what at Real they called *espectáculo*, was so important in terms of a football club's global appeal, Landor found, that it might even have been more important than victory. An integral part of the 'show', as they had also understood at Real Madrid, was the charisma of the showmen on display. The greater their charisma the more they were talked about, the bigger the reach of their own name and that of the club they played for. 'Football players,' the Landor report said, 'seem to be the world's favourite subject of conversation after the weather (sometimes ahead of it), and certainly more volatile and disputable.' When people talked about football players, they really engaged, they put their self-esteem, and the esteem with which they were held by others, on the line. As the Landor report laconically put it, 'Providing a brief commentary on football players without putting one's personal and/or professional integrity at stake is a real challenge.'

Despite the volatility of the debates on the relative merits of players, the report found that some players stood out above the others in the global markets surveyed. These were Zidane and Roberto Carlos (then at Real), and Beckham and Ronaldo (not yet at Real). Zidane was king among football fans, the only player to appear consistently at the top of all five geographic zones surveyed. 'In these times of tough talk on immigration and tension between the West and Islam,' said the report, venturing unasked into political terrain, 'what a vote of confidence for culture and colour-blind meritocracy in football!' The report might have added that the choice of Zidane, whose father was Algerian, as the world's favourite football player revealed that in the end what captivated fans was talent; sheer, raw talent. Zidane was not necessarily the world's most effective player in terms of getting a result. He had never been a great goal-scorer, for example. But he was the great football artist of his generation and the fact that fans around the globe equated his artistry with their judgement on who was the world's best player could very plausibly be interpreted by Pérez and Sánchez as a vote of confidence in the new football model they were propagating.

The Siemens board was convinced. And what convinced them in large measure was the synergy they perceived between their own desire, as all big western multinationals desire, to expand into Asia and the phenomenal growth of football there. Beisswanger negotiated with Sánchez over two months and a three-year sponsorhip deal between Siemens and Real Madrid was signed (Beisswanger had the

date indelibly fixed in his mind) on 16 July 2002. From this date on
the Real Madrid shirt would carry the words 'Siemens Mobile' blazed
across the front. Beisswanger could not believe his luck – just as the
Audi people could not believe theirs twelve months later with
Beckham – when a month and a half later Real Madrid bought
Ronaldo.

What associations did the words 'Real Madrid' conjure in people's
minds and how did that work in terms of Siemens's objective of
livening up their brand? Beisswanger's response was a statement of
faith in the new vision his friend Sánchez and his boss Pérez had
brought to the football world.

'Real Madrid means best in class,' Beisswanger said. 'It means beautiful football of a type to which people everywhere are emotionally
committed. It means playing with fun and adventure. They do not
take a methodical, strategic, results-driven approach to their football,
as you find with Italian or German teams. Florentino Pérez says he
wants to play attractive football to make people happy, period. And
that's it, not like in Italian football, in particular, where it is all so
tactical and planned, so targeted at stopping other teams playing, so
focused on not losing by putting up an impenetrable defensive wall.
With Real Madrid the idea is also not to lose, of course, but the
emphasis is totally on winning by attacking and scoring one more
goal than the rival. People everywhere see and understand this and
love it.'

To Beisswanger's delight, everybody within Siemens seemed to
see this too. 'We made a video internally for the company of recent
Real Madrid goals, ten or twelve of them, and our people loved
them, all of them. Goals by Raúl, Beckham, Figo, Ronaldo, Zidane.
Everyone loved the video: so creative, spectacular, so different from
goals you see in other leagues, other teams.' More to the point, as
far as the Siemens board was concerned, since the Real Madrid deal
the company's mobile phone sales had risen dramatically all over the
world. Beisswanger was thrilled, having met the objective for which
he had been hired. 'Yes, that's right,' he said. '"Be Inspired": now it's
a perfect fit. Now we come across as an inspiring company. Siemens,
this giant multinational, has completely changed its image with one

marketing tool, Real Madrid. This is the reason why I receive invitations all the time from all over the world to go and speak at marketing forums. And now of course we have David Beckham: what an add-on!'

Beckham was an add-on whose value to Siemens would endure as long as their association with Real Madrid, and beyond the player's retirement. In 'universalising' Real's name, as Pérez put it, not only did you capture more sponsorship deals and sell more shirts in the short term, you consolidated the power and appeal of the club years, possibly decades, into the future. Nearly half a century later the Real brand was still reaping the benefits of the club's association with Di Stefano, Puskas and Gento. Manchester United would not have become as big had their own holy triumvirate of Bobby Charlton, George Best and Denis Law not excelled for them together back in the Sixties.

What about Manchester United, I asked Beisswanger. There had been some dispute as to whether they or Real Madrid were the world's richest club, the answer usually depending on what methods were employed to do the adding up and subtracting. But, whatever the case, had Siemens not thought – at least for a while – that the big English club, with its established penetration in the Asian market, might be as good a bet as Real Madrid? 'That is a good question,' Beisswanger said. 'Because, yes, when I took this job I saw there were only two brands that could do what we wanted, which was to transcend local markets and really appeal globally, Real Madrid and Manchester United. But all our inquiries, including that Landor research, led us to conclude that Real were far bigger.' *Far* bigger? 'Yes, and I will tell you why. First, there is the history of Real, the nine European Cups, the great players of the past. Football people everywhere know that; it means something to them even if they do not know the details. United cannot compete with Real at this level. Second, look at the individuals in the current teams. Who can name the United team these days? People know a few players – van Nistelrooy, maybe Giggs and possibly Scholes, Keane. But the Real Madrid players are worldwide household names. Ask any kid in the world, any kid, to name five Real Madrid players and he will be able to do so. And third, United used to be bigger in the countries of the North and Real of the South. But that has changed since Beckham arrived. Real enjoy a monopoly on both. Man United lost fifty per cent of their brand value when Beckham left. In marketing terms, without Beckham they are worth half what they were.' Beisswanger might have been exaggerating a bit when he said any kid in the world would be able to name five Real Madrid players. Beckham, though, everybody knew. And I mean everybody. I have accumulated Beckham stories from all over the world. I have a friend who saw Beckham shirts for sale in the single most remote corner of Madagascar. But the most remarkable Beckham story of all, in my experiene, came in an article in the *Jordan Times* that I stumbled across on the internet one day. It was a first person account dated March 2002 by a Lebanese journalist called Hala Jaber about a visit he made to a hide-out of the Palestinian 'Al Aqsa Martyrs Brigade' in the Gaza Strip.

The suicide bombers, young martyrs-in-waiting, told Jaber of their eagerness to blow themselves up and kill as many Israeli civilians as possible. Invoking God and love of the fatherland they told the journalist of their desire to hear Israeli mothers scream. They spoke also of the reward that would await them in the Islamic heaven, the unimaginable beauty of the 'houri' virgins who would minister so devotedly to those carnal pleasures the sons of the Prophet had been denied on earth. At which point someone – another of the so-called 'fighters' – burst into the room.

'I have very important news,' he cried. Everyone stopped what they were doing. Conversation ceased. The Al Aqsa martyrs had been waiting anxiously for this messenger. The blessed virgins, the screaming Israeli mothers, the holy Palestinian cause all ceased, for one deliciously earthly moment, to be the be-all and end-all of all life, or even death. The whole room hung on the new arrival's words.

'Manchester United 5,' he declared. '. . . West Ham 3!' The result, from that very afternoon's Premiership action, was greeted with murmurs of satisfaction. But there was more news, more reason to rejoice. 'David Beckham scored twice!' the bearer of glad tidings cried. 'Very good, Manchester!' Very good indeed! Cries of pleasure filled the underground death chamber. And then a chant arose. "Allahu Akbar! Allahu Akbar!" – the ancient chant of victory they entone when news arrives of a successful result on an Israeli bus: God is great! God is great!

Almost as surprising was the news that Beckham was making an impact in the one country where the football religion – football as spectator sport, that is had failed to penetrate – the United States. 'But you know,' Beisswanger said, 'there are signs of change. A friend in New York City called the other day to ask me for a Real Madrid shirt. He said that in New York's coolest, hottest clubs THE thing to be seen wearing was the Madrid number 23 Beckham shirt!'

In Asia you didn't have to go to the coolest, hottest clubs to see Madrid number 23 Beckham shirts. They were everywhere. Within a week of Beckham signing for Real Madrid the eighty shops in Singapore that sold the team's shirts reported they were running out and desperate for more. Adidas Singapore reported that due to Beckham's arrival they expected to sell forty per cent more Real shirts over the next three months. Future Brand, another brand design consultancy, expained that because fans in Asia tended to be loyal to players rather than to clubs, by signing Beckham Real Madrid could expect to win over immediately almost five million of Manchester United's sixteen and a half million Asian fans. In Japan they understood this very quickly, a major TV station there immediately snapping up the rights to carry Spanish league games live and paying eight million euros for a thirty second spot Beckham did to promote la Liga, half of which, of course, ended up in the coffers of Real Madrid. José Angel Sánchez confirmed that from the moment the Beckham deal was announced in June 2003 the calls had been pouring into Real Madrid's marketing department from Asia. By the end of the year, he said, half the business he was doing was with Asian clients.

Given all this, I expected Beisswanger to share the view, so prevalent at Real, that they had bought Beckham for a song. 'Do I agree? Of course I agree! It is mind-blowing how cheaply Real Madrid got him. Mind-blowing! Of course, Real's big advantage was that United wanted to get rid of him, made it plain they did not want him any more. But still . . . There's no bigger catch in the world of sports marketing. I will give you the example of my Australian wife. She has told me she wants to go and watch Real when they come and play Bayern Munich so that she can see Beckham – and she knows nothing and cares less about football.'

The story about Mrs Beisswanger is telling. It reveals the emergence of a new global trend that might not have hit the radar screens of the marketing consultants yet but on anecdotal evidence that I have come across is growing and not insignificant. Adults are converting to the game. Women adults, long-suffering females who for years have uncomprehendingly endured their male mates' obsession with football are increasingly beginning to get it, are tuning in more and more. The movie star quality of Beckham catches their attention, draws them in and soon enough they start to develop an interest in the less obvious but arguably more refined charms of Figo, Ronaldo, Zidane. (There is a strong and burgeoning body of female opinion out there, as I have discovered on my world travels, that holds to the view that Figo is better looking than Beckham.) Once these football-awakened females start to attach names to faces, they find themselves developing a dawning interest in the game itself, keeping their eyes on the television screen for a moment or two rather than turning their heads away in exasperation when Ronaldo scores a goal and Beckham jumps joyfully on top of him, closely followed by Figo and Zidane. Before they know it these female apostates will start asking their startled and delighted mates to explain the finer points of the offside law, all the better to follow the action next time a game comes on. The final stage of conversion comes with the female insisting that no, let's not go out to the movies tonight, let's stay at home and watch the re-run of last weekend's Barça–Madrid game.

Such an exchange might seem fanciful, but it has surely been seen in a few hundred – or even a few thousand – homes already. And will be seen in more. And Real Madrid's Galácticos will play a large part in ensuring that the trend really does grow. For which reason, as well as many more, they are so pleased with themselves at Adidas for having had the wit back in 1998 to sign a ten-year sponsorship deal with Real. At the time it looked like a good idea. In retrospect it was the best idea the company ever had. And what about this notion, put forward by Sánchez as well as by Landor, that with these players in your team, success, in the obvious definition of the word, was not so indispensable a requirement? Was it true that the secret and genius of Real Madrid's new football model lay in its resistance to results, in the idea that because it bet on talent its appeal was more enduring? 'True, in terms of the brand's value, of the appeal the club has globally,' said Adidas's head of football Gunter Weigl. 'You can go three, even four years without winning trophies and it is not so important if you have players of that calibre.'

As for Beckham, if Real Madrid was the best institution Adidas ever signed up, the England captain was their most valuable player. Weigl told me an anecdote about Beckham that had become a legend at Adidas's German headquarters. It happened in Tokyo on the trip Beckham made to Japan just after the deal had been concluded for his transfer from Manchester United to Real Madrid. Adidas invited Beckham to go and see their main store in downtown Tokyo, promising that they would keep the visit top secret and would close the doors to the public for an hour so that he could shop and look around in peace. The problem was that within a few minutes of him arriving someone spotted him through the store window. 'Before twenty minutes had passed the traffic in downtown Tokyo had come to a standstill,' Weigl recalled. 'Word had spread like wildfire and there were 20,000 people gathered outside the store. Beckham remained a prisoner inside for five hours. He spent a good part of his time filming the crowds with his video camera, as if wanting to register the truth of an event that maybe otherwise people would not believe.'

The fact that he had by now left Manchester United, who had a deal with Adidas's biggest global rival Nike, made this spontaneous expression of Japanese adoration for Beckham all the sweeter for the Germans. 'The simple fact of the matter is that having both of them together in the same team, Beckham and Real, is marketing heaven,' Runau said. More to the point the success of the marketing plan had been demonstrated in the company's returns. Runau said that 2003 was a year in which they had hugely exceeded global sales targets, a lot of which had to do with the image of the company projected by that Beckham–Real Madrid partnership. 'Beckham's global appeal,' Weigl said, 'is unlimited. Truly unlimited! He is even breaking into the US. The film *Bend it like Beckham* has had American teenage girls going crazy; there are Adidas billboards with his face on them all over Los Angeles. The phenomenon continues to grow. The people he reaches on and off the field: no other athlete has anything close to the same global impact. No one else can stop the traffic in central Tokyo. People mention Tiger Woods. Beckham is much, much bigger – apart from anything else because the sport he plays is the world's most popular by far.'

Another measure, apart from the phenomenal shirt sales, of the commercial impact of the Beckham factor was the fee Real Madrid charged to play exhibition games. Carlos Martinez de Albornoz, the club's managing director, said that the pre-season friendlies they had played in the summer of 2003 in Asia had brought in 1.5 million euros per game. 'That was already a lot more than anybody else was getting,' said Albornoz, a graver, older man than Sánchez, the type you want running your company's financial operations. 'Manchester United were charging between 400,000 and 600,000. Milan too. Now, for the friendlies we are planning this coming summer of 2004, we're going to be charging – and getting – five million euros a game. And maybe more: we've signed a contract for next year's summer tour of Asia – travel, accommodation, everything included – that will net us 14.5 million euros for, as the contract says, "two or three games"'. Why had there been such a massive increase since the previous summer? 'Must be Beckham,' Albornoz shrugged.

The happy irony in all this for Real was that while they were Manchester United's sporting benchmark, Pérez had identified Manchester United on taking over at Real in 2000 as his model of effective big-time football management. 'Their figures were available easily because they are a listed company and Florentino studied them.

Manchester United were the world leaders in exploiting the commercial possibilities of a football club,' Albornoz said. 'Florentino was
intrigued by how they divided their income into three areas: TV,
Stadium/Tickets and Marketing/Commercial. We've done much the
same, drawing up graphs accordingly.' And the graphs, which he
showed me, revealed an astonishing evolution between 2000 and 2004,
with the financial year in each case beginning on 1 July and ending
30 June. In the financial year 2000/2001 the club's income was 138
million euros. Income for the year 2003/2004 was 240 million euros
– and that excluded 'extraordinary' income from sales of players.
Money from ticket sales increased by fifty per cent in this period; TV
rights had risen markedly too but the vertical ascendancy was especially sensational in the section marked Marketing/Commercial, this
having been a source of income the club had virtually ignored prior
to Pérez's arrival. 'As Florentino said when he arrived,' Albornoz
recalled, '"Hang on a minute, we are a huge international brand, the
very image of Spain abroad for tens of million of people, and we are
making no money from this."'

By the middle of the 2003/2004 financial year revenue from
Marketing/Commercial sales – which meant sales of merchandising
and income from sponsors like Siemens and Adidas – amounted to
forty per cent of total income, as opposed to less than ten per cent
when Pérez arrived. Particularly gratifying to Pérez was the fact that
this forty per cent figure represented a sizeable increase over
Manchester United's twenty-seven per cent cut from marketing-
related income over the same period. Pérez did not come out and
say it but he derived a lot of satisfaction from having leapt ahead of
the big English club at the game which, within the football world,
they themselves had practically invented. The satisfaction was all the
greater at the club for the belief that Real would continue in the
following years to race ahead of the competition.

'The prospects here, especially internationaly, are practically unlimited,' Albornoz said. 'We have this virtuous circle whose secret is to
deliver a football spectacle of the highest quality, a football team with
extraordinary players. With these core elements at our disposal we
ensure that the club becomes more and better known. As the club's

fame and reputation grows our capacity is boosted to generate income from merchandising and to charge sponsors higher amounts, which in turn allows us to invest in more extraordinary players, which in turn extends still more the club's global reach. And so it goes on.'

The belief that they truly had hit upon a recipe for printing money encouraged José Angel Sánchez and Pérez to plot all manner of leaps into previously uncharted territory. The two biggest schemes involved, first, developing Real Madrid's projected new *Ciudad Real Madrid* (Real Madrid City) into a theme park which would draw tourists to the Spanish capital like never before; second, expanding Real Madrid Television beyond Spain, into a global pay-per-view channel.

'We've studied the economics of setting up satellite communications with the rest of the world and found it to be more accessible than we had at first imagined,' said Sánchez. 'The idea will be to allow people everywhere – in the US, in China – to access our programming via their national digital platforms. So if you're sitting in your home in Louisiana or Shanghai and you fancy watching Real Madrid's latest game live, or highlights, or interviews with the players you do much what you would do to sign up for a pay-per-view film or a local sports programme and there you have it. In time, of course, we may be able to sell advertising space on our international TV station.' And as for the *Ciudad Real Madrid*, this would be first and foremost the club's training headquarters, for the first team and the entire youth set-up. But there would also be a Real Madrid museum, a theme park, a hotel, streets and shops and the whole complex would occupy prime land on the edge of Madrid, near the airport, covering an area four and a half times bigger than the next biggest training centre in world football, Manchester United's Carrington complex. Real Madrid were in discussions with Disney to explore the possibility of working together to exploit the theme park possibilities to the full. Sánchez's experience with cutting-edge games technology at Sega encouraged him to imagine all manner of possibilities: animated films with the Galácticos transformed into cartoon characters, for example, or virtual games that allowed real children to imagine they were exchanging passes in an indoor pitch with Ronaldo and Zidane.

And on top of that Sánchez and his marketing team were keeping a close watch on developments in mobile phone technology, with plans afoot to deliver Real Madrid 'content' – be it the highlights of a game or a message from a player – straight to one's handset. Pérez wanted Real Madrid to be prepared to exploit the opportunities that science would open up. 'Technology works in our favour,' Pérez said. 'Some day anyone anywhere in the world will be able to choose a game to watch merely by pressing a button on a computer. And that will really be to the advantage of a global team like Real Madrid.'

The perception that Real Madrid would have a ready market for these and other schemes the club was plotting was encouraged, in José Angel Sánchez's mind, by the idea that the assembly of superstars at Real Madrid would prove irresistible to children the world over. 'In ten years' time, if we can carry on bringing in the most charismatic players, we're going to have half the world supporting Real Madrid if we're not careful!' Sánchez said. 'The concept extends to adults in the immature football audiences, such as in Asia. Today the loyalty is to individual players but, in future, as people's relationship with the game matures, it will be with clubs.'

Translating the planetary emotions Real Madrid generated into financial gains depended first of all on the club's global reach. But it was the nature of the message that Real Madrid conveyed that determined which companies would be prepared to pay good money in sponsorship deals. 'It is the combination of the vast numbers of people that we deliver and the quality of responses the club generates that has persuaded the best multinational companies to associate their names with ours,' Sánchez said. 'Take Audi, they are a classy, distinctive, aspirational brand. In us they see a perfect fit.'

Jesús Gasanz agreed. 'Real Madrid represents values we ourselves identify with. The idea of being the leader, the best, plus that unique sense of style. To be a Real Madrid fan or to own an Audi car is to show discernment, class. That is why we pay Real Madrid good money: to make that identification between them and us explicit.'

One thing about Real Madrid that particularly struck the president of Audi in Spain was the same thing that struck the former Spanish prime minister, José María Aznar: that people in China or Rwanda might not know where Spain was but the name Real Madrid immediately hit a chord.

'Real Madrid places Spain on the map,' Gasanz said. 'The club avoids the need for the country to spend large sums of money promoting itself. I will give you an example of what I mean. Next week sixty Chinese Audi concessionaires are coming to Madrid to see the launch of a new car. In previous years Audi would have staged an event like this in London or Paris. But now Madrid has become a centre for the development of the Audi brand. Now Madrid is where our Chinese concessionaires want to be. They will stay at the Ritz, see the Prado museum and the Bernabéu. They will go and watch a league game at the weekend. And, I promise you, they will tell their grandchildren about it.'

5: Proving a Point

Asked by a journalist in São Paulo for his views on David Beckham joining Real Madrid, Roberto Carlos had this to say: 'Now that Beckham's coming there are finally going to be two good-looking guys in the team. I am so glad, because I felt so lonely being the only handsome player in such an ugly team.'

I quoted those lines to Beckham at the beginning of the television interview we did on the morning of his official presentation as a Real Madrid player. Normally so restrained in his public appearances, so robotically in control of his off-field celebrity persona, Beckham shook with laughter, revealing for all the world to see his not quite perfect teeth.

Tony Stephens, in the studio watching the interview off camera, laughed too. With relief as much as anything else. He had been nervous about what I might do to his boy. With Alex Ferguson out of the picture, Stephens was Beckham's father-figure-in-chief. Before the interview began he had come up to me and said, 'So, um, tell me . . . what sort of questions do you think you'll be asking David?' Tall, soft, white-haired, Stephens had the benign, venerable manner of a bishop. I told him he should relax. I was not going to ask Beckham about his parents' recent divorce, his views on homosexuality or the rationale behind his latest hairstyle. I wasn't even going to ask him the question that had been animating the great British public these six or seven years past: 'Who wears the trousers in the Beckham marriage, David or Posh?' No, I assured Stephens, the plan was to talk football.

Stephens let out a gentle sigh of relief. This interview was a big deal for his star client. Quite apart from the fact that substantial extracts from it would be shown in every country in the world where they had TV, there was for Beckham himself a more pressing concern. He was anxious to know how the Spanish public in general, and the Real Madrid fans in particular, were reacting to the news of his move. In England they were crazy about him, but here, who knew how they might respond? This was uncharted territory. He did not speak the language and could not read the papers, much less understand all that babble on the radio and TV. He was in the dark. He was not – perfectionist that he famously was – at all on top of this situation. It was important that he made a good impression. For this interview, which would not only be broadcast with subtitles but carried in full the next day in the two big national sports dailies *Marca* and *AS*, was his personal introduction to his new public. Would they like him? Or would they conclude that he was, as many had already been conditioned from a distance to suspect, a good-looking twerp, a not especially brilliant player who for some reason drove teenagers wild the world over? They'd seen some of the hysterical scenes he had provoked on the trip he had just made to Japan and Vietnam, they had read about him filling a stadium in Ho Chi Minh City with 40,000 people who had come simply to gawp at him, to watch him doing a sort of victory lap around the stadium – without a football in sight – in an open-topped car. They had seen him arrive the day before in Madrid as if he were the King of England, driving around the city with an escort of police motorbikes. And many suspected the worst. The media, by and large were well-disposed towards him; prepared to give him the benefit of the doubt. Some were prepared to give him a lot more.

'Beckham arrived barefoot, like Christ,' one over-excited Spanish radio commentator was to say later, commenting on the moment of his apparition before me and the other twenty or so people milling around the studio where the interview took place. And true enough, he wasn't dressed in what one might in a gentler age have described as his Sunday Best. He was shoeless and sockless, and his faded jeans were strategically torn at the knees. But he shone. Hard as he had endeavoured to look, from the waist down, like one of the wretched of the earth, he shone brighter than the rest of us in the room. Maybe it was a trick of the mind. Maybe because you expect him to have a special sheen about him, he does. Or maybe it's that uniquely charismatic people like him do indeed shine brighter, and *that* is why they stand out the way they do, rather than the other way around. Sven-Goran Eriksson, the Swedish manager of the England team, reckoned in an interview he gave *Marca* some months later that it was something innate. 'David Beckham has charisma,' Eriksson said. 'If he were in this room, we would all be looking at him. That's something you're born with.'

Or maybe it's just the way he looked and the way he dressed. Perhaps it was that he was wearing an all-white Real Madrid tracksuit top – clean and new and with no holes in it – and that he wore his blond hair long and that he had startlingly fine-featured, film-star looks.

Among the Spanish population, a number of people did make the point that all Beckham needed to take his angelic place in the celestial throne was a good pair of wings. The bare feet, meanwhile, were a start. I made no comment on the feet, as if it were the most natural thing in the world for him to turn up for an interview without shoes. That's the thing about celebrities. They set the agenda. They dictate what is fashionable and what is not, what is cool and what is old hat. And Beckham, perhaps more than anyone else alive, had become the glass of global fashion, the mold of popular taste. Maybe within twenty-four hours half the world's youth would be walking the streets barefoot, joining the other half who had no choice in the matter. What was certain was that young men everywhere would be imitating his swept-back pony-tail look. And as for the spotlessly white Real Madrid tracksuit top, they'd had trouble shifting it at the Bernabéu's big merchandising store. Within forty-eight hours of that interview they had sold 4,000.

For all that, you could tell he was nervous. He had never been interviewed for half an hour on television on his own before. He knew he wasn't the world's greatest conversationalist, that he was far better doing his talking – as nature intended that he do – with his feet. Some light exchanges between us, some talk about the joys of rearing bilingual children before we went before the cameras did perhaps ease the mood but it was that Roberto Carlos crack, celebrating the end of his beauteous solitude, that really did it.

'I don't know,' said Beckham, spluttering with toothy laughter
barely one minute into the interview. 'I just don't know what to say
after that . . . No, but he's a great player and I'm pleased, really pleased
I'm playing in the same side as him now. AND he's very good
looking, of course.'

Beckham only ventured one more joke after that but it was plain
sailing from then on. My first questions centred on why he had
joined Real Madrid, what was so special about the club for him,
and he lapped this stuff up. 'This was the only team I wanted to
come to,' he said. 'Real Madrid excited me. They're a great club –
massive club – and this was the only team that actually excited me.'
I put it to him that people sometimes forgot with all the other
madness in his life that he was a footballer. 'Yeah', he said, more to
himself than to me, 'yeah . . .' in a short, breathy, exhaling sort of
way, as if expressing relief that someone had finally figured it out.
And they forgot also, I continued, that he was a fan too, a football
fanatic. So that it was almost as much of a thrill for him to be playing
with these fantastic Real Madrid players as it would be for any ordinary football-loving Joe. 'Oh, of course!' he replied. 'That was the
whole excitement for me about joining Real Madrid!'

I reminded him about the two games he had played against Real
Madrid barely two and a half months earlier, especially that first game
at the Bernabéu where he and his Manchester United teammates
had spent much of the time being spectators. 'Yeah, I'd probably
compare them to the Harlem Globetrotters,' he said, stealing a line
from his friend Gary Neville. 'They play amazing football, exciting
football, but effective football as well. Playing against them at the
Bernabéu was a very, very difficult game. I think in the first half the
football that they played was absolutely amazing, and astonishing. For
me now being part of that – hopefully being part of that – is a very
proud time for me.'

Hopefully? 'Yes,' he said. 'I have to fight for my position, and the
other players do as well. That's what makes them – us – a successful
team, you have to fight for your place. I'm not coming to Real
Madrid expecting to step straight into the team. I'm expecting to
fight for a position.' So far, he wasn't putting a foot wrong, dashing

any notions Spaniards might have had that he was a supercilious Englishman by the clear admiration he felt for the club and the pleasingly humble doubts he was expressing about his future place in it. And as for his new teammates he was, if not quite in awe of them, genuinely bowled over at the prospect of playing alongside them. We ran through the better known of them.

Roberto Carlos: 'He is a great player. Obviously he's a left back, a defender, but he goes forward like a left winger and a forward. He's probably more of a forward than he is a back but that's a great advantage. He is a great player, and the nice thing about him is that every time I've come up against him there's never been any nastiness. Obviously he's very professional, we tackle, but there's always a handshake and a hug after the game. And that shows me there's a nice man there as well.'

Ronaldo: 'Well, he's the best player in the world at the moment and he's proving it, the goals he's scored this year. He's been absolutely immense and I'm looking forward, hopefully, to putting balls through for him to score goals . . . To come back from injury the way he has done, and to come back the player he has done, is absolutely amazing.'

Raúl: 'He is a very different kind of player . . . You know, they all work hard of course, but you look at Raúl and he works harder than most of the players, probably. He drops into positions. He has a great football brain and again he is a nice person. He is very quiet, but he is some player.'

Figo: 'I think once people saw I was coming to Real Madrid they said I was going to replace Figo out on the right. Well, that never entered my head. I want to be in the same team as Figo, because he is one of the best crossers in the world, one of the world's best players, and to be in the same team as him would be a great honour.'

Zidane: 'He's, he's . . .' (For a moment Beckham was lost for words, as if stunned just thinking about how good Zidane was.) '. . . You know, I describe him . . . when I talk about Zidane, I say he plays football like a ballerina. He glides across the pitch: the way he plays football, his first touch, his passing of the ball with both feet, the way he controls the game – everything. Amazing! For me he is one of the best – if not the best in the world.'

What? So both Ronaldo and Zidane were the best in the world? 'I'm glad,' he said, smiling just a tad coyly, as if caught out in a few too many superlatives for his new teammates, 'I'm just glad I'm in the same team as them, anyway.'

I asked him whether, in the light of all these extraordinary players who were already at Real Madrid, he found the prospect of playing with them a little bit daunting. I put it to him that he had been brave in deciding to come to Real Madrid, when maybe he could have gone to a club in which he would have been a bigger fish in a smaller pond? 'At the end of the day, you know,' he replied, not disputing the justice of the question, 'me coming to Real Madrid is not about me coming to be the main star. It's joining a whole team of stars. And my thing about coming here is to play football and to play good football and that's what they do – and that's what we do now. That's what I'm looking forward to more than anything. The football side is the most important thing for me. Always has been, always will be. I'm not coming here to be the main star. I'm coming here to enjoy playing with these great players and be in this great city.'

The second and last joke of the interview came when I asked him if there was some aspect of his game that he thought was good but was not sufficiently valued by other people. 'My tackling,' he replied, with a self-mocking little smirk, as if knowing that everybody would get the joke. 'I think I'm a great tackler.' Little did he know that in due course he would be asked by Real Madrid to tackle more than he ever had before in his life, that he would be playing in a more defensive role than he would ever have imagined. Had he known that he might have hesitated a little more before declaring that if there was one thing really driving him to succeed it was the people, most of them in England, who said he would fail. 'There have been people who have doubted me coming here and performing in Spain,' he said, his eyes narrowing, his look hardening, revealing a shadow of a hint of the steely resolve that lurked inside the man, beneath the soft voice and the bland exterior. 'It would be a great thing for me to quieten these people and play some good football. The whole challenge of being here is playing with the great players.' So he wanted to prove a point? 'Of course. It's always good to prove points to people and I'd like to do that here. Even though maybe I don't have to prove points to my closest people and family. But there are still some people out there who doubt me and, yes, I'd like to do that.'

Those who doubted him in Spain, where most people knew little about him as a player, had no idea that beyond his ability to strike a ball more cleanly than perhaps anyone alive, he was a supremely fit player, known always to have possessed more stamina (a fact Alex Ferguson had corroborated) than any contemporary of his during his thirteen years at Manchester United. As a child he had been a cross-country and 1,500 metres champion. 'I've always liked running quite a long way, and I seem to do the same thing on the pitch as well, you know. I work hard. I'm a team player more than anything. People might think otherwise, but me, personally, I love being involved with the team, I love playing with great players and I love working hard for the team – and, well, that's me.'

Again, Beckham was saying just the right things to ingratiate himself with his new public. No one likes a show-off but the Spanish like them less than most. In contrast to the United States, but also England, Spain is a country where it is considered in bad taste to flaunt your wealth. Rich people go out of their way to appear more modest than they are. The same principle applied to top football players. For Beckham to say he saw himself as one more of the bunch won him a lot of points from his Spanish audience. As did his claim that he always stayed behind to practise his famous free kicks – his trademark as far as the Spanish public were concerned – at the end of training, even after his teammates had headed off home. 'I still practise every day with the free kicks. When I'm training, after training, I always take twenty, thirty free kicks. And I always will do. I don't ever think you can practise enough, even with stuff that you're good at. You can always get better. The free kick at Old Trafford against Real Madrid was one of my best free kicks and I was really pleased with that. Obviously not starting the game then coming on and scoring two goals, and especially one of them being a free kick, meant a lot to me.' Why had that free kick been one of his best? 'One, it was special to me because it was against one of the best goalkeepers in the world and one of the best teams in the world.

Two, because I hadn't started the game and I felt that I had to come on and prove a point to some people. And three because looking back on it it's one of the best free kicks that I've actually taken.'

It was when I asked him the straightforward question whether it had sunk in yet that he was no longer a Manchester United player that he let slip how long the wound Ferguson had inflicted on him had been festering. 'No,' he replied, 'probably a year – probably six, seven months ago I probably wouldn't have even thought that it was possible. But if I was going to leave Manchester United I wanted to leave for Real Madrid. Simple as that.' Why 'six, seven months', I asked? 'No,' he replied, collecting himself, 'just because everything was going smoothly then and I wouldn't have expected to be putting put on a Real Madrid shirt at the start of the season, not because I wanted to leave then because nothing went on until two, three weeks ago when it was all discussed with Man United. I said six, seven months ago because it was all running smoothly then.'

He was not going to be particularly candid about his relationship with Fergsuon either. I reminded him that his father, Ted Beckham, had told the press that Fergsuon had hounded him out. 'Well, honestly you have your ups and downs with your manager in all walks of life, and I'm no different and the other players are no different. But all I can say about that is that Sir Alex Ferguson has been a major part of my career, of my life, for thirteen years. He was one of the reasons why I signed for Manchester United, he was one of the reasons why I got in the team at Manchester United and he was one of the reasons why I stayed in the team at Manchester United. He has been a sort of father figure for me all the way along and that is one thing I will always remember.' Yes, certainly, but being dropped for that huge game against Real Madrid at Old Trafford, wasn't that a bit of a betrayal by the father of a favourite son? 'I'm sure,' said Beckham, playing yet another impeccably straight bat, 'that it was more professional than anything. Obviously I wanted to play, more than anything, because I'm – as you said – a footballer more than anything else and football is the only thing that matters to me, bar the family. It was disappointing not to start the game but I felt I came on and tried to prove a point.'

It was the third time he had come out with this idea of 'proving a point', reminding me how proud a man he was, how persistent. Here was the player speaking who after being left out at the start of the Real Madrid game at Old Trafford had come on and scored twice; the one who had been sent off for England against Argentina in 1998, been publicly pilloried for his irresponsibility and who had bounced back the next season to win the famous 'Treble' with Manchester United, to become England captain and to score the winning goal against Argentina in the World Cup rematch in Japan four years later.

What people in Spain might worry about, though, was that, admirable as his track record might be, his celebrity persona would swallow up his game, do as Ferguson said it did and undermine the quality of his contribution to the team. Was it not true, I put it to him, that the frenzied mobs he generated everywere he went were a sign that things in his life had got out of hand? 'No, Not out of hand,' he replied, 'because I always feel that I'm in control of it, because I never let myself get carried away – even though being in the Far East just recently was a pretty amazing experience, being there on my own instead of being there with Man United or England. But I always feel that I'm in control of that side of my life. I never let it affect my football side because my football side is the most important thing, I have to stress, for me. The reason I have these fans and have had so many different things outside footbal is because I'm a professional footballer and because of what I've done in football and I realise that, and that's why I feel I have total control of the events that surround me.'

'Total control'. It was an important notion for Beckham, who may well be what Freud calls an anal personality. (Perhaps part of the reason for the personality clash between Beckham and Ferguson was that they were both control freaks.) Beckham himself became aware over the course of the various books and documentaries made about him that he was obsessively neat and tidy, that at his home every suit, every shoe, every sock always had to be in its place. It was a trait his family spotted in him from an early age – as a child he was so prim, his mother said, that he used to fold his dirty clothes before he gave them to her to wash – and that his teammates at Manchester United always used to tease him about. (Ryan Giggs used to like telling how when Beckham used to give them a ride in his car he would plead with them not to scuff his shiny leather seats.) When he became famous, that impulse to keep everything absolutely under control extended to the management of his fame, of his public persona. That meant in his case projecting an image – always, unfailingly – of a thoroughly nice, polite, decent, honourable young family man who also happened to be the trendiest thing on two legs. And who played football like a Trojan.

Had he created a split personality for himself, then? Had he managed to make a complete separation between one aspect of his life and the other? 'I'm quite a level-headed person, I've got a very strong family behind me, a very level-headed family behind me. I go out to the Far East but then I come home to my sons and my wife and it's a normal family life. I try to do the normal things in life. I like to go to the grocery store and things like that. I like to do those things still. I just keep the two as far apart as possible, and that's important to me and important to my new set of fans because I am sure they see that part of it and worry. But – trust me – they don't have to worry about that because the football side and the other side are totally different. The football side is the serious part.'

Eric Cantona, his former teammate at Manchester United and a man Beckham much admired, that very week of our interview had said, 'I left Manchester United because I lost my passion for the game, because I did not master the merchandising side. At one stage what mattered was Cantona the Product, the Profit – and then I had to go.' Did he ever worry about Beckham the Product, I asked Beckham? 'No, I don't. Because I just see myself as a footballer more than anything and the other side is a bonus. That's the way I actually look at it. The stuff that goes on around me is a bonus, and the reason it's a bonus is because I'm a footballer and that's the way I treat it.'

We switched to talking about his family and his thoughts about moving to Spain. It was a surprise to hear how sincerely enthusiastic he felt at the prospect – not the reaction you would normally expect from an English football player. Beckham told me that learning Spanish was 'something I want to do as soon as possible'; that it would be 'an amazing experience' for his two little boys to be able to speak two languages.

'It's a challenge on the football side,' he said, 'and it's going to be a great experience off the pitch because obviously my family are moving over, my children are going to go to school and it's going to be an amazing experience for us all . . . I'm definitely going to enjoy playing football over here and my family is definitely going to enjoy living here . . . My family are going to be happy anywhere. My wife's going to be happy here, she is going to work from here and London and America and my two boys are going to go to school over here and they're going to have a great life and me, finally, me I'm here to play in a great team, to play great football – to play beautiful football, like they do – and just to win as many trophies as possible.'

Only once it was all over – once we had shaken hands and Beckham had taken turns, with infinite patience, to have his photograph taken with everybody in the room, and once he and Tony Stephens had walked out, relieved I am sure that the whole thing had not turned out to be a dreadful fiasco, was I able to pause and reflect on how masterly Beckham's performance had been. Listening to him talk in his not always impeccably grammatical English, in that far from booming voice of his, your first impression is not that you are in the presence of a guileful communicator, as rigorously 'on-message' as the canniest politician. But you are. And the fact that you don't realise it, that he comes across as so boyishly artless, only makes you succumb all the more to his wiles. When people asked me – as they did all the time, all over the world, for months after that interview – what he was like, what he was *really* like, I always had a stock answer ready. I said that what most came across was his sweetness of nature – a sense that, unless you had had a personal run-in with him, it would be very difficult to dislike him. I said that he came across as a Walt Disney prince, the type who comes on at the end of the film, whisks way the princess and marries her in his castle: good, in other words; good looking, dashing, but, like the Disney prince, some doubt remained as to how much content there was in there, exactly.

But that was my stock answer, when I didn't want to labour the point too much. Examining that interview more closely, watching it again, I concluded, as did friends who watched it with me, that he is a lot more thoughtful than people imagine. No doubt he has had some training in these matters, having been excruciatingly tongue-tied in his first TV appearances, when he was becoming famous in England but was still a couple of years short of becoming a global celebrity. No doubt too Tony Stephens gave him a briefing, setting out a few basic objectives, before the two of us went before the cameras. Though I had a feeling that at this stage of the game Beckham did not need much prompting. He knew perfectly well that from his point of view the purpose of the interview was to insinuate himself into the graces of, first, his new public and, second, his new team-mates; to lay a solid foundation on which to mount an important new phase of the continuous public relations offensive that the life of a soccer showman – the greatest soccer showman of all – required.

In the event, he achieved all of these objectives. It was like one of those clean, solid games of his in which he dispenses tidily with each ball he receives. He came across as likeably humble, joking about his famously poor tackling, stressing several times that he did not take for granted his place in the Real team, that he would have to fight for his place. He also had the wisdom and self-knowledge to make the important point, sometimes forgotten amidst all the celebrity broo-ha-ha, that he was not *such* a fantastic player; that he is not (while he did not say it, he implied it) in the same league as far as talent is concerned as Ronaldo and Zidane; that the idea of him taking the place of Figo, the world's greatest winger over the last decade, was preposterous; that he was first and foremost a hard-working team player. And that, for all of these reasons, it was brave of him to choose to come to Real Madrid.

And he did what any good diplomat does on arriving in a new country and proclaimed his pleasure at the prospect of living in the 'great' city of Madrid, declaring his intention to raise his family in the Spanish way. As for the football, no amount of rehearsing could have conveyed the message more convincingly. He was itching to get started; he was going to play the most beautiful football he had ever played; he was going to have the time of his life. He really believed he was.

6: The Revolutionary in a Suit

Outside his home he always wore a grey suit and a blue shirt. He probably wore a grey suit and a blue shirt inside his home too. It was difficult to imagine him in anything else. A businessman of medium height, medium looks, in his mid-fifties, he was the enemy of ostentation. The anti-Beckham. And yet everywhere Florentino Pérez, the president of Real Madrid, went he was mobbed. Teenagers screamed his name, begged for autographs, implored him to pose for pictures with them.

There had never been anything quite like it. Not in the world of football, at any rate. People know tons about the game: they remember who scored the winners in cup finals played thirty years earlier, and in what minute of the game; they know the dates of birth and favourite colours of their favourite strikers; they have informed opinions on young players coming up through the reserve teams of the clubs they support. But they know nothing, nor do they want to, about the people who run the clubs. At most they might be aware of the name of the president, or chairman, but otherwise the men in suits remain dim and distant figures, unrecognisable in crowds.

Pérez was something else altogether. I travelled with him to Real Madrid away games, went with him to ceremonial openings, sat with him at restaurants and bars. It was impossible, unless his security chief deliberately kept people at bay, to sustain an uninterrupted conversation with him in public. He oozed power in a way that people do who really have it. Something about the sense of entitlement with which he slipped into the back of sleek, chauffeur-driven cars oblivious to the presence of the bodyguards who held doors open for him. The bodyguards were no luxury item. He needed them as all

captains of industry did in Spain because of the threat from the
Basque terrorist group ETA. And yet for any seriously determined
terrorist he was a sitting duck. He was continually out on the streets
and under siege. Teenage girls and boys, their fathers and mothers,
their grandparents. Everybody wanted a piece of him, the way everybody wanted a piece of Beckham. Or perhaps not in quite the same
way, or to the same degree. Pérez would not have stopped the traffic
in central Tokyo; he was not a household name in Shanghai. It was
only inside his own country that his face was as well known as the
incumbent prime minister's. Pérez – whose surname is more humdrum
in Spanish than Smith is in English – was a celebrity in his own
land. And he was a good celebrity too. A good sport. He had spent
most of his life toiling obscurely, if enormously successfully, in the
construction business, but he turned out to be a natural at the fame
game. At restaurants he would cheerfully interrupt his dinner to sign
napkins and menus. He would sign photographs of himself, specially
brought along for the purpose, for the thrilled waiters and kitchen
staff. Very late at night once at an airport, returning from an away
game, I stood and watched as he posed and posed with a patiently
benevolent smile for two teenage girls whose camera – to their
absolute despair – refused to work. I have been with him in the
middle of dense crowds when he has gone to open a new Real
Madrid football school and heard people screaming out his name,
'Florentino! Florentino!', as if he were a pop star. Or another Galáctico.

Which, actually, he was. Luis Figo said once in a radio interview
that never mind him and his fellow superstars in shorts, the man in
the grey suit was the true Galáctico. Figo was right. Pérez was the
father of the Galácticos. Without Pérez's extravagance of vision, we
may never have seen such a cartoonishly improbable collection of
footballing superheroes in the same team. To have gathered together
such a larger than life set of players you needed a larger than life
imagination. And the conviction and drive to make it happen.

Had he never had the idea of running for the club presidency
Real Madrid might have gone on and won quite as many trophies.
They might even have won the admiration of football fans every-
where, the way teams like Arsenal and Milan did. But they would

not have excited the football world in the same way. Real Madrid fans understood all of this better than anybody. On becoming president of Real Madrid in the summer of 2000, Pérez promised he would restore the club to its former glories, that his Real would shake the world the way Di Stefano's had. Three years later, Pérez had largely fulfilled his grand pledge. He might end up falling some way short of winning five European Cups in a row, but in a very short time he had achieved an implausible amount. He had become one of the commanding figures in the game and the team he built, *el Florenteam*, as they called it in Spain in grateful acknowledgement of its parentage – had captured the imagination not only of Spain, but of the world.

The world's best players were queuing up to play for this team. Ronaldo had asked if he could come; so had Zidane; so had Beckham. Francesco Totti, Italy's best player, said around the same time that the one team in the world that he would leave his beloved Roma for would be Real Madrid. As for Fabio Capello, one of the two or three most respected coaches in world football, he declared on Spanish television that he frankly envied Carlos Queiroz. 'Real Madrid is the team all coaches would most love to manage, that most great players would like to join,' Capello said.

That the luminaries of the game considered Real Madrid, without a doubt, the greatest in turn generated a great deal of resentment, especially in Spain where envy – as the Spanish themselves always say – is the national disease and where for every *Madridista* there was an *anti-Madridista*. Pérez's Galáctico Real Madrid was not a club that left people cold. You were either for them or against them. And because no one in Spain was in any doubt that the Real Madrid of Zidane and Ronaldo was the brainchild of Pérez it was on him that much of the rage was heaped. It was not just the adulation that he shared with his famous players, it was also the abuse. Sitting near him at away games, it was staggering to see how much foul language was hurled his way, and at the slightest excuse. The referee gave a throw-in Real's way when (in the opinion of the home fans) it should have been given the other way; the referee missed a perceived foul by a Real player; a Real player fouled a home player; Real scored; Real won: each time, unfailingly, a contingent of the home fans within earshot of him would turn away from the game, glare at him with hatred in their eyes and shout: '*Hijo de Puta Florentino*' and '*Me cago en tu puta madre, Florentino.*' 'Son of a bitch, Florentino' and 'I shit on your whore of a mother, Florentino.' And they weren't drunk, or young and thuggish necessarily. The abuse hurled his way was but a twisted expression of admiration, of course, an implicit recognition of his power, audacity and imagination.

Because, as all those bitter rival fans knew, Real had achieved what they had in the Pérez era thanks almost entirely to Pérez himself. Yet, in terms of the rest of the man's achievements, what he had done at Real was almost the least of it. Compared to his day job, running his huge ACS global construction company, Real Madrid was, in business terms, small potatoes. Running the biggest institution in world sport was something he did as others might collect stamps. 'Running Real Madrid,' he told me, in all seriousness, the first time I met him, 'is my hobby. I am essentially the president of ACS and my leisure moments, instead of dedicating them to something else, I dedicate to Real Madrid. For me, dedicating that time to the club is a privilege and a pleasure.'

Our first meeting was not at the Bernabéu, where he has an office that he rarely has time to visit, but ten minutes away by car at the headquarters of ACS. We sat at a round table of polished wood in a large air-conditioned room on ACS's solemn, hushed executive floor. Pérez himself, in his grey suit and blue shirt, was not solemn at all. He did not know me but, as relaxed as if he were inviting a friend into his home, he instantly adopted the informal and familiar *tú* form of Spanish in conversation, instead of the formal *usted* I had been expecting. His first question to me was whether the air-conditioning was at a comfortable temperature; the second, whether I would like some tea or coffee. Never less than courteous, in an old-fashioned Spanish sort of way, he was respectful and warm at the same time.

A boyish gleam came into his eye when he talked about the fabulous players he had brought to Real and it was with the same delight that he confided to me that once a year he made a point of summoning his star players to have lunch with him here, at the very table where he and I were sitting. At the end of our hour and a half together not only did he escort me to the lift, when the doors opened and I went in he reached inside to press the ground floor button for me, as if this were an indignity to which his guests should not be expected to stoop.

It was the summer of 2003 and right around the time when we met – never mind his recently completed Beckham purchase – Pérez was putting the finishing touches to a merger that by the end of the year would place him at the head of the third-largest construction conglomerate in Europe. 'Yes, we're going to be very big,' he said matter-of-factly, making it plain he was not too interested in talking about his day job. How big? 'A turnover of 12,000 million euros, nearly 100,000 employees, operations in seventy countries,' he shrugged. Suddenly the commercial dimensions of deals involving the purchase of football players for 35, 40, 60 million euros were put into perspective. Those sums didn't amount to a whole lot for a man routinely obliged to compete with other multinationals for contracts to build bridges and motorways hundreds of miles long and billions of euros in costs. He himself, as executive president of ACS, was reckoned by the Spanish financial press to be worth at least 600 million euros. Quite a haul for a man who had entered the business world only twenty years earlier, whose experience before then had been limited to politics and the civil service.

In 1983 Pérez left politics and bought a small, bankrupt construction firm for one peseta. The rest is history. In two decades he achieved success of the sort you are not surprised to encounter in an inveterately optimistic and mobile free-market society like the United States, but you rarely find in western Europe, where the economic and social structures – and the ways of thinking generally of the people – are more rigid. Pérez belongs to a class of Spaniard not known abroad but common, even typical, in the Meseta, the arid plains of Castille. He is hard, dry, austere, persistent, driven. You looked at him and you understood a little better how a handful of his compatriots once sailed off in small wooden boats and conquered Mexico and Peru.

The US army had a motto during the Second World War that was supposedly first coined by Napoleon. 'The difficult we do immediately; the impossible takes a little longer.' Pérez's career at Real Madrid, as in the world of big business, was Napoleon's bon mot made flesh. In his first three years as president he did the impossible several times. Starting with the very fact of getting elected to the job in the first place. When he threw his hat into the ring for the summer 2000 election, you would not have bet one penny on him winning. He had already had a go and lost – amid suspicions that he was fraudulently denied victory – in 1995.

But that first time conditions had been a lot more favourable for him. Real Madrid had gone twenty-nine years without winning the European Cup, a trophy the club and the fans still insisted perversely in imagining that they somehow owned. And while they were doing well in Spain, there was little about the team then to excite people, to make them imagine that the glory days might finally be around the corner again.

In 2000, by contrast, Pérez was running against an incumbent, Lorenzo Sanz, who had delivered glory. Not only had the team finally won its coveted seventh European Cup under his reign, in 1998, they had won their eighth a matter of weeks before the election, in May 2000, after defeating Valencia 3-0 in the tournament's first all-Spanish final.

There were a number of explanations as to why Pérez defeated Sanz, all of them to do with the peculiar nature of the Real Madrid fans. The voters in the election were not shareholders, as they would have been at Manchester United which is a private company. The voters were the club's 83,967 paid-up members. For Real Madrid, big as the brand name might have become, remained a sports club in the amateur sense of the word – a non-profit-making institution run for the benefit of the members. In this case the members were the club's hard-core fans, season-ticket holders who occupied the majority of the seats at the Bernabéu. The difference with these fans, what set them apart from just about any other set of fans in the world, with the exception of fans of the Brazilian national side, was that for them winning was not enough. They were winning trophies, the most sought-after trophies in the game, but the problem for Sanz – and it was a problem no other president of any other club in the world would have encountered – was that Real Madrid fans felt they were being short-changed. Winning and not losing was important, yes. But what really mattered was how you played the game.

If you won the league playing defensive counter-attacking, Italian-style football – as Real did with Fabio Capello as their coach in 1997 – that didn't count. Style was indivisible from substance. For Madrid fans getting their money's worth meant knowing that when they turned up at the Bernabéu, or watched Real on TV, they would be treated to the best football show on earth.

Pérez convinced them that he was the man to give the *Madridistas* what they wanted, that he would bring back the magic of Di Stefano and company. Real fans had been irredeemably spoiled by those all-singing, all-dancing, all-triumphant teams they had in the Fifties when Di Stefano and his team bestrode the football universe. The fans feasted on football paradise for those five years when their team won the European Cup five times and from then on, even among those too young to have seen that team play, the idea became fixed in the collective memory of paradise lost, a paradise that had to be regained and one day would be. And until it was – until Real Madrid won playing with art and glamour – their fans would never be fully satisfied and Real would not be Real, would not have its *Madridista* soul back.

'The reason I presented my candidacy,' Pérez told me, sipping a coffee at his round wooden table, 'was that I felt that *el Madridismo* had lost its way and had to recover certain values it had lost. We had departed from the orthodoxies that had made us great.' It is fascinating this habit people have in Spain of referring to their football clubs in ideological and cultural terms. You have *Madridismo* and *Barcelonismo* and even *Valencianismo* as you have Communism, Capitalism, Fascism. If you were to go into a pub in England and ask people if they were Manchesterites or Arsenalites, you would get some very funny looks. If you went on to inquire as to the proper definition of Manchesterism or Arsenalism they would very quickly be calling for the men in white coats. Spain is different. When I asked Pérez to define *Madridismo* for me, his response was simply to purse his lips and nod, in solemn acknowledgement of the gravity of my question.

'For a start, it means to have a clear sporting project,' he said. 'In our case this meant having a team that did not win games by chance or because we had one brilliant player, but a team that had a clear identity and knew where it was going. Identity is the thing. Identity. Real Madrid's identity is based on playing attacking football. Other teams have a defensive style and it works fine for them. Not for us. That is why our project is based on having the finest players available in the world, players of superior talent. Our purpose is to provide an artistic spectacle with a touch of magic to it. Winning is important, but more important still is consolidating a style of play that is of the highest quality. The values on which we draw are courage, leadership, desire, solidarity among the players and respect for your rivals. All that had been lost when I made my bid for the presidency. Now I believe we have recovered it. That is why when people ask me how I have done what I have done I reply that it has been very easy. I have simply been faithful to the history of the club. I have done nothing else.'

If there was one word in Spanish that summed up the qualities he wished to see once again in his Real Madrid, and that defined the character of the great team of the Fifties, it was, he said, '*señorío*'. *Señorío* is an old-fashioned word. It means something like lordliness, dignity, bearing, stateliness, or majesty – with suggestions of honour, elegance, pedigree, nobility, class. Pérez did not say it himself but it was obvious that his predecessor did not possess these qualities in abundance. Lorenzo Sanz was a sleazy character, a man who could – and did – make a 2,000 euro suit look cheap. Pérez, who would not dream of spending a quarter of that on a suit, projected an image of grave, gentlemanly restraint.

Which was why he struggled a little when he started talking about Real Madrid, why there was a clash between his own personal restraint and his immodest vision of the club's true worth.

'Real Madrid is more than a well-known football club. I say it is the best brand in the world,' Pérez said. 'I understand how people can accuse you of being arrogant when you say something like this. But I say it in all humility. Besides, it is the best brand in the world that asks you for nothing in exchange. Of course Coca-Cola is a huge brand too, but you have to pay and then you derive some physical satisfaction from consuming the drink. But Real Madrid satisfies your heart, your sentiments. It fills not your stomach, it fills your soul. It is a brand that is in the hearts of so many millions and millions of people everywhere but asks for nothing in return. People identify with Real Madrid not merely because we win, but because they relate to the club as they might, in a way, with religion. People sometimes say to me, why don't you make Real Madrid into a limited company? Well, believe me, no one believes more in limited companies than me. Here I am with a limited company that is on the stock exchange and is very big. But these things that move people's sentiments and emotions: you can't have them in the hands of one individual. For example, if the Catholic church belonged to one man, it would be – to say the least – odd. Well, this is something similar. Real Madrid belongs to everyone. While I am president I am merely the caretaker and interpreter of a heritage that belongs to all *Madridistas* – and I don't just mean the members, but all those followers the club has in Spain and all over the world.'

Pérez's zeal for Real Madrid was matched only by the diligence of his personal self-denial. His dress, his style, everything about his demeanour was low key. It had a lot to do, it turned out, with the admiration he felt for his father. 'My father always said that what you had to do above all was behave like a normal human being,' said Pérez. 'You should never think yourself more important than other people, you should always keep your feet on the ground.'

Pérez had striven to emulate his father and live like a man obliged not to have a moment's rest. His constant claim to be 'normal' was misleading. He was not normal at all. For a start, this business about him speaking 'in all humility' was nonsense. Pérez may indeed dress in such a way as to pass unnoticed in a crowd. But the truth was that, just as he was the enemy of ostentation, he was the enemy of humility. You could not be humble and at the same time be as spectacularly successful in business as he had been. Neither could you be humble and be president of Real Madrid. *Madridismo* was about *señorío*, said Pérez, and one of the defining qualities of *señorío* was an unshakeable belief in your untouchably aristocratic pre-eminence. Time may pass, teams and players may come and go, you may languish thirty years without winning a European Cup, but there were certain verities that were eternal, chief among which was the innate superiority of Real Madrid over all other football clubs. Pérez held to this belief as fervently as any season-ticket holder at the Bernabéu. He felt about Real Madrid the way Pope John Paul II felt about the Roman Catholic church. A faith, a love, an esteem, a belief in superiority that was absolute, and therefore way beyond arrogance. Humility didn't enter the picture.

But Pérez was quite abnormal in his personal habits too, which were often closer to a monk's than a successful business mogul's. Quite apart from the fact that he stopped working only to sleep (quite aberrant behaviour in Spain), how many men were there who only ever wore the same blue shirts? And always a conventionally unassuming sky blue. 'Why complicate your life?' he replied, when I asked him about this. He didn't drink either. 'I am completely abstinent,' he said. Neither was he very interested in food. In so far as he had a favourite dish it was, he said, egg and chips.

As for other sensual pursuits, he and his wife María Angeles Sandoval have three children. 'His only vice,' she would say, 'is being president of Real Madrid.'

But while his habits may have been dull, Pérez was not. He had a relentlessly wry sense of humour, the permanent glint in the eye of a man always ready to find something to smile at in his own behaviour, as well as the behaviour of others. And he did have some passions, apart from Real Madrid. He liked to sail on a luxury yacht that he kept moored in Mallorca. He was a collector of modern art, with works on the walls of his home by Warhol, Rauschenberg, Chillida and Barceló. Another distinctive touch was Pérez's passion for dogs. He owned three. 'I love them,' he said. 'I love them so much that, while I sometimes find it embarrassing to admit it, they do actually condition my life. There are times I won't go out so as not to leave them alone. I won't go on a trip so as to not to leave them alone . . . And when I return from a trip it's always a joy. There they are waiting for me.'

People always said Pérez was ruthless. And – never mind the dogs – they were right. Which was why he had beaten the odds to do what he had done in business – and to get himself elected president of Real Madrid. But how exactly had he done it? How did Pérez pull off the miracle? How did he convince club members that he was the man to make their nostalgic dreams come true?

The answer lay with one man – Luis Figo. Captain of Portugal and King of Barcelona, the idol of the Camp Nou, Luis Figo was a man who, in his noble bearing as in the talent in his play, was the living expression of that identity and those values Pérez chose to believe were the birthright of Real Madrid. The truth was that anyone who loved football had to love Figo. Pérez did some research among Real members prior to launching his election campaign and one of the questions he asked was which player they would most like to see at Real Madrid. The response, by an overwhelming margin, was Figo. Whereupon Pérez took a deep breath and declared, 'I promise the club's members that if they elect me I shall bring Figo to Real Madrid.' And they believed him. Why? How come? I asked him. 'Because I have credibility as a businessman,' replied Pérez, modestly, 'but more important because I promised them that if I were elected and did not bring him I would pay their membership fees – all their membership fees – for the next year out of my own pocket.' Duly elected, Pérez fulfilled his pledge. He prised Figo away from the old enemy, Barcelona, for 60 million euros, breaking what was then the world transfer record.

Pérez got his man because he was obstinate and cunning, and because he was prepared to spend all it took to get him. And also because he took the considerable risk of putting down tens of millions of his own money as a guarantee to the bank which came up with the cash to buy Figo. Pérez took the risk because he under-stood that Figo was the heroic figure around whose talent and drive Real Madrid fans would allow themselves to dream of greatness once again. By announcing his determination to buy the most desirable player in the world at that point, Pérez was signalling that he was daring to think big; that he meant to do what he said – restore Real Madrid to what the club saw as its rightful place: indisputably the greatest and most exciting club in world football.

What Pérez did not know when he took over Real Madrid in July 2000 was that the institution as a whole was in urgent need of an overhaul. He had been aware that things were bad with the club's economy. But he had no idea how bad. The Sanz stewardship had been a disaster. The club was desperately deep in debt. As the managing director Carlos Martinez de Albornoz told me, 'When Florentino arrived we didn't have enough money to buy a biro.'

Pérez found himself in a similar predicament, in other words, to the one he had inherited when he bought a bankrupt construction firm in 1983 for one peseta. Only this time the challenge was a hundred times greater. After winning the Real Madrid presidency and buying Figo – Pérez now had to make the club profitable again. What he did was as brilliant as it was controversial. He sold the land where Real Madrid had their training complex, *la Ciudad Deportiva*, to developers. But before selling it he saw to it that the land was rezoned for commercial use. The value of the land catapulted, Pérez sold, and Real Madrid got 480 million euros. The debts (amounting to 270 million euros) were cleared in one Herculean stroke, the players and staff received their wages on time and the way was paved for what would turn out to be a mightily profitable restructuring of the club.

I put it to Pérez that some saw this life-saving business manoeuvre as evidence of corruption, that an inside deal had given Real Madrid in effect, a giant state subsidy.

Pérez rejects that claim. 'What we have done with *la Ciudad Deportiva* is exactly what others have been doing over the years who have owned land in this part of the city. We sought rezoning permission and, quite naturally given the location of the land, we got it. And then we sold the land – not to the Madrid municipality as some seem to think, but to third parties. To big private companies. And obviously, at market price. So what's the problem?'

The tremendous global success of Real Madrid has had a mighty beneficial impact on the city and on Spain, both in terms of international status, profits, tourism and a happy sense of self. The mayor of Madrid would say in a speech at the end of 2003 that Pérez, as president of Real Madrid, had become the city's 'best ambassador within Spain and in the rest of the world'. 'Obviously it was great for us to have sold off *la Ciudad Deportiva* the way we did,' Pérez told me, 'but it's also been a marvellous operation for the city. That's why everybody agreed with it, not least the federation of neighbours of the area. The fact of the matter is that there has never been an operation of its kind where there was greater consensus or transparency.'

Others, depending on the football tribe to which they belong, might not be so convinced. But no one – not even the *Ciudad Deportiva*'s neighbours – had lost out from the deal. And lots of people had gained from it. After all, had Pérez not pulled off that mother of all land deals the world would have been deprived of the chance to delight in the spectacle of Figo, Zidane, Ronaldo, Roberto Carlos, Beckham and Raúl all playing in the same football team.

7: Revolutionary Ideology

The most conclusive evidence that whatever else Pérez was, he was not humble, was that he presumed to have come up with the formula for footballing success. In this most capricious of sports, in which results so consistently surprise you, he believed he had come up with the answer. Daring to defy the football gods, Pérez believed he had hit upon the Promethean formula. Prometheus was punished by the gods, chained to a rock for eternity, for his impudence in seeking to steal their secret knowledge of life's mysteries. Pérez, his *señorío* run rampant, was convinced he had defeated the gods, that he was beyond their wrath. He had overcome every obstacle to triumph in business. He had cracked that code. Now he would do the same in football. As the president of the biggest club of all, and thanks to him one of the richest, he had the planet's players at his disposal. And he did not hold back.

His recipe was so simple it was subversive. Buy the world's greatest players – the most charismatic ones, the most brilliant, the most flamboyant, the best. Put them on the pitch and let them get on with it. The orthodoxies be damned. Talent counted for far more than the perspicacity of the coaches – those 'messiahs', Pérez would say – who pronounced on the game as if they had invented it, who attached more value to man-made 'tactical' inventions than to the natural-born genius of their players. All the talk, built up over the years to a philosophical certitude, about the coach's paramount importance: pure gobbledy-gook as far as Pérez was concerned.

Those who uttered the most mumbo-jumbo – with their talk of 'systems' and the need for a team to have 'balance' and so forth – were charlatans. And here Pérez included those legions of pundits – the former players and the football writers, as well as the coaches – who made a living out of pontificating on the game *Los futboleros* was the name he gave to these high priests, these false prophets, who purported time and again to pass definitive judgement on a team or a player, or even predict the shape and outcome of a game, and every time got it as wrong or as right as anybody else ever did.

Pérez, who enjoyed seeing himself as a bomb-thrower, as a destroyer of received wisdom, had no time for the footballing intelligentsia. He saw them at best as a necessary evil, as forces built into the architecture of the game that one had to put up with but whose judgements one should on no account bother to listen to, much less respect. He was an engineer, a practical man who worked from basic principles. Football for the Real Madrid president was a simple game. The formula for success boiled down to this: the greater the players/the greater the spectacle/the greater the success/the greater the club's global reach/the greater the profits/the greater the capacity to buy more great players. Add all that up and what you got was *ilusión* big time, permanent *ilusión* in bright shining lights. That was the new football formula. Simple as that. If you understood the formula you understood the great Pérez riddle: the most expensive players in the world were the cheapest.

'And the reason why is that they generate the greatest profits,' he told me. 'Because the relation between money out and money in is the most favourable. The best players are the most profitable players in every possible sense.' But where did the profits actually come from? Shirt sales? TV rights? How did the addition of a player like Zidane translate into hard cash?

'Let me explain,' said Pérez. 'When I arrived three years ago the club was bringing in a regular, working income of 115 million euros. Next season we shall be bringing in more than double that: 240 million. So, what difference do these star players make in real money terms? The answer is: something quite extraordinary. A massive phenomenon. So massive that five years ago Real Madrid never once filled the stadium and now, for each game, we have 200,000 requests over and above the Bernabéu's capacity; we used to take in less than 30 million euros in ticket sales, now it's nearer 70. So massive that now that everybody knows the passion for Real Madrid extends beyond Spain to the whole world, the big companies are coming to blows for the privilege of advertising their products with us, to associate their names with Real Madrid.'

If the projected overall annual income now stood at 240 million euros, I asked him, and 70 million came from ticket sales, where did the rest come from? 'Approximately thirty per cent comes from tickets. Thirty per cent audio-visual rights. And forty per cent from everything relating to marketing. Everything. Merchandising.'

Pérez's early experience in the job reinforced his view of the rightness of the path he had chosen – and confirmed his suspicions about the *futboleros* who purported to have a higher understanding of the game than the rest of us.

A close friend of his told me over lunch in Madrid some months after that first meeting I had with him that when Pérez began in the job he said he would abide by the decisions of the club's coaching staff. This meant that when they issued him with advice on what new players to buy he would not say 'no' – at least not flatly. The close friend recalled overhearing a telephone conversation between Pérez and a former Real captain called Pirri, who was much admired in Spanish football and occupied the job of technical director at the club, until he left, following Valdano's appointment, at the end of 2000. Pirri told Pérez that if he bought Claude Makelele and Flavio Conceiçao from Celta de Vigo he would have, without a shadow of a doubt, 'the best midfield in the world'. 'Pérez was doubtful,' said the close friend, 'but he went ahead. He stood by his word and signed them both, despite harbouring especially serious doubts about the value of the Brazilian Flavio, who was going to cost 24 million euros – not much less than Real ended up paying later for Beckham.'

Makelele proved his worth. But Flavio struggled to win a place in the team. A couple of months into the season Flavio had still not found his way into the starting eleven, and was coming on only sporadically as a substitute. Whereupon one day Pérez went up to del Bosque, who had also been keen on Flavio initially, and asked him what was going on. Del Bosque replied, in the laconic way he has, '*No lo veo*' – I don't see it. A couple of weeks passed and Pérez repeated his question. Back came del Bosque's answer one more time: '*No lo veo.*' Pérez went to Pirri next, eager for an explanation. Pirri did not mince his words. 'In the game of football signings,' he told the incoming club president, 'there is a mathematical rule. Three out of five fail.'

Pérez was appalled. To pay 24 million euros for a player who, it rapidly turned out, was surplus to requirements struck him as the most idiotic investment he had ever been involved with in his life. 'The way Florentino saw it,' his friend said, 'if someone at his construction company urged him to buy a machine that cost that much money and the machine did not work, that someone would be asked to go out personally and push the machine until he did make it work.'

Pérez learnt from the mistake. He drew from it what he considered the most valuable lesson he would learn at Real Madrid. That in football as in all other spheres of life 'it is the simple things', as he would say, 'that work best'. The Flavio mistake was replicated by the in-house 'gurus' not only at Real Madrid, but also at Manchester United, Barcelona, Juventus – everywhere. Time and again, season after season, clubs invested massive amounts of money in players whose potential contribution to the team they completely misjudged, whose talents they lamentably overestimated. Alex Ferguson was a prime example. The grand old man of British football, the man credited with wisdom that way surpassed ordinary football people's understanding, got it spectacularly wrong in the transfer market time after time. Juan Verón, for whom he paid 10 million euros more than Real Madrid paid for Beckham, represented his most embarrassing failure of judgement. But the purchase of the Uruguyan Diego Forlán for 7.5 million pounds was almost as inexplicable. And then, when Beckham went, he bought five players in his place. In strict adherence to the Pirri principle, two succeeded and three failed.

Experience showed that in so far as the question of judging football talent was concerned these 'experts' who thought – or wished people to think – that they had such a keen understanding of the game, in practice knew no more, as Pérez himself would say, than the kid collecting pictures of the Real Madrid stars in Tokyo or the average taxi-driver in Madrid. What you had to do – and Pérez elevated this to an article of faith – was only buy Galácticos; buy those who were, beyond all debate, already proven as the greatest players in the world.

'Florentino has a simple, common sense view of football,' José Angel Sánchez once told me. 'It is a view in stark contrast to that of the members of the *futbolero* sect, the chosen ones, the keepers of the temple, who consider themselves the sole guardians of the game's deepest and most secret truths.'

A point that Pérez and Sánchez perhaps failed sufficiently to take on board was the important social service the *futboleros* provided. Irrespective of whether they were right or wrong, they knew how to talk about the game and as such set the conversational agenda for planet football. They were more articulate than others on the subject of football and spoke with a greater conviction because of the credibility they had won either as players, coaches or football writers. And this is not a negligible thing. It was perhaps worth the decent living the *futboleros* made out of peddling their expertise. You need people to lead the conversations, to stoke up the debates. If only to have someone to disagree with. Because for the fan football is more about talking than anything else.

Football fans only spend a small part of their lives actually watching games: they spend far, far more time talking about football, a game whose greatest value to humanity, perhaps, is that it does us the immense service of giving us a limitlessly fertile subject of conversation, giving us an activity which is entertaining, inspiring and – even – fraternally binding. Football allows people to reach out to one another like maybe nothing else can. What else could have allowed me immediately to connect with a busload of Kenyans en route to a slum ravaged by AIDS? Only football binds men and women so regularly, regardless of race, creed, tribe, religion, language, social class. Football is globalisation. It is the dominant world culture. Beyond humanity's immediate animal or domestic needs, there is nothing that interests more people more keenly than football.

If you are sitting next to a stranger in a bus station in São Paulo, a dockside bar in Marseille, an airport lounge in Kuala Lumpur, and

you are bored and feel you would like to while away the time talking
to this stranger, the one subject in the world with the best chance
of eliciting not only an informed but an amicable response – the
one subject that would strike up a bond of fellow-feeling, of instant
solidarity, between the two of you – would be football. If you had
asked the stranger in question in São Paulo, Kuala Lumpur or
Marseille in July 2003, just after the Beckham transfer had gone
through whether Real Madrid had bought a really great player or
merely pulled off a *coup de théâtre*, the odds were that within no time
you'd be chatting so animatedly that you'd both forget to get on
your bus, boat or train.

Many of the *futbolero* critics served this social function we speak
of, delivering meaty subjects of conversation for people, by arguing
that the purchase of Beckham was a mistake. Just as some of them
had said that buying Ronaldo ('too injury prone', 'over the hill') and
Zidane ('he's coming to Madrid to retire') had also been essentially
exercises in media marketing. The criticism levelled at Pérez in Spain
was that he was too commercially driven in his purchases, too set
on buying what they dismissed as *mediático* players: those whose
appeal to the media, whose celebrity, overrode their talents as players.
Beckham was of course perceived as the ultimate example of the
mediático. A huge name, a footballing Elvis Presley, whose chief value
to the team was as a seller of shirts and booster of international TV
deals.

Another thing was what sort of a team you built out of these fabulous players, how effective they would be as a unit. The big doubt
about the Florentino project was whether it had become too ideal-
istic, too refined, whether Real were too top heavy with attacking
superstars at the expense of defence. There was nothing in the team
even dimly resembling a 'holding' midfielder and the central defensive players in the squad were rookies, unknowns alarmingly lacking
in experience. It was the very antithesis of the philosophy of Italian
football – make the defence top heavy and leave it to a couple of
solitary scavengers up front to knock in the odd goal. Adriano Moggi,
director general of Juventus, spoke for the whole *futbolero* world when

he expressed derision at Real's decision to buy Beckham. 'In their place I would have reinforced the central defence and stiffened up the midfield,' Moggi said.

Millions would have agreed with him. Looking at the situation coldly, and if what you wanted above all was to win, the Italian approach looked shrewder than the Florentino one, which in turn was the rarified expression of the more generous attitude towards the game taken in Spain generally. Carlo Ancelotti, the Milan coach, accused Real Madrid of 'an excessive appetite for the aesthetic'. The reply to that was that his Milan demonstrated an excessive appetite for the pragmatic. Make war, not love, is the Italian footballing motto. On a football pitch you don't muck about, you don't tamper with the tried and trusted rules. It is the very opposite of the Pérez philosophy, equally taken to extremes. The weakness of the Italian model was that it bet all on avoiding defeat. If you lost there was nothing left, nothing to savour, to cause *ilusión*. Hence the constipated style of play that characterised Italian football and had made the Milan–Juventus Champions League final the previous season a balefully dull affair. Outside Italy, the game was universally deplored, consigned to the dust heap of football history. The Champions League clash of the season was, of course, the quarter-final between Real and Manchester United. And as for the final the year before that, when Real Madrid had beaten Bayer Leverkusen in Glasgow with that goal from Zidane, that volley from the edge of the penalty box into the roof of the net – that game, because of that goal, would echo for the rest of time.

Pérez understood that this was the way of the world and it was on this understanding that he based his entire approach to the game. He once defined his approach in a newspaper interview as 'the policy of Zidanes and Pavones'. The phrase stuck. It was so frequently repeated in the Spanish press that they shortened it to 'the ZP policy', or simply 'ZP'. As in a headline in *AS*, 'ZP For ever!'. So what did it mean? Pavón was the name of a young central defender who had come up through the Real youth teams. What Pérez meant by 'the Zidanes and the Pavones' was that he was prepared to buy the very best and most expensive players in the world in order, as he put it, 'to nourish the legend' – but only the very best. And, it seemed, only attackers – except perhaps for the rare event of coming across an exceptional defender like Roberto Carlos, who also happened to be one of the most electifying attackers in the world. What the Z part of the policy amounted to was making one big superstar signing a year – and that was that.

The P part meant depending for the rest on his youth team players, the ones who came up through the Real ranks and had the added merit, as Pérez saw it, of helping preserve the core identity of the club, not diluting it in a flood of foreign-born talent.

ZP was not only about ideology or, as some saw it, the capriciousness of '*el señor presidente*'. There was, as Pérez always insisted, an economic logic to it too. Real Madrid, for all its success, did not have bottomless pockets. They could not afford to buy, as Chelsea could under their new Russian owner Roman Abramovich, any player that caught their fancy. Pérez made the point that in order to keep Real going as a profitable member-owned club, as opposed to a private company 'that can be bought by any Arab sheikh or Russian magnate', he needed to put in place a viable economic project. The ZP approach was viable because the Galáctico signings paid their way. Other players were not only less dependable on the pitch, they were a drain on profits. They cost too much and they did not bring returns to the club, they did not enhance the brand. In order to keep the books balanced and the sheikhs and magnates at bay, the more utilitarian players should be obtained free from Real's youth team, rather than purchased expensively from other clubs.

The events of the season would tell whether this was a winning formula in terms of trophies, or whether those who said Real would have been better off buying an experienced centre half rather than a luxury item like Beckham would see their arguments vindicated. Although the Pérez position was that he had been vindicated already, irrespective of the fickle business of results. Beckham's presence at Real would seize the imagination of people the way, say, Alex Ferguson's five signings at Manchester United would not.

Santiago Segurola of *el País*, the most authoritative sports writer in Spain, liked to argue among friends that Pérez had a Freudian relationship with Real Madrid, that the ZP philosophy emerged from his association between his love for his father and his love for the club of his life. Pérez forged his relationship with football, his almost religious ideals, watching that mythical Real team of the Fifties as a child at the Bernabéu. He started going to the Bernabéu with his father (and with his mother, who was also a keen Real fan) on a regular basis from 1951, when he was four years old. His memories begin to get vivid around 1955, by which time he was playing football himself with his friends every day. The next five years were marked indelibly in his mind. In the company of his adored dad, a fully paid-up member of the club, he experienced a euphoria so unbeatably intense that he was condemned throughout the rest of his life to seek to recreate to it. And once having done so, having brought Di Stefano, Puskas and Gento back to life in the shape of Zidane, Ronaldo and Figo, he offered his gloriously restored Real Madrid as a gift of love to his father. So went the Freudian interpretation of the unconscious driving force behind the Pérez presidency.

The fact was that for fifty years Pérez had been going to watch Real Madrid play, home and away, in Spain and everywhere else in the world, with the regularity of a practising Catholic going to mass. Football was his life's passion and the football he first experienced in his childhood was the best football he ever saw, never mind the new sophistications the game's theorists may have divined in the game since then.

As I discovered that first time I met him, Pérez was as sentimental – with his dogs, with his football – as he was pragmatic; as quixotic – madly prizing attack and spurning defence – as he was cold and calculating. Real Madrid was the outlet for the wild inner man – it was the bright fuchsia shirt, the three-star Michelin meal, the Burgundy Grand Cru that he never allowed himself in real life. If the construction business was the prose in his life, I put it to him, football was the poetry.

Pérez smiled, as if found out. 'All of us who love the game have a poetic, romantic connection with it, I would say. And, yes, for me football's always, always been a passion.'

Pérez's popularity at home, and acclaim abroad, was at its peak in the summer of 2003, at the beginning of the new season. Everything, he knew, could change from one moment to the next. Football people live in the present; in and for the day. They forget triumphs and defeats with casually ruthless rapidity. They make their judgements and shape their moods according to what happened in the previous game, or at most the previous two games. The fact that Real Madrid had won the league the previous season, clinching the championship in a nail-biting couple of final weeks, had been practically forgotten. Fewer than three months had passed since the Real players had hoisted aloft the biggest trophy in Spanish football and yet people were only thinking of this coming season, of this new, Beckham-reinforced team. If things went badly in a month from now, the glory days would be forgotten, swept away in a tidal wave of disappointment and regret. And possibly even abuse. For all that, though, Pérez had the feeling that he was creating something more lasting at Real Madrid, that he had helped bring an aura to the club that offered some protection against the tyranny of results. And, from my own experience at least, he was right. I remember a friend of mine, Pedro the eminent Malaria doctor, saying before the very last game of the 2002/03 season, one Real Madrid had to win to have a chance of winning the Spanish championship, that he was not too bothered about the result. No other fan of any other club would have said such a thing. But he meant it. 'It has been such a joy watching them play this season that winning the league does not seem to matter so much all of a sudden,' he said.

Pérez himself had been hearing words like those from fans like Pedro ever since he had bought Luis Figo. 'People don't come up to me and say, "Congratulations on winning the league,"' Pérez told me, marvelling at the way the Madrid fan's mind worked. 'They say something that is more flattering and even – dare I say it – enduring. They say, "Thank you for restoring the spirit of *Madridismo*."'

Which had been a revolutionary, audacious and solitary act. Pérez had scorned the high priests of the game, shunned their received wisdom, ruled Real Madrid according to his simple faith in the virtue of talent and the beautiful game, the bullfighting, dancing, attacking game. 'But *futboleros* don't always understand that, it seems.'

Or maybe it's just that these *futboleros* Pérez had in mind simply talked too much. Because it doesn't matter how rigorous-minded you are about obeying footballing conventions, there is no one – no one – involved with the game in any way, shape or form who does not succumb to the charms of football the way it was played by that great Brazil '70 side, or Cruyff's Ajax, or as Zidane and Ronaldo played the game at the turn of the twentieth and twenty-first centuries. The kind of football these people played was beyond dispute, beyond discussion, beyond all talk.

Pérez's uncluttered mind had zeroed in on this large essential truth about the game. He knew what his basic principles were. Taking decisions, therefore, was straightforward. Pérez looked at a problem, saw which solution corresponded most clearly to those principles, and acted accordingly. That was why he did not go backwards and forwards debating whether he should or should not buy Zidane, Ronaldo and Beckham. It was clear as day to him that he should. As José Angel Sánchez described him to me, 'He is a man of action. He is busy consciously making history.'

No, Pérez would not be held up or forced to deviate from his path by the thumb-sucking theoreticians. 'Hang ideas!' says the narrator in Joseph Conrad's *Lord Jim*. 'They are tramps, vagabonds, knocking at the back-door of your mind, each taking a little of your substance, each carrying away some crumb of that belief in a few simple notions you must cling to if you want to live decently and would like to die easy!'

Pérez, with the vision in his mind of an eternal Real Madrid, clung to his simple notions, saw with unambiguous clarity what the way forward had to be. And he went for it. With all the conviction, *élan* and sense of purpose of the Florenteam in full flow.

8: Beckham is from Mars

Alfredo Di Stefano is a gruff old dog. Much as they shall always revere him at the Bernabéu, the affection Real Madrid's seventy-seven-year-old president-for-life elicits is tempered by the complete absence of any effort on his part to ingratiate himself with anybody. An individual with a temperament more different from David Beckham's would be hard to imagine. Di Stefano also happens to be an Argentine, and we all know what the Argentines think of the English. 'Pirates', 'hypocrites', 'pompous asses' are some of the gentler descriptions you will hear on the streets of Buenos Aires of the usurpers of their cherished Malvinas.

All of which made you wonder when you watched Di Stefano hand Beckham his white number 23 shirt at his ritzy unveiling as a Real Madrid player on 2 July 2003, an event that had the second biggest live TV audience ever after the funeral of Princess Diana, what the glum expression on his face really meant. Was the club's grand old man signalling, as many of us there suspected, disapproval and distaste? Or was that just the normal face Di Stefano wore in public? Maybe that was all there was to it; maybe he was as happy as any man could be in those circumstances when his favourite pastime was to sit in an old-fashioned bar, far from the multitudes, with a cigarette in his hand. And yet, as the bulbs of 300 cameras flashed, as the triumphant music blasted away in the background and as Beckham – beautifully stage-managed as ever – uttered his first words in Spanish, '*Hala Madrid*!' (Come on Madrid!), you had the distinct sensation that the living legend wasn't entering into the spirit of things; that the man who led Real to five successive European Cups was privately thinking, 'Good grief, what a circus! And this

Beckham bloke with his pony-tail and his flashy clothes: he's not fit to tie my shoelaces, let alone wear the hallowed white of Real Madrid.'

Maybe I am being a little harsh on Don Alfredo here. Maybe I am unfairly decrying his judgement. But whatever he himself might have been thinking, the fact of the matter was that Spain's football establishment was not, by and large, too impressed by the arrival of David Beckham. He had come across well in that inaugural interview I did with him. But while being a nice guy with a good attitude was most welcome, his human qualities didn't count for very much where it mattered, on the football pitch. The general view, and it extended to many fans, was that the Englishman was not a top-of-the-range Real Madrid player; that he had been bought to sell shirts and to stick it to the old enemy, Barcelona. I know for a fact that there were people high up the Real hierarchy who argued strongly against signing Beckham on precisely these grounds, that Pérez had to go to war to persuade the board to back him. Beckham's detractors knew from watching Manchester United in the Champions League that – yes, sure – he was a sweet striker of the ball, good at corners and free kicks. But did he have much pace? Had he ever taken on a defender and beaten him? And by the way, as men in bars were asking the length and breadth of Spain, wasn't he also a little bit of a *maricón* – a ponce? And what about this business, reported in the glossy magazines, of him wearing his wife's knickers? And those earrings, and the haircuts, and the Indonesian skirts . . . ?

No, the thinking went, Pérez had let his business brain get the better of his football heart. He and his boy wonder José Angel Sánchez had bought Beckham to enrich the club's global brand, to open up new markets in China and Japan. Pérez could not possibly believe, surely, that the man they called 'Goldenballs' back home in England was capable of competing as an equal on a football pitch with the likes of Zidane, Ronaldo and Figo.

El País summed up well the prevailing view in an article published a few weeks before Beckham's signing was announced, while his move to Real still appeared to be in the balance and the possibility still seemed to exist that Pérez might be prevailed upon to change his mind. Certainly, *el País* conceded, the acquisition of Beckham might do wonders for Real's bank balance.'But do the same favourable conditions exist on the footballing as on the economic terrain? No. Beckham is a player for whom there is no need in this Real Madrid. Nothing that he does adds footballing value to the team.'

Similarly disparaging noises were heard outside Spain. Uli Hoeness, the Bayern Munich general manager, said Beckham's signing confirmed his view that Real Madrid had 'turned themselves from a football club into a circus act'. Pelé trotted out the old cliché, music no doubt to Alex Ferguson's ears, about Beckham's problem being that since he married the Spice Girl he had becomes more of a pop star than a footballer.

There was a countervailing view, expressed most convincingly by those who knew his qualities as a footballer best: his own former teammates at Manchester United. Gary Neville wrote a moving testimonial in *The Times* to his best friend, the player he had sat next to in the team bus for twelve years. Neville recalled how as a teenager Beckham, slender as he was, could always kick the ball further than any of the rest of the United youngsters. It was a point that other contemporaries at United always made about him. That range of his. A funny thing for a professional footballer to comment on, at first sight, but on reflection the relevance of the point becomes clear. Because if you have the power in your legs to kick the ball very far it means that over a distance that would be far enough for an ordinary player but is well within your capacities, say fifty metres, you would be able to exercise so much more accuracy and control. Another thing that struck his teammates was Beckham's ability to hit a long straight pass without a run-up, from a standing position, barely swivelling his body. In other words the power derives from the leg itself, and the ankle, discarding the added momentum that most players require from the movement of the body from the waist up.

Yet, according to Neville, what would surprise them most at the Bernabéu would be 'his character and spirit'. 'It is the Englishness in him,' Neville said, 'the willingness to do whatever it takes when the chips are down; the way he seeks the ball. He just wants to play, wants to win. It is an honesty and determination on the pitch and it is infectious. In a United shirt, the 1999 European Cup final was probably as good an example of those qualities as I can remember. He was our best player that night.'

So what would it be? Would it be the pundits or the footballers who would be proved right? Would Beckham rise to the greatest challenge of his footballing life? Would he cut it at the best football team, man for man, in the world? Or would Alex Ferguson be vindicated? Would it actually turn out that United had made a brilliant sale; that far from paying peanuts for Beckham, Real Madrid had splashed out far too much?

This Manchester United team were not Real Madrid. They had put on a fantastic fighting display in that second Champions League quarter-final at Old Trafford but the gap in class had yawned wide from the minute the whistle blew in the first game at the Bernabéu. Being a star at United offered no guarantee that you would be a star at Real.

The odds were stacked against Beckham. The mountain of prejudice he had to overcome was only part of it. Solid, practical difficulties loomed large, on and off the pitch.

The world-famous but far from worldly lad from Chingford, Essex, was moving to a new country for the first time in his life, and doing so with a fame-seeking wife who had enjoyed some celebrity outside the UK during her Spice Girls days but now, as far as Spain was concerned, glittered only in the reflection of the person to whom she was married. He had a reason to be in Madrid; she did not. Standing self-sacrificially by her husband would be a novel challenge. Their two little boys, Brooklyn and Romeo, might find it hard to adjust to school in a foreign country, especially if their mother was going to be spending a lot of time, as Beckham himself had said, in London and the United States. Even in the best of cases, with the whole family as gamely committed to the Spanish enterprise as Beckham himself, adjusting to a new language, new customs, new food – new paparazzi – would be tough.

In football terms, he would have to adapt to a new set of players after leaving a club that had been like a family to him for nearly half his life. These were really big players – real 'bigheads', as Ferguson might say – who might resent, or perhaps sneer at, the gap between his celebrity and his talent. If there was one area of his game where Beckham really could compete with the very best – in which he probably was *the* best in the world – it was in his crosses from the right, his famous 'half-goal' centres. The terrible thing was that neither of Real's two central forward players, Raúl and Ronaldo, seemed to have the dimmest clue how to head a ball. The one player who would have thrived on Beckham's crosses was Fernando Morientes, a tall, classic centre forward – almost of the old English school – with a good jump, great power in his neck, and a long history of powering or glancing headers into the back of the net. But Morientes, who had won three European Cups as part of the Real squad of recent years, had been loaned out to Monaco, the club having decided that with Ronaldo in the side he was surplus to requirements and so why not save a bit on the annual wage bill? The wisdom of that decision would be judged as the season unfolded but meanwhile Beckham had no choice but to rue the fact that perhaps the most effective element of his football repertoire would be going to waste. He would have to reinvent himself if he was going to succeed.

And there was the Figo issue. The Portuguese team captain occupied the very same position as Beckham, out on the right wing. If he replaced Figo, a popular figure among players and fans alike, the weight of expectation would be enormous; the willingness to jump down his throat at the first suggestion of failure, irresistible. If he did not replace Figo and played in a central midfield role that would be better, but then the task of adapting to his new teammates would be complicated by his own need to adapt to a position which he liked, which he wanted to try out, but had played in only rarely. Again, the risk of failure was great.

There were plenty of doomsayers in the British press who, assessing all these factors, really did feel that it was not Beckham who was going to have the last laugh here, but Alex Ferguson; that the Pelé consensus would be proved right and the English wonder-boy would be exposed for all the world to see as more pop star than footballer. And failure did indeed seem like a safer bet. One really did suspect that, impressively as he had overcome the previous obstacles life had thrown before him, this time he might have bitten off more than he could chew. Beckham, as even his most passionate detractors back home conceded, had been very brave in joining Real Madrid. But there is a fine line between bravery and foolhardiness and in joining not only the most glamorous club in the world, but the one with the greatest concentration of natural-born footballing talent, Beckham seemed to have crossed it. He said he approached the enterprise humbly. The question was, would it prove the most humiliating experience of his life?

Two things happened early on that did him no harm at all. First, there was Real Madrid's pre-season tour of Asia, a part of the world where the suggestion that Beckham was not, in every respect, the greatest human being alive, would have been widely considered a sacrilege. Second, Real surprised the football world by signing Carlos Queiroz as their new coach. Queiroz not only spoke good English, Beckham liked him from the year he had spent the previous season at Old Trafford as number two to Alex Ferguson. The day the two first came across each other at the Bernabéu they embraced warmly.

The Asian tour of China, Japan and Thailand did not provide any conclusive answers, though the fact that every single member of the Real team resisted the temptation to strangle Beckham, on whom so much adulation was focused that the likes of Ronaldo and Zidane would pass through Bangkok airport as anonymous as package holidayers, was in itself encouraging. The frenzy that greeted Beckham everywhere he went, whether it was in deepest Kunming in southern China, Beijing or central Tokyo, were unlike anything anyone ever recalled seeing in the inscrutable east. Matthew Syed, an Asia expert and three times Commonwealth table-tennis champion, wrote in *The Times* that one should not rule out the possibility of one day Beckham's image replacing Mao Zedung's as the most ubiquitous and well known in China.

'It is possible that Beckham is the most popular Englishman in China's history,' Syed wrote. 'Certainly his presence has comprehensively overshadowed the carefully choreographed visit of Tony Blair last week. It is not just the England captain's presence on newsstands, buses or Chinese television that attest to his popularity, or even the fact that eclipsed superstars such as Ronaldo, Zidane and Figo have been reduced to being mere witnesses in what has so far become the Beckham tour. No, the most telling insight is gauged by the reaction of ordinary people – neither fans nor journalists – mulling around the shopping districts and working in offices. This is a culture very different from our own: few faces betray a flicker of recognition if one attempts to communicate in English. But they light up at the mention of Beckham's name (rendered Da-wei Bei-ke-han-mu in Chinese). In one tall office block where I had a meeting on my first day here, I was stunned to find that two of the female employees had built mini-shrines to their hero at their desks, consisting of posters and, in one case, a home-made statuette.'

Things on the football field went well for Beckham too, chiefly because his performances in the four games he played served to question the general preconception back in Spain that he was a strutting nancy boy. Queiroz eased his entry into the team by starting out playing him in his habitual position on the right of midfield, pushing Figo – who unlike Beckham is strong on both feet – over to the left. No surprises there. Neither did it come as a surprise to anybody when he scored from a free kick in a 3-0 victory against FC Tokyo, bending the ball round and over the defensive wall. But what really did raise the eyebrows of players and fans alike was the amount of running he put in. At Beckham's medical examination prior to signing his contract with Real, the club doctor had pronounced him to be 'fit as a bull'. Already, just three friendly Asian games into his new career, the club's in-house statistics proved it: Beckham covered more kilometres per game than anyone.

AS, the most shamelessly pro-Real Madrid of Spain's many sports dailies, went further. They spoke of their surprise at how 'the delicate sex symbol' became transformed on the pitch into 'a building site labourer' and then went on to note that when Beckham moved during that Tokyo game from his habitual position on the right to central midfield – which Beckham had long thought of as his natural position – 'the team's sails puffed up, the ship flew'. The other players were impressed, not least by a facet of his game not normally asso-

ciated in Spain with English football: the intelligence of his positioning. Iván Helguera, Real's articulate centre half, noted with admiration that 'you can see he's been taught to think tactically since he
was a little kid'.

And so, among his teammates, whatever initial suspicion there
might have been about Beckham the Celeb, it quickly faded. First,
because as he had told me in our interview, he did not play the
Celeb. As a pleasantly surprised Real player observed in those early
days: 'In the dressing room he is shy. He does not talk much at all,
even in English. Eyes down usually, when he looks up he looks up
sideways. But he is always nice to everyone. We see him as a good
bloke.' But the main reason why he won over his fellow players was
that he sacrificed himself for them on the pitch, he covered back
when Michel Salgado, the right back, went on a forward run; he was
happy to do the unglamorous, stuff, let the others have the glory.
He lived up to his billing of himself as a team man, and they appreciated him.

Raúl, the Real captain and three-time European Cup-winner, was
never the most effusive of characters. But with Beckham he did not
hold back. 'I can see David already helping me be a more effective
player because of his quality and vision, and because those passes he
makes are magnificent for a forward,' Raúl said. 'Also physically he
is very strong. He has won the respect of all his teammates and the
fans.' The highest praise came from Ronaldo, who evidently saw him
as one of the gods' chosen few. 'He is so good,' Ronaldo said, 'he
could have been born a Brazilian.'

Beckham fell to earth with a bump on his arrival back in Spain,
on his first game on Spanish soil. It was a pre-season friendly against
Valencia, in Valencia, on a balmy August night. Valencia's left back,
the thirty-seven-year-old Amedeo Carboni, promised to stitch
Beckham up before the game and stitch him up he did. Playing in
his customary position out on the right, Beckham was embarrassingly ineffective. His shortcomings were miserably exposed, his strong
points nowhere to be seen. Most alarming of all, his first touch –
the first thing you look for if you want to judge a player's class –
looked clumsy. The ball seemed to bounce awkwardly off his shins,

not stick to the feet as it did with his teammates, who played as if they had velcro on their boots. As Zidane glided past players without losing the ball, or wriggled free as they clustered around him, Beckham would perform these clumsy reverse movements you sometimes saw in him when he was in trouble at Manchester United, spinning backwards 180 degrees, but far from beating his man, keeping him right there, dead in front of him, poised to go in for the kill. Whereupon he either did something very simple, like slip it to a player more accomplished in the arts of ball control than he, or attempted a clever pass that, on this night, invariably went astray. His weakness, as he jokingly acknowledged when I interviewed him, was his tackling. The problem was that he had this terrible tendency, amazingly never beaten out of him by Ferguson or any of his assistant coaches, to go crazy when he lost the ball, to try and retrieve it by any means possible. Which showed admirable pluck, for sure, but because he tackled so badly, because his timing was often so off, he often commited a foul, frequently a bad one. As he did on Vicente, the excellent Valencia left winger, a player with many of the attributes that Beckham patently lacks – great turn of pace, the ability to beat a man. Beckham kicked him so hard in the ankle he was lucky not to be sent off. The upshot was that Beckham spent much of the game shaking his head in frustration. You wondered, watching him, might he perhaps be feeling that the move to Real Madrid had been, after all, a mistake? That these players were so much more talented than he was. That his debilities were being cruelly exposed? That in this company he was, in short, out of his league?

Things only got worse in his second game, this time a serious competitive fixture, the first leg of the Super Cup (Spain's Charity Shield – league champion versus cup winner), away to Mallorca. Beckham again looked out of his depth and Queiroz took him off thirty-five minutes before the end. Michel, a former Real Madrid star and Spanish international who heads the commentary team on Spain's main state television channel, crowed: 'Beckham looked like he did whenever Manchester United played in Spain. The Englishman couldn't adapt to the Iberian pace, passion, pressure – or greatness.' Despite Real losing that Mallorca game 2-1 Beckham did have the

gumption to appear before the press and confess that he had not
played well. 'I can do a lot better,' he said. 'It's a tough challenge but
if I didn't believe I could do the job I wouldn't have taken it on.'
People were not too convinced. Not even Queiroz, who sought to
calm nerves but only raised more alarm bells when he said: 'I have
spoken to David and told him not to worry about trying to be like
Zidane or Figo. I also told him not to worry about the criticism.
You don't climb a mountain in one step, you have to go bit by bit.'

If ever the time was right for Beckham to make good on his
promise 'to prove a point' in Spain, his Real Madrid début at the
Bernabéu four days later, in the second leg against Mallorca, was it.
The omens were appalling. The word on everybody's lips was that
Florentino Pérez had blown it, that it was all very well monkeying
around and scoring from free kicks against weak teams in the Far
East – teams whose players had pictures of Beckham and the other
Real players on their bedroom walls – but here in Spain, in what
every Spaniard solemnly agreed to be the best football league in the
world, the crudity of the English game would be shown up by the
inability of the nation's captain to live up to the mighty standards
expected of a Madrid player. But it was worse than that. The day
before the game came the news that Claude Makelele, the Zaire-
born Frenchman with whom Beckham imagined he would be estab-
lishing a fruitful partnership in midfield, was leaving for Chelsea.

Makelele had become an indispensable player at Real. The two
games which they had lost in the Champions League the previous
season – against Milan in the early stages and against Juventus, calamitously, in the semi-final second leg – happened not coincidentally to
be the only two European games in which Makelele did not play,
due to injury, all season. Makelele was no Galáctico. He competed
with the left back Michel Salgado for the title of most rustic player
in the team. But frills would have been an inconvenience in the part
he played. He was a combine harvester of a player, a defensive midfielder
who, covering back and tackling, did the work of two men. The ball
having been recovered, his next move – based on a wise understanding
of his limitations – had the virtue of simplicity. He would release the
ball swiftly and accurately to the nearest available talent, usually

Zidane. You could see him doing much the same with Beckham, whose defensive deficiencies he would compensate for, whose midfield bodyguard he would effectively become. The beauty about Makelele had been that he provided a hard protective core around a central defence softened by the toll time had taken on the once excellent Fernando Hierro, whose contract Pérez had not renewed in the summer. Not only that, Makelele's industry liberated Zidane, Figo and the others to do their stuff up front without having to expend valuable energy tracking back.

Makelele left Real Madrid because Chelsea offered him a lot more money. For some months he had been grumbling that he was not paid enough by Real, that his contribution to the team was such that he merited at least half what the Galácticos were getting. Pérez was not having any of it. The Galácticos each got paid a net salary of 5.5 million euros a year and the rest of the team got paid a quarter of that or less. To make an exception for Makelele would be to risk severe disruption among such non-galactic, but critically important, players as Helguera and Salgado and Guti, who had resigned themselves with good grace to the indignity of having to make do with a weekly income of 20,000 euros, one million a year. Pérez understood that Makele's loss would weaken the team's already wobbly defence, but the potential damage would be greater, he calculated, if he surrendered to the Frenchman's financial terms.

Roman Abramovich, Chelsea's Russian owner, entertained no such scruples. A thirty-six-year-old Russian oil magnate, the second-richest man in his country and the richest in Britain, he owned a home in London's Belgravia, a 440-acre Sussex estate and had a fortune estimated to be in excess of 10 billion euros. Pérez had a lifelong attachment to Real Madrid and to a game he played practically every day until he was eighteen, but Abramovich bought Chelsea not out of love, nor even because he had any particular interest in football, but because, as he himself said, after 'exploring the market' he found the club to be a good buy in terms of 'price and quality'. Which was a peculiar thing to say for a man who seemed to have lost all sense of money's value. Having bought Chelsea, traditionally a London club with big pretensions but small success, for 220 million euros in July

– in fact on the very day that Beckham was officially presented as a Real Madrid player – he set about acquiring players with the reckless capriciousness of Imelda Marcos buying shoes. Within two months he had spent 155 million euros and brought in fifteen new players: a world record unlikely ever to be beaten, except perhaps at some later date by himself. The funny thing was that none of the players were global household names; only two or three of them had big reputations in the European football world, and some of them were discards. Juan Sebastián Verón, Alex Ferguson's worst-ever purchase, was sold to Chelsea by Manchester United for half what they had paid for him two years earlier. Hernán Crespo, another Argentine, arrived from Inter Milan, where it seemed they had finally rumbled the central truth about him, that he was the most overrated striker in the world game. Joe Cole, one of the English purchases, was similarly afflicted. Having spent seven years wallowing in the title of 'potentially England's best player of his generation', it was becoming increasingly evident that he was not quite going to make the grade. Geremi, a Real Madrid reject, looked like a sound enough bet for midfield, but an odd acquisition for a club with the highest possible aspirations.

Five years earlier Chelsea had set their sights on becoming 'the Manchester United of the South'. Under Abramovich, governor of the Arctic Russian region of Chukotka and the 60,000 people who lived there, the stakes were raised. The aim was to become Real Madrid. The Russian had formed this aspiration on the night of 23 April at Old Trafford, where he watched United and Real's epic encounter. Abramovich knew little about football. He had never even played the game. They didn't in Chukotka, a barren tundra landscape inhabited for centuries only by reindeer herders where the temperature fell in winter to minus forty degrees centigrade. And while Abramovich had been toying for some months with the idea of investing in a professional football club, it was only after watching what in Spain they had described as 'a spectacle to waken the dead' that he decided to come in from the cold and enter the great community of nations, that good half or more of the human race that is hooked on the beautiful game.

Abramovich's philosophy was borrowed wholesale from Real Madrid. Buy big name players, win things putting on a great show, and watch the revenues from merchandising, sponsorship, stadium attendances and TV go through the roof. To that end he tried buying Raúl from Real Madrid. Raúl may not have been the most technically gifted player in the team, but he was the club's emblem, the Madrid-born lad who had won the three European Cups of the modern era. To steal him would have been to prise away Real's soul. That is why Chelsea approached Raúl's agent in mid-July and indicated they were prepared to offer Real a world-record shattering 100 million euros for him. The agent rang up Raúl who flatly said thanks, but no thanks. Leave Real Madrid for Chelsea? He wouldn't do it for all the oil in Russia.

With all that money Abramovich had to splash around there was a new rumour every day. He wanted to bring Beckham back to England, he wanted Ronaldo, Roberto Carlos, Figo – anybody. Just give me a piece, Abramovich seemed to be screaming, of Real Madrid. As if having got that one piece he might decipher its DNA and construct from the genetic information it supplied the mutant replica he ached to posses. In the event all he got was Makelele. To get him he had to offer him a Galáctico salary and pay Real Madrid a price as unbelievably high as Beckham's had been unbelievably low. Whether Peter Kenyon was advising Abramovich is not certain, but it is a fact that exactly one week after the Makelele purchase Kenyon joined Chelsea as chief executive, the Russian having offered him double the salary he earned at Manchester United. Makelele was thirty-one years old and by no stretch of the imagination could he be described as box office, yet Chelsea paid 24 million euros for him – practically the same, minus bonuses, as Real had paid for Beckham.

Pérez and José Angel Sánchez had another of their shake-of-the-head-in-disbelief chuckles over that, but Queiroz – who had banked on having Makelele in his team – was not laughing. And nor was Beckham. And nor, for that matter, was Di Stefano, who placed such a high value on Makelele that he would tell his friends, only half jokingly, that he would go to church on match days with the express purpose of praying that Makelele would not be injured, that he would be fit to play. None of the players who had played with him over the previous three seasons were happy either. They all valued Makelele, whose contribution on the pitch they viewed as practically irreplaceable. They were right to be unhappy, too, as Pérez had no intention of buying another defensive midfielder. Pérez bought great attackers, period. And now Real Madrid had no defensive midfielders at all. Not one, unless you pushed up Helguera, an unusually good ball-playing centre half. The problem for Beckham was that, in the very likely event he ended up playing in central midfield, he would have to reinvent himself as a player: at this advanced stage of his career he was going to have to try and learn how to tackle; he was going to have to cover for the Zidanes and Figos; he was going to have to transform himself, up to a point at least, into another Makelele.

Add to all this the sceptical press Beckham had received following those first two abysmal games he played on Spanish soil, never mind the radio phone-in programmes where people were calling in to say he was a show-horse and a *maricón* (prompting one British tabloid rather prematurely to coin the headline, 'Beckslash!'), and you could see things turning out very bleakly indeed for the princely Englishman. The prospect of going out and making his début in a Real shirt at the Bernabéu, twenty-four hours after the news that Makelele was on his way out, would have made a less stubborn man jump on the first plane back home, never to return. But play he did, from the start, in that second leg Super Cup game against Mallorca, with Real obliged to make up the 2-1 deficit from the first game. It was the first trophy Real Madrid were competing for in the Beckham era and it would be a bad portent for the season ahead if they didn't win. As if the pressure were not already bad enough, the two big sports dailies, *AS* and *Marca*, carried big photographs of Beckham on their front covers that morning, with stories inside quoting him saying how much he'd love to score on his début, and football writers reminding readers how he had said when he scored from that free kick in Tokyo that what would really count was his performance at the Bernabéu. Well, the time had now come, the moment he had been saying all summer that he had been waiting for.

The fans greeted him correctly. They were not wildly enthusiastic

– they rarely are at the Bernabéu – but they did come up with a polite enough cheer when his name was called out, together with the rest of the starting line-up, over the stadium's loudspeaker system. They had their doubts but naturally they wished him the best. Someone high up behind one of the goals had even had the consideration to make a big banner for him. It read, in English, 'Beckham. Welcome to the Galaxy. From Red Devil to White Angel.' Whether it was that he read those words, or that his son Brooklyn was in the stadium wearing a white Real kit, or that on that very day Mars, the Red Planet, was the closest it had been to earth in 60,000 years, or that he possessed that unique presence of mind and sense of drama that allows a truly top performer to rise to the occasion when the expectations are highest – whatever it was, he played a blinder.

Not a hint of first night nerves, Beckham looked poised on the ball right from the start, doing the simple things well, striking every pass true, strolling when strolling was appropriate, running hard when he had to across the billiard-table smooth Bernabéu turf. It was as if he had metabolised all that pressure and transformed it into high-energy fuel. Ten minutes into the game he had the Bernabéu fans – the most exquisitely fussy fans in the world – in his pocket. Real Madrid got a free kick on the edge of the Mallorca penalty area, but wide out to the left, nearer the corner flag than the 'D'. Few other players would have considered a shot on goal from there. Beckham did, sending the ball skimming over the point where bar meets post, with the goalkeeper quite beaten. Real players clutched their heads in despair at the near miss. The whole stadium cried, 'Uuuuuuuuuuuuuuuy!' And then, immediately and for the first time ever, a sector of the Real Madrid crowd started chorusing his name. He may have thought for a moment that he had died and risen to heaven. The state of bliss, the celestial choir, the white angels: they were all there.

For the rest of the game he didn't put a foot wrong. He dictated the tempo in midfield behind Zidane, Real's rapier; he made three or four of his trademark pin-point passes, fifty yards long from the right touchline to the left; he covered every blade of grass ('He left his skin on the pitch,' the Spanish papers said next morning), but added to his game a new propensity to tackle back. That desire won over the fans. If there is one thing fans everywhere, no matter how lowly or exalted the club, value even more than talent it is a player who shares their will to win, who is the incarnation on the pitch of their competitive passion. Fans can sense whether a player has that honesty immediately. It is an instinct, as reliable as the sense of smell. And instinct told them that Beckham was a true son of the Real Madrid soil, that he was prepared to die for the cause if need be.

With Real 2-0 up in the second half but still vulnerable, Iker Casillas having been obliged to pull off a couple of heroically implausible saves, Beckham won the *Super Copa* for Real by rising to – of all things – a Ronaldo cross and – miracle of miracles – heading the ball into the back of the net. This was not the way it was supposed to happen. It was supposed to be Beckham laying on goals for Ronaldo. Besides, no one had any recollection of ever having seen Beckham score a goal with his head. As the man from *Marca* wrote: 'Blessed madness!' Or *AS*: 'That ball will end up at Sotheby's.'

Here was evidence once again, in case anyone had forgotten, that Beckham most certainly led a blessed life. Not for the first time, the timing of his great act of derring-do was memorably dramatic. There was that last-minute goal against Greece that sent England through to the 2002 World Cup finals, his performance against Bayern Munich in the 1999 European Cup final, the winner he scored for England against Argentina in the 2002 World Cup (revenge, just like in the movies, for the red card fiasco four years earlier), the two goals he came on and scored after Ferguson had left him on the bench against Real Madrid. And now here he was, on his début at the Bernabéu, with all the odds seemingly stacked against him, and he goes and scores the goal that gives Real their first trophy of the season. The only man who was as happy as Beckham, and quite possibly more relieved, was the man whose controversial decision it had been to bring him to the Bernabéu in the first place: Florentino Pérez. Approached by the press for his reaction after the game, he got it just right. 'Beckham's début could not possibly have been more successful,' he said. 'Beckham's goal was like the final scene of a script that had already been written.'

But the big point about football, the reason why it is such an enormously popular spectator sport, is that it is so maddeningly unscripted; that it provides the most suspenseful live theatre on earth. In no other sport is the outcome more consistently unpredictable right to the very end. South Korea knocked out Spain in the 2002 World Cup. In 1966 North Korea knocked out Italy. In 1950 the American national soccer team beat England 1-0, a defeat for the game's inventors so utterly unimaginable that bookmakers offered odds beforehand on it happening of 500–1. Results almost as unlikely as that one repeat themselves over and over every weekend in football games across the world. You never know what might happen in the same way that you are never certain of a result during the course of a game until one team is winning 3-0 and there are five minutes left to play. That quality of relentless drama and continual capacity for surprise is something you do not find, to anything like the same extent, in rugby or cricket or baseball or American football, much less in individual sports like tennis or running or golf.

Beckham celebrated his goal that night like, well, like players do when they have scored the winner in a cup final. He ran to the corner, raised his eyes and arms to the heavens and let out a cry of euphoric triumph and defiant rage that you could have heard in Manchester – or would have done had not the rest of the stadium and the Real players, who swamped him with the unalloyed love all players feel for a teammate who has won them a cup, been shouting almost as loudly as he was. The fans saw his passion and loved him for it all the more. He really was one of them, they could see it. I spoke to a friend called Juan who watched the game in a bar in Cádiz, where he was on holiday. He spoke for all *Madridistas*, I think, when he said that what had most thrilled him about Beckham's performance had been how over the moon he looked when he scored. 'It was his reaction to the goal, to victory, to winning the cup that did it for me,' Juan said. 'It was the pride he felt in wearing the colours of Real Madrid, his sheer joy at winning.' But it was more than that. Talking to my friend Sebastián, a season-ticket holder at the Bernabéu, I understood why it was that Beckham was destined to be loved by the Real Madrid faithful, why Pérez's instincts had been so absolutely right. As Sebastián explained, 'Yes, Beckham has those "*ganas*" – that lust to win – that all fans always demand in their players. But he has an extra quality that Real Madrid fans specifically require from their idols: he has elegance, he oozes class. Watching him strike the ball is a thing of beauty. And then add to that the glamour – the fact that he is a world-famous celebrity, that he is incredibly good looking – and that he is the England captain – because, the truth is, scratch the surface of any Spaniard and, whatever they may say, they do admire the English – so, well, add all that together and you have a recipe for total adulation.'

Beckham had won the game for the fans, for the team, for Florentino Pérez – but most of all for himself. One lesson he had learnt from Alex Ferguson was to put his competitive paranoia to good use. Indeed, it had been Ferguson himself who had warned in his autobiography that 'one should never underestimate David Beckham'. He wrote those words in 1999. Four years later he had forgotten them so completely that he did not just underestimate him, he grossly undervalued him. Beckham reacted the way Ferguson always did to what he perceived to be an affront to his self-worth. Ever mindful of his detractors, driven to ferociously ambitious heights by them, Beckham had elevated this obsession of his for 'proving a point' into a philosophy of life. He said as much, in words that in a less amiable character might have sounded chilling, in a brief exchange with reporters the next day. 'I like to correct people's wrong impressions of me,' he said. 'My life and my career has worked this way until now: proving wrong those who do not believe in me.'

The front page of *Marca* next morning read, 'Beckham Conquers the Bernabéu!' The other newspapers offered variations on the theme. 'Beckham Joy', 'Beckham Rejoices', 'Beckham Glory'. Hugo Gatti, a celebrity back home in Argentina and a former goalkeeper for the national team, watched the game live on TV in Buenos Aires then wrote this in a column for *AS*: 'The good-looking one is the one who fights the most. I was happy for him. What a great footballer!' The doubters – the few that dared now to raise their heads – did venture the thought that perhaps this first game had been a flash in the pan, that one swallow didn't make a summer, and so forth. No,

they said, the real test would come three days later in the first league
game of the season against Betis, a tough team full of talented players
with a good coach who many fancied to do great things in the
2003/04 season.

And what happened? What happened was beyond improbable.
Any bookmaker would have offered you anything you wanted –
1,000–1, 10,000–1, whatever, so long as you were foolish enough to
drop some money on him – on Beckham scoring in his first two
games at the Bernabéu, each time from a Ronaldo pass. But that
was what happened and more. Beckham did not just score again
from a Ronaldo pass, he scored the first goal that anybody scored
in the Spanish league that season. Within three minutes of the start
of the game. And he played a commanding role throughout. Along
with Ronaldo he was the best player on the pitch. *El País*, whose
position on Beckham before the signing was well known, suddenly
declared him to be 'an excellent footballer'. Carlos Queiroz, his new
coach said, 'Beckham will be very valuable, because he will bring
the British footballing mentality and values like determination and
bravery to the club.'

After the game, which Real won 2-1, a Betis player, Capi, further
reinforced the dawning perception among delighted Real fans that
Beckham, contrary to all initial expectations in Spain, was no shirker.
'Apart from striking the ball well,' said Capi, who had been on the
wrong end of some tough exchanges with Beckham, 'he knows how
to put the boot in when he has to.' John Toshack, former Real Madrid
coach and another of the legion of football luminaries who warned
that Beckham would not make the grade in Spain, had said before
the game: 'It is very difficult for Beckham to play in the centre of
midfield.'

But it was from that very position that he delivered a pass in a league
game two weeks later that God himself would have stood up and
applauded. The rivals were Valladolid – respectable mid-table performers,
never an easy team to beat. Real beat them 7-2 and it was fireworks
all the way but the one truly lasting memory of that game will be the
fifty-yard pass Beckham launched from a position inside his own half,
to the right of the centre circle. He struck it hard and true, arrow

straight. It was the archetype of the trademark Beckham strike Valdano referred to when he wrote in a book, long before Real Madrid had even thought of signing Beckham, about his admiration for the Englishman, and about his certainty that all his life Manchester United had been playing him out of his natural position. 'He is a central midfielder exiled to the wing,' wrote Valdano. 'A player with vision, competitive courage and a striker of the ball so clean that the fans, following the ball's trajectory, can read on it the name of the manufacturers. Beckham's defining characteristic is that he hits the ball like no one else does, filling it with privileged information.'

He aimed the pass at Zidane who was sprinting towards goal down the inside left channel, looking behind him as he ran, watching the ball in the air, hoping – daring to think – that it might land just right for him to catch it on the volley. The question was how would the ball fall? Would it drop hard or would it drop soft? It dropped, as a friend of mine called Luis Angel put it, '*como un flan*' – like a crème caramel. Luis Angel was born in Málaga but lived a lot of his life in Argentina, where he played on the wing for the national universities eleven. Which meant he was as good a footballer as it gets without being a professional. I asked him to explain to me, if he could, the crème caramel aerodynamics of that Beckham pass. This is what he told me: 'For it to work, for it to land in such a way that you maximise the possibilities of a goal resulting from it, you have to get the ball to brake just before it drops on the boot, or rather to decelerate. And to descend at something close to a vertical angle. If not, if the ball arrives at high speed, still flying almost horizontally, it is almost impossible to avoid sending your shot flying high and wide into the crowd behind the goal. But in this case Beckham did get the ball to slow down for Zidane, allowing him to get into position, to get properly balanced and described the up and down arc with his leg necessary to dispatch the ball precisely where he intended. The effect, in other words, is the same as if you had thrown him the ball with your hand from two metres away, dropping it perfectly at his feet for him to smash it exactly where he chooses to. The difference here was that the ball had already travelled fifty metres by the time he hit it.'

So how do you achieve that effect? Was it just luck, or was it technique? 'It's technique. A gift that only very, very talented people possess,' replied Luis Angel, who is a writer, a lecturer, an internet whizz and understands, among many other things, the laws of physics. 'The story of that pass was this: Beckham struck the ball extremely hard in order to get it to travel as far as it did in the air, but at the same time he put back spin on it. If you were to train a camera on the ball during its flight you'd notice that it only began to spin right at the end, barely four or five metres before impact, as it was beginning to come down over Zidane's right shoulder towards his left foot. That spin slowed it down – decelerated the ball, as I say – and allowed Zidane the milliseconds he required to adjust his stride and his body for the shot.'

And what a shot! If there was genius in the pass, there was at least as much in the way Zidane plucked the ball out of the air and hammered it, low and true, and across goal, past the goalkeeper's flailing dive left, into the back of the net. Maybe no other player in the world could have made a pass like that; maybe no other player could have made contact with that ball with the same laser-guided ferocity.

After the game Beckham said that might have been the best pass he had ever made in his life. 'And that is certainly the greatest goal anyone has ever scored from a pass of mine,' he added. 'What Zidane did was a dream.'

The whole game was a dream. Fantasy football. Raúl scored a hat-trick, each goal a delicate little work of art. And Ronaldo, receiving another perfectly weighted pass from Beckham (this time along the ground), scored one of those rampaging goals of his, running on to the ball, advancing into the area, making as if to hit the ball with his right, checking himself at the very last instant, turning, then striking it with his left just inside the post for goal number six of the night. It seemed hard to believe watching the Brazilian in action that it had taken the Bernabéu crowd a good nine months to take him to its heart, that it wasn't until he won that game for them at Old Trafford with his famous hat-trick that the jeering of the Real Madrid fans – who kept complaining that he did not try hard enough

– finally died down. But, more like opera buffs than football fanatics sometimes, Real supporters are so demanding – so damn spoilt – that it even took them three or four months to come around to the idea that the purchase of Zidane was a good idea, to be convinced that he had not come from Juventus to Madrid to enjoy a premature retirement.

The staggering thing about Beckham, a point incredulous Spanish commentators kept making, was how quickly he had won the fans over. By the time the final whistle had blown on that Valladolid game, within two weeks of the start of the season, there was no room for further discussion. They had made up their minds. They loved him unconditionally. The day after the game, Sunday 14 September, I spoke to Angel Moreno, a taxi-driver from the southern province of Murcia who lives near Barcelona. He had seen the game on TV at a bar called La Amistad in a town called Roquetes. La Amistad, which means 'Friendship', is an enclave of *Madridismo* in the heart of Catalan country. I have met football fans as passionate as Angel, but none whose life is more intimately intertwined with the fate of his team – in this case Real Madrid. The stubborn intensity of his commitment is all the greater because of where he lives. Fútbol Club Barcelona amounts to a pagan cult in Catalonia. Angel, a squat feisty man in his mid-forties, is a heretic in this land, defiantly flaunting the enemy flag.

So what had he made of that Valladolid game? 'What a glorious night!' he cried. 'I'll tell you something I thought I'd never imagine I'd say: with games like that and goals like that it almost doesn't matter whether we win the championship or not. That goal of Zidane's: all I can say is that we are lucky to be alive at this time to have been able to witness it. Raúl: magnificent, as ever. Eternal. But Beckham! Beckham! What a player! How he has managed to integrate himself into the team in barely a couple of weeks, as if he were the most veteran member of the team! You'd think he was the captain from looking at him. What a fighter, what desire, what *ganas*! And how he strikes the ball: that right foot of his is a glove, a white glove.'

Angel told me that *La Amistad*, whose walls are covered with framed photographs of great Real teams past, had been packed. There had even been three Barça fans there. 'Me and my friends we were watching them watch the game,' he told me, chortling like a madman. 'We'd say to them, "Here, mate, take a serviette to wipe the dribble from your lips. Go on, clean it up."'

'The charge of the white cavalry,' *el País* called it. *AS* described Beckham's performance in particular as 'imperial'. 'The fans see him as a jewel,' it said. 'And they love his warrior spirit.' *AS*'s editor, the veteran Alfredo Relaño, described him as 'the marshal' of the midfield – 'as if he had been the first player to arrive, and the rest of the team had been built up around him.' As far as *Marca* was concerned, the verdict on Beckham was already in. 'Beyond the ad campaigns, the dyed hair, the changes of look and the famous singer wife,' *Marca* said, 'the Englishman is making it plain that he is also a quite fabulous football player.'

A friend of mine, a Barcelona fan called Mundo, summed up the gap between the expectations Beckham had created among football fans in Spain and the player they had come to know. 'We thought he was Little Lord Fauntleroy,' my friend said, 'but it turns out he is a Welsh miner.'

Florentino Pérez was exultant. And not just because his wisdom in buying Beckham had been vindicated in the face of the *futboleros*'s scepticism, but because through the Englishman's seamless adaptation to a successful team he was proving his revolutionary theory that if you had great players in attack you did not have to worry about the defence. Pérez's football was a take-no-prisoners, do-or-die game. And in those early days of the season it was working.

The terrific start Real Madrid made in the league, and especially Beckham's start, did have the effect of quietening the critics of '*el Proyecto Florentino*' for a while. But soon the muttering began again. Wait till the Champions League began, they said, then the team's deficiencies will be cruelly exposed. In the view of those who lacked faith in the project, the team lacked that essential article of *futbolero* belief, balance. Too many pianists, in a phrase French football people used, but not enough people to carry the pianos. The answer was provided promptly enough, on 16 September, and against France's biggest club, Olympique Marseille. Real Madrid's 'unbalanced' team dismissed the doubters exactly the way Pérez fantasised that they would. In the first game against Olympique the French did have the temerity to score first, but their joy lasted exactly two minutes. Because Real unleashed a whirlwind. Roberto Carlos smashed in the equaliser, a volley from the edge of the box, the ball laid on a plate for him by a Beckham cross. Then a couple of minutes later Ronaldo put them ahead. They went 4-1 up, then relaxed a bit and, as was their habit, made a defensive mistake that let the French make the score look like less of a slaughter than it really had been. A slaughter to music. Ballet music. Zidane was in what his number one fan, David Beckham, would have described as full 'ballerina' mode. An *AS* writer suggested that people back home watch Zidane in the the video of that game to the accompaniment of Tchaikovsky's *Swan Lake*. 'Go on, try it. See how delicious it is', the *AS* man said. As for Beckham, the *AS* writer continued, it turned out that he was 'an improved version' of an earlier Real blond, Bernd Schuster. Schuster, who played for Real and Barcelona, was one of the greatest German players of all time. Beckham, though, was 'better looking, passes the ball better, plays like a gladiator and has more charisma'. A friend of mine who was at the game, a season-ticket holder called Sebastián, scoffed at the idea of needing Makelele to bring order to the midfield. 'Who's Makelele? We've got Beckham now,' said Sebastián. 'It's what we're all saying up on the stands. We're playing better than ever with the Englishman. So Makelele's gone? Better! Great! Beckham's played four games and he looks like he's the most veteran member of the side. He's made us better. Much better. Now it really does not matter if they score against us, we will score more. Four, five – whatever. To hell with order and balance in a team. This is art!'

And fun. The whole team played with smiles from ear to ear, none more so than the toothy Ronaldo, who summed up the Pérez philosophy Brazilian style when he said, 'Our objective is to score more goals than the other team. We are a lot of us in attack and we're always going to have difficulties defending, but that is the way Real Madrid play football. We always play attacking football, we always try and score goals and that is the way it has to be.'

It was a remarkable beginning to the season. In two games, in three days they had scored eleven goals and conceded four. The players, the fans, Pérez were in football heaven. Football really was a simple game. You got the best players, you put them on the field and they won, giving you along the way the best show on earth. *Le Monde*, a solemn newspaper not given to lavishing praise on mere sportsmen, delivered a metaphor-mixing symphony of a paragraph on Real's demolition of the biggest team in France. 'Professional football can still be a fount of pleasure. To see it is true one need look no further than Real Madrid. When the soloists play to the same tune – a fast, fluid, attacking, perfectly controlled game – the feast for the eyes is total.'

It was with these two games, against Valladolid and Olympique, and barely two and a half weeks into the season that Beckham, outrageously prematurely, consolidated himself as a key member of the team, as a player who brought substantial added value to 'the Galaxy'. He showed spirit, composure, vision, poise and skill. He was playing with authority and verve. It seemed an extraordinary thing even to think, but he was looking a better, happier, more complete player than he had ever done at Manchester United. Which meant that he had fitted into his new team with almost miraculous ease. He might not have spoken more than two or three words of Spanish but his fluency in the language of football was complete. The thing about Beckham was that he grasped every nuance of that language, he spoke it with such mastery that, having achieved his ambition of playing in central midfield, he was demonstrating for all to see that this was where destiny intended that he should have been playing all along.

Chatting with José Angel Sánchez in his office a few weeks into the season he told me that the secret of Beckham was his pride. 'I've got to know him quite well, I've observed him,' said Sánchez, who is a clever observer and was as close as anyone at Real to Beckham in those early days. 'He loves being in this team with these players. He is gaga about Zidane. Like a regular fan. But the players have come to love him too. This is what the people in the club closest to the players tell me. It is because he is a humble, regular guy when he is with them but also because he makes so many sacrifices for

the team on the pitch. And he is so, so happy. It was so, so important to him, I know, that he should be seen to be capable of playing
at this level. It was maybe the greatest challenge of his life, the one
that carried with it the most damaging risk of failure. For Beckham
to join Real Madrid was to have a crack at climbing Everest. Real
Madrid was his Everest. And he scaled it, in record time, with grace
and skill.'

I spoke about Beckham to Vicente del Bosque. Having been
sacked within days of the announcement of Beckham's transfer, his
judgement of the Englishman might have been a bit twisted. But it
wasn't. Far from bitter, he quite candidly admitted that he regretted
not having had the opportunity to coach a player who he had long
admired. If he had stayed in the job and not been replaced by
Queiroz, del Bosque said, he would not have hesitated to play Beckham
in the middle. 'Beckham's great merit has been to adapt himself to
the needs of the team, play in that new role as if he had played there
all his life when before he had always played out on the wing,' del
Bosque said. 'I was sure that he would end up playing in the centre.
At Manchester United he was not playing in his natural position.
He is a player who has to be where the ball is. He is very tactically
involved, very plugged into the action and wants to participate in
the game all the time. A player who nature has intended to play out
on the wing has another type of mentality – he is more patient, in
a certain sense. Beckham is greedy to be in on the action throughout
every one of the ninety minutes.'

And he showed it game after game in those early weeks of the
season, putting in another masterly performance in the second group
game in the Champions League away to the Portuguese champions
Porto. Porto were a strong team, UEFA Cup-winners the previous
season. They were fast and skilful and well organised by their excellent young coach, José Mourinho, later to become manager of Chelsea,
who had started off his football career ten years earlier as a translator for Bobby Robson when the former England coach arrived to
take up a job with Sporting Lisbon.

After a bright start, after having the impudence to go 1-0 up
within seven minutes, Porto were no match for Real Madrid. This

time the glory fell to one of the more unsung but most consistently valuable members of the team, the eternal susbtitute Santiago Solari of Argentina, who scored twice in a 1-3 Real victory. But Mourinho did not fail to draw generous attention to Beckham's contribution in his otherwise shell-shocked after-match comments. 'Beckham never ceases to surprise me,' Mourinho said. 'Millionaire, galactic, famous, but he is the player who works hardest of all on the pitch.'

The statistics backed up Mourinho's perception. At Old Trafford Beckham seemed to have dwindled during his last season with Manchester United into a dead-ball specialist – like a kicker in American football – whose function it was to take corners and free kicks. Three weeks into the season the figures showed that he was the Real Madrid player who had had the most shots on goal, had made the most passes into the penalty area and, after the right back Michel Salgado, had committed the most fouls. That confirmed the impression that in addition to the talent he brought, Beckham was infusing his team with something of that never-say-die inspiration habitually associated with his old captain at Manchester United, the pugilistic Roy Keane.

The game after Porto in the Champions League was at home to Partizan Belgrade, one of those tricky, gritty opponents against whom, on an unwary night, anything can happen. Real won 1-0, which meant that if they only drew the return two weeks later in Serbia; their place in the last sixteen would be assured. Draw they did, 0-0, in a crude, rough, rain-soaked game which sealed Beckham in the eyes of his harshest critics as the buy of the season. Booed by the Serb fans from beginning to end, assaulted with intent right from the start by the Serb players, Beckham played like one of those battle commanders that seizes the regiment's flag and leads the troops over the trenches into the enemy guns. 'Through thick and thin, he was the best Madrid player,' wrote *el País*. 'When courage was needed, he put his tibia at risk with admirable conviction.'

Jorge Valdano was effusive. 'Beckham,' he said, 'has given us some-thing we needed. A willingness to sacrifice himself for the team in midfield and bags of quality. He is one of those rare players who give you both quality and quantity. He has competitive courage, an amateur spirit of love for the game and a capacity to cover an extraordinary amount of ground in the course of a game. And on top of that, I have to say since Maradona I have not seen anyone who strikes the ball like Beckham.'

It would have been worth Beckham's while to have learnt Spanish simply to have been able to read what another Argentine, grouchy old Alfredo Di Stefano of all people, had to say about him. Asked in an interview with *el País* a week after that Valladolid game what he thought of the new addition to the team, he was at pains to put the doubters in their place. 'Everybody was wrong about Beckham,' Di Stefano said. 'He is a worker of the old school. Apart from that ability to strike a ball that he has, he is the first to press when the opposition has the ball . . . This boy does not stand out as a seller of clothes. He stands out as a footballer . . . This boy is committing himself unconditionally and with extraordinary effort to the team. People are surprised at how well he is doing. This is a source of great satisfaction for the club and for the president, who signed him . . . Buying him has been a brilliant move for Real Madrid.'

9: Marseille in Medellín

I watched Real Madrid's fifth Champions League game of the season, away to Marseille, in Medellín, Colombia, where I had travelled to do a completely unrelated newspaper story about love, death and cocaine. Medellín, the dark heart of the international drug-trafficking business, had acquired a reputation over the previous couple of decades as the murder capital of the world. It was an extraordinarily dangerous place, made all the worse by that fact that Colombia had been engaged for forty years in a savage civil war that was fuelled less by ideology then by an interminable cycle of revenge and the endless supply of weapons that drug money can buy. Someone in Colombia once described these rival armies as 'autistic', living in a closed world where killing became an end in itself.

Football was Medellín's window on an outside, saner world, a saving vision of something beyond the tawdry barbarity destiny had chosen for the city's inhabitants. To my delight I discovered that the Marseille–Real game would be shown live on Colombian television. I watched the game in my hotel room with an unemployed journalist called Luis David Obando, his son Jorge Andrés and the son's friend Juan Diego, both fifteen. I looked at these boys and I worried about them. I sensed that their lives would be so precarious. If your family was wealthy you could find some shelter from the dangers and nefarious influences that preyed on teenagers in Medellín. But these boys' families were struggling, they were on their way down, not up the ladder. What awaited them below? What alternative was there to the favourite cocktail round these parts: guns, drugs and extreme violence?

I might have been worried about them, but they were worried about something else: they wanted to see Real Madrid win the game. They knew pretty much everything there was to know about Real – as much certainly as your average reader of *AS* and *Marca* back in Spain.

There was no need for me to do any explaining of any kind. As in that minibus ride in Nairobi I experienced the mildly belittling sensation of realising there was not much of value I could offer these people on the subject of football in general, or even Real Madrid in particular. How come they were so well informed? The TV, the radio, newspapers, the internet, they explained. It was all out there these days. All you had to do was look. It was yet another example of the new global football village, where knowledge of the game and team loyalty were no longer limited by geography. It was the reason why Pérez's new football model, based as it was around the world's most famous and charismatic players, was achieving its objective of creating '*ilusión colectiva global*'. Here it was, happening right before my eyes, in my hotel room in Medellín.

The first question that concerned the boys was, how Zidane would be received by his compatriots. It was answered promptly. He received an ovation from the Marseille fans even before the game had started when his name was announced in the staring line-up over the loudspeaker. The boys and their dad and I were able to discern the odd dissenting noise but overall the *Marsellaises* seemed to be happy to be welcoming back their favourite son, even if he had returned with the express purpose of killing off their chances of progressing in Europe's leading football competition.

In the first half hour Marseille shot five times on goal and received no reward for their pains, in large part because the Real goalkeeper, Iker Casillas, was going though a patch of form so brilliant, the saves he was making were so miraculous, that teammates and fans alike had taken to calling him 'San Iker', Saint Iker. After thirty-five minutes Real finally stirred themselves for an attempt on goal. Beckham took a free kick on the edge of the Marseille penalty area. It was a classic. He bent the ball round and high over the defensive wall, arching it over the goalkeeper's outstretched left hand, until the top spin kicked in and the ball dropped like a guided missile – as if someone with a remote control radio were instructing it – shaving the underside of the bar before crashing into the top right-hand corner of the net for a goal. All the Real players rushed to embrace Beckham, none with more love in his eyes than the usually diffident Zidane, who had indeed come to Marseille with murder in his heart.

The two Colombian boys jumped up, mouths open, their hands on their faces in a classic gesture of stupefaction. They both played football themselves at what was considered a high level locally. They both dreamt of becoming professional players one day, but they were both in awe of the genius in that goal. '*Cómo la hace caer!*' they both kept repeating over and over. 'How he makes it drop!'

That goal was the green light, as it so often tended to be with Real, for Zidane and Roberto Carlos and Figo to start doing some showing off – the little backheeled one-twos, the flicks over defenders' heads, the general taunting of the opposition. '*Olé!*' said the two Colombian boys in response to one particularly impudent little flourish from Zidane. The older Luis David could not resist a smile.

'I love football but I must tell you that I love the *toros* more,' Luis David said. 'Watching Real Madrid I am reminded of the bullfight. Often much of the action is a disappointment, a yawn. The bulls are often sluggish, only occasionally are they lively and aroused. But the whole thing is justified, the price of the ticket is entirely warranted, when suddenly the bullfighter flicks his wrist in a particularly daring and delightful way and makes a beautful pass. The whole evening is salvaged and you go home with a memory to treasure, your life enriched, a smile on your face.'

After that goal, and until Marseille equalised half an hour later, the game did indeed risk descending into a bloodbath. The Marseille players, angry as gored bulls, and barely more rational, abandoned all attempts to kick the ball and opted for less mobile targets: the Real players' legs. Zidane and Figo were clobbered so hard the team doctor had to rule them out of the Spanish league game coming up that weekend. Beckham survived but only after looking one of his assailants in the eye and calling him, so deliberately we could lip-read it from Medellín, an '*hijo de puta*' – son of a whore – the first sign I had seen that the Englishman was getting a grip on some practical footballing Spanish. Luis David guffawed and the two boys roared with delight.

With seventeen minutes to go Beckham won the match for Real. He had been playing at full throttle which meant in Beckham's case, given his genetically freakish stamina, that he ran twice as much as anyone else on the pitch. He runs and runs but does so, when he is at his best, with the economy that only a high footballing intelligence imparts.

All these finer qualities of Beckham's game were expressed in Real's winning thrust against Marseille. Chasing back into his own penalty area, he mopped up a dangerous ball. But then instead of doing what nine players out of ten would have done in the same situation, which was to boot the ball safely into the stands, he spun round and delivered a perfectly weighted, in-curling, forty-yard pass down the line to Figo who ran on to it inside the Marseille half, slipped it inside to Raúl, who passed it to Zidane, who immediately released it back to Raúl, who rolled it forward to Ronaldo – who scored. Half the Real team rushed to embrace Ronaldo; the other half rushed to embrace Beckham.

I chatted to the two boys after the game. They had been impressed by that capacity of Real's to go up a gear when they needed to. But they warned that things could come unstuck later on, at the sharp end of the season, once Real came up against the really tough teams, the Milans, the Arsenals and determined rivals in the Spanish league, like Valencia and Deportivo la Coruña. 'I still reckon Makelele is going to be missed,' Juan Diego said. 'They depend too much on Casillas pulling off those miracle saves of his. With Makelele, Casillas didn't have to be so busy. There's no one in the team that defends the back line like Makelele. Beckham does it because he is a trier, but it's not his job. It's not what he does best, or even well.'

Jorge Andrés suggested, rather more controversially, that the weak link was Raúl. He was right, Raúl was playing poorly, his worst start to a season after years of sustained brilliance. But Raúl was Real's sacred cow. It didn't matter how badly he played, the fans and the press in Spain never criticised him. As the top scorer in the history of the Champions League, as the winner of three European cups by the age of twenty-five, he had earned the right to be, at least for a while, untouchable. 'Look, it's true that since Figo and the rest of the superstars arrived at Real Madrid there's been no team in the world better to watch,' said Juan Diego, who was an impressively thoughtful young man. 'But I wonder if they have the strength in depth you need to win the trophies their talent deserves. Florentino Pérez talks about his Zidanes and Pavones, but are the Pavones good enough? If a player like Ronaldo gets injured and is out for a month, or someone like Zidane or Beckham is suspended for an important Champions League game, the whole thing could fall apart. And what about Roberto Carlos? Who can replace him if he is injured?' It was another telling point. Maybe all football fans everywhere spoke of the need for 'balance' between defence and attack; maybe they all felt the need for a labourer or two – or a water-carrier, as the World Cup-winning French captain Didier Deschamps, now Monaco coach, used to describe himself – in midfield.

Pérez would get impatient with this kind of talk. When it was put to him once that he might want to consider buying Gennaro Gatusso, Milan's combative midfield water-carrier, his reply, was, 'Sure, to carry the players' kit'. The intriguing thing about Pérez was that while on the one hand he was the most hard-nosed capitalist in the world, on the other he was a starry-eyed romantic. No one was more professional in his methods; no one more amateur in spirit. He was striving, with great success, to make Real Madrid into the most profitable machine in world sport, yet his personal approach to the game was childlike, dispensing as it did with grown-up notions of tactical orthodoxy, resting on the belief that if you reduced the game to its brilliant essentials, if you put the fantasy footballers on the pitch, you would – as night follows day – triumph. The temptation to succumb to that Freudian analysis of his relationship with Real Madrid, the expression of an unconscious yearning to relive his happy Bernabéu childhood, was strong. But did all this mean that Pérez, of all people, would be exposed in time as being naïve? As a dreamer?

Certainly that had been the thought in quite a few minds a couple of weeks before that Marseille match when Real suffered their first serious reverse of the season. With Roberto Carlos out injured and the right back Michel Salgado suspended, the thinness of the squad was cruelly exposed. Sevilla, eternal mid-table battlers, thrashed them 4–1.

And it could have been worse. Sevilla were 4–0 up at half-time and I remember thinking that if they did not take their feet off the pedal in the second half we could be in for a repeat of Deportivo la Coruña's scandalous 8–3 defeat at the hands of Monaco in the Champions League four days earlier. Queiroz played Pavón, the original Francisco Pavón, out of his usual centre half position at right back and the poor lad was roasted by Sevilla's outstanding left winger José Antonio Reyes, whom Arsenal would buy for 22 million euros a few weeks later. The game was a fiasco and for another of the Pavones, a burly young man called Rubén drafted into central defence alongside Helguera, a piteous débâcle. The gentle giant was taken off by Queiroz after half an hour, with Real already 3–0 down, and he wept and wept and wept. Rubén had sensed – correctly – that his career at Real Madrid was over; that the great dream of his young life had bitten the dust.

I found myself having a conversation about this very game with the porter at my hotel in Medellín. A small wiry man in his late fifties, his name was Orlando and he was one of those people whose range of responses to the sport was vast, from unbridled enthusiasm over Beckham's goal against Marseille ('That's a goal one could watch and watch and watch over and over and over again!') to coldly critical analysis of what he described as 'a timebomb' in the Real Madrid set-up: the wide gap in class that separated the front rank players and those on the bench.

'There is no cover in defence!' Orlando cried. 'Florentino Pérez has taken the view that you can afford to lose your best centre half, Hierro, and your one defensive midfielder, Makelele and then *not replace them*! Well, OK, you've got Pavón, and Rubén and Raúl Bravo and I think some other young guys but they're just *potentially* good players at this point, not the finished product, like Hierro was. So you've got this weak centre and then – I repeat – no Makelele, no midfield armour, to protect it. Last night against Marseille they looked good, thanks to Beckham mainly, but they were also lucky. Marseille could easily have drawn that game.'

But the problems were not only in defence, Orlando said. 'Why, why, why did they loan Fernando Morientes to Monaco?' he wanted to know. 'The money you save there could be lost later if the results don't go with you. The fact is that Morientes would be an excellent replacement on the bench for Ronaldo or Raúl.' Repeating the point that the young Juan Diego had made, Orlando said he feared for Real in the event of injuries or suspensions later on in the season. 'Maybe these guys are so magical, so galactic, so not of this earth that they won't ever get injured, but unfortunately I doubt it.'

These were the arguments the *futboleros* back home in Spain were making. The better the Florenteam did, the less vocal they were. But the muttering never quite stopped. Pérez was not totally naïve. He had actually tried to buy a top-class centre half to replace Fernando Hierro, whom he had pensioned off in the summer. He had wanted to buy Fabián Ayala, who was the main reason why Valencia had consistently enjoyed the best defensive record in Europe since the start of the millennium. Ayala, the Argentine team captain, was fast, tough, wily and excellent in the air. And that was another thing: with the possible exception of Iván Helguera, there was no one in the Real team who could head a ball. Not only was there no one to take advantage of Beckham's corners up front, there was no one to stand up to big attackers in defence. Valencia had flirted with selling Ayala to Real but, fearing a fans' revolt, decided at the last minute not to let him go.

The upshot was that Real's coach, Queiroz, would have to make do with what the Real youth team could deliver. Raúl Bravo, who had started off life as a left back, was reinvented by Queiroz as a central defender. He was strong and fast and, in the absence of anyone else, he would have to do. Bravo had been loaned out to Leeds United the previous season and had failed utterly. He played a few games, was dropped to the bench and was then dropped altogether from the team. Now Leeds were having a miserable season in England. They were facing the serious prospect of relegation. And here was Bravo at the top of the Spanish league, cruising along in the Champions League.

While that happy state of affairs persisted there was nothing for the doubters in the Spanish press – if not in Medellín – to do but shut up and wonder whether perhaps they had been wrong all along, whether Pérez was indeed privy to a superior wisdom that they themselves lacked the wit to glimpse. And if in the looming *superclásico* Real Madrid managed to beat Barcelona in Barcelona, that would be the end of that. Game, set and match – for a while at least – to Florentino.

10: The First Galáctico

Roberto Perfumo, a former captain of Argentina and one of the toughest defenders his country ever produced, joined the glamorous Buenos Aires club River Plate three-quarters of the way into his career. The fans of Racing, the club where he had made his name, were outraged. The first game he played back at the Racing stadium in the River colours he, and his poor blameless mother, were subjected to every insult imaginable. Perfumo's response after the game was to shrug and say, 'I never knew that they loved me so much.'

Whatever abuse Perfumo endured that day it was as nothing compared to the rage and hatred heaped on Luis Figo on his first appearance against Barcelona, in Barcelona, wearing the colours of Real Madrid. The football was the least of it at the Camp Nou on the night of 21 October 2000, three months after he had sold his soul to the detested Castillians. The atmosphere at Europe's mightiest modern amphitheatre evoked images of the bullfight, of Greek tragedy, of Christians at the Colosseum. The bare sporting statistic – Barcelona 2 Real Madrid 0 – masked the true nature of a spectacle whose purpose was not so much victory as a blood sacrifice to requite and ease the pain of the 105,000 souls packed into Catalunya's holiest temple. They bayed for the blood of the traitor, the man who had dealt the most painful blow anyone could remember to that famously prickly pride of theirs. Other players had defected from Barcelona to the old enemy, but none had been more esteemed. Figo had a unique style on the ball, more rugged than you would expect from a player blessed with that most cherished and most classic footballing attributes, the ability to beat his man time and time again. He was not silky in his movements like Zidane, or bullet-fast like Beckham's former colleague –

and proclaimed admirer of Figo's – Ryan Giggs. There was something workmanlike as well as quietly menacing about him, like a brooding blacksmith with two days' dark growth on his face. Yet he was as good as any winger ever was at the critical business of accelerating and stopping dead, feinting right and going left, twisting defenders inside out and then crossing the ball with an accuracy, flight and pace that only Beckham could improve on. Not merely a supremely talented performer but a warrior too, a take-no-prisoners competitor who had saved the day in a hundred battles, Figo had been Barça's favourite son for the last three of the five years he had been at the club. He could have gone to Milan or Manchester United, and the fans would have been upset, humiliated, hurt. But they might have forgiven him, in time. But to quit Barcelona for Real, and to have done so – as everybody chose to believe, as a hundred banners at the Camp Nou proclaimed – for a few pesetas more was a sin so epically unpardonable it only bore comparison with Judas' betrayal of Christ.

One banner said it best, capturing the poignant essence of the outrage. 'We hate you so much,' it read, 'because we loved you so much.' Perfumo had it right. Hell hath no fury like a football fan scorned. Every time Figo touched the ball the decibel level at the Camp Nou became so searingly intense you could have imagined, if you had closed your eyes, that a dozen jumbo jets were on the grass, revving their engines for take-off.

How did Figo himself react? With more aplomb, astonishingly enough, than any of his teammates. The whole Real team had made Figo's plight their own, it seemed, had collectively been worn down like a bull by a toreador – goaded, bloodied, dizzied by the malevolence seething from the stands – until they were helpless to resist the kill. But Figo himself refused to be bowed. He never shirked, he never stopped looking for the ball. 'If I don't have the ball I go mad,' he once said. It did not matter that every time he got involved in the play the jumbo screech became unbearable, became almost physically painful: he kept playing his hungry natural game. 'They are making me feel as if I were a murderer,' he had said before the game, amid the hysteria his return to the Camp Nou had been generating all week. In the event he played like a murderer too, a cold-blooded one.

Poker-faced throughout, his expression revealing not a hint of fear or anger, he gave his marker, Carles Puyol, a punishing night out. 'The thing about Figo is that he never, ever stops moving, pulling you this way and that,' Puyol, regarded by many as the best defender in Spain, said after the game. 'But the really amazing thing about tonight was that despite that brutal pressure he was under he kept asking for the ball all the time, as if nothing out of the ordinary were happening.'

Three years later, the hatred had barely abated. If in that first game back Barça had been the matador and Real had been the bull, for the 2003 rematch the roles were reversed. Roberto Carlos applied the *coup de grâce* but Figo played the part of the picador, the man on the horse who digs, digs, digs the tip of a spear into the animal's back.

The Portuguese captain was often accused during his career of hogging the ball. This might also have been taken as a compliment. To play at the highest level of the game and be able to keep possession of the ball as long as he could – longer than anybody else – was a sign of genius. During this Barça game he kept the ball at his feet for such long stretches, especially during the first half hour of the game, that – beyond selfish – it was plain rude. He was guilty of insulting behaviour towards his rivals, both players and fans. Which was precisely his objective. As it had been when, in violation of an agreement the Real players had made before the game, he took the first corner. The rumpus the year before, when the game had to be suspended for fifteen minutes because Barça fans were hurling all manner of objects at Figo every time he went to take a corner, had persuaded the Real camp that it would be best if Beckham took all the corners this time around. But when the first Real corner was awarded, Figo, in an act that blended heroic defiance with outright provocation, raced to the flag and took it himself. And then, as if asking the enraged crowd to do their worst, came the hogging, the twisting this way and that with the ball seemingly tied to his bootlaces, running up the byline and then down again, in a spectacle that made a mockery not only of his Barça tormentors but of the whole concept of football as a team game.

Beckham, vivid memories no doubt coming to mind of the savage abuse he had endured from crowds back home, loved it; marvelled at his teammate's brazenness. He too had faced down his tormentors, had weathered the storm and come out the stronger for it. Their pride, in each case, was what carried them through. Like all top sportsmen, they were proud by definition. What drove them, in large measure, were oversized egos and paranoid levels of competitiveness, manifested in a horror of failure.

Yet the personalities the two men projected off the pitch could not have been more different. Beckham was sunny and uncomplicated; Figo, dark and gloomy. Beckham loved the stage lights; Figo shunned them. Beckham could hold that radiant smile of his all day long; Figo, the Galáctico of the sad countenance, had been known to smile in public, there had been sightings. But it was not so much joy or celebration that he transmitted on these rare occasions as wry acknowledgement of life's bitter mystery.

Put him in shorts with a ball at his feet, though, and he was quite as expressive as anybody else. He did agony well, he did ecstasy, but what he was particularly good at was incredulous rage directed at yet another in a painfully long line of referees who, inexplicably, had failed to give a foul against him. He did not do badly for himself, though. Accused always by rival fans of being a serial diver, he was the player who season in, season out in Spain received the most fouls. That was the price you paid, as his footballing hero Diego Maradona always used to find, for being so good.

Figo cost 60 million euros when Pérez sensationally filched him from Barcelona in the summer of 2000. An only child born into a respectably-off family in Lisbon (his father owned a bar; his mother worked as a seamstress) he was identified as a potential footballing superstar aged twelve. Four years later he was playing first division football for Sporting Lisbon. When he was twenty-three, Johan Cruyff signed him for Barcelona in 1995 and from then on he was consistently the best winger in world football, capable of operating on both sides of the pitch, almost as lethal with his left foot as with his right. Winner of the European Footballer of the Year award in 2000 and FIFA World Player of the Year in 2001, Figo's eminence at Real Madrid was exceeded only by his eminence in Portugal, where he was a celebrity as big as Beckham was in England, as well as the star and talisman of the national football team.

The first time I met him was towards Christmas-time in 2003 at a hotel outside Lisbon where he was gathered with his Portugal teammates. Arriving early for our appointment, I saw him in a lounge just off the lobby watching TV. A dozen other players were watching TV too. From the ribbing, gesticulating and general air of hilarity I deduced they were watching themselves on the news. But Figo, who was sitting on the best chair in the room with his legs stretched out proprietorally, registered no emotion at all. Grim melancholia was his natural, resting expression and grim melancholia was what I saw. Young players freshly arrived in the national squad found him intimidating, I had been told. In Portugal he was a national institution, the big difference with Beckham in England being that whereas Beckham went out of his way to break the tension his fame generated, Figo remained icily remote. They used to call him the Lion King when he was at Barcelona. He was that, all right. The undisputed leader of the pack. But what made the effect all the more forbidding was that Figo, who unusually for a footballer enjoyed reading novels, was also Hamlet: a man apart, self-involved, seemingly wrapped in gloomy contemplation.

Slowly and with no attempt to disguise his reluctance he lifted himself from his seat in the TV room, greeted me without enthusiasm and led me to a stark room around the back of the hotel where we spent the next hour talking. That is about three-quarters of an hour more than most football players are ever prepared to give people from outside the professional footballing fraternity. Football players do not like interviews. You can see their point. It is not something they tend to do well.

Figo understood that for a footballing superstar to spend an hour talking to a writer was to risk diminishing your image. But he also knew, or he ought to have known, that in his case this was not a cause for concern. There were not too many players with whom you began a conversation asking them in all seriousness whether they would prefer to speak in their second or third language. Figo spoke fluent Spanish, having lived in Spain eight years. But he also spoke fluent English, which was fairly remarkable given that he had no English family members and had never lived in an English-speaking country. Portuguese was his native tongue. I did not speak Portuguese. He did me the kindness of offering to talk in one of the languages with which I was familiar.

We spoke in Spanish, deviating into English only when an English word seemed to express a thought better. What about his great *traición*, I asked him? How did he justify what would always go down in Catalunya as his great act of betrayal? I expected him to shrug, raise his eyebrows, look away in semi-despair at the tedious predictability of a question I felt I had to ask. I expected wrong. This was his reply: 'Look. In this football world what you learn, in the end, is that you have to put yourself and your family first. Of course, I understand the fans. The fans with me have always been fantastic. I have nothing to reproach them with, but in a way I would like them to see that they should not reproach me either. Because . . . well, look at the football world: I've had teammates who have been ten, fifteen years in one club but suddenly they just kick them out, not recognising all the effort and all the sacrifices they have made. And then there are others who are in a club for three years, for whatever reason never get a game and then at a certain moment they kick them out too. So as a player you have to distinguish between the human relationship with the fans and the professional relationship with the directors, who in the case of Barcelona did not value me. Now, of course, I want the respect and affection of the fans. Of course I do. But I know I won't have it the moment I start to play badly. That's the way it is in football. So I figured I had to think first of all of myself, be a little selfish if you like. And I decided to do what was best for me.'

All that brooding: it was not a pose. He did chew on things. He was the reflective type. And while I had heard from journalists who covered Real Madrid for a living that Figo was a disagreeable, suspicious character who treated people he did not know with something bordering on disdain, it turned out that he was not as stand-offish as the image he projected would have suggested. He spoke in a deep-voiced monotone, but was not as perfunctory in his replies – or as self-evidently bored – as other players could be.

'Doing what was best for me' is what all players do, if they have any sense. It is endearing how football people cling to the notion

that players owe as much loyalty to their clubs as the fans themselves. However much they love the game, football for the players
never ceases to be a job. For the fans it is a religion. It is only by
an extreme leap of faith that fans are able to cling to this notion
that the players share their passion for the club colours. Because
rationally, given the abundance of evidence to the contrary, it is quite
inexplicable. A particularly compelling example was provided after
the final whistle blew in Figo's first game back at the Camp Nou.
As the Barça fans revelled in the stands, gloated over Real's battered
white carcass, each and every Barcelona player made a special point
of seeking out Figo and embracing him. The fans evidently chose
not to understand it, and they may never understand it, but that was
the worst, most enduring betrayal of all. Never mind the fantasies of
the football follower, the message the players were sending was that
professional footballers were not, in fact, a people apart. They were
like everyone else. Their first loyalty was not to their club any more
than than the average football fan's first loyalty was to the company
that employed him. Before that came your loyalty to your bank
account and to your friends and your family. The Barça players,
without necessarily meaning to, were reminding the Barça fans not
to kid themselves. Figo remained their old pal and if the right,
improved offer came along they too would sin as he had done.

Just how mad the fans are, though, was revealed to me one afternoon at Madrid airport in the summer of 2000 just four days after
Figo's move to Real had been announced. Fernando Redondo, hitherto a loyal servant of Real, was packing his bags and leaving for AC
Milan. The Real fans had insisted on convincing themselves (quite
wrongly as it turned out, but that was another story) that he had left
for the money. At the airport I came across an Italy-bound Redondo
pursued by a small group of Real fans hurling abuse at him.
'Golddigger!' cried the outraged innocents. 'Scum!' These were the
very same fans who had thrilled to the news the Monday before that
Real had acquired the services of Figo, who was in turn receiving
the very same abuse from the fans at Barcelona. All of which goes to
show, once again, that football fans are the most irrational people in
the world, incapable of anything dimly resembling objective thought

once their lives' ruling passion, the club they support, hoves into view. Sanity, you would think, would demand one of two responses. Either football fans start seriously waning in their devotion towards the star players of their favourite clubs; or they do as the sensible Japanese do – follow players, not clubs, and when a player switches club, cheerfully switch with him. (Thus was Japan converted overnight, with Beckham's arrival, into a nation of Real Madrid television watchers.)

I talked to Figo about Beckham, beginning by putting it to him that on the evidence of the season so far it seemed to be he and the Englishman who drove the Real team on when things got tough, when the team was behind with fifteen minutes to go playing away in the cold and the rain. That they were the foreigners in the Real team who delivered the Spanish '*furia*'. 'Yes. You're right. Neither of us likes to stand still. We are not the tranquil types. In fact,' he said, offering another surprise, a conspiratorial smile, 'I think that maybe the Portuguese and the Englishman are the most hot-blooded players on the team.'

Another quality Figo said he had in common with Beckham was the constant desire to become a better player. But could a player like him really still improve at this late stage of the game? 'Yes, you always can. Every day.' In what? 'In everything. In all technical aspects. Headers, striking the ball better.' Dribbling too? 'Dribbling too. Everything,' said Figo. But football was more a gift than an acquisition, surely? 'I believe it is a gift. It is fortunate to be able to play football. It is not something that you can learn, like, say, mathematics. With football it is predestined; you are born with it. When you see a kid you can tell immediately whether there is a clumsy player there or whether he has ability.' Yet you could work at striking the ball better, after all these years? 'If you are not born with an aptitude for the sport it is no good but if you have the basic qualities required then you can always work at your game. So yes, if you spend all day striking the ball, logically you will get better all the time.' So that means he struck the ball better now than before, than say five years ago? 'Yes, probably . . . yes. Yes.' As well as Beckham? To that he replied nothing; just a shrug, and a bashful smile.

Following the Englishman's transfer there had been a lot of talk within Real Madrid about Figo and Beckham and how they would get on. There was a prickliness to that pride of Figo's sometimes, they said. Possibly what drove him was that deep down he was more insecure than he would have liked to admit. I heard a story from someone at Real about his reaction to the arrival of Zidane in the summer of 2001. A few weeks into the season Zidane met with Florentino Pérez. Pérez asked him how he was settling in and he said fine, except for one thing. Figo simply refused to pass him the ball. Time and again when the simple and natural thing would have been to give it to him, he gave it to someone else. Pérez went and talked to Figo. Not revealing that Zidane had been complaining about him, Pérez asked him why he did not pass the ball to his new teammate more often. Figo responded as one might have expected. With indignant denials. Pérez said nothing and let the matter drop. The next time Real Madrid played, Figo, on first receiving the ball, passed it to Zidane. The second time, again to Zidane. Third, to Zidane again. Whereupon he turned towards the stands, to where Pérez was sitting, opened his arms, palms outspread, and shrugged, in a gesture intended eloquently to put it to Pérez, 'What the hell are you talking about, *señor presidente?*'

Figo's response to Beckham's arrival was, if anything, more blatantly competitive than it had been to Zidane's. But this time his response was to play out of his skin. Right from the moment the team set off on its tour of pre-season friendlies in Asia Figo ran and battled for the ball like a man possessed. Beckham talked about his need to prove a point; Figo went out of his way to prove it on the pitch. Because Beckham had always played in Figo's position, out on the right, at Manchester United, the question on everyone's lips was whether Real would be big enough for the both of them. The question I put to Figo was whether his self-esteem had been pricked by the Englishman's arrival, whether it was right to have inferred from his performances in those early days that he had been goaded into demonstrating that he was the better player?

'No, look, I will explain,' he said. 'In football you always have to show your worth. Day in day out. But for me this challenge was nothing new, because I was the first to arrive, then came Zidane, then Ronaldo, then now Beckham. But I have always felt confident in my abilities. As a professional football player I have known perfectly well from the day I started playing that every day I had to fight for my place. So yes it was one challenge more. I should immediately say that for us it is good that David is with us because he makes us much stronger, we are more competitive and better but, yes, in a sense it was one more challenge for me because he is a new teammate and you have to continue fighting to continue playing. But, all that said, more than anything else what drives me is that I play for myself.'

He was not smiling now. As he talked what came through once again was that tremendous pride you saw on the football field. He had said something similar in an interview with *el País* three years earlier: 'I have achieved what I have on my own. No one has ever handed me anything on a plate. My greatest obsession in football is to play well; what most worries me is not being able to do my job well.' He wanted to be in on the action. He wanted to strut his stuff. And that was why he was the Alpha male pack leader type. Pride, an occasionally chippy pride allied with huge ambition, was what distinguished him. It is what distinguishes the ordinarily successful player from the superstar. It was why he had been captain of the Portuguese national team since the age of twenty-three; why he said of Portugal's chances in the European championships the coming summer that while there were better teams around 'I will fight to the death to win – whatever it takes'. That lust to prove himself and triumph: it was what Beckham had. Failure for Beckham was not an option. Had he not made it at Real he would have been humiliated, crushed. It was a question more of willpower than of talent. In Figo's case there was more talent to carry him through but he too feared, more than anything, the prospect of being deemed a failure. How could this happen after so glorious a career? It could happen in the event that Real Madrid chose to discard him, to sell him the following summer to the highest bidder. That would amount to a rejection, which meant failure, which for Figo would be unbearable. He had talked to Pérez about this. He had a special connection with Pérez, having been his first Galático, his first-born after he became father of the great Real Madrid '*familia*', as he he used to like saying. And Pérez had told him not to worry, that he would stand by him, that there was a sentimental bond between them that was unbreakable. And when he said it he meant it. Not only was Figo the signing that gave Pérez reason to believe he could achieve his dreams at Real, Pérez admired him for the courage he showed on the pitch, for his fighting spirit when a game was going badly. But Figo, whose vanity was flattered by the friendship the president showed him, remained wary. As he had said to me, he had seen players unceremoniously tossed out of clubs after fifteen years of loyal service. Fernando Hierro, his captain at Madrid during his first three years at the club, might have been in his mind when he said that. Besides, he was thirty-one and while, yes, he remained a formidable player it was not beyond the bounds of the possible that Real Madrid might decide to make some money on him while they still could, especially if things changed and the season did not end as gloriously as it seemed now, December 2003, that it would.

All of which helped explain why Figo made a point every now and again of dropping hints about his desire to play in England. As he did to me. 'There is a tradition and a culture in English football – an intensity in the way fans follow the game – that is special,' he said. 'The Spanish relate to the football spectacle in a very different way. In England, you can be losing 2-0, 3-0, and the fans are still cheering on their team. In Spain, it would be the opposite; they would be jeering. This is not to criticise. It has to do with different cultures, different ways of being.' He volunteered the thought that a particular reason why he himself was attracted to English football was that it had a big impact on him when he was a boy genius, chased by the top clubs in Portugal. 'In the years when I was getting started in the game it was the English teams who were at the peak in Europe. Those were the days of English domination: the late Seventies and early Eighties. Clubs like Liverpool became my reference point in the game.' When I asked him where in England he might like to play, he did not hesitate. 'London,' he said. London? 'Yes, if you really want to know, London.' But would it ever happen? 'In this game anything can happen. But when I say I would like to play in London some day I am expressing merely a dream, and dreams don't often come true.' Figo said this kind of thing quite often to journalists during the course of the season. He was toying with them, using them to send messages to Florentino Pérez, to Roman Abramovich, to other potentially interested parties. But above all he was engaging in these flirtations as a sort of emotional insurance scheme, so that in the event that Real did decide to sell him he would be in a position to say that, no, he wasn't pushed, he had jumped. That it was at his initiative that he left. The truth was, you sensed, that really what he most wanted was to remain at Real Madrid. Chelsea might pay him well and London might be a great city, but in football terms, in historical terms, glory terms, it would be a sad come-down after Real.

A friend of Figo's, a former Portuguese national team press officer called José Carlos Freitas, said that his *amor propio* – his self-love – was enormous. 'That is why I think he sometimes talks about going to play football in England,' Freites told me. 'Some might think he would not fit in, that his tricks – the time he spends on the ball – would not work out, but for him it is a challenge and something he feels he could overcome. But I don't think he will go. For him Real Madrid is *the* club. He was a big fish at Barça, a bigger fish in the sense that the goals, the plays, the action centred around him. But for him it is a challenge to play in a team of big stars like Zidane. He likes to test himself at the highest level.'

As for celebrity, yet another point of contact with Beckham, Figo took a rather different approach. He was huge in Portugal, the number one national star. I remember the very first thing I saw on arrival at Lisbon airport to interview him was a large billboard with his face on it advertising some local product. But he was much bigger than that, bigger than Beckham was in England, in fact. He was so big that if, for example, the King of Spain came on a state visit, the president would invite him along. So big that when elections came around the whole country waited to see who he would come out and publicly support. In the previous national election he had given his endorsement to a Socialist candidate. When he failed to give it to the Socialist in a subsequent election for the mayor of Lisbon there was an outcry. And yet, in contrast to the treatment Beckham received in England, the press in Portugal left him respectfully alone. Figo was good looking in a classically Latin tall, dark and handsome sort of way. He was also a snappy dresser. But the intrusion into his private life was minimal. This was partly because of the nature of the Portuguese media, partly because neither he nor his wife – a beautiful Swedish model – invited intrusion the way Posh and Becks did.

Some within Real Madrid said that, notwithstanding Figo's apparent indifference to publicity, he was secretly envious of all the attention Beckham received; resentful of the unavoidable fact that every time the team made a public appearance all eyes were on Beckham. If all that were true, he did not reveal a glimmer of it. I asked him what Beckham was like, whether anything had surprised him about his newest colleague at Real Madrid? 'Yes, sure,' he replied. 'You always have an idea that is not entirely real when you don't know the person. I obviously knew his qualities as a player but in terms of personal contact now I can say that he is a great professional, who is always available on the pitch to his teammates and in terms of daily contact the same. He is a person who does not speak very much but who is very *simpático* and always ready to help in anything. It would be very difficult to dislike him.' He said Beckham made the Real team stronger. (Indeed four years earlier, before he had any notion he would ever play alongside him Figo had nominated Beckham as one of the three best players in the world, alongside Rivaldo and Raúl.) What specifically did Beckham bring to Real, I asked him? 'Chiefly, quality in the pass, fighting spirit and a great first touch.'

As far as Figo was concerned the secret of this Real Madrid, the reason why at their best they played the best football on the planet, was, precisely, the supreme quality in the first touch of so many of their players. 'I think the most important thing in football is that first control,' he said. Figo himself did indeed possess an extraordinarily feathery first touch, a genius for achieving complete mastery of the ball however difficult the direction or pace of the ball he received, as well in his case as a deceptively easy talent – for he lacked the blistering turn of speed of Beckham's former colleague and proclaimed fan of Figo's, Ryan Giggs – for getting past defenders. But he stressed that the soul of Real's game, the team's ability to move the ball around the pitch accurately and at speed, was that ability the star players had to control a moving ball, to stop it dead. 'A good first control is the difference between winning and losing, between scoring and missing a golden chance. Without doubt this is the most important thing, for me.'

A few days before our meeting in Lisbon FIFA had announced the results of its World Player of the Year 2003 awards, the outcome of which was decided by the votes of the coaches of all the world's national teams. Zidane had come first, Thierry Henry of Arsenal second, Ronaldo third. An even more telling statistic was this: of the top eleven in the world, six had been Real Madrid players, Figo inevitably among them. Whereupon it surely followed, if six members of the world's ideal eleven played for Real Madrid, that Real Madrid were the best team in the world, right? That was what Florentino Pérez said, as well as Beckham and pretty much everybody in the football world that you cared to ask. But Figo was not so sure. 'That's what the president says,' he said, smiling. 'But I don't know. Yes, I am playing with some truly magnificent players now but as to whether this is the best team only time will tell.' All right, then, but were they at least the best collection of individuals he had ever played with? 'Well, yes, I do think that in terms of individual quality this is the best team I've played in. But in collective terms will we continue to win . . . ? There are a lot of factors you can't control, starting with the fact that – as sometimes people seem to forget – we are normal people, we are human. Still, the fact is that the balloon has really been inflated and now in what is left of the season we will have to see if we deserve it.'

What Figo said made perfect sense. In fact, he was stating the blindingly obvious. But his words still took me aback. One had become so programmed to talk and think of Real Madrid players in galactic superlatives that the very suggestion of their humanity came as a surprise. That's what football people do, what the football press do: always magnify, exaggerate. Either a player or a team are brilliant, superb, out of this world, or they are rubbish. On Real Madrid we had all decided to bestow the mantle of greatness; we had chosen them to satisfy this seemingly perennial human need of ours for heroes. So we put them on a pedestal, we imagine them in the clouds and we keep doing this despite the fact that self-evidently they are human, they have bad days. The impulse is to preserve the memories that reinforce the ideal, and discard the rest. Like that famous first half against Manchester United

at the Bernabéu in which Figo himself scored a cracker. 'That's right,'
he said. 'We had a brilliant first half in which it all came together. I
think that was a case when everything works out the way you want
it to and it is fantastic football to watch. But there are also days when
things don't work out and it is horrible to watch us. We are not
machines that can be programmed. With the quantity of games we
have there will be some days when we play badly. That's natural. You
can't programme your body to be in peak condition for eighty games.
That's what happens. Some days there will be three or four or five
players who are not in the best shape, or we'll have players out with
injury, and that's when we will lose.'

And that was precisely what happened after that win against United.
They went on to the semi-finals and lost to Juventus, a manifestly inferior team man for man that just a couple of months earlier United had
beaten 3-0 away. At this point of the 2003/04 season, having qualified
easily for the second phase of the Champions League, they were again
most people's favourites to win the European Cup, although a note of
caution was injected into the debate by the bad news in mid-December
that Real's rivals in the first knockout stage of the competition would
be Bayern Munich. The Germans were always exceedingly tough rivals
and even were they to beat them Real would have the likes of Juventus
waiting for them in the next round. And Real looked, for all their brilliance, to be a less compact, less reliable team than Juventus. 'Yes, sure,
but there are no perfect teams,' said Figo, offering still more wisdom.
'The mistake is to imagine that perfection is possible when the very
idea is unthinkable. On the other hand, while we may not have the
defensive capability that Juventus have we perhaps have arguments in
attack that Juve lack.' Eight arguments, he might have added. Eight
players out of eleven committed to attack, while Juventus typically
fielded eight whose primary mission was to stop the other team from
playing. Marcello Lippi, Juventus' coach believed that there was a recklessly impractical, art-for-art's sake quality to Real Madrid; a principle
that it was not worth winning if you were not going to win well, if
you did not combine efficiency with panache. 'That's right,' said Figo.
'That is our philosophy and the characteristic of our team and of our
players. And, look, it has yielded results.'

11: The Bullet Man and *el Superclásico*

It was a Wednesday morning. The Barcelona–Real Madrid game wasn't being played till Saturday night but that morning's four big sports dailies were carrying sixty-four pages between them on the big match. They were not saying anything that had not been said a thousand times before. But they were saying it anyway. One paper had an 'exclusive' interview with Ronaldo who, at twenty years old, was the top goal-scorer in Europe. Question: 'Do you want to take on Real Madrid?' Answer: 'Yes. I really want to beat them.' This translated into a screamer of a front page headline. 'RONALDO: I WANT TO TAKE ON REAL MADRID.'

The year was 1997. Ronaldo was playing in the claret and blue colours of Barcelona, his one season at the Catalan club before moving on to Inter Milan. He would score the one goal of the game, helping extend Barça's unbeaten run at home against Real Madrid to thirteen years.

More than six years would pass before the Brazilian played again at Barcelona's Camp Nou. This time he was wearing the white of Real Madrid. On the day before the match, 6 December 2003, the four big morning sports dailies carried sixty-eight pages on the *superclásico* One of them featured an interview with Ronaldo who confessed that, yes indeed, he was 'really looking forward to taking on Barcelona'. But this time they did not use that line for the front page. This time they had something even better. Ronaldo was making a prediction, like Muhammad Ali used to do. Real Madrid would win 1-0 and he would score. '0-1: MY GOAL' screamed the headline over a photo of the Brazilian. Roberto Carlos added to the pre-match frothing. Real's other – and in his own way no less remarkable – Brazilian had played against Ronaldo in the Real defeat in Barcelona in 1997. Now he proclaimed that with Ronaldo on the same side, the Real team would finally put to an end two decades of humiliation in Barcelona. Real Madrid had not won once in twenty years of matches away against Barça at the Camp Nou. The stakes for both clubs were, as was always the case, shatteringly high.

The two teams had played hundreds of games since their very first encounter in 1902, when Barcelona won 3-1 at home, but the game this weekend, on this night of 6 December 2003, was *el Partido del Siglo*, the Game of the Century. Or at least it would be until the two sides met again at the Bernabéu the following April.

There is no rivalry quite like it in European sport. Manchester United v Liverpool, Milan v Juventus: they don't come close. (Beckham himself was quoted as saying how underwhelming his past duels for Manchester United against Liverpool seemed compared to the game that loomed at the Camp Nou.) Celtic v Rangers in Glasgow may have something of the same edge, because of the religious rivalry, but even that fixture has lots some of its heat since Rangers started admitting Papists and Englishmen into the ranks.

So what would an apt comparison be? The World Cup final? That's showbiz. For serious fans, club excites deeper passions than country. A general election? For the supporters of Real and Barça the outcome of this match mattered far, far more. My brother-in-law Chema, a *Madrileño* who used to work in Barcelona, put it best. 'It's like France versus England,' he said. 'In the time of Wellington.'

I remember talking to Bobby Robson about the Barça–Madrid rivalry before that game in 1997 in which Ronaldo scored the winner for the Catalans. Robson, previously an England player and England manager, was the Barcelona coach at the time. When he took on the job, after nearly fifty years as a professional in the game, he knew he was taking on a mighty responsibility. But he did not know how mighty. 'I've seen football all over the world, I've watched games between all the famous rivals, but this is something else altogether,' he told me. 'And you know why?' Robson, nearly seventy but always bursting with furious energy, leant towards me and dropped his voice, as if to confide some dread truth. 'Because it's two countries. *Two countries*, do you understand? It's not two clubs in one country. It's not just Real Madrid and Barcelona. It's Catalunya against Castille. They've fought wars with real armies and soldiers in the past. We fight the wars for them now. Our team is the army of Catalunya. This is our army, our air force, our navy. And I'm the British general commanding the Catalan troops.'

Having lived through more than a dozen of these epic contests I have tended to the view that they feel the rivalry that little bit more keenly in Barcelona than they do in Madrid. There's more rage among the Catalans than among the Castillians. The Catalans have been on the receiving end of more grief over the years. They were invaded and conquered by the Castillians during the early eighteenth century and the memory of Franco, who prohibited the official use of the Catalan language and stamped hard on anything that smacked of an autonomous impulse, remained fresh. Franco's death opened the floodgates and since then, in a fervour of over-compensation, Catalan flags have been almost as ubiquitous as the Stars and Stripes in Florida, every street sign in Barcelona has been rendered in Catalan, political parties have continued seriously to push for independence from Spain.

But still the historic *victimismo* lived on, no matter that Catalunya was now ruled by an autonomous parliament and was the richest region in Spain. The sense of unrighted wrongs and continuing 'oppression' was reinforced by Barcelona's failure on the football field to match the accomplishments of Real Madrid, which happened to be fixed indelibly in Catalan minds as the team of Franco, of the 'royal' (to turn to the original meaning of the Spanish word 'Real') and ancient oppressor. The loathing Real Madrid fans feel for Barça is, I think, more a response to Barça fans loathing of them, than anything else. Loathing feeds on loathing after all.

Thank God for football, though. Football, the great depository of national pride, channeller of collective rage. Nationalist radicals in Northern Ireland had the IRA and in the Basque country they had ETA. The most extreme expression of Catalan nationalism was FC Barcelona. Catalans – radicals and moderates – had their very own football army to engage in war by other means.

Ferguson and Beckham out of love.

Beckham and Roberto Carlos exchange shirts after Manchester United
go out of the Champions League 2003 to Real Madrid.

Morientes, Ronaldo, Beckham and Raúl at a happy pre-season press conference in Hong Kong.

Zidane takes Beckham's 50-yard ball on the volley for a goal v. Valladolid.

Figo, Ronaldo and Raúl preening for Real Madrid sponsors, Audi.

Real Madrid fans in Beijing.

Beckham fans in Japan.

Beckham at a press conference after the Madrid train bombs.

Roberto Carlos and Luis Figo celebrate the Brazilian's lucky equaliser
in the Champions League v. Bayern Munich.

Beckham sent off against Murcia for insulting a linesman in Spanish.

Rebecca Loos, Victoria Beckham and Romeo watching Beckham play.

Florentino Pérez at the Bernabeu flanked by his four Galáctico acquisitions.

By one of those mad perversities that the football fan's mind is prey to, and evidence of the blinding influence of tribalism in football (as in all things), the Real Madrid player that the Barça faithful had most consistently loathed over the previous six years had been Roberto Carlos. They had grown to detest him. Raúl, the very expression of Castillian Spanishness, the captain both of Real Madrid and of the Spanish national team, would have been a more likely target for pent-up Catalan resentment, you would have thought. But the Camp Nou had no problem with him. They left him respectfully alone. By contrast every time Roberto Carlos so much as got near the ball, the howls of derision and rage would rain down from the ramparts.

Maybe – for much the same reason that rival fans abused Florentino Pérez's mother – because he was so good; because they would have so loved to have had him on their side. They would have been right to feel that way. No player in the world was more fun, more exciting, to watch.

My friend Sebastián, the Bernabéu season-ticket holder, always used to say that on the day that Roberto Carlos left, or retired, there would be a vacuum on the left side of the Real team. 'We'll feel orphaned the day he goes,' Sebastián would say. 'After he leaves they should play without a left back for a year so we can try and forget him, though we never will. His departure will be desperately sad, like a little death for us fans who have savoured him – we have almost come to take his genius for granted – down the years.'

Sebastián was right. Funnily enough, Orlando the hotel porter in Medellín, had said almost exactly the same thing. He was not Spanish, he had never been to the Bernabéu, but when I asked him who his favourite player at Real Madrid was, this was what he said: 'Look, people talk a lot about Beckham, Raúl, Zidane. But for me – for me – Roberto Carlos is the man. How that player manages to exercise such an influence over the game from left back is for me one of the wonders of the world. He has given me so much pleasure over the years. I dread the day he stops playing. I really dread it!' I put it to Orlando – we could have spoken all day the two of us, though we knew nothing about each other's lives – I put it to him that Roberto Carlos had one grave problem in life: he played so well always that his Spanish fans, and maybe fans elsewhere, got used to him and stopped noticing just how good he was. Orlando nodded vigorously in agreement. 'It is a terrible injustice, you're right,' he said. 'I don't think people realise as much as they should just what a gem he is.'

Vicente del Bosque did, though. The coach was his biggest fan during the three and a half years they worked together. 'He is unique. Irreplaceable. A complete footballer,' del Bosque told me. 'I used to say to him that if he set his mind to it he could be a striker and be the top scorer in the league.' Was he as valued by the *Madridistas* as highly as he ought to be? I asked him. 'Not always. A year and a half ago I remember I was at a dinner for Real Madrid veterans and one famous ex-player whose name I won't mention but who played as a forward said that Roberto Carlos was not good in defence. At which point José Antonio Camacho, who don't forget was not only a great defender for Real Madrid but for Spain, turned to this famous player and said, "Listen, my friend, you and I are not worthy of tying Roberto Carlos' bootlaces." And he was right. The truth is that he is very good in defence and outstanding in attack. When he goes, yes, he will be the player that the fans will most miss. I agree with that. And you know what else, he is addicted to football. The ball is like a drug to him. He can be playing with a ball for an hour and a half before the start of a game. He is mad about the game, and it shows in everything about the way he plays it. And his impact is shown in the statistics. All the great triumphs of Real Madrid recently, he's been there, along with Raúl.' If he had to sum up Roberto Carlos in one sentence, I asked him, what would he say? 'He is two players in one,' del Bosque replied. 'Simple as that. And amazing as that.'

That was why pound for pound Roberto Carlos may have been, with the possible exception of Alfredo Di Stefano, the best purchase Real Madrid ever made. Eight seasons after Inter Milan let him go for the grotesquely cheap price of five million euros, he had broken Di Stefano's record of most games played by a foreigner for Real Madrid. The thing about Roberto Carlos was that – more than Di

Stefano, or Puskas or Zidane or anyone – he was a complete original. There had never been a left back like him in the history of the
game and there probably never would be again. He scored an average
of seven times a season when most left backs would be lucky to
score seven times in a career. And what goals! Always, without fail,
they were spectacular, screamers smashed into the back of the net
with extreme power, usually from outside the penalty area. 'He scores
incredible goals but he is also a super defender, and on top of that
he always puts on fantastic entertainment for the fans,' said Ronaldo,
talking about his Brazil and Real teammate in the week before that
superclásico against Barcelona. 'And he keeps up the same level game
after game. It is extraordinary. It is as if he gets younger every day.'

Ronaldo said that Roberto Carlos was his choice for the 2003
FIFA World Player of the Year (it yet again went to Zidane), whose
identity would be revealed later that month. Sven-Goran Eriksson,
the England manager, and Giovanni Trappatoni, the veteran coach
of the Italian national team, each pledged their votes for Roberto
Carlos. It was a scandal that he had never won it before. No other
player had a trophy haul more impressive. Since joining Real Madrid
in 1996 he had won three Spanish leagues, three European Cups
and played in two World Cup finals, one of which he won. People
used to say Ronaldo was a 'phenomenon'. They were wrong. It was
Roberto Carlos. He was a phenomenon of nature, a primal force.

Maybe it was because as a child, so the legend went, he played
barefoot and the ball he used was filled not with air but with sand.
Or maybe it had to do with the fact that from an early age he was
a sort of human ox, spending hour after hour in the fields alongside
his father carrying outrageously heavy loads of sugar cane. I talked
to him once about his childhood after training and he told me he
had been born on a large sugar estate, that his father had been a
desperately poor cane-cutter living and working on the estate, that
he had started working alongside his father at the age of twelve. 'It
was hard, hard, hard work,' he said, 'and I am sure it contributed to
making me the player and the man I am now. Though I do think
most of it was genetic, from my father, to whom I am physically
similar in many ways.'

Whatever the reason, Roberto Carlos's thighs were a wonder to behold. The Brazilian Football Association reported at the start of the 1998 World Cup that he owned the most thickly muscled thighs in the national squad, by some margin. At twenty-four inches in diameter, they were the same size as Muhammad Ali's when he was heavyweight champion of the world. Which might not have been all that remarkable were it not for the fact that at his peak Muhammad Ali was 6ft 3in and fifteen stone, while Roberto Carlos was 5ft 6in and ten stone.

The reason to dwell on these almost freakish vital statistics is that they have a direct bearing on the defining quality of Roberto Carlos's game. They called him *el hombre bala* – the bullet man – in Spain and he was, quite simply, the most explosive player in the world. For three reasons, all of them intrinsically connected with those legs of his. First there was his electric, almost Olympic sprinter's, pace. Anyone who had watched him pelt up and down the left wing at the Bernabéu down the years would not have been amazed to be told that he had been timed doing 100 metres in 10.6 seconds. Second, there is his long-distance runner's stamina, the reason why he is able to give his hyperactive all at the beginning as well as at the end of a game, a quality that won him the undying love of the Real Madrid faithful from day one. And of the players too. (Figo once joked to me that Roberto Carlos had 'no merit, no merit at all'. When I asked him why, Figo said that he was so naturally fit that unlike himself and all the other players who had to work hard in training to keep in shape, 'Roberto Carlos can just step off a plane after a fourteen-hour overnight flight from Brazil, go straight to the stadium, play 90 minutes and win the game for you on his own.')

And the third reason is the fierce, devastating power in that left foot of his. According to various detailed studies, he routinely fires the ball at a dumbfounding 105mph. And that is not all. Roberto Carlos imparts a unique 'bend' to the ball when he takes his famous free kicks, crazier even than anything Beckham can do. And because of the length and speed of his run-up, the effect was more than explosive – it was thrilling. Every free kick he took, anywhere in the world, caused the crowd to respond with a special sense of anticipation. It was not just the excitement, or trepidation, at the strong likelihood of the ball crashing into the net. It was also a sense that something bordering on the superhuman might happen. Because everywhere where they loved their football, the memory lingered of a stupefying free kick in a game between Brazil and France in 1997 when he bent the ball, defying every law of football physics, around the outside of a defensive wall with the outside of his left foot, from thirty-five yards, past a mute, helpless and utterly immobile Fabien Barthez and into the back of the net. There has never been a free kick like it, before or since.

To those seeking to make sense of the science of that left boot of his (a very small left boot, incidentally, the smallest in the Real Madrid dressing room), Roberto Carlos explained once that he was in the habit of striking his free kicks with his three outside toes, leaving the big toe and the index toe out of the picture altogether. 'I take a run-up of between six and eight metres to pick up speed,' he said, 'and I hit the ball dead centre, but always with the outside of the foot so that it will spin that way from right to left.'

If you caught him in a less guarded moment he would give you a less scientific explanation. As he said after scoring a goal against China in the 2002 World Cup, 'The truth is that I just fix the position of the target in my mind, close my eyes and try to hit it as hard as possible.'

What makes Roberto Carlos so thrilling to watch, as thrilling as anyone in the game, is that in addition to all that power and pace and speed of shot, he is a classically Brazilian player in the tradition of the generous artists who won the World Cup in Mexico in 1970. There have not been too many players since then, Brazilian or otherwise, who would have slotted into that team alongside Pelé, Tostão and Rivelino. But Roberto Carlos would have done so seamlessly. No one-dimensional piledriver, he flicks and backheels the ball as joyously as Zidane, crosses it (almost) with the accuracy of Luis Figo. Unlike Figo, whose on-field personality is morose, Roberto Carlos never ceases to exude good humour. He possesses in abundance that warm, tropical Brazilian *joie de vivre*. He seems always to be smiling, joking, laughing. Even when things are going badly for his team he will find time to make a sporting gesture to his rivals. Football for Roberto Carlos is circus as well as sport. And in this, his Brazilianness meshed with the time-honoured spirit that Florentino Pérez had striven to restore to Real Madrid. As a defender whose natural function was to attack, Roberto Carlos was the living expression of what the *el País* writer Santiago Segurola described as Real's 'congenital imbalance'. Which was exactly what one might have said about that Brazil 1970 side. Then there was his cavalier recklessness in defence. As the ever-acute Segurola also has observed, Roberto Carlos can be a danger not only to his rivals, but also to his own team. A textbook left back in the Paulo Maldini mould he is not. No one ever accused him of possessing an impeccable sense of positioning, of diligently preserving his defensive shape, of obsessively sticking to the coach's tactical formations.

Which is perhaps why he only lasted one season at Inter Milan, having previously triumphed in Palmeiras, where he twice won the Brazilian championship. Curiously, though, it was an English manager whom he blamed chiefly for what turned out to be his unhappiest year in football. Roy Hodgson, then Inter coach, did not seem to know what to do with him. 'It was a disaster,' Roberto Carlos said at the time. 'I need to play with freedom, and Hodgson didn't let me cross the halfway line.' So Inter sold him to Real Madrid at the end of the 1995/96 season. It was a huge mistake, as an Italian journalist from the newspaper *Tuttosport* was quick to point out. 'So he didn't enter into Hodgson's tactical scheme? When you have a player like Roberto Carlos in your team you don't have to adapt the footballer to the system, you adapt the system to the footballer.'

It was an Italian coach, Fabio Capello, who did just that for Roberto Carlos when the Brazilian player came to Real Madrid in 1996. The four coaches who followed Capello at the Bernabéu were equally wise. They let Roberto Carlos do his stuff and what they found, by and large, was that while his defensive acumen might not have been up to the highest standards of diligence, he made up for his tactical deficiencies, as well as for what some considered to be his excessive enthusiasm for joining the attack, by his sheer speed of recovery and fearsome power in the tackle.

Roberto Carlos's goals, his passes for goal, his passion for the game – contagiously transmitted to his teammates – were indispensable to Real's success over the years. Maybe Raúl was as important a figure. Maybe the previous captain Fernando Hierro was too. But the Brazilian was fireworks. No one outdazzled him.

This was remarkable, because his position was, after all, left back. There had never been a left back who tackled and covered as demonically as he did while exercising such a dominant influence over a game, posing such a permanent threat in attack. The most amazing thing about Roberto Carlos, more amazing even than his thunderous thighs, was that in reality he played in not one but three positions. He was, as they said in Spain, a footballing holy trinity. He was a defender, he was a midfielder but he was also an attacker – a winger who made and scored goals. In short, a terror to all rival teams.

Which in turn explained why at the Camp Nou they detested him so much. They detested him all the more after the game of 6 December was over. All Roberto Carlos's qualities were on dazzling display that night in Barcelona. Remorseless in defence, pitiless in attack, he won the game for Real. The final score was 2-1 for Real Madrid – putting to an end the sequence of twenty straight losses at the Camp Nou.

Roberto Carlos scored the first and set up the second. The goal, in the first half, was a Madrid classic. Fifty-yard pass from right to left by Beckham to Zidane. Control by Zidane as if someone had placed the ball on his foot with their hand. Roberto Carlos steams up like a locomotive behind Zidane's shoulder. Zidane slips it with perfect weight and direction in Roberto Carlos's path. Roberto Carlos lashes it from twenty-five yards into the back of the net. Then in the second half, after another charging run down the left Roberto Carlos opts, instead of going for another screamer himself, to do the sensible thing and slip the ball across to Ronaldo who, unmarked in front of the goalkeeper, tucks the ball away for goal number two. In between his two stellar cameos he played in defence like a man possessed, defying the baying hordes, cutting down his opponents in full flight, blessedly fortunate to get away with just the one yellow card.

12: Apotheosis Beckham

The instant the whistle blew signalling the end of Real Madrid's victory over Barcelona at the Camp Nou Beckham rushed towards Roberto Carlos and took him, with a cry of primal delight, in his arms, then kissed the top of his head and danced a little jig with him right there, in conquered Catalan territory, over the enemy grave. It was an image that, outside Catalunya, made all the front pages next morning. 'The fans loved David for that,' José Angel Sánchez, staggered by Beckham's capacity to win over the *Madridistas*, told me later. 'That image of him and Roberto Carlos jigging at the Camp Nou: the fans see that and they see that he is a fan too, that he understands what it means to beat Barça in Barcelona, that he has made the history and tradition – just like that – his own.'

But greater love had no fan for Beckham than Beckham had for Roberto Carlos. The two had a special bond in the Real dressing room. Beckham had said in an interview the week before the Barça game that the person who had had the greatest impact on his life since arriving in Spain had been the Brazilian. 'Roberto Carlos,' said Beckham, 'has treated me as if I were his son or his brother.'

A few years earlier the two were in America doing a photoshoot for Pepsi-Cola, a company that sponsored them both. It was a team photograph, with two or three other players in it. The American photographer apparently had little idea of the significance of the individuals he had before him.

Not only was he not impressed with these football luminaries, he was downright disrespectful, making some disparaging remarks about Roberto Carlos's small size. It seems the Brazilian was spoiling the symmetry of the image, and so the photographer made some crack about making 'the short guy' stand on a crate of bottles. Roberto Carlos did not understand. But Beckham did and he immediately let the photographer know it, stepping towards him angrily and ordering the bewildered photographer to watch his mouth or the two footballers would walk off the set. Roberto Carlos was confused, but when it was explained to him what had happened the seeds of a friendship were sown.

Real's director of sport Jorge Valdano's loyalty to Beckham was growing by the day too. I found myself sitting in the back of a car with Valdano in Barcelona the weekend of that 2-1 victory over the old enemy and I took advantage of the moment to ask him for his highly specialised assessment of Beckham's start at Real. I knew that originally he had not been entirely sure it was a good idea to buy him. I also knew that there was no more articulate football analyst than Valdano alive, none that combined his extraordinary experience as top-flight player and coach with such an intelligence and facility with words.

Had he been surprised, I asked him, at Beckham's management of his twin personalities, the celeb and the footballer? 'Beckham has a natural talent that you very rarely see in players for this business of projecting a public image,' Valdano began, 'but the most remarkable thing about him is that when he goes into football mode, when he is in the dressing room just prior to a game, he leaves all that completely behind. You're in the dressing room and you see him sitting down with his eyes fixed on a distant place. He has this gaze that tells you he has shut off the rest of the world, that he is focused completely on the game at hand. As if he had flicked a switch in his brain and now, beyond the game, there was nothing else, only darkness. Before a game I look at the players, I wonder what their state of mind is. I worry about some of them. Are their minds really in it, heart and soul? But with Beckham I have no worries whatsoever. His concentration is absolute.'

What did Beckham bring to the team that was new? 'Real Madrid is a team with a lot of unravelled threads. He knits the team together,' Valdano said, drawing a circle with his finger, indicating that what the Englishman did was cover the whole pitch, knitting – tidying up loose ends – everywhere he went. 'He is everywhere, like the Holy Spirit. And he's got that quality that you find in Argentine players of commitment, seriousness, pride, hating to lose. But he is cunning too, he has an intelligent football brain. He knows what the team needs and he does it.'

Perhaps Beckham's defining quality, Valdano said, was that he was a very 'primary' footballer. 'For all that gloss off the pitch, on it – when he is in his footballer persona – there is something pure and elemental about his relationship with the game. Maybe it has something to do with the English and the special connection they feel with the game they invented. There is a special love for the game in England and Beckham incarnates it. That's why it was so savage, so cruel of Ferguson to drop him for that game against us last season.'

I put it to Valdano that maybe the most remarkable thing about Beckham was this apartheid, this separating wall, that he seemed to have built in his mind between Beckham the footballer and Beckham the celebrity. 'Yes. Because the amazing thing is that despite all that other stuff, despite the fact that no one in the team generates anything like as much hysteria as Beckham does, he is the most professional player there is,' Valdano replied. 'You can't get more professional than Beckham. Other players moan and beef about how long the season is, how many games they have to play. He doesn't. When he is injured he insists on being allowed to play. He complains, he argues, he gets angry. He wants to play always. He's a boy who understands how fortunate he has been in life. He understands it very clearly. He knows he is one of the privileged of the earth. And he is never, ever going to complain again. With some players, yes, you find this culture of complaint. With Beckham it is quite the contrary. His enthusiasm to get on the pitch and play is constant and total.'

As for Beckham playing out on the right wing, Valdano – like del Bosque – had never understood what he had been doing out there in the first place. 'The games in which Roberto Carlos marked him in recent years – there were four or five, between Manchester United and England games, I think – Beckham was shown to be quite ineffective out wide. Roberto even gave him a few yards' start to make it more interesting but he always had him sown up. Beckham does not belong there, he hasn't the pace or the dribbling ability.' Playing deeper in central midfield, Valdano said that Beckham had become for Real something similar to what Roy Keane had been to Manchester United, the team's driving force.

The notion that Beckham should play on the right wing seemed quite ludicrous now, four months into Beckham's Real Madrid career. In fact, Queiroz had tried it once, when Figo was out injured, for an away game against the Pamplona side, Osasuna. Or rather he had tried it in the first half. Beckham looked out of sorts, clumsy, underemployed and Real Madrid went into the break 1-0 down. The evidence of those forty-five minutes had revealed once and for all how unsuited Beckham was to playing on the wing. Wingers, if they do nothing else, can take on players and beat them. They have liquid hips, fast feet and a sharp turn of speed. Beckham has none of these things. He is the field commander who directs play, with stiff elegance, from the middle. Queiroz switched him back there for the second half and within minutes he had laid on a *pase de fantasía*, as a Spanish sports newspaper described it, from which Ronaldo scored the game's equaliser.

In this honeymoon stage of Beckham's relationship with Real Madrid, when the team played well, Beckham played well. When the team played badly, Beckham played well. Games that the previous season would have ended in defeat for Real, ended in draws now that he was in the team. And games that would have ended in draws, ended in victory.

The fans understood this, not least my friends round at the *La Amistad* bar, my favourite *Madridista* enclave in Catalan country. I went round there a few days after that victory against Barcelona to revel in the gloating and to watch what was a pretty meaningless last Champions League group game at home against Porto, Real having already assured top place.

There must have been a dozen *Madridistas* there, all working-class men, mostly immigrants from other parts of Spain, like my friend Angel the taxi driver and his best buddy, and dominoes partner, Rafa. I conducted a little poll. I put the question to them, Who had been the best Real player of the season so far? Never mind Roberto Carlos, or anybody else – the consensus was absolute. Everybody agreed that the best player of the season so far had been *el Inglés*. These men loved nothing more than to have a raging argument about who was best and who was worst and whether Helguera's natural position was midfield or central defence and so forth, but here there was nothing to talk about. Why? *'Porque tiene un par de cojones, aquel inglés.'* 'Because he has a pair of balls, that Englishman.'

As it turned out, Beckham – along with most of the Galácticos – was rested for that game against Porto, which ended 1-1. He was on the bench, though, and it did look at one point as if he might come on. Right at the end he began limbering up as if he were going to trot on for the final minutes. The crowd got excited, a buzz went around the ground, but in the end Queiroz decided to give him the night off. Tomás Roncero, the *Madridista*-in-chief at *AS*, lamented Beckham's no-show. 'Because going to see Real Madrid without Beckham,' Roncero wrote, 'is like going to Paris and not seeing the Eiffel Tower.'

Beckham did play five days later in the home game against Deportivo la Coruña. It was his Madrid apotheosis.

The stadium was packed, as usual, but there was a special air of expectancy. Along with Valencia, Deportivo had been consistently Real's toughest league rivals over the previous five years. Like Valencia they were a compact team, hard working, speedy, as strong in defence as in attack. Just a year and a half earlier they had ruined Real Madrid's centenary celebrations by beating them in the Spanish Cup final, the *Copa del Rey*, at the Bernabéu.

Playing according to conventional rules of football engagement, with a fraction of the budget, based in a city with twelve times fewer inhabitants than Madrid, Deportivo had become a force not only in Spain but in Europe, counting Manchester United and Arsenal among their recent Champions League scalps.

But Deportivo did not have Beckham and Roberto Carlos in their team. And they didn't have Beckham and Roberto Carlos for the fans to feast on during the pre-match warm-ups. One of the pleasures for me of watching Real Madrid live, in the stadium, was this warm-up, and in particular a routine that the England captain and his Brazilian chum always engaged in for three or four minutes before heading back to the changing room.

Beckham would position himself on one touchline, Roberto Carlos across the pitch on the other and they would float fifty-yard passes back and forth to one another. It was a joy to behold. Roberto Carlos's passes were always pin-point accurate, but sometimes they landed a bit short, more often a little long, at waist or shoulder height. Every single Beckham pass – it was uncanny – landed metronomically at Roberto Carlos's feet, dropping always in such a manner as to minimise the effort required to control it. Like that 'flan' – that crème caramel – pass he had made for Zidane's volleyed goal against Valladolid. The trajectory of Roberto Carlos's passes, by contrast, was flatter. Beckham's rose higher, carried more spin. I was so engrossed watching the elegance, artistry and precision of the two of them stroking the ball back and forth to one another before the start of that Deportivo game that a journalist friend tapped me on the shoulder and, laughing, suggested I close my mouth so as to keep out the flies.

Re-reading a wonderful book on football by Eamon Dunphy called *Only a Game*, I understood a little better just why I had been so rapt watching them. It was that I had been privy, like a voyeur, to an intimate moment between them. 'If you are just knocking a ball between you, on a training ground, a relationship develops between you,' writes Dunphy, a wonderfully gifted player in his day who played professionally in England and for the Irish national team. 'It's a form of expression – you are communicating as much as if you are making love to somebody. It's an unspoken relationship, but your movements speak, your game speaks. You don't ncessarily become closer in a social sense, but you develop a close unspoken understanding.'

The unsurprising fact is that footballers are very rarely masters of the spoken language. Interviews with famous footballers, so vigorously sought by journalists, are usually a disappointment. Speaking well is not what most footballers do, any more than playing football in front of 80,000 people is what journalists do. A major exception was Jorge Valdano, who even in his playing days would read – among many other things – the Byzantine works of his Argentine compatriot Jorge Luis Borges, on whom Valdano became something of an authority. When he was playing for Real Madrid in the late Eighties, Valdano once wrote a column in *el País* criticising US policy in Central America.

But Valdano was, in that respect, an aberration. Beckham and Ronaldo, Zidane and Roberto Carlos and most other professional footballers – do not read Borges. Nor do they dedicate their time off the field to analysing the finer points of international diplomacy. But they are masters of that football language Eamon Dunphy speaks off.

I watched the football bards in action at the Real Madrid training ground the day before that game against Deportivo. I kept my eyes particularly on Beckham, for whom English was of little use. What became immediately obvious was that he had shed whatever timidity he may have had in his first weeks with his teammates. His Spanish was not up to much, though, so he talked with feet and ball. It was fascinating to see how he did it, how he made jokes with his passes, how he teased teammates with his shots on goal.

Casillas the goalkeeper would have his back to him and, from ten yards or so away, he would hit him with the ball on the back of the legs. But gently. Casillas would look around to see who it had been. Beckham looked away, continued solemnly with his training routine, playing the innocent. Then he caught Casillas's eye and laughed. Casillas shook his head, pretended to look annoyed. And so it went on. He kidded around worldlessly with his teammates. More often than not I noticed that Beckham engaged with the lesser figures in the team, the reserve goalkeeper Cesar, or the beningly oafish fourth-choice centre half Rubén who suffered so in Sevilla.

As if to reinforce the point that he did not see himself as a super-ior figure, for all the celebrity and acclaim. As if to make the point that he really did see himself, within the team, as one more, which went down well with all the players, the Galácticos included. Where the Galácticos were in a class of their own was in their passing the ball around to each other. Iván Helguera once admitted in a press conference early on in the season that for him to go and train with the likes of Zidane and Figo was a refined form of spectator sport. 'I could just stop what I'm doing, sit down and watch them all day,' Helguera said. That was how I felt watching Beckham and Roberto Carlos before that Deportivo game. I didn't even need the game to start. This was entertainment enough.

When I read the line-ups of the two teams I did receive a bit of a jolt. Not for the first time I was struck by the callow leanness of the Real Madrid bench, compared to the Deportivo one. Real's first eleven were on another planet, of course, but their bench consisted of Miñambres, Rubén, Borja, Cambiasso, Solari. The last two, Argentines both, had been around but the first three – pure Pavones from the Real youth ranks – had no more than about 200 minutes of first-team playing experience between them. The Deportivo subs – Cesar, Pandiani, Fran, Munitis and Victor – may not have been exactly house-hold names beyond their home town but they were massively expe-rienced, with about 1,000 completed First Division games behind them. Not for the first time the thought struck that this team could find itself severely caught out in the event of a Galáctico or two being ruled out of action. The thought seemed quite redundant, banished to the deeper recesses of the mind, a couple of hours later, as all those of us who watched the game basked in the afterglow of a pulsating clash, which Real won 2-1, and another masterpiece from Zidane. Beckham was commanding and combative in midfield, as the Bernabéu now expected him to be, but as he himself knew better than anybody he was not in the same bracket as Zidane in terms of sheer art. Theatre, though, is one thing the Englishman does well. And we saw it once again at the end of this game.

The whistle blew and he headed purposefully, at a fast walking pace, towards Lionel Scaloni, an Argentine Deportivo player with whom he had been having a bit of a running battle – a yellow card each included – in the last minutes of the game. Knowing full well that the eyes of the stadium's 80,000 fans were on him, he squared up to Scaloni, chest to chest. It was a classic act of old style Spanish machismo, of male honour displayed, sated, satisfied; but done in the correct and most demanding old Spanish style – with class, with authenticity, with flourish; and without fear, looking the adversary straight in the eye.

And then, just when things threatened to get nasty, he looked away, turned his gaze towards the fans massed around the mighty stage and, with masterly composure, raised his hands in grateful applause for their support. The matador, had gone nose to nose with the sweating bull, flaunting his control and superiority, and then disdainfully turned away to receive the acclaim of the multitudes. That Beckham, a working-class lad from London and new arrival in

Spain, should instinctively have understood all of this and then pulled it off, offered a clue as to the success of his celebrity persona, revealed very strikingly that his natural-born talents did go beyond kicking a football. Beckham, playing the part of the ancient Spanish *hidalgo* to the hilt, had faced down the foe and vanquished them in a way that Spain still cherishes and celebrates – not with brutish blows but with nobility, refinement, grace and courage. With *señorío*.

The Bernabéu loved it and repaid the compliment with full-voiced tribute to the man who, more than any other, had played all season as if winning were a matter of life and death. As he headed down towards the players' tunnel the chant 'Beckham! Beckham! Beckham!' rung around the ground.

He should have had his mobile phone with him. He had done a TV commercial a few weeks earlier for Vodafone that had enraged Alex Ferguson. It showed him, Beckham, house-hunting in Madrid on a bright sunny day. He is on his mobile to his two big mates at United, the brothers Gary and Phil Neville. They are huddling from the Manchester rain in what looks like a bus shelter. Beckham sends them a photograph of the sunny blue sky from the camera built into his phone. When Ferguson saw the commercial he went 'berserk', according to a report in the *Guardian*, 'because he thinks it high-lights the perception of Europe's elite that bugs him the most – that Manchester United are inferior to Real Madrid'.

Imagine Ferguson's feelings had he witnessed Beckham, the last man off the pitch, that evening. It was Beckham's great moment of glory, an ovation as heartfelt as any he had received. It was the moment he understood, if he had not before, that in barely five months they had come to love him as much at Real Madrid as they ever had in thirteen years at Manchester United. He almost recognised as much in a newspaper interview published on 29 December. 'I'm proud,' he said, 'about the way I've responded to the challenge and it thrills me to see how the Madrid fans have responded to me. I couldn't be happier than I am now in Madrid.' And the great thing was that he had proved that point of his. 'There were people who said before I came that I wasn't good enough to play in Spain but these five months here have been unbeatable for me.' As for the highlight of those five months, it was that send off he received after the Deportivo game. 'That moment,' he said, 'was right up there with any of the best things I've done.'

I spoke to Pérez that very day the interview came out in his office. He was thrilled at the memory of that ovation his fourth Galáctico had received from the hard-bitten Bernabéu faithful, but glowing still more at the recollection of that wholehearted reaction of his – that embrace with Roberto Carlos – to victory at the Camp Nou. The warmth of that cherished moment, coupled with his gratitude to Beckham for having delivered all season on the faith he had invested in him, and his appreciation of the manner in which he had absorbed the emotional significance of beating Barcelona away – all of it and more combined for this dry, self-denying grey-suited businessman in a blue shirt to say to me, with feeling, 'You know, I am in love with David Beckham.'

And Beckham, as he had revealed in that end-of-year interview, was in love with Pérez and Real Madrid. What he had achieved in those few months since the day of his inauguration as a Real player, the day he said to me in that television interview that his dream was to prove a point by finding his way into a permanent position in the team with the greatest players on earth, had been – to repeat the most overused word in the Spanish media when they talk about him – extraordinary. In terms of solitary feats – for while he played a team game the courage and talent and personality he showed had been his own – what Beckham had done at Real Madrid ranked among the great sporting achievements of recent memory. After that Deportivo game Roberto Carlos told an interviewer in São Paulo that he had been stunned by his new teammate's level of play. 'If Beckham continues playing like this he will soon be the best player in the world,' the Brazilian said. That might have been a slight exaggeration, an overeffusion of camaraderie. Beckham summed up his start at Real less grandiosely, but with greater force. With the pride of a man who has swept away all the doubters and well and truly proved a point, he said, quite simply, 'I am in the best team in the world and I have shown that I know how to play football.'

13: The Coach as Martyr

The word tragedy derives from the Greek word *tragoedia* which means 'goat song'. No one knows for sure why a play in which the hero invariably ends up getting killed should be associated with goats or songs. But the generally accepted conjecture is that in ancient Greece the custom existed of sacrificing goats as a placatory offering to the gods; the sacrifice of the tragic hero held the same symbolic meaning as the ritual slaughter of the goat: it purged a people's sins, restored health to society, got the gods on their side once again.

Sophocles, Euripides and company were on to something there. In the family, in politics, at work: people always need someone to blame. Once the guilty party has been identified everybody else feels much better. In football, it is the same. When teams lose it is important for the mental health of the fans to find an individual on whom to pin the cause of failure. Ninety-nine times out of a hundred this individual will be the coach. Sooner or later, since all human enterprises – football being no exception – are doomed to failure, he is subjected to the ritual sacrifice colloquially known as getting the chop. At which point order – or its appearance – is restored; and hope springs anew.

What it is that constitutes a successful coach, fleeting as success inevitably is, is one of the game's great enigmas. People have their theories. They say a coach ought to have a better than average understanding of how to organise a defence, how to assess a player's abilities. That he should be a natural leader, able to enthuse. But lots of coaches will claim to have these qualities – vaguely defined as they are – and little good does it do them. What the formula for success consists of, nobody knows. There is only one thing that one can say with any certainty: that some coaches will work well with certain players in certain teams for a certain period of time. And that's it. After a while the team, and with it the coach, will start to fade. A coach that has been successful with one team will move to another and, likely as not, be a miserable failure. It happens all the time. It is the rule.

But there is one rule that applies still more pertinaciously; one rule, and one alone, that applies always and everywhere. It is this: that the chief function of a football coach is to provide an emotional outlet for frustrated fans; that he is there to be whipped; that he is there, when the time comes, to be sacrificed. In short, he is a professional scapegoat. Martyrdom is his ineluctable fate because the bad times shall assuredly come and it is only once he has fallen that the gods may be prevailed upon to smile on the team once again.

Things were going great for Real Madrid when I went to see Carlos Queiroz in his office one afternoon in early February 2004 after training. They were top of the Spanish league, in the semi-finals of the Spanish Cup and heading confidently for their big game, when the Champions League resumed a week later, with Bayern Munich. The other newcomer, David Beckham, had inevitably gathered all the attention. The Englishman's start at Real had been phenomenal. But what about Queiroz? His achievement had been at least as impressive, surely? Little known in the broad football world when he left his post as number two to Alex Ferguson – having previously been an itinerant coach in places as far afield as South Africa, the United Arab Emirates, Japan and the US – he seemed to provide yet another example of the Pérez Midas Touch. Queiroz had been at first sight an eccentric choice as Real Madrid coach. It was Valdano who had picked him out, detecting in him a blend of experience, intelligence, sensibility and worldliness – not only had he worked in five continents, he could communicate in five languages – that seemed to mesh well with Pérez's large global aspirations. More importantly, he fitted in with Pérez's notion that players of Galáctico calibre barely needed a coach because by definition they were so intelligent and so self-motivated. What this Real Madrid team needed, Pérez said, was 'minimum orders and maximum freedom'. 'You couldn't possibly have the Italian regimented type of coach, or an overbearing personality like Alex Ferguson, with players like these,' Pérez told me. A big name, a Galáctico coach who would wish to impose his own hard-and-fast methods on the Galáctico players, was therefore decidedly not in line with the Pérez dogma. Free expression was the key. Tactics were of overwhelming importance when you had ordinary players in your team; they were secondary when your players were world stars. The low-key Queiroz seemed, in all of these respects, to fit the bill perfectly.

Getting the Real Madrid job, he told me, was 'a gift from God'. But he was not smiling when he said it. It was a statement of fact rather than an expression of joy. Queiroz might have chosen to see his first seven months at Real as God's reward for his courage in accepting the job, for the application he had shown in his coaching duties, for the inventiveness he had shown – given Florentino Pérez's refusal to buy him defenders – in redeploying Beckham as a defensive midfielder, in making a central defender out of Raúl Bravo, who had previously peformed as a singularly unimpressive left back, and in dredging the promisingly cocky Alvaro Mejía up from the reserves to join Bravo when needed in central defence. But Queiroz refused to be impressed by his own achievements. Rather, there was an aura of provisionality about him when I met him, a resigned air, as if he were steeling himself for the day when he would add his carcass to the charnel house of slaughtered football coaches.

Queiroz wore a wary expression on his face for much of the two hours that we talked. Nothing to do with me. It was the way he was, or that his experience of war and football had taught him to be. His eyes said it all. He was an intriguing-looking man: tall, lean and grave, with a spartan air like a priest, but what really struck you when you saw him in the flesh were his remarkable eyes. They were a watery blue-grey with a hint of purple and tucked deep as caves on a cliff face under two heavy, jutting brows. They were alert eyes but mournful, brimming with the wisdom that comes from having suffered some hard knocks.

How did he deal, I asked him, with the constant complaints a coach is fated to receive? 'Have you heard the story,' he shot back,

as if ready for the question, 'of the donkey, the boy and the old man?'
No I had not. 'Well, the boy was riding the donkey and the old man
was walking alongside. They came across some people on the road
who said, "How can it be that the old man is walking, at his age?"
So the boy got off and the old man got on the donkey. Then they
came across some more people who said, "How can that boy be
walking, him being so little?" So they both got on the donkey and
they came across some more people, who said they thought it was
unfair on the donkey to be carrying so much weight, so then they
both got off, but people still carried on complaining . . . Well, you
see. This job is the same. That's the way it is and you have to accept
it. The trick is not to pay too much attention otherwise you'll never
get anything done.'

If things did end in disappointment, I put it to him, he might at
least have the consolation of finding allies when the time came to
point the finger of blame at Florentino Pérez and his insistence on
playing such a recklessly attacking game. The coach of Osasuna, the
outspoken Mexican Javier Aguirre, had recently said that Queiroz
had done a brilliant job, especially given the *embolao* – the dog's
breakfast – Pérez had bequeathed him. What, in fact, did Queiroz
make of the Pérez revolution?

'What the president thinks, his style and opinions, we must respect,'
he replied, like the good soldier that he was. 'The president is like
an ideologue, he has an ideal project in mind. But he is also – don't
forget – an engineer by training. He must understand that you cannot
just have dreams, you have to build them. Jules Verne dreamt of going
to the moon but science, the engineers, provided the mechanisms
to get there. The president has a dream, say, to win a contract with
his company to build a train line that goes to ten cities – but in the
end it is his engineers who will tell him how to do it, millimetre
by millimetre. My opinion, the way I follow my president, is this: I
too believe that traditions are made to be broken. Old routines belong
to the past by definition. But – but – what you cannot do is change
the nature of the game. Verne had his dreams but the nature of the
moon is such that there is no oxygen there, and that you cannot
change. The nature of the game of football is that the ball is round,

and a game has two moments, when you have the ball and when you don't. Therefore you must be able to attack and you must be able to defend. My duty as the engineer in this case is to find a solution in defence with Zizou [the name in the dressing room for Zidane] and Guti and Beckham. You cannot change the nature of the game: it is about winning, and we have to beat Bayern Munich, because the sense of joy in football in the big competitions is that which is associated with winning. So while this Real Madrid team is something wonderful, something unique in the world, for this project to succeed we must always strive to find the right harmony between breaking traditions – smashing orthodoxies, if you like – and showing respect for the nature of the game.'

Queiroz's reply was so artfully constructed as to admit the possibility, in a literal interpretation, that he was perfectly happy with his *embolao*. Yet the message he was transmitting was clear enough. Without saying it in so many words, he did feel that that harmony he spoke of was lacking at Real Madrid; that had he been given a replacement for Makelele to shore up the defence from midfield, or a top-class central defender to plug the gaps the midfield had left, he would have been a happier engineer, would have felt more confident of achieving his president's celestial ambitions. 'What we try and do is minimise the areas where we are less strong. And we do that not by asking Zidane to become Makelele but by asking all six players in front of the defenders to contribute to the cause when the other team has the ball.' His fear was that in a month or two, at the sharp end of the season, in March, the unnatural effort players like Zidane had been making in defence would begin to tell; that injuries and suspensions would disrupt the team's already fragile equilibrium. Yet it all seemed to be going well enough at this point. No wonder Pérez did not feel it necessary to heed his and Valdano's clamours for new players. Queiroz was on course for all three trophies Real were competing to win, and – on the surface, at any rate – there seemed little reason for him to be hang-dog about the team's prospects. In fact the *futbolero* fraternity as a whole had rolled over, the sceptics had accepted that under Queiroz's wise guardianship the Pérez model was – in violation of all the orthodoxies – working. The doubters in the Spanish sports press had given up complaining about the team's lack of balance and submitted to Pérez's superior wisdom. Alfredo Relaño, the editor of *AS*, had spoken for many in his profession when he had declared five weeks earlier at an end of year journalists' lunch that all their convoluted theorising about football had been revealed to be hollow words by Real Madrid's scintillating performances on the field. 'Florentino,' Relaño declared only half-jokingly, 'has exposed us!'

Queiroz did not buy that. He refused to share in the spirit of complacency that seemed to have enveloped the club. He insisted to me that there were reasons for concern. Quite apart from his fear that the team's defensive frailties would not stand up to the rigours of an increasingly difficult schedule, he worried that the players' bodies might not sustain the required level of competitive ferocity over the course of a full season. 'They do not always have fresh legs or fresh minds,' he said. 'It is not the players' fault, or – for that matter – the coach's. It is the system: all these games! It would be interesting to see what happened if you asked Pavarotti to sing at Barcelona's stadium and then asked him to perform two days later in a bar before forty people and two days after that in a hotel and then at the Bernabéu. It would tell you something about Pavarotti's levels of motivation. It would tell you that he cannot sustain the same high level each and every time.'

How were these guys up close and personal? How was it to coach those he himself described as this 'unique and wonderful' set of players? 'It is – I must use the same word, forgive me – a unique experience. You cannot apply the lessons here from other coaching experiences. This is different. There are huge personalities here, some of the most important individuals in the game. Some are more than players, more than men: they are events, companies, some are individual industries. The secret to dealing with them as a coach, I believe, is to combine freedom and respect for the individual with a sense of team harmony; to establish the space and limits of our common interest. Very important to define this idea of the common interest, which is not a question of rules or authority but of shared commitment to an objective, and it is this that makes us work together. That team pride is the thing. They really, really understand this sense of common interest; they know that individuals alone cannot satisfy the champion spirit, because you cannot be champions alone. Therefore the task for me is simple, because they really are champions, they really are big stars. Which is different from people who think they are big stars but are not.'

What was a big star? Were these Galáctico players of his in the first instance special humans, bountifully blessed by genetic fortune? 'Yes,' said Queiroz, solemnly. 'Yes they are . . . You see, in the end I am a football romantic. I am as one with the bedrock philosophy of this club, of the president. I am not as concerned with the league or the European Cup as I am with playing great, quality football. Of course, I believe that if we play beautifully – if we follow the example of the great Brazil side of 1970, which shaped all my foot-ball dreams – our chances of winning are much increased.' Talk about your beautiful players, I said to him. Having enjoyed the privilege of watching them up close, closer than anybody, those previous seven months, how did he define their genius?

'First,' he said, really warming to his subject, 'they are the finest athletes. Independent of the sport they happen to be playing, they are champions. You find football players who are great at what they do but are not champions, which means having a winning mentality.

'Second, they are more than professional players – they are masters of the game; teachers of the game. Zizou, Figo, Roberto Carlos: hundreds of coaches around the world and millions of players are following them on television, watching their every move, learning from them. Every game they invent a new play, every day there is something new, different from what the rest do. They continually reinvent and regenerate the game – the old game which some of us thought had nothing new to teach us.

'Third, they have different skills and above all a different vision of the game. They can see things more quickly than others, assess a situation more quickly, see things that we cannot see in a game. Imagine two cars colliding, for us it happens at normal speed; they see it in slow motion, they catch a lot more details in the same time as us; they can compute in their minds more details than you and I can see. Therefore they have more time than others, the great ones. They see the game in slow motion but it is really in normal time.'

More than anything else the quality that Queiroz the coach, as opposed to Queiroz the fan, most valued in the Real superstars was their authenticity. I put to him Florentino Pérez's point that it was a mistake to distinguish between celebrity players and great footballers; that one by definition went with the other. 'I agree completely,' he said. 'They have got to where they are, they have become world famous, because in the end they are the real professionals of the game. The difference between a professional and a guy who is paid to play football is a difference in attitude. A professional for me is a player who always plays at the extreme of his ability, to the limit, always gives his best, someone who was born with the ability to fly, and so asks the question, "Why walk?" And, let me say this right away because people say a lot of silly ignorant things: it is not a question of money or recognition or receiving honour. No. It is about passion for the game, it is about pride. These top, top players have a profound awareness of their specialness, of their unique talent, that goes beyond arrogance: that just *is*. You cannot lie to the game. You especially cannot lie to the other players. They know the real thing when they see it, and these guys are it.'

14: The Dancing Master

Hundreds of years from now museum visitors will stand in reverent silence before the collected works of Zinedine Zidane. They will admire video sequences of goals the French master scored, supreme among which will be the volley from edge of penalty area to roof of net that won Real Madrid the European Cup against Bayer Leverkusen in Glasgow. But connoisseurs of the ancient discipline, future footballing PhD's, may form a more lasting attachment to the rarer points of Zidane's art; they may be more taken by the subtleties of his cushioned first touch, more entranced by the great goals that never were.

Irrespective of anything else that might have happened in the football world in 2004, and long after everyone had forgotten who won what, Zidane conjured a moment of magic that you knew – right then and there – would stand the test of time. The date was 1 February and Real Madrid were away to Valladolid, the team against which Zidane had contrived another masterpiece – the volleyed goal on the run from a fifty-metre Beckham cross – in September. The build-up before Zidane became involved was in itself a thing of beauty. Guti, an unpredictable player of exquisite touch, beat a man in midfield then, precise as a billiard player, rolled the ball to Ronaldo on the D of the penalty area. The Brazilian, with three defenders around him, placed his foot on the ball, then – in a flash – rolled it with his studs into the path of Zidane, who arrived over his right shoulder like a train. The Frenchman had a Valladolid player to beat before he could have a clear shot on goal. What the big man did next would be imprinted for ever in the memories of all those who saw it. He did not feint right, to go left. He did not feint left, to go right. He did not attempt to slip the ball through the defender's legs. He performed, instead, a piruoette; a 360-degree spin in the penalty area that left his rival for dead.

Collecting Ronaldo's pass on the run, floating as he always seemed to be one inch above the ground, he pinged the ball from his right foot to his left, at the very same instant initiating an anti-clockwise rotation of his body. Halfway through the electric-quick turn, in the split second when his body was turned towards his own teammates, he slid his left foot back over the ball, dragging it along in the direction of the rival goal. The momentum of the swivel allowed him to complete the pirouette and now he was facing again in the direction in which he started when he received the pass from Ronaldo, but with only the goalkeeper to beat, the defender he had squared up to a millisecond before having been calamitously wrong-footed, lost, fatally out of the picture over to his left. Zidane should have shot immediately but did not, as if wishing to savour for one instant more the magnificent bravado of the moment, as if paralysed by the collective intake of breath of the 26,000 souls packed into the ground. The hesitation lasted no longer than the pirouette but it was enough to give the goalkeeper a chance to come out and narrow the angle, force Zidane a degree or two wider than he would ideally have wished, obliging him to strike the ball a shade off-balance and send the shot just wide, just high of the goal.

No matter. It had been a moment of pure magic. The praise rained down from the football firmament, none more heartfelt than from the best judges of all, his own Galáctico teammates. 'There is only one word for that, fantastic,' said Ronaldo, who scored two fantastic enough goals of his own that night. 'That could have been the greatest goal in the history of the game.' Roberto Carlos said there was 'only one word to describe something like that, genius'. Raúl shook his head in wonder and said, 'Only Zidane is capable of doing a thing like that'. As for Beckham, Zidane had merely offered him further confirmation of why he had been right to move to Real Madrid. 'It's just a delight to be there on the same pitch watching him play,' said the Englishman who had once described him as 'a ballerina'. 'He's just so beautiful to watch. Stunning!' Figo, who was reputed to have been jealous of Zidane when he first arrived at Real, did not hold back either. 'What can you say about a player who can do things like that? It's incredible. He's out of the movies.'

Valdano, who could usually be relied upon to come up with a choice phrase at moments like this one, did not disappoint. Comparing Zidane's Valladolid effort with a similarly memorable miss by Pelé in the 1970 World Cup, Valdano said the Frenchman represented 'the aesthetic summit of the game, a synthesis between the harmony of the players of the Danube [meaning Hungary] of the Fifties, the cunning of the Argentines, the skill of the Brazilians'. What you ought to do with Zidane, the ever-metaphorical Valdano said, was 'take out the black box and create from it a football textbook'.

Somewhere in the cortex of his brain rested the black box that contained the mysteries of the Frenchman's flight. But we had no idea how to decode it, any more than we were able to define in human language the balletic genius of Rudolf Nureyev. Zidane himself – as prosaic off the field as he was poetic on it – would not get close, though he did have his theory, his one theory of what it was all about.

I spoke to him once. Just once. The Greta Garbo of football, he shunned interviews. He was the most expensive player by far in the history of football. His face was among the ten best known in the world. In his own country, where victory in the 1998 World Cup was greeted with scenes not remembered on the Champs Elysées since the liberation of Paris in 1944, he was practically a national monument. A poll at the end of 2003 found him to be, unsurprisingly and not for the first time, the most admired individual in France. And yet he was a man who had never sought, much less wanted, celebrity. A quiet family man whose wife one never saw, he did not feel comfortable talking about himself. He did it because he had to, because it was part of his job as a Real Madrid player and Adidas name. Ushered into a room at the Real training centre to talk to me by a Real employee who had acted as intermediary between us, he looked as if he had been dragged in at gunpoint. Leaner and younger in the flesh than he looked on television, he shook my hand thinly, eyes searching not mine but the room. Dressed in a dark suit and tie, for he had an official Real Madrid function to attend later in the morning, he could have been a shy, middle-ranking corporate executive. Once we got talking he was – while never brimming with enthusiasm like Raúl, or oozing light charm, like Beckham – attentive enough, respectful in his replies. That was a big word for him, respect, one whose importance was drummed into him from an early age by his Algerian immigrant father. In the interviews he had been obliged to give since propelling himself to world fame with the two goals he scored in France's 3-0 1998 World Cup final victory over Brazil, respect was a recurrent theme. He was right. Lack of respect probably accounted for ninety per cent of the conflicts humanity was prey to – as well as for a good number of defeats by strong football teams to weaker ones. 'You must be respectful of others,' he said, as if this were a lesson he felt obliged to preach when preach he had to.

But what I wanted to know about was that nearly-goal against Valladolid. That move, had he practised it a thousand times, I asked? 'The roulette, you mean?' Yes, I said, guessing that must be his name for it, the roulette. 'No, not a thousand times. More than a thousand times. Much more. Thousands and thousands of times.' When did he first practise it? 'That particular move? Since I was fifteen or sixteen, half my football life ago. I have repeated it over and over again. But in that game you speak of there was no goal. It was pretty, but no more. A gesture, that's all.'

Geste was the word in French. Gesture was the correct translation but it did not quite catch the meaning of the original, which conveyed an idea of motion with elegance. It was a word he used often, for example in a DVD in which he did his own explanation of the 'roulette' – 'A *geste* which I like a lot and love pulling off. It consists of beating your opponent by making the turn of a wheel in the direction of the rival goal. As I am right-footed I take the ball with the right foot, pass it to my left and, turning at the same time, off I run with it. It's something to do to have fun with your friends in the neighbourhood. But in a stadium it's difficult. I only do it if I am absolutely sure of my mastery over the ball, otherwise you run the risk of looking ridiculous.'

Far from ridiculous, the roulette against Valladolid had been breath-takingly memorable, something the likes of which had not been seen in a stadium before. Surely that was enough? Surely he should not lament, the way he seemed to, the fact that it did not end in a goal? 'The important fact is that it did not end in a goal,' he said, putting an end to the subject. 'So it was only a *geste*.'

Being respectful seemed to include, in Zidane's mind, being humble. Which was probably right, because if he were not humble with all that talent he possesed, if he were straightforward, he would never cease to intimidate. Juanma Trueba of *AS* once made the wonder-fully well-observed point that after Zidane scored one of those goals of his that only he can score 'he laughs, but not without a hint of embarrassment'. As if he were not comfortable drawing attention to himself, as if he had done something boastful that was not in tune with the sort of person he was or wished to be. Zidane, perhaps more than any other sportsman since Muhammad Ali, floated like a butterfly and stung like a bee. But he would never say as much. He would never have cried, as Ali always did, 'I am a dancing master, a great artist' – though he was both of those things.

Thus it was that when I asked him about another magnificent *geste* of his, but this time one that did end in goal, like an Ali knockout punch, his instinct once again was to deflect attention away from his genius. I meant the volley in the first game against Valladolid at the Bernabéu. 'Yes, it was a good goal, but the most important thing was the pass,' he said. 'It was so perfect. It fell so well for me.' As if it had been placed there for him with the hand rather than a kick fifty yards long, I said, remembering my friend Luis Angel's aerodynamic analysis? 'Yes, that's right' he said, smiling for the first time, revealing a perfect row of white teeth and a face as handsome as that of the man who made the pass, but so much more discreetly concealed. 'It was as if he had passed me the ball with the hand, that's right. That's why what David did was the most important element of that move.'

But what, I asked, was the most important requirement to become a great player like him? What would be the most important piece of advice to a child who wished to play the game well? Zidane did not hesitate. 'Work, work, and more work. Simple as that,' he said.

'And then you have to be very serious and very committed, as well as very respectful of other people'. Yes, but, this was true for all lines of business, not just football. What did he specifically mean? 'Look at that volley against Valladolid,' he replied. 'I struck it with my left foot, which is not my natural foot to kick a ball with. But I struck it well, as well almost as if I were left-footed. How did I manage to do that? Because from a very early age I practised and practised and practised using my left foot. My left, my left – again and again. I worked hard to defeat the limitations of my nature. I worked against nature. And now I can play equally well with both feet, which undoubtedly gives me an advantage and is a very, very important part of my game.'

It gave him a huge advantage, because one of the surprising things about the professional game is how few players could play well with both feet – never mind brilliantly well, like Zidane. Beckham was a fabulous striker of the ball with his right, but his left served – as they said in Spain of one-footed players – merely for him to stand on. Roberto Carlos had a piledriver of a left foot but his right was, if anything, more useless than Beckham's left. Raúl was OK with his right, but far better with his left. It was no accident that Real Madrid's three Galácticos in chief, the expensive ones that Pérez bought in his first three years as president, happened all to play equally well with both feet. Zidane happened to play on the left and Figo on the right, but they could easily interchange positions, and did. It was inconceivable, on the other hand, that Roberto Carlos should play on the right and Beckham on the left. Ronaldo was naturally right-footed but his shots on goal were just as lethal with his left.

But Zidane's repertoire was wider than either Figo's or Ronaldo's. There were more things he could do with a ball – or more things that he could pull off at speed, surrounded by defenders. Juergen Klinsmann, the blond striker who won the World Cup with Germany in 1990, told me once that what made Zidane unique was his ability to get out of problems, or to beat three players, while keeping his 180-degree vision. 'The few players who can do what Zidane can do, who can take on and beat three players, do it then they lose that vision, and everything becomes a blur for them,' Klinsmann said.

'Zidane retains his composure when all around him are losing their heads because the game is so second-nature to him.' And the game was second-nature to him because, as Queiroz said of him and the other superstars, he had more time than ordinary players to do what he did, because his control of the ball required critically fewer milliseconds, because instinct took over and his brain remained clear to calculate the next move. Like the roulette, there were lots more tricks he had internalised and automated, lots of feints and dummies and wiggles of the hips to round defenders. But what really stood out was the first touch. It did not seem to matter whether the ball was rolled to him at perfect speed to his feet, or hurled at him at knee or waist height by the goalkeeper, or powered in his general direction on a treacherously bobbing pitch: he controlled the ball as if his foot were a feather cushion. Instant and total dominion. So instant and so total – so instinctive – that he had time to look up and ponder, even before he had received the ball, his next move, when almost all other players would be deploying every last ounce of concentration in their mind and body in the struggle to bring that ball under control. He was also arguably the best passer in the game. Long or short; outside of the boot, inside or backheel (a thirty-yard pass once to Roberto Carlos with the heel was yet another cameo that all those who saw it won't forget); left or right foot: the weight and direction of the ball were invariably impeccable. And he could even head, which Figo and Ronaldo could not. The two goals he scored in the World Cup final against Brazil were both headers. Of course, he was genetically blessed, but he worked at it with mechanical persistence. He had a brilliant indolence about his play that masked the years of toil he had put into it. He made the game look easy, because he had worked at it so hard.

'What would happen as I was growing up was that I would maybe see a piece of play in television or – more likely – among the older boys of my neighbourhood and I would go away with my friends – or alone – and imitate it. But not for five minutes, or half an hour or half a morning, but all day long. And not just that, I never stopped practising my basic skills. When I was at Cannes, my first club, I'd train three times a day. I'd spend hours working on my ball control, hitting the ball against a wall, with my right foot, them my left, my right, then my left. Over and over, until I felt I'd got it right.'

He never ceased trying to get it right. Aged thirty-one, he was still relentless with himself. You saw him in training and you were surprised to see how seriously he took the little skips and jumps, the hoops the players were routinely put through by junior members of the technical staff applying his own 'work, work, work' dictum to the letter.

'Zidane is a player who is very, very respected by his teammates,' Vicente del Bosque told me. 'Very professional. Severe with himself, even, I'd say. He takes tremendous care of himself – with his food, his rest, his training regime. He is truly a great, great professional. And he can play in every register, implement every move. He lacks nothing. Passing, dribbling, control, vision of the game. He is perfect. He has it all. He has that ability that Netzer had (Gunter Netzer, the brilliant German who played for Real Madrid alongside del Bosque in the Seventies) that even if he were surrounded by rivals you could pass him the ball knowing he would control it, shield it, not lose it. Zidane does everything well. Tell me something he can't do: you can't. There is nothing he cannot do.'

Del Bosque's comparison with Netzer was just right in the sense that whenever a Real Madrid player was under pressure and had to release the ball, almost without fail, the player he would look to was Zidane. Typically at a throw-in, against which defenders were always able closely to patrol the players of the team in possession, you gave the ball to Zidane and he would contrive a way to hold on to it. The same went for the goalkeeper Casillas who seemed nine times out of ten to throw the ball out to Zidane, considering him to be not only the best initiator of an attacking move, the dancing master around whom all things turned, but the safest pair of feet. As Queiroz said of Zidane, 'He is the conductor of the game, the most apt person in the world for the job.'

Were there boys he played with when he was young, when he was in his teens, who were better than him, I asked, wanting to test this contention of his that his genius had been less inspiration than perspiration. 'Lots,' Zidane replied. 'Lots who were more talented than I was. But you also have to be lucky, as well as working hard and having a clear road ahead, a vision. You need to be very concentrated on what you are doing to go far in football and that's difficult when you are fourteen, fifteen, sixteen years old.'

Especially difficult when you grew up in one of the rougher areas of Marseille, a port city Zidane once compared to Liverpool. Zidane was raised by his Algerian parents – of Berber, not Arab extraction, with their own non-Arabic language – in a crime and drug-infested immigrant neighbourhood called La Castellane. Life was hard and football invested life, as it did for millions of poor people worldwide, with a joy and a dignity – and in special cases like Zidane, a hope – it would otherwise have lacked. He was a shy, scrawny teenager who nevertheless conveyed to his contemporaries – this, at any rate, was the folklore that came to be received as fact in La Castellane – a sense that if anyone among them would escape life in the ghetto and triumph it would be the boy with the circus magician's name, Zinedine Zidane. The steel in Zidane so well hidden under that gentle monkish demeanour came, so his family in Algeria liked to say, from the tribe into which he was born. The small town of Aguemoune in the Kabyle region of Algeria was where the Zidane family was from. An old uncle of Zidane's told *el País* once that the town's most honoured inhabitant was the way he was because he bore, in their finest expression, the characteristics of the Kabyle people. Zaïd Zidat, who said the old family name was changed to Zidane in France by the immigration authorities, said the Kabyle people were famous for their warriors and poets. 'That is Zidane for you. He is a fighter on the football field, but one who knows how to create beauty,' the old uncle said.

Berbers are traditionally fairer and taller than Arabs. Zidane was especially tall, more than six foot. And his feet were big by any standard, by far the biggest in the Real Madrid dressing room. He took a Continental European size fifty. These details are significant in that they reveal once again how successful his battle was against nature, as he put it, to triumph in the manner in which he did. Lanky sportsmen with almost freakishly large feet tend to play basketball. When they play football they are usually clumsy of movement, more reliant on power than finesse. Zidane is a big man who treads softly, who seems to hover across a football pitch, his movements becoming all the more airily Fred Astaireish when he has the ball. His big feet, in others a clownish detriment, became in him a virtue, prehensile shovels with which to enhance rather than restrict his range of options.

Florentino Pérez may have lacked eyes to see the value of a heavy-footed defender whose chief purpose was to stop others playing but if there was one thing he understood when he became president of Real Madrid it was that he must have Zidane in his team – and at any cost. 'The reason why we had to have Zidane,' Pérez told me at one of the meetings we had at the round table of his office, 'was contained in something a young Madrid supporter told me once. "Our grandparents always, always told us 'you never saw Di Stefano play'", the young man said. 'Well, now we will be able to tell our grandchildren, "We saw Zidane!"'.'

Pérez smashed the world record for the French captain. He paid 75 million euros for him, more than twice what Beckham cost. 'We had to have him.' Pérez told me. 'He is the Di Stefano of our age. How could we not bring him to Real Madrid?'

Happily for Pérez the desire was mutual. Zidane, having spent five years in Juventus since leaving his first big French club Girondins of Bordeaux, was languishing away in cold, dark Turin, pining for a class of football that would allow all that laboriously acquired talent of his to flourish. All those '*gestes*' of his were not appreciated in Italy, or if they were, they were not seen – the way Pérez viewed them – as the very soul of the game. The spirit of *Serie A* derived from Machiavelli, whose guiding doctrine he defined in his masterwork on statecraft, *The Prince*, in the following uncannily prescient way: 'In the actions of all men, and especially of princes . . . one judges by the result.' Make war, not love, was Italy's footballing motto. But Zidane, good Berber that he was, wanted to make both. And Real Madrid was the club of his dreams.

'When the Juve people sold Zidane to us,' Pérez told me 'they thought they had pulled off the sale of the century. They were going to build a whole team with that money, they said. But they were quite mad. They missed the point that in football the same basic rules of life apply. In what other sphere of life are you going to despise talent? In none, yet football people sometimes seem inclined to do so. Agnelli [owner of Fiat and president of Juventus] understood though. He said that when Zidane left, Juventus lost its heart. You cannot let players like Zidane go. You cannot.'

Pérez was so excited when the deal finally went through that on the morning of the day Zidane was due to arrive to sign the contract he and a friend stole into Zidane's room at the Ritz Hotel and lovingly, reverently laid on his bed a Real Madrid shirt with his name on it. 'The thing about Zidane,' said Pérez, for whom the Frenchman was the living emblem of the spirit of Real Madrid, the expression of his 'Florenteam' project, 'is that he delights himself with the ball. He is not merely a footballer. He does what he does for the human species.'

Valdano, usually more poetic than Pérez, was not so high-flown. He recognised that there were games in which Zidane did little for Madrid fans, let alone this species. Away from home in the league he often played some way below his glorious best. 'But you see,' Valdano explained, 'Zidane is an artist. He needs the big stage to display his talents and the Bernabéu is it for him. Winning is not as paramount for him as it is for say Beckham, Figo or Raúl. He is more of a pure artist. Now, of course he wants to win. And when you combine artistry with efficiency, as he did most famously in that Champions League final in Glasgow, then, well, football has nothing more to offer.'

And the football world agreed. No one since Maradona had received such warm, widespread and unanimous acclaim. Figo, when I spoke to him in Lisbon, was almost at a loss for words, which was eloquent in itself. What did Zidane have? I asked him. 'Zidane . . . Zidane . . . Zidane has . . . football!' he laughed, delighted with the clear-sighted simplicity of his remark. Pressed a little, he could only add this: 'He has huge quality. What defines him is how he makes the transiton from defence to attack and for that what matters is his control, which is extraordinary. And . . . well, what what more is there to say?' Another illustrious teammate, Thierry Henry of Arsenal and France, was no less admiring, but in this instance more lucid when interviewed by *Marca* in January 2004. 'What a pleasure it is to play with Zidane!' said Henry, the second-best French player of recent times. 'He does things with the ball that it would be tricky to do with your hand. He makes what's difficult look easy. The remarkable thing is that he has already become a historical figure when he still has years to go before he retires.' Ryan Giggs, the most talented British player since Paul Gascoigne, was unusually loquacious when asked for his views on Zidane in December 2003, 'Every season you see him doing amazing things with a ball that you hadn't seen before and every season he just seems to get better,' Giggs said. 'I know for a fact that David Beckham is astonished with what he sees him do every day in training.'

If Pérez was concerned going into 2004 as to whether Beckham would see out his four-year contract with Real, he was thrilled in February when Zidane signed an extension of his contract until 2007, practically committing himself to the club for the rest of his football life. He had no intention of ever going anywhere else. As Zidane said when asked at the press conference when the contract extension was announced whether he would listen to an offer from Chelsea's Roman Abramovich, 'I would speak to him respectfully but I would say no. I am not moving from here. In Madrid I am happy.'

Alfredo Relaño, editor of *AS*, wrote a warm editorial rejoicing in Zidane's decision to remain at Real. 'The news confirms that talent will continue to be the cornerstone of Florentino's Madrid,' Relaño wrote. 'It confirms also how happy Zidane is here. Never had he played so well as he has done at Madrid. Never until now has he had the freedom to unleash fully his inspiration. What is asked of him is so radically different from what was required of him (or prohibited him) in Italy that the freedom he now enjoys has translated into a sort of permanent creative euphoria . . . People sometimes debate the question, who is better Ronaldo or Zidane. They are so different it is hard to compare. Tossing a coin, I'd go for Ronaldo. But when the choice is to go and watch the game at the stadium, or put some money down on pay-per-view TV, Zidane mobilises the masses more than anyone. After that "roulette" of his against Valladolid a football connoisseur I know rang me to say,

"We've got to get rid of the goalposts. The game is an end in itself."
And that's right. If Ronaldo's game reaches its peak when he scores
a goal, when we are presented by the spectacle of Zidane playing
football the result ceases to have any relevance.'

For the purist, like Relaño's friend, for the fan in whom the game's
tribal overtones do not drown out the aesthetics of the spectacle,
Zidane is an end in himself. Those of us who have been lucky enough
to see him in full flow will cherish through life the magical images
he has left us. We'll remember, and talk about until we are very old,
the volleyed goals against Bayer Leverkusen and Valladolid, the
'roulettes', the unfailingly feathery first touches, the waltzes and
minuets into which he would convert the most banal footballing
manoeuvres.

But I'll stay with a delicious little cameo he performed in Real
Madrid's last game at the Bernabéu of 2003, a 2-1 victory against
an excellent Deportivo la Coruña. It was Real's best performance of
the season thus far, the best they had played since the Manchester
United games back in April. And the main reason they played so
well was that the dancing master – 'Nijinsky in boots', Santiago
Segurola of *el País* called him – was at his most brilliantly inspired.
Everything Zidane did was perfection. His full repertory was in display,
the flicks, the feints, the impossibly easy controls, the arrow-straight
fifty-yard passes, an impeccably executed 'roulette' (but this time only
in the centre of midfield), the reducing of his opponents to flailing
shadows. With the defenders who tried vainly to repress his style he
was like the torero with the bull: respect and disdain at the same
time. The bull is there to be feared but more importantly to give
the fighter the opportunity to display his art.

In the particular moment that I shall always treasure, the role of
the bull was played by Deportivo's fast, skilful and doggedly accomplished right back Manuel Pablo. It was the forty-fifth minute of the
first half. Zidane received a long pass from Helguera on the run out
on the left wing. He controlled the ball, or rather gathered it as if
his left foot were a basket, but then momentum propelled him
forward in such a way that he risked running on and leaving the
ball behind him, of looking – a risk he himself said you always ran

when you tried something really clever in game – ridiculous. But no. In a second and entirely seamless movement, using the spur of his right foot he forward spun the ball in the direction that his feet were taking him – a '*geste*' which left the poor Pablo so baffled, bewildered and dejected that he fell helplessly flat on his back, leaving the field entirely for Zidane. That was the moment when he needed that 180-degree clarity of vision Klinsmann spoke off. Any other player, after a trick like that, hearing an ovation all around him from the Bernabéu equivalent to the one you heard when you scored the winner in a cup final, might have been forgiven for allowing his eyes to blur. Not Zidane, he ran on towards the left-hand edge of the penalty area and, spotting Ronaldo in the middle, by the penalty spot, made aim. But not like a football player makes aim. Like a golfer with a putt. In the fraction of a second – though you couldn't see it at the time as you saw it later on slow-motion TV replays – he angled his head ever so slightly to one side the better to calculate his direction, speed, range and – for all we know – windspeed and atmospheric pressure. And then he slid the ball to Ronaldo who had nothing more to do than stick out his foot and allow the momentum of Zidane's pass to steer it effortlessly into the back of the net.

Valdano, in his post-match comments, got it right once again. 'What Zidane does is another profession, no one else does it like he does,' he said. 'No one in history controls the ball the way Zidane does. Football is also about memories. And what Zidane will leave us will be his marvellous control.'

The next day Zidane was named FIFA World Player of the Year for the third time in six years. Tomás Roncero of *AS* celebrated it best. 'Welcome to the Real Madrid of Marvels. Let the band play on.'

15: White Munich

The chartered plane that flew the Real Madrid party to Munich for the game against Bayern was a heavy, four-engined Airbus but the mood in the cabin was so buoyant I had the sensation that the engines could fail and we'd still remain airborne. The players were laughing and joking and horsing around; the Spanish press were in remarkably chirpy mood given it was only 11.30 in the morning on a Monday; and as for the club directors and their wives, they were so euphoric they were practically levitating. Even Carlos Queiroz was smiling.

It felt as if we were on our way back from a famous victory. All that was missing was the champagne. There was no indication during the two-hour flight that mighty serious business still lay ahead; that the following night Real would be playing their most important game of the season so far, the first leg of a last sixteen Champions League knockout tie against a rival that always, unfailingly, gave them a very difficult time. Bayern Munich were Real's bogey team in Europe. Especially at home in Germany, where not only had Real never won, the record stood at seven games, seven Real defeats. Once again the Germans stood in the way of the biggest prize of all.

There should have been some sign of nerves, some sense of foreboding, but, if there was, nobody aboard the plane was letting on. Then again, there did exist sound enough reasons to be cheerful. Barely thirty-six hours earlier Real had pulled five points clear at the top of the Spanish league, having beaten Espanyol 4-2 away. They had made it to the final of the Spanish Cup, beating powerful Valencia 5-1 on aggregate along the way. And they had after all been the first of thirty-two teams competing in the Champions League to qualify for this second knockout phase.

Things could not get much better. The empire Florentino Pérez had built held the football world in sway, the doubts about his revolutionary model had all but disappeared. For what could you do in the face of such facts? I remember a lunch I had in Madrid with one of the most admired sports writers in Spain, a man troubled by Florentino's footballing heresies. We were chatting, as one did, about who Real's big signings might be in the summer. We mentioned the usual suspects – Thierry Henry, Francesco Totti and Ruud van Nistelrooy. Both of us agreed that Henry should be first choice, though he would probably be unavailable. Between Totti and van Nistelrooy, Totti seemed to us to be a better bet. Not only was the Italian captain a more complete and skilful player than the Dutchman, he was more elegant and had film-star looks. A perfect fit for the 'Florenteam', we both agreed. And yet, my friend said, he had heard in the previous week that in fact Florentino's first choice was van Nistelrooy. 'Doesn't make much sense to me,' my friend the veteran sports writer said, 'but if that's what Florentino believes, we must accept that he is right.' My friend was only half joking. He spoke like a man ruefully acknowledging defeat, like a preacher (and a much-respected one at that) whose articles of faith had been demonstrated to be flawed by a newcomer who possessed a superior intelligence, who was more in touch than you were with the religion's elemental forces.

L'Equipe had published a huge 'special' on Real Madrid at the end of January. In an immensely detailed sixteen-page report – covering everything from the name of the company that made the club's travel arrangementes to the annual salary each squad member received to the names of the two in-house falcons (Figo and Zidane) charged with keeping down the pigeon population of the Bernabéu – the most interesting piece was an editorial on Pérez headlined '*Un Homme Dangereux*'. The tone was satirical, the ridicule aimed not at the Real Madrid president but at those who questioned the wisdom of his ways.

'Florentino Pérez is an evil genius,' the editorial began. 'Beginning with his accountant's talent and his gift for marketing . . . Graver still, since his accession to the Real Madrid presidency on 16 July

2000, he has transformed a relic threatened by bankruptcy into the most powerful institution in the world of spectator sports. In terms of individual skill and collective imagination, prowess of play and clinical efficiency, the epic twenty-first century Real Madrid places itself as the rightful heir of five-times World Champion Brazil, the Ajax that gave the world "total football" or the levitations of the Chicago duo, Jordan and Jackson. For all this, may Florentino Pérez be reviled!'

With praise of this type ringing, from all quarters, in the minds of everybody on that Munich-bound plane, praise made all the more enjoyable by the comforting conviction that the Spanish title was already in the bag, the feeling had taken hold that Bayern would be easy meat: one more lamb for the Galácticos stylishly to slaughter. Besides, the latest news from Munich had been highly encouraging. All commentators agreed that the great old Bavarian club were fielding their weakest team in years. Seven points behind the leaders in a German league generally acknowledged to be decidedly inferior to *la Liga*, Bayern were reported to be a lacklustre, disjointed team, lacking in morale, desperately dependant on the inspiration of Roy Makaay, the Dutch striker they had bought in the summer from Deportivo la Coruña. A story was doing the rounds among the Spanish journalists that a Real spy sent to watch Bayern's league game the previous week had been unable at times to contain his laughter, so scornful was he of the Germans' game, so sure they stood no chance against the Galácticos. The story might have been an exaggeration, but the willingness of the plane's passengers to believe it revealed their state of mind.

As for Beckham, he had more reason than most to look forward to playing once again at Bayern's Olympic Stadium. He had not been playing all that well since the turn of the year. He seemed to have lost the zeal that had driven him to prove himself a worthy Real player during those spectacularly successful first six months at the club. Maybe it was the consequence of an ankle injury he had suffered just before Christmas. Maybe rumours of problems in his marriage were true and the flights he was finding himself having to make back and forth between London and Madrid were exacting their toll.

Maybe it simply was not possible for a player to sustain the intensity he had shown at the start, to play game after game at the very peak of his abilities. But now he had reason for cheer. His memories of playing, first, against Bayern and, second, in this stadium were very happy ones indeed. Bayern were the rivals when he won his one and only European Cup, with Manchester United, in 1999. The last time he had played at Bayern's stadium it had been as captain of England in a World Cup qualifier, when England, in an unforgettable afternoon for the nation's fans, beat the old enemy 5-1 away in a World Cup qualifier. It had been one of the great days in Beckham's football career, one of the worst in the life of the German goalkeeper, Oliver Kahn. Kahn was going to be in the Bayern goal for the game against Real. Reports from Germany reaching happy Madrid followers was that his recent form had been atrocious.

For all that, Kahn, the Bayern captain, was one of the big names in German football. A European Cup-winner with Bayern, he was the main reason why a poor Germany team – the very same one that had lost 5-1 to England – had reached the World Cup final in Japan in 2002. (Though another thing no one in the Real party forgot was that Ronaldo had scored two goals against him in that final, winning the trophy for Brazil.) But now, at thirty-four, age seemed to be catching up with Kahn. He kept having back problems. He made bad mistakes. But he was brave, dogged and defiant. The word was that he'd had fifteen injections over the weekend to allow him to be sufficiently pain-free to play on the Tuesday against Real Madrid.

It was that spirit that explained why before the game he had felt compelled to break with what had clearly been laid down as the Bayern party line. The word from the top was that Bayern should adopt the role of underdogs – or, worse, no-hopers – in the face of the Real dream machine. Kahn was having none of it. Bayern Munich might not have been playing well but they would rise to the occasion, Real would see. 'A good racehorse jumps highest when it needs to,' he declared, in words that would come back to haunt him. 'We are Bayern and we know when to win.'

Everybody else in the club was scrupulously playing the part of the victim. Karl Heinz Rumenigge, the Bayern chairman, said his team could not win even if they played at 100 per cent of their possibilities. Franz Beckenbauer, the club's president, was more stark. 'There is no belief, no hope, no form, no logic to suggest we can beat the mighty Real Madrid,' said the man they call the Kaiser, the greatest player in German history. As for Uli Hoeness, another distinguished former player now general manager at Bayern, he said in an interview with *AS* that Real Madrid were the best team in the world and were therefore clear favourites. 'On paper,' Hoeness said, 'Bayern stand no chance.'

The Real players read *AS*. They were reading that interview on the plane on the way over to Munich. Hoeness knew they would be reading it. Anyone with any sense would have known that, while no doubt believing much of what he said, he was also toying with his rivals' minds, trying to to soften their resolve. Bayern were not exactly novices in international competition. They were the biggest club by far in a country with a formidable footballing tradition. If you were to add trophies won in international competitions – the World Cup, the European Championships – to trophies won at club level, only Italy among the northern hemisphere nations had been as successful. England lagged way behind. The self-deprecating remarks of Rumenigge, Beckenbauer and Hoeness – big contributors all to the glory of both club and country – reeked not only of false, but of carefully choreographed, modesty. The Real players knew what the Germans were up to but it was difficult for them not to succumb, to some degree, to their blandishments. After all, they did know they were superior to Bayern, they did believe they were the best in the world, they did feel they were the masters of the football universe. And Hoeness's humility, so undeniably justified, did serve subtly but surely to reinforce their complacency.

As the plane began its descent into Munich the air was dense with cloud. Only once the wheels had been lowered did land become visible, all of it blanketed in snow. '*Alemania Blanca!*' shouted some wag at the back of the plane. '*Sí! Alemania Blanca!*' another voice cried, to triumphant laughter all around. The joke, as everybody instantly understood it, was that Germany had dressed herself in Real

Madrid white in homage to the Spanish invaders. It was Napoleon's *grande armée* at the gates of Moscow, oblivious to the wintry perils ahead. The weather – temperatures well below zero were expected on Tuesday night – might rather have been expected to make my fellow revellers on the plane pause, wonder for a moment how the Brazilian contingent (for example) might be affected, whether the elements might shift the balance alarmingly in favour of rivals accustomed to playing in the extreme cold. But no, '*Alemania Blanca!*' it was, as it would be again in a Spanish newspaper headline the next morning. The old enemy had surrendered, had bowed before Real's supremacy, before a ball had been kicked.

Still more evidence of Teutonic self-abasement was provided upon arrival at Munich airport. No sooner had Beckham stepped off the plane than he was pounced upon by three large policemen. Meek as schoolboys, pens and exercise books in hand, the *polizei* in green implored the England captain for an autograph. The scene, as familiar to Beckham as his face in the bathroom mirror in the morning, repeated itself all the way down the passenger ramp, along the airport's long corridors, down the escalators, out of the airport doors until he found refuge in the team bus. If it was not policemen it was airport staff, if it was not airport staff it was screaming women and children. The weak or the faint-hearted or the merely unlucky, settled for an autograph from Figo, Raúl or the great Zidane. Those who did get Beckham's autograph, or better still a photograph (the man's patience is heroic), walked away in a happy daze, clutching their scraps of signed paper as if they were treasure from King Solomon's mines.

Last out of the plane was Ronaldo. He received the Beckham treatment and, like Beckham, he too obliged every supplicant. The difference was that for Ronaldo there was less screaming. And the TV camera crews did not get quite so goatishly excited as they had done when they caught their first sight of the Englishman. A Spanish TV cameraman, veteran of dozens of these airport scenes down the years before Champions League games, told me later that day that he had been amazed at how many German crews had turned up. 'Usually it's four or five,' he said. 'This time it was eighteen or nineteen.' Why? 'It's the Galácticos and their growing reputation, for sure. But it's mostly to do with Beckham. You should have seen the women reporters out there preening themselves, touching up their hair, when word got out to us that the Madrid plane had landed.'

The players boarded the team bus, the official Real team bus driven from Madrid to Munich to carry the kit and make the players feel at home, and serenely it set off down the icy airport road followed by another couple of buses ferrying the directors and press, and a convoy of three imposingly black Audis with Florentino Pérez and other Real bigshots inside, towards the luxury Mandarin Oriental Hotel, in the centre of town. A small crowd waited in the falling snow across the road from the hotel entrance, foremost among them two small boys bearing a sign that read 'David Beckham: you are the best'. Once inside the hotel, the players withdrew into their usual cocoon on these occasions, either inside their rooms – where they watched television, played with their gameboys or talked on the phone – or in a lounge specially allocated for them to eat or discuss plans for the game with Queiroz, and sometimes Valdano. The cocoon is almost impenetrable. Florentino Pérez might slip in for a moment, but only for a moment. He understands as well as anybody the unwritten rules here, the inviolable halo that surrounds the team in the thirty-six hours before a big game. It is like a religious retreat, or the reverent preamble to a holy ceremony. It is all quite mystical and, for the players, very boring. Yet they would not have it any other way. It is the way things are done in the football world, an away game ritual that must be solemnly observed. One would have thought – or a journalist might, at any rate – that this might be the ideal time, for example, for a player to sit down and do something useful, like a newspaper interview. Forget about it. The very notion, to all but the uninitiated, is utterly preposterous.

Pérez and his people were also in the habit of creating a little cocoon for themselves during the day and a half they spent in the team hotel before an away match. It was the Real president's habit to hold court in the lounge adjoining the lobby – invariably a plush room with chandeliers, soft carpets, deep chairs and quietly efficient waiters who deliver coffee in silver pots. At the indulgently overstaffed Mandarin Oriental, the circle over which Pérez presided was wider than usual. With him were not just the two or three club directors who attended, as he did, each and every Real away game. Now his family were here too. Playing Bayern was a big occasion, made bigger than usual this time by the happy anticipation of a famous victory. Accompanying Pérez were his thirty-one-year-old son, Florentino, who had grateful memories of Germany, having been successfully operated on for a brain tumour by a German surgeon the summer before; his daughter Cuchi and her husband, recently married; and Pérez's wife Pitina, who goes with him to most games. And his brother Enrique was there too, with a couple of friends. It's a Spanish thing. It doesn't matter whether they are wealthy magnates or plumbers or peasant farmers. The most sociable of social animals, Spaniards are never happier, whether home or away, than when seated in a circle sipping and nibbling together. And if it's family, so much the better.

Jorge Valdano stood outside the circle, busy on his mobile phone. As is invariably the case, he was the most dapper man in the room. But the Argentine was as precise in his thinking, in his choice of words, as his impeccably tailored suits. One sure sign of his unusual intelligence was that he admitted to not having all the answers to life's – or for that matter football's – questions. 'I can't make up my mind whether winning the league back home as easily as we seem to be is a good or a bad thing,' he told me. 'On the one hand the players are more physically and mentally rested than they otherwise might be; but on the other hand you worry that when they come to a big Champions League game they might have lost something of that necessary competitive edge. Is it best to be relaxed or to be tense? I'm not sure.' If Valdano, who had seen everything in football, wasn't sure then you could be certain that no one else knew either. But the best thing, in the end, he said, was to place trust in the instincts of the extraordinary collection of players Real had assembled. 'These are top, top guys who know how to administer their energies, their tensions, their commitment. See how in game after game this season, they have raised their game in the second half; how they've gone into the dressing room at half-time a goal or two down and come back in the second half, banging in three, four goals in twenty minutes. Being able to step up a gear when you need to: that is the sign of true greatness.'

Outside the hotel Real's German fans gathered to catch their own glimpse of that greatness, as people do when a pop star is in town. Except that for Real Madrid the age spread of the fans was wider, the range more diverse. Children and elderly men, teenagers and women with babies in prams waited side by side in the snow for a glimpse of their white heroes. They waited and waited. I saw a couple of teenagers, in despair as the afternoon wore on and no one of note emerged, take turns photographing themselves against the background of the blue, white and gold Real team bus. Eventually the players did come out, boarding the bus at six in the evening for their first training session at the Olympic Stadium, where the game would be played the following night. Ronaldo had to make an exit before them, having been appointed to speak to the world on behalf of the players. The one officially sanctioned break with pre-match purdah, the one small concession to the hungry media, and the hundreds of millions who they in turn feed, was made on the evening before the game. One player was served up for a brief, banal but invariably hugely well-attended press conference.

Slipping out unnoticed by a hotel side door, Ronaldo stepped into a waiting Audi. Invited by the Real Madrid press chief Paco Navacerrada to join them, I sat in the back seat. Ronaldo sat in the front, large as a heavyweight boxing champion in a thermally padded tracksuit, next to the German driver. It was already dark but the car drove through the snow-powdered, sometimes icily crunchy Munich streets as fast as if it were a bright summer's day. We shook hands. I reminded him that I had interviewed him in Milan, while he was still at Inter, just before the 2002 World Cup. (He had forgotten.) And I told him I thought it was strange how people, in talking about how well he was playing these days, forgot how back then when we met he was coming out of a terrible injury, how uncertain his professional future seemed. He nodded, grave as a Buddha, and mumbled, 'Yes, they forget, they forget, they forget . . .' And then he went quiet – a quiet I knew better than to disturb. It would have been more than improper, it would have been profane for me to interrupt the great goal-scorer's inscrutable thought processes. In a deep pre-match trance, he went silent, his big head immobile. It was a meaty boxer's head, the flesh visible beneath his stubble cut, except that you knew he was not a boxer because even from behind – it was the shape of the ears, small and jutting – he was so instantly recognisable to anyone who had taken the slightest interest in football these last eight or nine years. Three-quarters of the way to the stadium, he did emerge from his trance to say one thing. He turned his head a fraction in the direction of Paco Navacerrada, seated next to me at the back, and he asked, 'What's the date of the first game we'll play in the next round of the Champions League?' 'The quarter-final, you mean, after Bayern?' 'Yes.' 'A week after the final of the *Copa del Rey*, on 24 March.' 'Ah, OK.'

At the press conference itself he wasn't quite so cocksure. He did half pretend, in a diplomatic gesture to his German hosts, that he thought there might be a dim possibility of Real not qualifying for the quarters. All the praise being showered on Real by the German camp – Hoeness had declared Ronaldo himself to be, quite simply, 'the best forward in the world' – was 'a pre-game strategy', he said. Bayern were a team that had to be treated 'with great respect'. But then in response to a question about Real's poor record at the Olympic Stadium Ronaldo could not resist the impulse to declare, with the defiant confidence of Muhammad Ali before a big fight, 'We're going to change history tomorrow night.' Not that, in any other respect, there was anything about the press conference that even remotely suggested the fireworks and pizzazz of one of Ali's public performances.

Ronaldo's appearance before the world's media – and there must have been 120 journalists and more than twenty TV cameras present – lasted barely fifteen minutes. He looked, for the most part, bored, impatient to be somewhere else. If the journalists looked less bored it was not so much because of what he said (though the *AS* crowd were deeply grateful for that line about changing history, which next morning they splashed on the front page) as because they too are fans, almost as agog to be in the presence of footballing greatness as the policemen who asked for the autographs at Munich airport.

When Ronaldo stepped out on to the Olympic Stadium pitch at around seven in the evening to join the rest of the Real squad in training the thought perhaps occurred to him, for maybe the first and last time in his life, that he might actually have preferred staying in the warm press room taking more silly questions from reporters. It was absolutely freezing. Beckham, born in a colder latitude than any other member of the team, was the only player wearing shorts and the only one who seemed to be enjoying himself, hurling snowballs in the direction of Raúl and other not entirely amused teammates. The temperature was five below zero. The forecast for the game, due to start just over twenty-four hours later, was seven below. When the session was over Roberto Carlos and Figo walked off arm in arm, propping each other up, as if congratulating each other for having endured and come through a heroically daunting ordeal.

The players returned to the hotel, had dinner monastically together and went to bed. Florentino Pérez, Valdano, Carlos Martinez de Albornoz, and a couple of other Real grandees had made a protocol visit to their Bayern counterparts and then regrouped around midnight in the hotel, pitching their tent once again in the Mandarin Oriental's soft-carpeted lounge. Pérez invited me to join them. The mood was jollier than ever. Pérez was especially thrilled to have his family with him. 'Isn't this great?' he said to me. 'Here we are in Munich and look, there's my daughter at that table with some friends; there's my wife at that other table, playing cards; and here's my son sitting with me over here.' Pérez was even happier when he saw José Angel Sánchez arrive warmly wrapped, fresh from Madrid, through the hotel doors. Sánchez is almost an adopted son to Pérez, his favourite executive at Real, the man with whom he is most in tune, whose judgement he most values and with whom he is most at ease.

Sánchez took his seat in the Pérez court – he played the clever court jester, licensed to joke, to Pérez's king – and the banter began. Pérez proposed what he considered to be a brilliant new idea to swell the Real coffers. 'Since we have demonstrated that we can win paying only minimal attention to defence,' he said, mischievously deadpan, 'I suggest that from here on in we play with one central defender instead of two. We will then sell that eleventh place in the team for one million euros. It's like what they are doing in space, selling places in spaceships to people who want to be astronauts for a day. We'll be giving people – OK, filthy rich people – the chance to make their greatest fantasies come true and I don't really believe it'll make much difference to the result. We'll leave Zidane and Ronaldo to take care of that.' Everyone was chortling away at Florentino's wacky inventiveness, all except Sánchez who, entering into the spirit of the game by also keeping a straight face, said he reckoned it would not be necessary to keep the eleventh man on the pitch for the whole game. The sheer thrill of being able to put his head to one cross from Beckham would be worth a million right there. He could be substituted after a few minutes with a proper professional and that would be that – the players' salaries for the week paid off at a stroke. 'No, no,' rejoined Pérez. 'The substitute will be another playing guest. You see, these guys will be exhausted after fifteen, twenty minutes. We'll be able to get four of them on per game. Four million euros!' I suggested that for *Copa del Rey* games, seeing as how they were not exactly top priority for Real, he could rent out a place in the team to not one but two millionaires. Play with just nine pros. Pérez thought this an excellent idea. And so the delirium went on – unaided, in Pérez's if not Sánchez's case, by the influence of alcohol. The Real president kept calling the waiter over, but all he asked for each time was a small bottle of mineral water.

The evening with the Bayern crowd had had a pretty heady effect of its own, though. Rumenigge had spent much of the time singing Real's praises, congratulating Pérez for having assembled such a stupendously talented team. It was all part of Bayern's deliberate buttering up exercise but, as with Uli Hoeness's remarks in the interview with *AS*, because it was flattery it did not mean it was not true. Pérez recalled the moment when he told Rumenigge, a fabulous player twenty years earlier, that if he had been Real president then he would not have hesitated to sign him up for the Galácticos. 'Rumenigge really lit up,' Pérez recalled. 'He was so pleased I had said that. It was the clearest evidence all night that these Bayern people were sincerely impressed with what we are doing at Madrid.'

Into his fourth bottle of water, at around two in the morning, Pérez made a confession. 'My secretary Conchita tells me that there is a danger of all this going to my head, driving me mad. Or that at the very least it's going to affect my judgement. And it's true that sometimes when I think how big Real Madrid is getting, how many people's lives it touches all over the world, I feel almost overwhelmed. I feel the possibility does exist of going bonkers.' Not that he seemed too worried about it for in a moment he was galloping off on another rant, with Sánchez once again geeing him on. This time the theme was the club's burgeoning global appeal, a phenomenon some in the Spanish press described as '*el Real Madrid Planetario*'. He reminded me of a fax he had received a couple of months back when I was with him in his office. It had been from an Iranian journalist asking whether he had some comment to make, some words of comfort to offer, following a terrible earthquake there had been in the town of Bam that killed thousands of people. Right there and then Pérez had drafted a reply, not only offering Real Madrid's and all the players' condolencies but promising also to set up a Real Madrid football school in Bam at the earliest possible opportunity. (A couple of months later he and Alfredo Di Stefano met with the Iranian ambassador in Spain formally to announce the Real Madrid Foundation's decision to inaugurate said school.) The club already had sports schools bearing the Real Madrid name in Bolivia, Chile, Argentina, El Salvador, Morocco and, even, Iraq. 'Real Madrid is the universal club,' Perez told the assembled company, a number of whom had heard this speech before. 'The trouble is that when we say this it sounds presumptuous. Well, it's true. There is nowhere on earth where people don't know the line-up of our team, where people do not get excited at the thought of owning a club shirt. Real Madrid is in the hearts of a lot of people, including lots of poor children in Africa who don't have enough to eat and whose satisfaction in life comes from football and the great players we have here in our team. For me there is no greater satisfaction than to know we're bringing smiles to those children's faces.'

That was Pérez in solemn, borderline messianic mode. But he quickly snapped out of it, reverting to the whimsical tone that had been defining this cheerful pre-match soirée. The way things were going, he declared, what with the club's appeal being so universal and all, he reckoned that by the year 2018, when the fans of today's team reached adulthood, everyone in the world would be supporting Real Madrid. At which point, he said, the game would cease to be, for there could not be a game without rivals. 'Then we'd have to play without goalposts. Just performance art,' suggested Sánchez. 'Quite so,' Pérez, laughing, agreed. 'In a way we are doing that right now, with the players we have. Maybe it doesn't matter any more if we win or lose . . .' At two-thirty Pitina, his wife, came over, and informed Florentino it was time for bed. Next morning, she reminded the miscreants, they had meetings, starting early, with their three big Bavaria-based sponsors: Siemens, Adidas and Audi. Pérez cracked one last joke then did as he was told. Caesar always had a man on hand to remind him that he was human. Pitina, a laconic woman, not easily impressed, exercised much the same function with her imperially aspirant husband.

Next morning in the lobby Sánchez related the previous night's babblings to Valdano. '*Delirium tremens*,' was Valdano's amused commentary to the two of us. 'Yes', retorted Sánchez, 'but we need to do this, don't you see? We have one of these sessions at least once a week where we sit back and try to put into perspective our own roles in all this, where we register our amazement and disbelief at what we have created here, at the power and reach of Real Madrid. We have to play the fool in order to stand back from it all. We have to put some distance between ourselves and this monster we are creating; this monster that is only going to get bigger. If we didn't joke about it all we really would go mad. Imagine if we didn't laugh at ourselves. Imagine if we took ourselves deadly seriously, if we were building all this with unsmiling solemnity. Then we really would be nuts. Then they really would have to take us to the lunatic asylum.'

Further evidence of Pérez's sanity was provided that evening, as the club directors and other visiting Spanish dignitaries waited to board the convoy of buses and Audis that would deliver them to the Olympic Stadium for the big game. Pérez confessed for the first time

to feeling nervous. 'It's bloody cold out there already and the temperature seems to be falling by the minute. Some of our players are not
going to like that at all. And besides, let's not forget: Bayern might
not be very good, but they are Germans . . .' The thing about German
teams, as everyone in the football world knew, was their uncanny
capacity to overcome their limitations, make the best of what they
had and, somehow, win. Often against teams technically much better
than they were. It was not pretty. Michael Ballack, the one Bayern
player you could maybe imagine making it into the Real Madrid
forward line, put it this way in an interview published that morning
in *el País*: 'We're a German team: first, discipline; second, fight; and,
only in last place, style, technique. That's the way it is. That's our
tradition. You have to respect it.'

Did the Real players respect it, as far as this game was concerned?
Yes and no. Waiting in the hotel lounge to catch our bus to the
stadium, Valdano told me that at this stage of any match-day, with
two hours or so to go to kick-off, the players always felt a surge of
anxiety in the pit of their stomachs; and all the more so in a Champions
League game. Valdano recalled how José Antonio Camacho, the tough
Real defender from the Seventies who played for Spain nearly a
hundred times, used to throw up, without fail, before every single
game. That said, it did not appear that the players were preparing for
this game with quite the trepidation it merited. 'This afternoon
they've been taking bets on the score,' Valdano told me, shaking his
head, not at all happy at the mood of complacency all around. 'Some
are saying 4-0, others 3-1.' And what about the cold weather, weren't
they taking that into account in their wagers? 'It's true. The weather
won't help us,' Valdano said. 'But the players will be as well wrapped
up as they can be. And they put this cream on their feet that helps
the circulation and stops them from getting cold. It should not affect
them too much.' Francisco Gento, the left winger from the great
Fifties Real team, the man with the unmatched record of having
won six European Cups, was there in the hotel lobby, part of the
official Spanish delegation for the match. How did he think the cold
would affect the players? I asked him. A small man in a thick black
coat, smoking cigarette after cigarette, he made light of the icy

temperatures. 'The problem,' he said, 'is when the wind blows. Then you haven't got a chance to build up a sweat and you freeze. There doesn't seem to be any wind tonight. It won't be a problem.'

Gento, born three years before the Spanish Civil War in 1933, looked like a man made of sterner stuff than some of the present Real generation. As far as the cold was concerned, sterner than the Brazilians, that was for sure. For Ronaldo and Roberto Carlos it was a long way from Copacabana. But at least they could run around. It was harder for the spectators in a stadium originally designed for the summer Olympic games, barely fit for human habitation in winter. A whole half of the stadium was completely uncovered. And while it was a mercy that it was not snowing, most of the spectators were cruelly exposed to the elements. No fears for the VIPs, though, I – rather inappropriately – among them. We had a thick red blanket waiting for us on each of our seats. Before going out to watch the game we were able to snuggle up in a warm lounge where waiters served mulled wine as well as champagne and there was plenty of hot food.

Three surprise visitors were in the VIP lounge when we arrived with the Pérez retinue for what would turn out to be a historic – if not particularly eventful – football summit. Peter Kenyon, the ex-Manchester United man installed barely two weeks earlier as chief executive of Chelsea; his enigmatic boss, the billionaire Russian Roman Abramovich; and an attractive young woman with short blonde hair who never left the Chelsea chairman's side and who was, it emerged, his wife. Pérez, and then Sánchez, greeted Kenyon like an old friend. He in turn introduced them to Abramovich. Pérez spoke to him in accented but perfectly respectable English. To Pérez's surprise the Russian did not immediately respond. It turned out that he did not understand what Pérez was saying. The blonde was translating for Abramovich. When she had finished he nodded, with what seemed like embarrassment; smiled, with what seemed like deference, and uttered some pleasantry back in Russian, which the blonde in turn translated for Pérez.

It was a strange encounter. Pérez and the man who would be Pérez. The Russian oil tycoon who purported with his money to transform Chelsea into Real Madrid, into the world's biggest football club. He had only bought Chelsea FC the previous summer but already he had spent more money on new players than Pérez had since he had taken over at Real in the summer of 2000. He was a predator with bottomless pockets and while he was around no rival team's player, so long as he was good enough, was safe. Every time a rumour arose that a Real player might be leaving the club the first thought in the minds of everybody in the football world was 'Abramovich'. He had already snatched Claude Makelele and been turned down by Michel Salgado. But barely a week had passed since then without either Roberto Carlos or Luis Figo or Ronaldo or even Beckham himself being rumoured to be moving to Stamford Bridge. Pérez kept his thoughts to himself about Abramovich, though it was hard to escape the conclusion that he must have viewed him as a rather annoying whippersnapper. First, because he coveted Pérez's players and he had the presumption – as president of a club whose one and only English league championship victory had been in 1955 – to imagine himself to be a serious rival. Second, because in financial terms he really was a serious rival, a potential menace to Pérez's project. Third, because he looked so absurdly callow for an individual of his power and wealth.

Anyone who had not known who Abramovich was would have imagined him to be there in the Bayern VIP lounge because he was someone's son. Perhaps Kenyon's, who looked every inch the venerable patrician next to his boyish employer, a slender, physically unprepossesing individual of medium height sporting a wispy little Sixties fringe curiously at odds with his mousy, close-cropped hair. He looked ill at ease, lost in there in the company of so many established figures in the world game – Rumenigge popped in, Gento was there, Valdano, the whole Real crew. Unable to understand a word anybody was saying, a large television set up on the wall offered him the only means of escape. Amid the buzz of incomprehensible chatter he sat down and trained his eyes on the screen, where images began to appear of Champions League goals past. Suddenly Zidane filled the screen, the fantastic volleyed winner against Bayer Leverkusen in Glasgow. And then more Real goals, crackers by Ronaldo, Roberto

Carlos, Figo. Shown again and again, from every angle in slow motion. Abramovich was riveted. Pérez, seeing him, turned to Sánchez, Valdano and I and, in mock horror, cried, 'Stop! Stop! Tell them to turn off the TV! Turn it off! We can't have this guy watching this stuff . . . !'

The game began shockingly for Real Madrid, Roberto Carlos nearly scoring what would have gone down as one of the great idiotic own goals of all time. The ball came to him in the air a couple of steps back from the penalty spot. There wasn't a Bayern player near him but instead of heading it away or controlling it on his chest then booting it out of the danger area, he took the ball acrobatically on the volley, lashing it with his left foot. It was pure showing off. Which is part of what makes Roberto Carlos such a joy to watch. When he does this sort of thing though, it can also mean he is nervous, as a member of the Real coaching staff said later. In such circumstances he overcompensates, tries to cover up his nerves with false *bragadaccio*. Which is also fine, if it comes off. But this time he miss-hit the ball horribly. Instead of belting it upfield, to his right as he had intended, he sliced it. The ball scurried past a horrified Casillas half a metre wide of the post.

Five minutes later Zidane tried a little slice of his own. It was a piece of unbelievable skill. One of those things that you don't ever recall having seen on a football pitch before. Receiving a pass from Ronaldo on the edge of the penalty area, he struck it first time with the outside of his right boot, imparting a venomous side-spin on the ball that delivered it past two German defenders perfectly into the path of Ronaldo, who had kept running into the penalty area. Instead of shooting, Ronaldo struck the ball left across goal towards Raúl, who was waiting alone in front of Kahn. Ronaldo should have shot. A German player just got a leg to the pass, sending the ball ricocheting for a corner.

Unfortunately for Real it was the Roberto Carlos incident, rather than the moment of genius from Zidane, that defined the night's proceedings. Which side more consistently wins the fifty-fifty balls is as reliable an indicator as any of what the outcome of a football game might be. The side that does is the one that's hungrier, braver, more focused. Exceptionally with Real Madrid the fifty-fifty test, however, is of little value. Because such is the precision of their passing and the quality of their first control, they do not have to worry as often as other teams about fifty-fifty balls. This time, though, the passing was, by their standards, all over the place. And there was no question which of the two sides was hungrier, braver and more focused. The cold, minus eight degrees in the second half, had its effect. (Ronaldo, in black leotards, looked a mildly ludicrous shadow of his usual panther-like self.) But above all it was the pre-game phoney war that was yielding its effect. The Real players, hard as Queiroz and Valdano had tried to convince them that they were in for a hell of a fight, had not entirely expunged from some treacherous corner of their minds that pernicious notion that Bayern were simply not in their league, that the gap in class would be decisive, that they did not have to do too much more than show up to win the game. The Bayern players, on the other hand, had two things going for them in the mental contest: their pride – they were wearing the colours of the legendary Bayern Munich at the legendary Olympic Stadium after all; and the comforting belief that they had nothing to lose, that they had all to play for, that if they gave it their best shot and were defeated there would be no recriminations, while if they won against opposition of this rare class and style they would be heroes in Munich for the rest of their days.

Frozen in mind as well as body, Real were bundled aside by the superior desire and muscularity of the Bayern players. It was with relief, and thanks to a couple of good saves from Casillas, that they went into the break without conceding a goal. But no sooner had the game restarted than Real again found themselves under siege. Instead of raising their game in the second half, going up that gear Valdano talked about, they wilted, disconcerted by the rugged confidence of Bayern. They had prepared in their minds for some token resistance, not much more. But they had discovered, as Bayern pounded the Real goal with howitzer after howitzer, that they were in the Battle of Stalingrad. Thanks to Casillas, Real held on for thirty minutes. But then, in the seventy-fifth minute of the game, Makaay got away from Helguera and rose to head the ball commandingly into the back of the net. With just fifteen minutes to go everything indicated that if there was to be another goal it would be Bayern who scored it. As Bayern grew in confidence, Real looked panicked. Suddenly the prospect of the Galácticos falling at this early stage of the competition, of not making it into the last eight, seemed embarrassingly plausible. The golden rule in these Champions League knockout games was to score a goal away from home, because in the event of a tie away goals counted double. Thus if the score stayed at 1-0 and Real won 2-1 at the Bernabéu Bayern would go through.

You could almost hear the pundits back home in Spain, the old school *futboleros* which *l'Equipe* had mocked in its editorial, saying, 'You see, Florentino? You see? We warned you that your great experiment would sooner or later be revealed as a romantic dream. The beautiful game will only take you so far. Against the big Champions League teams you can't allow yourself the indulgence of playing without defensive midfielders, with an inexperienced centre half.' Florentino had been proving the orthodox believers wrong all season long, but watching the rabble to which they were being reduced, helpless before the Bayern blitzkrieg, you had to wonder once more about the wisdom of playing Guti and Beckham in the conventional midfield 'holding' position typically occupied by hard nuts like Roy Keane, Juventus' Gatusso or Bayern's very own Demichelis, who was not only tough but wily too, as Argentine players tended to be. I was reminded of Carlos Queiroz's point, which he said Pérez had refused fully to take on board, about football being by nature a game of two parts: one in which you have the ball; another in which the other side has it. The problem now was that Real, lacking the ball-winners required for a scrap like this one, were simply not getting possession. Whereupon the Pérez notion, mimicking the philosophy of the great Brazil side of 1970, that if you score two, we'll score three, if you score three, we'll score four, was being rendered crushingly academic. As for Raúl Bravo at centre half, the young man looked all at sea, dizzied by the pace and power of the Bayern attack. It was his confusion that led to the cross that led to Makaay's goal. That German discipline and fight Ballack had talked about before

the game were having their effect, suffocating Real's style and technique. The Madrid players were like Olympic ice-dancers who turn
up at the skating rink to discover that they have been requisitioned
to take part in one of those bone-crushing games of NHL ice hockey.

In a measure of just how bad things were, and how incapable
Roberto Carlos in particular had been of adapting to the conditions,
how rattled he was, he did something very uncharacteristic: he struck
out with his fist at Demichelis after the Argentine had clattered into
him hard. Demichelis did his best to make a meal of the incident,
holding his hands to his face as if he'd been hit by Mike Tyson. To
his disappointment, however, the Norwegian referee did not see the
punch. It was the turning point of the game. Quite undeservedly,
the luck was with Real Madrid. With seven minutes to go to full-
time Roberto Carlos, who should have been sent off, was lining up
alongside Beckham to take a free kick from some five yards outside
the Bayern penalty area. That was the closest Real had got to the
Bayern goal since that one-two in the early minutes between Ronaldo
and Zidane. It seemed far too far away, though, to pose any serious
threat to the night's most under-employed individual, Oliver Kahn.
Beckham made as if he were preparing to curl one of his benders
over the wall but Roberto Carlos took the kick, low but seemingly
harmlessly – he miss-hit the ball, caught it too heavily, making a
shade too much contact with the ground at the moment of impact
– in the direction of Kahn's goal. The Brazilian, knowing immediately that this had not been one of his walloping specials, turned
away, like a golfer who knows his drive is headed into the rough.
What happened next was the golfing equivalent of the ball catching
a lucky bounce off a rock, spinning back on to the fairway, then on
to the green and into the hole. Neither Roberto Carlos, nor any of
his teammates, nor any of the Bayern players, nor – for that matter
– anybody in the ground could quite believe for a second or two
what had happened. Only Kahn did. Only Kahn, lying in a dejected
heap along the goal line, understood, in that bewildering first instant,
that he had let the ball squirm under his body into the net. That
Real Madrid had scored the equaliser.

The whole mood of the game changed abruptly. They say about

golf that it's all in the head. It is in football too. A great deal of it. Until that twist of fate the Bayern players had reached the point of imagining, with even more conviction than the Real players had felt before hostilities had begun, that they had the game in the bag. After that Makaay goal, though there was only a one-goal difference in it, it was they who succumbed to the demon of overconfidence. The Madrid players, meanwhile, had become as dejected as the Bayern lot claimed to have been during the build-up to the game. Everything had been turned on its head. Losing 1-0, not conceding another goal, had seemed just a few moments ago like a pretty desirable result, the way things were going that cold and frosty night. But that bolt from heaven, that catastrophic mistake by the man the English press had dubbed 'Oliver Can't' after that 5-1 German defeat, had transformed the psychologies of the two teams. Now it was Bayern whose heads were down; now Real became Real again, holding on to the ball with almost contemptuous ease, looking suddenly the more likely of the two sides to score a second goal. Some residual anxiety from the mauling they had received during the first eighty minutes perhaps held them back; or the knowledge that if they played out the draw that one goal they had scored would practically be worth two for the return match at the Bernabéu. So they didn't go in for the kill, as they would have done had they really had to. They played keep ball, tormenting their dispirited rivals, until the final whistle blew. Kahn, staring at the ground with his hands on his head, was a picture of despair. Not one Bayern player went up to console him. The former Bayern and Germany captain Lothar Matthäus explained why in televised comments just after the game: 'In recent years he has criticised his teammates and not one of them has forgotten it.'

No one, certainly not in the press contigent, even seemed to feel sorry for Kahn. Valdano did, though. 'They say he is a son of a bitch but as a former player myself I cannot but acknowledge that he was the victim of a very cruel stroke of fate tonight,' Valdano told me on the way out of the stadium to board the team bus. 'Yes, I must admit it. I do feel sorry for him.'

It was minus ten degrees and well past midnight by the time he, the players and the rest of the Real party arrived at Munich airport for the flight home. Ronaldo's prediction had been right, if not exactly in the manner he had anticipated. History had indeed been made: Real had managed not to lose to Bayern at the Olympic Stadium. And they had pulled off a result that did position them now, by any cool appraisal, as favourites to qualify for the quarter-finals. That 1-1 draw had been, in short, a very good night's work. But the mood on the Airbus home was a lot less exuberant than it had been on the way in. In other circumstances after such a result the players might have been laughing noisily the whole way home. But they were subdued, smiling – if smile they did – in the slightly furtive manner of people who know they have been fortunate way beyond their deserts. The directors and their wives weren't joking anymore either. If they talked, they talked about things other than the game. Those who could sleep did so, grateful to be able to forget the night's sobering lesson. Beckham, who was always so wired up after a big game that hours passed before he could go to sleep, sat part of the way home reading – or looking at – the previous morning's *AS*. Whether he understood much of what he read it was hard to tell. If he had understood he would have had cause to reflect on the gap between the paper's almost tauntingly cheery pre-match histri-onics and the present post-match blues. He himself – though no more than anybody else – had played poorly.

The game had been a footballing morality tale, a retelling of the old saw that pride comes before a fall. And a reminder too that the men in white were as capable as anybody of playing football badly. This game against Bayern had been Real's most important by far since Beckham's arrival in the summer and yet they had failed to rise to the occasion. Whatever the excuses, chief among them the weather, the fact was that they had fallen humbly short of the hype, of the legend their famous names had spread to every corner of the globe. The Galácticos were of this earth after all, as prey to bad days and to human frailty as any other player. And as vulnerable, too, to the whims of fortune. Had Kahn stopped a shot he would usually have saved with his eyes shut – or as he himself put it later, that 'a man without arms and legs' could have stopped – it would have been the Real players and not he who would have ended the night in despair.

Real Madrid were the world's most charismatic club; they had the best players; they played the most beautiful football – but not always, and neither did they always win. They were not great, as they seemed partially to have come to believe before the Munich game, by fiat, by God-given right. Player for player they were miles better – worth many millions of euros more – than their German rivals. Hoeness had not lied. On paper Real were indeed far superior. But where it counted, on the grass, they had received a reminder of what they already knew but perhaps had temporarily forgotten, that you have to demonstrate how good you are every single game, that you have to earn the acclaim, that you have to live with the weight of expecta-tion to perform – game after game – sublimely. The wonder is that usually they responded to the pressure, that they did live up to expec-tations. But sometimes they failed, they let down their growing legion of fans. Just as well. Otherwise that late night prediction of Pérez's about the game as we knew it coming to an end by the year 2018 might not have been quite such a big joke after all.

16: The Spirit of Michel Salgado

Two calamities befell Real Madrid that psychologically turned the tables for the return leg against Bayern at the Bernabéu. A UEFA disciplinary committee had a look at the video of the first game and decided to impose a two-match ban on Roberto Carlos for punching Demichelis in the face. And Ronaldo got injured playing in a league game against Racing de Santander, ruling him out of the Bayern game. It was a big loss, in part because of the ability each had to decide the outcome of a game on his own, but most of all, as Figo explained, 'because they are two players who are very integrated in the mechanism of the team'. Without them, in other words, the team's choreography would be less automated; the parts would not move with the same clockwork precision.

For all of which reasons Bayern arrived in Madrid in much the same mood that Real had arrived in Munich two weeks earlier. The enforced absence of the two Brazilians seemed to have amply made up for the misfortune of that Kahn howler at the Olympic Stadium. Raúl would have to operate as the lone striker and, as everybody knew but – because he was so revered in Spain – nobody liked to say, he had not been at his best for months. The season before the team captain had scored nine goals in the Champions League; so far this season, in which he had been dogged by ankle injuries and problems generally with his feet, he had scored just one. He had not played against Racing because of the injury and there were doubts as to whether he would last the full ninety minutes against Bayern.

The Spanish sports newspapers on the Wednesday morning of the game ran with Figo's assessment of Real's two requirements for victory. '*Casta y Calidad.*' *Calidad* means quality. That's clear enough. *Casta* is an altogether more interesting, more layered word – but just the right one to define what was needed on a day when many of the Madrid faithful were going wobbly at the knees. (I reached Florentino Pérez on his mobile telephone that morning. He refused to acknowledge that he was worried. But his reflexively jokey response – 'What? Do you mean am I afraid that we might win 2-0 instead of 3-0?' – offered the surest sign that he was on edge.) The literal translation of *casta* is 'caste'. What the word really means is a combination of things in English, chief among them fortitude, perseverance, discipline – characteristics which everybody in the Real team knew they would have to display, and in abundance, if they were to defeat the old German enemy.

This time the conditions were perfect for football. The temperature was about ten degrees, the sky was clear after a brief afternoon squall and there was a mild breeze. No advantage for the Germans there. Neither was there much comfort for them up on the stands. Some 3,500 red-shirted fans had made the trip from Munich but otherwise the stadium was a ferment of white *Madridismo*. Moments before the game began, with the players already limbering up on the pitch, a massive banner, fifty yards across, appeared behind one of the goals. '*Silencio*,' it read, '*Comienza La Décima Sinfonía*'. 'Silence, the Tenth Symphony is About to Begin.' The allusion, picked up by all in the ground, was to Real Madrid's tenth European Cup, nine having already been won. But if the wits behind the banner were trying to be cocky, no one at the stadium was fooled. This was not going to be one of those Bernabéu opera nights. It was not going to be a spectacle for dilettantes, for Real fans – cigar in one hand, glass of brandy in the other – to engage in the luxury of complaining about their team's lack of artistic accomplishment, jeering Guti when he lost the ball, booing Figo if he tried to get too clever and made a hash of things. Tonight the fans would set aside their customary fussiness, forget about beautiful football and concentrate, like all normal fans everywhere, on getting a result. This was the biggest and toughest game of the season and they knew that this time they had a part to play; that they had a duty to stand by their team through thick and thin, like the English did, and rouse them on to victory. Tonight was the night when the fans of Real Madrid would reacquaint themselves, for the first time all season, with that staple of football fans everywhere: suffering – ninety minutes that seem like ninety years of relentless, stomach-churning, heart-pounding suffering.

The team that suffered less would be the team that displayed the most *casta*. And *casta* was precisely what the Bernabéu got from every member of the Real team, but most of all from the less celebrated players. It was the night of the Pavones. Sadly for him, Francisco Pavón himself was not there. The player doomed chiefly to be remembered by posterity for giving his name to that Pérez formula 'Zidanes and Pavones' was considered by Queiroz to be surplus to requirements on this big European night. His place at centre half taken by another 'Pavón', a young *madrileño* named Alvaro Mejía.

It was a risk. Mejía had never played in a Champions League game before. He had only made his début in the first team two months earlier. But, appearing out of nowhere, he had looked good. Stylish for a defender, composed for one so inexperienced. Still, to play his first European game against Bayern of all teams in a life-or-death Champions League decider: that was to ask a lot of a twenty-two-year-old rookie. But Queiroz had taken a good hard look at him and decided that, both as a player and as a man, he would do. If Mejía failed, if Bayern won, the heat would not be on him, it would be on Queiroz – who would either be fired on the spot or, at the very latest, at the end of the season. Which is why it was a bigger game for Queiroz than for anybody else connected with Real. Pérez would remain president, Beckham would not willingly be sold. For Queiroz, condemned by the Pérez model to run a team long on quality but short on quantity, there would only remain, for the rest of his life, bitter reflection on what might have been.

He had to put Mejía in the middle of the defence because he had to shift Raúl Bravo to left back. In the absence of Roberto Carlos, Bravo was the only player in the Real squad with experience in that position. Not that he was much good there. Bravo is a big, strong, fast player who no one will ever accuse of possessing a light touch on the ball. But he did not put a foot wrong against Bayern. Even on the two or three occasions when he tried to do a lightning raid down the left, à la Roberto Carlos, he did not disgrace himself. Mejía was extraordinary. Comfortable on the ball in a way centre halves rarely are, he looked perversely relaxed during large chunks of the game. Which was either a sign of a man too unintelligent to understand the world around him, or a mark of incipient genius. By contrast the four Galácticos on the pitch – Figo, Zidane, Beckham and Raúl – looked taut from beginning to end, so set were they on fulfilling their unaccustomed obligation to stop Bayern from playing, as if they were concentrating hard throughout every one of the ninety minutes on the novel lesson their coach had tried to impart before the game about keeping their position, tackling back. 'Rarely have I seen Zidane tracking back so much to win the ball,' an amazed Franz Beckenbauer, the Bayern president, would say later. 'Rarely have I seen Real Madrid demonstrate such discipline in defence.'

The lynchpins of the Real effort, though, the heroes of the night were Iván Helguera and Michel Salgado. Mejía and Bravo, Queiroz's two great providential discoveries of the season, might or might not keep their places the following season. You never knew with these things. But Helguera and Salgado had been fixtures in the team, unchallenged members of the starting eleven, for the five years each had spent at the club. When the team was in full symphonic mode, they played second fiddle. On a night like this they were the lead violins. The rest of the team took their cue from them.

Helguera is a player who may not always have his fists clenched, his teeth gritted, his sleeves rolled up and his socks around his ankles – but he looks as if he does. He plays football as if he were big and tall, but he is neither. He is oddly wiry and a far from commanding five foot eleven. But he more than compensates for his lack of bulk by being, in all other respects, the ideal defender. A fearless, furiously committed fighter he is a good header of the ball whose uncannily intelligent positioning must make his often frustrated opponents wonder whether he wears some sort of hidden homing device designed to steer all attacking balls in his direction. Especially in the big games against German or English teams that pound the defence with aerial balls, Helguera's head always seems to be there first, clearing away danger. Rarely injured, he has become an indispensable man in the Real team – so indispensable that one had to wonder how he puts up with being paid less than twenty per cent of what the Galácticos made. Asked as much at the beginning of the season, asked why he was content to receive a mere one million euros a year while Beckham and company received nearly six, he replied in just the way you would expect from a player who on the pitch is guts and nobility personified. 'I signed my contract with Real Madrid a couple of years ago because here I felt valued and loved,' he said. 'Besides, while I do make good money, what you gain here at Real Madrid as a player is quality of life, which is more important than money.'

Quality of life was precisely what had drawn Beckham to Real Madrid at the start of the season, what had drawn Ronaldo and Zidane, what would continue to draw the world's best to the club. The quality of life of knowing that you are not just making money, you're making history. Helguera, from Cantabria in the north of Spain, had won two European Cups since joining Real from Espanyol in 1999 for the trifling sum of seven million euros. He had played in midfield, where he had acted chiefly as a stopper but had scored some great goals, and was now settled as that ideal kind of centre half, the type that discharges his primary duties with rugged intelligence but has the skill to play the ball out of defence quickly, stylishly and well.

Quality of life was also what kept Michel Salgado at Real Madrid. Unlike Helguera he had received a concrete, hugely tempting offer from Chelsea in December and even though he would have been paid appreciably more – even though he was twenty-eight years old and he knew this was probably his last chance in life to make really big money – he said no. He forsook the Abramovich millions and signed a new contract instead for five years with Real Madrid. A philosopher, like Helguera, he took the view that money couldn't buy him love. 'It is true that I have lost money,' he said, moments after renewing with Real, 'but I have won in other things, such as the sheer enjoyment of playing here in the coming years.'

Salgado arrived from Celta de Vigo in 1999 with a reputation as a feisty and tireless, if rather rustic, right back. He knew, brave fellow, that he was destined never to benefit from the comparison with his opposite number over on the left side of defence, the remarkable Roberto Carlos. He was as small as the Brazilian, but stocky rather than athletic. Hard, yes. (Steve McManaman once said Salgado was the hardest man he had ever met.) But hard with bone rather than muscle. Roberto Carlos rippled; Salgado seemed knock-kneed. Roberto Carlos could have been an Olympic sprinter; Salgado, all crouched and ungainly in his movements, might have had a better chance in the fifty kilometre walk. Roberto Carlos played with grace and fire; Salgado looked terribly busy always, in the way a carpenter might when sawing wood.

Though he won the European Cup in his very first season at Real the portents did not look good when Pérez took over in the summer of 2000. Quite apart from his lack of that artistry Pérez required, he had recently married the daughter of the man Pérez had ousted as president, Lorenzo Sanz. Salgado looked like he would be the first to go with the new regime. But two things happened that surprised people. First, Pérez was not as small-minded as Sanz, in a similar position, might have been; second, Salgado was determined to fight every inch for his place in the team. He wasn't a natural-born talent, but he was obstinate and proud and he would not give in. He would battle, as if his life depended on it, to improve his game. He would leave Pérez with no option but to keep him, his teammates with no alternative but to recognise his worth. One season gave way to the next, Galáctico piled on Galáctico, and each time he became more entrenched in what looked like the role of poor relation in the Real family – the one member of the team born in the wet, unfashionable, fishermen's province of Galicia. But despite continual rumours that he would be off-loaded he remained in place. Until, following Beckham's arrival, he suddenly grew to become as indispensable a member of the team as Roberto Carlos.

Whether Beckham had anything to do with it is not clear. Though the one thing that is certain is that the two did play side by side on the pitch, that they could communicate well thanks to Salgado's good English (he is the workhorse of the team but there is no one brighter than him at Real) and that Beckham did cover for him, did help him out in defence, allowing him to go forward on runs that at first bewildered opponents and teammates alike – so unused were they to see him play the all-singing, all-dancing Roberto Carlos role of attacker and defender so well. No one played so effectively, so consistently all season long. No one played more minutes than him in the whole Real team – in fact, the statistics showed that no player in Europe had played more minutes than he during the first four months of the 2003/04 season. And yet, unbowed by the physical strain, he flourished as a player, convincing Chelsea that he had become the best right back in the world market.

His teammates certainly thought so, and told him as much. He had passed from poor relation to mightily valued member of the team, by fans and players alike. And although he never kidded himself that he was a great star, he knew his worth and was proud to have won his battle to secure his place in this great team. All that was worth much more to him than money, as he explained after agreeing to that new deal with the once-sceptical Pérez. 'I'm never going to be a Galáctico,' he said. 'But I have achieved what I have always wanted, which is to be valued by my teammates – to whom I owe so much – and by the club, where it is now my dream to retire.'

Never did they appreciate him more than during that game against Bayern at the Bernabéu. If ever a game was made for a player of his toughness, of his *casta*, this was it. No Brazilians, no samba. That suited Bayern just fine. But it suited Salgado even better. Digging deep into all those reserves of grit that had served him so well in his arduous climb to the top of the Real Madrid tree, he led the charge that turned the game – and the psychological advantage – Real's way.

Salgado, a man famed more for his pluck than for his prowess in the air, had the temerity halfway through the first half to jump for a ball with the towering Bayern central defender Kovac. It was a loose ball that had ricocheted off another German player into the Bayern area from a Beckham cross. Salgado got his head to the ball first, nodding it across a perplexed Kahn towards the far post where Zidane was waiting all alone. The Frenchman just prodded the ball, which came to him gently at waist height, into the empty net. The fans, who until that moment had raised the average decibel level at the Bernabéu by a factor of ten, shook the walls of the old stadium with their celebrations. The players raced to embrace Salgado, the architect of a goal that was never on, that he made out of nothing, through sheer blind faith in the value of going for every ball, climbing every mountain. The rest of the team took their cue from him. For the frighteningly tense remaining hour of the game not one player went missing in action. Raúl's ankle hurt like hell but he stayed on to the end, battling back for every ball. Zidane adorned the game as always with his touches, providing the only suggestions of high art, but tonight he laboured like the best of them. Figo played with economy and discipline, only rarely trying to take on a man and beat him down the wing, which is the trademark of his game. Beckham hung back and covered, plugged every hole, disdaining personal glory in the higher cause of victory. Guti, whose hair is bleached blonder than Beckham's, who aspires to be a pretty boy too, fought in midfield like a Viking. And Casillas, the unfailingly miraculous 'San Iker', made a couple of saves to remind Kahn of the player he once was. What happened, in short, was that Real out-Germaned the Germans. Player for player, they covered more ground, they showed more determination, fight and discipline than Bayern in a game whose outcome was decided by the spirit of Salgado.

At the end the Real players hugged each other with the sort of intensity you only see after a team has won a major trophy. Every player embraced every other player. The game had provided a reminder once again that no matter what the respective fortunes of the teams at any given time, Real–Bayern was always a fearsome clash. But the players were not only celebrating a famous victory, or the fact that Real Madrid had pulled off the impressive new record of making it to the Champions League quarter-finals for the seventh consecutive season. They were rejoicing in the manner in which they had shown the world that, much more than a collection of individual artists, they were a great team. Florentino Pérez had told me once in one of the chats we had in his office that he saw the relationship between the players as one between a large family of brothers. 'There are rivalries, jealousies. Some get on better with one than with another. Some don't really get on. But when the chips are down, when there is a common enemy to face, they are bound together with chains of steel.' And against Bayern they played, as they say in Spain, with *cojones* of steel. They had shown *casta* and *calidad*. With their backs against the wall, missing their two inspirational Brazilians, they had known how to fight back together. One for all and all for one. The fans, too, had risen to the occasion, shedding their customary cool, abandoning themselves to the cause. The whole team went to the centre circle and did what Beckham always did on his own: they saluted the Bernabéu, thanked the crowd for playing their part in a victory which served as a reminder to all those of us who had been besotted by the natural-born talent of the Galácticos that skill alone does not guarantee victory, that to triumph in football you also need a big heart.

17: The Exterminating Angel

Fans of the Roman club SS Lazio were not famed for their toler-
ance or genteel manners during the years when Ronaldo played in
Serie A. Racial abuse was the local speciality, fines having been
imposed on the club by the Italian football federation after banners
appeared in the ground insulting blacks and Jews. Lazio's Stadio
Olimpico was not, therefore, the most auspicious setting for what
was billed as the Brazilian's definitive comeback after a year and a
half battling on and off to recover from a career-threatening knee
injury, especially since Ronaldo's skin pigmentation was a shade or
two darker than the southern European norm.

It was April 2000 and Inter Milan, the team Ronaldo had joined
from Barcelona in the summer of 1997, were playing against Lazio
in the semi-final of the Italian Cup. The comeback of the man they
had come to know in Italy as *il Fenomeno*, twice winner of the FIFA
World Player of the Year award and not yet twenty-four, lasted precisely
seven minutes. The first time he tried one of his trademark rampaging
runs, the first feint he attempted with the ball at his feet, his knee
gave way sickeningly, like a rubber doll's. It was the very same right
knee that had been operated on by a Parisian specialist four months
earlier. A hush so complete descended on the stadium that all around
the ground they could hear Ronaldo's screams of pain and despair,
and the shouts of the two Lazio defenders closest to him, calling for
medical attention. As the Inter doctor crouched over him, as one
minute, two minutes, three passed and Ronaldo remained immobile,
the Lazio *tifosi* began to emit groans of what could only be interpreted as genuine distress. When Ronaldo was eventually stretchered
away in a motorised cart, his knee heavily strapped, the atmosphere

in the stadium was funereal. All who witnessed the episode, whether at the stadium itself or live on TV, were filled with the heaviest fore-boding – a sense that Ronaldo's career was well and truly over, that he had been cut off in the full flower of his youth, that we would never see him play again.

But the doctors still thought there was a faint chance. Back in Paris, where he arrived on crutches, he had another operation to his knee. The pain was so great in the days after the surgery that Ronaldo was compelled continually to squeeze a pump they had put by the side of his bed to allow him to inject morphine into his veins. Nilton Petrone, the physiotherapist who took care of him during his conva-lescence and slept in a room next to his at the French hospital, told the Brazilian magazine *Veja* how very early one morning he was woken up by Ronaldo calling out for him. 'He was weeping like a child,' recalled Petrone, known to Ronaldo by his nickname 'File'. 'He cried out, "File, tell me that I am going to play again! Tell me, please!"' Petrone did what he could to calm him down. 'I am absolutely certain that you will play again,' he told Ronaldo. Yet, as he confessed years later, 'The truth is that I wasn't certain at all!'

What Petrone did not know then was how ferocious Ronaldo's will was to return to the playing field. For the next twenty months he spent six hours a day exercising his heavily scarred knee, often in excruciating pain, until the doctor who performed the operation judged him fit to play once again. This latest comeback was programmed for December 2001, away in *Serie A* to Brescia. This time he not only survived the ordeal, he scored – his first compet-itive goal in two years. Football fans in stadiums all over Italy turned away from the games they were watching to celebrate the news. Everyone inside the Brescia stadium broke into applause, not excluding the Brescia coach. Carlo Mazzone, whose team Inter would end up beating 3-1, declared in the after-match press conference that the pain of defeat had been tempered by the happiness he felt for Ronaldo. 'If we really had to concede a goal,' Mazzone said, 'then I'm glad it was he who scored it.'

The response of Gabriel Batistuta was no less elegant. Batistuta, who played for Roma, was the top marksman in *Serie A* and as such the player who logically would have felt most threatened by Ronaldo's return. Yet the response of the man they called 'Batigol' was one of unalloyed delight. 'I am very happy,' the Argentine hitman said, 'because Ronaldo is football.'

That was exactly right, and exactly why the football world – everyone, fans and rivals alike – responded the way they did to what in Brazil they described as his 'resurrection'. Ronaldo *was* football and everyone who loved the game understood immediately, instinctively, just what Batistuta was saying. Ronaldo was the game's distilled essence. He got the ball, he charged at the defence and suddenly he alone was the whole team. No other player at the top level of the world game could transform himself into a one-man band the way he could. No other player received the ball in midfield, with four defenders between him and the goal, and caused such panic, creating a sensation of such clear and imminent threat. The classic Ronaldo goal was one he scored for Barcelona in the 1996/97 season against Santiago de Compostela. He picked up the ball on the halfway line and ran and ran and ran, brushing off tackles like a rugby player, not so much weaving as cutting sharply in and out, never a thought in his head of passing the ball to a teammate, never a thought that wasn't of the goal, until he smacked the ball through a crowd of defenders in the penalty area into the back of the net. Ronaldo's coach at the time, the white-haired Bobby Robson, can be seen in the television footage of the goal clutching his head in disbelief, quite beside himself, at the spectacle he has just witnessed, the most remarkable individual goal he had seen in the fifty years he had spent as player and coach at the top of the professional game.

Or perhaps it bore comparison with the famous one Maradona scored against Robson's England team in the 1986 World Cup in Mexico. Maradona's goal was an impish slalom. Ronaldo's was a buffalo charge. It was what Valdano meant when he said once, 'When Ronaldo attacks, a herd attacks.' He scored goals like the one against Santiago de Compostela all the time. Usually it was not the entire defence he took on. Usually it was a mere thirty- or forty-metre run past three defenders – a rampaging run that combined power and finesse like nothing ever seen before, and that over the last fifteen metres was purely unstoppable. That was the essential Ronaldo and the reason why you felt on watching him that he was indeed 'football', the thing itself, was that it reminded you of your childhood when you played in the park or the school yard. There was always one boy who was better than the rest. There was always one boy who was so good that if, say, seven of you had turned up to play and you had to have two teams of four and three players, you would always put him in the team of three; or maybe you had to make it five against two, to even the odds. And that boy was so much more skilful and strong and fast on the ball than any of the rest of you, that he beat you single-handed every time, dribbling past one boy and another and another, scoring goal after goal. That is the crude, first experience of football we all have who played the game as children and that crude first experience was what Ronaldo replicated time and again, and for the rest of his life, when he went out on to a football pitch, however mature and experienced the defenders he faced, however exalted the stage. Always, from age five to ten to fifteen to twenty, at every phase of his evolution as a player he retained that gap in class between himself and the other players, none of whom ever quite caught up with him, all of whom he could, on his day, defeat on his own.

I spoke to Juergen Klinsmann, another great goal-scorer, about Ronaldo and he too found himself talking about the childlike quality in the Brazilian's game. Klinsmann was living in Los Angeles, California. Over lunch at the headquarters of the US Soccer Federation he explained to me his vision of Ronaldo's genius.

'All truly great players are unique at something. Ronaldo is unique because he executes, because he has one idea in his head when he gets the ball and he executes it. He does not know how, he cannot rationalise it, but since he was a kid he has done it. One day he had three or four defenders in front of him and he beat them and he scored. From that moment on he knew he could do it, and since that first time he has done it again and again and again. Because he *knows* he can beat defenders, he does really know it. He has a supreme confidence that is beyond arrogance that all the truly great players have. And on the other side the defenders know he has that total confidence and belief and they know he will try and do what others would consider so impossible they would not even dream of trying and so psychologically he has an edge over them the instant he gets the ball. Because he poses questions, causes fear. And he waits for the defender he is taking on to make the first move, and the defender knows he must not make that first move, but if out of fear he does make it, then he is lost, because Ronaldo's feet are quicker. Always quicker. And believe me, it all began when he was a little kid, the first time he did it, the first time he beat those three or four guys and scored. That settled it. Since then he has never stopped.'

He never had. And like the children who watched him do it that first time we remained agog each time he did it again, never tiring of his genius. He was such a lethal and supremely gifted exponent of the goal-scoring art – his shots on goal were aimed always with such laser predictability within inches of the inside of the post – that we all bowed down before him, we all wanted a share of him. He belonged not just to a club or a country, but – as Pérez said of Zidane – to the human race. Pelé was such a player. So were Di Stefano, Cruyff and Maradona. So in golf was Tiger Woods, or Jack Nicklaus. In cricket, Bradman or Sobers. Ronaldo had it all. He was tall, he was strong, he had devastating pace. He was a footballing god. The statistics revealed as much. In Holland, his first European port of call, he scored forty-two goals in forty-five games aged barely nineteen for PSV Eindhoven; he scored thirty-four goals in thirty-seven league games at Barcelona; twenty-five goals in thirty-two games during his first season at Inter.

I once asked Bobby Robson when he was still at Barcelona to compare Ronaldo with the much admired English goal-scorer, the best of his generation, Alan Shearer. The grand old man of English football, possibly repressing the urge to laugh at the ignorant banality of the question, replied: 'Shearer is a fantastic player but Ronaldo is six years younger and he can score goals that Shearer can't. He's the best player in the world and arguably the best player of all. But he will be the best, without a shadow of a doubt. When he's twenty-two, twenty-three, twenty-four, twenty-five, twenty-six – Wow! Wow! Wow!'

Except that, in footballing terms, twenty-two, twenty-three, twenty-four never happened. We had seen what Robson saw in him when he was nineteen, twenty, twenty-one and we wanted more. We wanted it never to end, and that was why everybody in the football world was so devastated when his knee crumpled beneath him at Lazio and was so overjoyed when the news spread that he had scored eight months later at Brescia. He brought out the best in us, a nobility that – in a game so often defined by the passion of its antagonism – went beyond our day-to-day tribal allegiances. We rallied around Ronaldo in sickness and in health because he embodied the qualities in the game that we most loved.

At the time he scored that comeback goal against Brescia, he was still not certain he would ever fully recover. Over the next three months, the first three of 2002, he continued to suffer relapses, to be taken off before the end of games, to be out injured for two or three weeks at a time. Come April, and with the World Cup just two months away, it was touch and go whether we would see him in the colours of every neutral's favourite football nation, Brazil; whether he would have the chance to make up for the disappointment of losing the previous World Cup final to Zidane's France in 1998.

I went to see him that month at the Inter Milan training ground, a beautiful spot set in lush green countryside within sight of the snow-peaked Alps. I remember how happy he seemed, bounding with confidence and optimism, every inch the footballing superhero. Mature, self-possessed, a man seemingly at peace with himself, he betrayed no sign of the anguish he had gone through. Was it over now? Was it really all over? 'Yes, yes,' he replied. 'Definitely. Now yes. It's been very tough. It's been two years of sacrifice. But now it's over. It's done. I've had a couple of muscular problems, yes, but regular, normal stuff. The serious injury has been defeated. I am ready to play.'

I put it to him that if he did indeed effect a full recovery, that if he had a healthy World Cup, he would go down as the patron saint of injured football players. He smiled, shook his head gently and said no, there were plenty of patron saints out there already. 'We've had lots of examples of great players who were seriously injured but made a complete recovery. I, for example, followed really closely what happened to Maradona when he was at Barcelona and broke his leg. What happened to Zico at Flamingo. And then when I myself was injured, I had a visitor at my house one day: Pelé.'

He was an assassin on the pitch – not a dancer like Zidane – but his conversational style was lazy in a sensual Brazilian sort of way. When he uttered the word Pelé, though, he paused for special emphasis, raised the volume an octave or two. Pronounced the name the Brazilian way, with a sharp accent on the final 'e': 'Pelé!' He was proud as a little boy that the greatest football legend in the history of his country had actually come to see him, at his house. 'Pelé told me that during the 1966 World Cup in England he got badly injured and that everybody told him he would never be able to play again. And two or three years passed and still nobody believed he would ever play at his best level again. But he did. He played in another World Cup, in 1970. He won the World Cup, he was chosen as the competition's best player. So, what I am saying is, examples like these – Pelé, Zico, Maradona – are what gave me the courage to persevere.'

Two other things he said at that meeting stayed with me. One, that he did not like Italian football – 'it's something like chess', he said – and preferred the way they played in Spain. Two, that not only was he confident he would win the World Cup with Brazil, that the best of his footballing life lay ahead of him. When I asked him, now that he looked as if he might finally be over his injury nightmares, what his biggest remaining ambition was, he answered with heartfelt simplicity, and without the slightest hesitation or doubt. 'To stay healthy,' he said. 'If I can stay healthy all the rest . . . all the rest I can achieve.'

He was as good as his word. Two months after we met he won the World Cup with Brazil, he was top scorer in the competition, he scored the two winning goals in the final against Germany and in December he was chosen for the third time in his life – but for the first time in five years – as FIFA World Player of the Year. And in between times he joined the club he most wanted to join in the world, Real Madrid.

Florentino Pérez had had his eye on Ronaldo, inevitably, before the World Cup began but until the competition had got solidly under way he remained unconvinced. Everyone remained unconvinced. Hurricane of a player that he was at his peak, he still seemed frighteningly fragile. The World Cup dispelled all doubts and come July 2002 the Real Madrid president had his ravenous eye firmly on Ronaldo and he was determined to catch his prey. It turned out to be a much more nail-biting drama than any of Pérez's other Galáctico swoops.

If José Angel Sánchez was the man Pérez dispatched to get Beckham, Valdano was the point man on Ronaldo. It all began, Valdano told me, when round about that time when I was interviewing Ronaldo in Milan. Inter had made contact with Real Madrid, offering him for sale.

'It was a couple of months before the World Cup when Inter put out feelers to us,' Valdano recalled. 'I made some discreet inquiries and discovered Ronaldo himself was dead keen to come. But we were not so sure because there was no certainty at that point that his knee was healed, and there was a suspicion Inter might be trying to do a number on us. But after the World Cup we decided we really, really did want him. And Inter, to our surprise, were still keen on selling. But the price had of course gone up.'

Operation Ronaldo, as the press called it, was a poker game that was to last through the summer, right up until the UEFA deadline for clubs to sign new players, midnight on Saturday 31 August. The breakthrough, or what looked like it, only came the day before when Barcelona joined the poker game, in what seemed like good faith. On that Friday, Barcelona's president, Joan Gaspart, talked to Pérez in Monte Carlo during a meeting of the so-called 'G14' – the richest football clubs in Europe. Gaspart informed Pérez that he wished to buy the Real Madrid striker, Fernando Morientes. Pérez struggled to contain his delight. Not only was Morientes very much on the market, his sale was the key that would unlock the door to Ronaldo.

The deal, announced as a *fait accompli* on the Saturday morning in all the Spanish newspapers, was a cash-plus-player arrangement that, for complex accounting reasons, would look like this: Real

Madrid would switch Morientes to Inter who would instantly sell him on to Barcelona; Real would also give Inter a large sum of cash; then Ronaldo would move from Inter to Real Madrid.

But during the Saturday afternoon, with the clock ticking, Pérez and Valdano smelt a rat – one with a familiar whiff to it. Barcelona started to haggle with Inter over Morientes's price, immediately prompting the Real twosome to suspect that Gaspart was playing dirty. Inter, far from heeding their warnings, were so convinced the deal would go through that they went ahead that very afternoon and signed Ronaldo's replacement, Hernán Crespo from Lazio, even before they had formally sold Ronaldo to Real.

'It was at five p.m. that our suspicions began to be confirmed that Gaspart had set an elaborate trap for us,' Valdano said. 'He announced that he wanted to pay Inter two million euros less for Morientes. This was a problem, but not an insoluble one. We resolved it ourselves by saying, Fine, we'll pay Inter two million more. An hour later Gaspart came back and said, no: two million more on top of that. We said, "We'll pay it.' The Inter people were beginning to get the picture, though they still struggled to believe that a club as reputable as Barcelona would behave in such an underhand way.'

Which was not to say that the Italians were pillars of business probity, virginally unaware that people could behave like this. It was to say that they failed to grasp, the way only a Spaniard could grasp, the depth of resentment Joan Gaspart and so many of the Barça faithful felt towards Real Madrid. As Ronaldo, who played for both clubs, would say much later, Barcelona had the idea lodged very firmly in the depth of the club's collective brain that they were the number two club in Spain – and this knowledge drove them at times to despair.

'It was not until ten at night,' Valdano continued, 'that Gaspart revealed his true intentions for all to see. There was no longer any doubt about it. He was seeking to scupper the whole deal by leaving things so late that meeting the deadline became impossible. What happened was this: we received a fax from Barcelona – at ten at night, I repeat – saying they pulled completely out of the deal. We were devastated but the Inter people were in even worse shape.

Massimo Moretti, their chief executive, was in what you would clinically describe as a state of shock. We were conducting this final
negotiation with him over an open phone line. Moretti asked for
five minutes to close the phone line so he could try and recover.'

Valdano, the coolest of men, confessed that he himself had been
sweating. Not Pérez, though. 'This was Florentino's moment. Pure
Florentino. Florentino at his best,' said Valdano. 'Everyone else's pulses
were racing but you had the sense that his blood pressure had gone
right down. The hotter the crisis, the colder his brain.'

Pérez called Moretti and said, 'Come on, let's get to work.' Pérez's
proposal was to offer Inter instead of Morientes another of a choice
of available players, the Argentine Santiago Solari being the most
likely candidate, in part exchange for Ronaldo. Either that or a
further ten million euros payable in December. 'We also got them
to knock a few million off their price,' Valdano said. 'We were not
the only ones that had to cede a bit here. They had the Crespo deal
poised too, hence their panic. But they also knew that Ronaldo
wanted to go and that the Inter fans, knowing this, did not want
him to stay – all of which meant that if the deal did not go through
we would have been terribly disappointed but they would have been
left with a terrible fiasco to deal with. Florentino had understood
all this, had judged the balance of power in the negotiations, in a
flash. Within forty-five minutes a deal was done. With enormous
relief on the Inter side and joy on ours, we got it all done a few
minutes before midnight.'

Everybody was happy except Barcelona and in particular Gaspart,
a man who had risen to the presidency of his club in the summer
of 2000, at exactly the same time as Pérez had taken over at Real
Madrid, and since then had found himself cast, with ever more
uncanny similitude, in the role of an envious, bitter, smarting Salieri
to Pérez's soaring Mozart. Nine months later the poor man was
driven, half-crazed, out of the Barça presidency, to be replaced
following fresh club elections by Joan Laporta, the man who lost out
to Real in the attempt to land David Beckham.

The timing of the announcement that the Beckham deal had been
clinched did not do much for Pérez's own popularity at Real. Not

with the players at least. The big news came on the Tuesday before the final game of the season, that following weekend. The rivals were going to be Athletic Bilbao, always a tough proposition, and Real had to win in order to be crowned Spanish league champions. The golden rule in such circumstances is that the club does nothing to upset the concentration of the players. Announcing that Beckham was coming, a news item more sensational than the upshot of any football game, was interpreted as a kick in the teeth by the serious minded Spaniards in the team. The likes of Raúl, Helguera and the then captain Fernando Hierro seethed with indignation. Ronaldo, on the other hand, asked on the Wednesday for his response to Beckham's arrival, had this to say: 'Terrific! He is a great player and a good guy. Besides, he attracts so many women that there are bound to be plenty left over for me!'

At the weekend Real beat Athletic 3-1. Ronaldo scored two of the goals. The team's other Brazilian, Roberto Carlos (who for his own more complex reasons was also pleased Beckham was coming), scored the other. Months later, well into the next season, I spoke to Ronaldo and Roberto Carlos at the Real Madrid training centre. The mood was playful and the conversation did have a habit of straying towards the subject of women, which seemed to be the natural connection they made in their minds whenever we started talking about Brazil. But I did manage to drag them back to football every now and again.

Ronaldo was even more deliciously lazy in his conversation, even more lethargically at ease with himself, than he had been a couple of years earlier when I had met him in Milan. You almost felt at times talking to him that he was going to doze off. Roberto Carlos was more taut, but not so much out of nervousness as because he had a tightly coiled, relentlessly highly-strung way of being happy. They were, in other words, the way they played. Roberto Carlos: perpetual movement – a human bullet train. Ronaldo: a prowler, waiting – all day if need be – to explode. He was the one player at Real Madrid who was completely excused defensive duties. The prize he offered – goals and, therefore, victory – was too precious to allow his energy to be squandered in any ancillary tasks. Queiroz did not immediately understand this when he arrived, which was why for the first competitive game of the 2003/04 season he asked Ronaldo if he could track back and keep an eye on a dangerous little Argentine midfielder called Ibagaza, who was well known and much respected in Spanish football. Ronaldo's response to Queiroz was, 'Who is Ibagaza?' Queiroz, puzzled that Ronaldo should not know, was at a loss how to react. Whereupon another member of the coaching staff said, 'Yes. Ibagaza. He wears the number ten on the back of his shirt.' 'Uh, no. I'm sorry,' Ronaldo replied. 'I can't see that far. My eyes aren't all that good.' And that was the end of that: the first and last time Queiroz ever attempted to persuade Ronaldo to violate nature and defend. If friends ever presumed to give him a hard time for not sharing the workload more with his teammates, he always had a cheeky reply. 'Running,' he would say, 'is for cowards.'

Florentino Pérez, who loved Ronaldo's brilliant idleness, who used to enjoy telling people how sometimes after matches Ronaldo did not even feel the need to take a shower, described him to me once as a lion. 'If you take your eyes off the ball during a game,' Pérez said, 'and watch him alone up front when our team is defending you'll see him walking slowly across the pitch from one touchline to the other, and then back across again. Then you look at the defenders and you see they are struggling to contain their fear and bewilderment, bordering on panic, as their eyes follow him in a state of hyperalertness, like gazelles or zebras who know there is a lion in the neighbourhood.'

He was a quiet lion. A thing about him that people sometimes commented on was his Buddha-like demeanour during a game. Most players shouted for the ball, offered instructions to their teammates, said things to their rivals. Ronaldo was completely silent during the ninety minutes, at his most histrionic when he made a gesture with his eyebrows, maybe, or the fingers of his hands.

But he was also a nice lion, a smiling king of the jungle. Everybody who knew him said he was the most likeable of men. Pérez described him as quite different from anyone else he knew. '*Un tipo feliz*' – a happy fellow, at one with the universe, immune somehow to the irritations and frustrations and minor distresses that beset ordinary mortals. He enjoyed the good life. He loved parties. He stayed up late. He had lots of women in his life. A man more different in his habits from Pérez it was hard to imagine. But they got on well. Pérez had come to understand that for Ronaldo to be useful to him, to be at his peak for Real Madrid, he had to be happy. And to be happy meant giving him the space in Madrid to be his lusty, epicurean Brazilian self. (Kiko Narvaez, a former player for Atlético Madrid, once captured Ronaldo's twin virtues as a seducer, on and off the pitch, when he said that while other players toiled and toiled all night to score, Ronaldo was 'like George Clooney, he winks and the girl is his'.) Pérez liked recalling the time when, jokingly, he lectured Ronaldo about the excessive number of beautiful young women in his life. To which Ronaldo responded, mock-beseechingly, 'But, *Señor Presidente*, you must understand: I *need* to make love!' To which *el Señor Presidente* – who you would no more imagine capable of having a fling on the side than the Queen of England – responded by cracking up laughing like he had never laughed before in his life.

Vicente del Bosque was another one who adored Ronaldo. 'He is not just a happy guy but someone who has a very clear idea of what life's about,' del Bosque told me. 'He has an instinct for foot-ball, and for life. He is different, singular – as a player and as a man. He could play as a midfielder or a centre half if he put his mind to it. He just happened to choose the glory position, the goal-scoring centre forward. He has a special gift for the game and for living with graceful ease. He knows how to live in a palace or in a slum. Everything he does he does with complete naturalness. He is a seducer – an enchanter – on the fooball pitch, and off it. I would be amazed to hear someone say they got on badly with him.'

Part of Ronaldo's charm, and that secret of life del Bosque said he possessed, was something he learnt during his years battling to walk again: a calm sense of perspective and balance based on his gratitude at the mere fact of being able to kick a football again; a sense that everything he was enjoying in his football life was a blessed and unexpected bonus. But another part of Ronaldo's charm, flowing from the same wise understanding, was that he had a giving person-ality, that he was generous in a low-key but meaningful sort of way.

After the terrorist attack on Madrid in March, the train bombs that went off on the very morning after Real's 1-0 home victory over Bayern, killing 192 people, the newly elected prime minister José Luis Rodriguez Zapatero went to a hospital to visit some of the injured survivors. He came across a nineteen-year-old Romanian boy whose leg had been shattered and who asked him whether, please, it would be possible for him to arrange for Ronaldo to go and see him. Zapatero called Pérez who called Ronaldo and the very next day Ronaldo was there, with Pérez, by the young Romanian's bed. The boy was thunderstruck to see his dream come true, comforted when Ronaldo told him how he too had endured his agonies with his leg and, not to worry, look how things had turned out for him – he'd be up and about playing football himself in no time.

When we spoke that time at the Real Madrid training centre he displayed that same generosity of spirit, but this time towards his closest footballing buddy, the player sitting right next to us. 'It's an injustice that I've won all these individual awards and Roberto hasn't won one. It's not right,' he said of the man with whom he plays for both club and country. 'Look at this guy. The world has never seen a player like him, and probably never will again. He's unique. The perfect modern footballer, who combines the technique of a Brazilian with the strength of a European. And he's won everything there is to win in the game. He's won more big trophies than I have. The only explanation is where he plays, that judges only look at players who score goals. Though come to think of it, he scores goals all right . . .'

Roberto Carlos was grinning as Ronaldo delivered what for him was an unusually long peroration on his footballing attributes. But Ronaldo hadn't finished. 'And the other thing is that he is in such extraordinary physical shape that he is going to continue playing at the highest level long after the rest of us have retired, he's going to break records, you'll see.' Then turning to his friend he said, 'So, when do you think you'll be playing until?' 'Oh, thirty-six, thirty-seven . . .' said Roberto Carlos, who was thirty at that point. 'And you?' he asked Ronaldo. 'Me? thirty-three, maybe . . .' Roberto Carlos was outraged, indignant. 'Thirty-three? No way! No way! I won't let you! You've got to keep going, do you hear me?'

It was as sincere a mutual admiration society as you could hope to find. 'Ronaldo is such a complete player,' Roberto Carlos said. 'He has such mastery of the ball. He has such quick feet. When he takes on a defender his movements are so short, so sharp, so fast that when he is in full flight there is very little you can do to stop him. In fact, when he is in full flight you can't stop him, however good a defender you are. There is just nothing to be done – not within the laws of the game, anyway.'

I reminded them of a goal Ronaldo had scored against Espanyol in a recent league game. Their faces lit up in instant recognition, just as they did in a wonderful photograph recording the moment when the ball crossed the goal line. Ronaldo is almost inside the goal, in the photograph, smiling broadly, Roberto Carlos is coming up behind him, running to congratulate him, laughing, his face a picture of delight.

Not as explosively spectacular as Ronaldo's 'attack like a herd' goals were, it would nevertheless remain for everyone who saw it one of the treasured memories of the football year. It was one of those goals that only Ronaldo could score; that made you feel that with him in the team you were invincible.

Running on to a pass that was going in a straight line for goal with only the goalkeeper to beat, he had two alternatives – or, at any rate, the only two alternatives any normal striker would have imagined possible: to shoot on sight or try and go around the goalkeeper and then shoot. Ronaldo, revealing exactly why it was no journalistic exaggeration to describe him as a player who operated on another dimension, chose a third option. He went straight through the goalkeeper without even touching the ball. He confused him so completely – feinting with a tremor of his hips and knees and ankles to go right, then left, then right, then left, all in a fraction of a second – that the poor man did not so much dive as collapse to his left. Ronaldo just kept going straight, only touching the ball for the first time once he had gone past the goalkeeper, who lay sprawled on the ground, past redemption, not the slightest notion in his head of recovery. Ronaldo slowed down, stopped altogether for a moment and then, grinning, walked the ball into the empty net.

I asked my friend Luis Angel, the Argentine universities international, to give me a more detailed analysis of that goal, one he had gaped in wonder at with the rest of us. 'The hidden story of that goal,' Luis Angel explained, 'lies in what is going on inside the goalkeeper's mind. He knows who Ronaldo is as well as any of the rest of us. But now here is Ronaldo galloping at full speed towards him with the intention of putting the ball past him for a goal. Three thousand possibilities come to his mind as to what Ronaldo might do, because he knows for a fact that Ronaldo indeed has 3,000 resources at his disposal in a situation like this. And all this is happening inside his head at the speed of light with the added distress brought on by the physical knowledge that a buffalo is advancing on him at frightening speed. But what he also knows is that this buffalo has a gyroscope inside his head, a device that is able to anticipate in which direction the goalkeeper is going to go and which in turn directs his own body with mechanical precision in the opposite direction. Add all those factors up, that torrent of thoughts and terrors in whose grip the goalkeeper finds himself in that millisecond of time, and the effect is a sort of paralysis of the man's brain, or perhaps an impulse to flee, to run, to dive out of the way.' And as for Roberto Carlos's reaction, the childlike delight, Luis Angel said that it could not have been any other way. 'It was a flashback to the school yard. One of those clever, ingenious, comical goals that had you all laughing with almost malicious delight.'

Ronaldo's recollection of the goal was happy, proud – and simple. 'I received a pass from Cambiasso running towards the goalkeeper at great speed,' he said, with Roberto Carlos listening, mouth open, all ears. 'And then . . . well, then with just one movement I made the goalkeeper fall to one side and I just kept going, down the middle. And then I scored.' Roberto Carlos applauded for joy. 'That,' he said, 'that is the beauty of football! That is the beauty of it all! That is Brazilian football! It is fun! It is our culture! It is life! A Brazilian player – with the ball or without the ball – creates fantasy!'

Vicente del Bosque, such a dyed-in-the-wool Spaniard, was with Roberto Carlos all the way. 'The fact is that – with respect to the English – the Brazilians are the parents of the game,' del Bosque told me. 'Look at Ronaldo. Other normal players from other normal countries are slow with the ball at their feet, fast without it. Ronaldo is slow without it, but give him a ball and he runs like lightning. That's what the passion for the game does for you. That's what happens when you have football in the blood, like these Brazilians do.'

Del Bosque had Real Madrid in his blood. He still harboured dreams of going back to work at the club in some capacity some day, despite the fact he had been sacked. And if he was, as many saw him, the living soul of the club, he had of necessity to love the Brazilian way of football. As Ronaldo and Roberto Carlos loved Real Madrid. When we reflected in our conversation how Roberto Carlos had spent eight years at Real Madrid Ronaldo could not repress a cry of envy. 'You're a lucky guy, you know,' he said, looking his friend in the eye, deadly serious for once. 'You're truly a lucky guy. You have played practically all you career at the best club in the world and for the best country in the world,' he said. 'I know,' the human bullet train replied, nodding. 'There is no better club for a Brazilian player. It is the same philosophy. Real Madrid is to club football what Brazil is to international football.' In the same way that Real Madrid went a long time without winning a European Cup, Brazil went a long time without winning a World Cup – 24 years, in fact, in which they never even made it to a final. Yet the lustre never wore off. Brazil always remained the world's most charismatic side, the one everybody – no matter what country they were from – wanted to watch. And that was partly, as with Real Madrid, because of the memory of their tremendous historical achievements but, more than that, because of the ethic Brazilian football enshrines. Winning was imperative but it was not enough. If you won playing dull, defensive football the merit in victory was diminished. What mattered was playing with dash. That message transmitted itself to the whole world and for that reason Brazil became, and for the foreseeable future shall remain, football's most potent global brand. What Florentino Pérez did at club level was to apply the Brazilian principles to Real Madrid, with identical results. 'That is exactly right,' said Ronaldo, nodding furiously in agreement. 'That is why they love Real Madrid in Brazil.

They love the fact that I have ended up playing for them. I am always being asked when I am back home which of the two is better, who would win a game. I say that if we had the full Real Madrid team, Real Madrid would win, because we play together all the time. The truth is that it's a privilege to play here.' Could he contemplate moving anywhere else, I asked him? Could either of them? After all, it had been no secret for some months that Chelsea's Roman Abramovich had cast his covetous eye on them.

'Look, yes, we do receive offers,' Roberto Carlos said. 'Yes, lots of offers,' nodded Ronaldo. 'But while I cannot say what my future will hold,' Roberto Carlos continued, 'you can't compare these clubs to Real Madrid. You can't compare any club to Real Madrid. You really can't.' 'No, you cannot,' said Ronaldo. 'All the top players in the world: this is the place they dream of playing in. As for me, there is no club better suited to my style of football than Real Madrid. None. And that is why I signed an extension to my contract in February till 2009. I want to finish my career at Real Madrid. I am quite clear about it. I cannot imagine anything more spectacular.'

And Ronaldo knew what spectacular was. It didn't get any more spectacular than what he did in the World Cup final in Yokohama on 30 June 2002, his two goals double redemption for the failure of the 1998 final and for four years of injury hell. I was at the game and I remember seeing him after the final whistle had blown, before the medals ceremony had begun, as the silver confetti and two million red and yellow and green origami birds rained down on the pitch and the tournament's joyous theme music blasted heroically around the stadium; I remember Ronaldo breaking away from Roberto Carlos and the rest of his cavorting Brazilian teammates and walking solemnly across to the other end of the pitch, on his own, to the German players and shaking each one of them by the hand, consoling them, reminding them that he knew better than anyone the taste of despair and defeat, but also that he knew better than anyone that if you hung on and had a little faith things could – and did – come right in the end.

18: April is the Cruellest Month

Early on in Raymond Chandler's *Farewell my Lovely* there is a scene in which a tough guy, a bouncer in a bar, meets his comeuppance. Arrogant, overconfident, he takes a shot at the wrong man and ends in a bad way, crawling along the floor 'like a fly with one wing . . . a man suddenly old, suddenly disillusioned'.

The mood on the flight from Madrid to la Coruña for Real's fourth to last game of the season against Deportivo recalled Chandler's fallen tough guy. It was the last day of April and the players, far from spoiling for a scrap against the gritty Galicians, gave the impression they wished it could all be over; that the season would just go ahead and end, that they could take off on their summer holidays and refresh themselves with dreams of the mighty feats they might achieve in the next campaign. Neither at Madrid airport while we waited to board, nor during the forty-five-minute flight north, nor upon arrival at la Coruña's miniscule airport do I recall seeing one smile. I remember Solari, the supersub, saying to everyone and no one in particular as we prepared to board the plane, 'OK, just three little points and we'll be in great shape again.' No one responded, no one even looked up. Somebody – I didn't see who, but it might have been Guti – emitted a grunt. And that was the way the whole trip went, the mood among these most fortunate of men heavy, dark and despondent. All they were going to do was play a game of football, yet you'd have guessed, if you hadn't known, that they were conscripts heading for the front line of a gruesome war.

April had been the cruellest month for Real Madrid – for the team as a whole, but particularly for David Beckham, who experienced more humiliatingly and painfully than ever before the pitfalls of celebrity; the price of wealth, good looks and fame.

Something had changed. Things in the Beckham-Real Madrid marriage, it emerged, were not going as swimmingly as they had been. Pérez was still in love with Beckham – but he was just not as sure as he had been that Beckham was still in love with him. The problem was the woman in Beckham's life, his wife Victoria, and her refusal to come and live with her husband in Madrid. It would not have been the business of anybody at Real, and no one would have cared in the slightest, had it not been for a dawning perception in the club that Beckham's matrimonial complications might have been undermining the quality of his performances on the pitch, as well as presenting what at this point was merely the hint of a threat – but a threat just the same – that Beckham might choose to leave Real at the end of the season and return to England, meaning in all likelihood to the only club with the money to afford the transfer fee, Roman Abramovich's Chelsea.

This was the state of play. Beckham had been enthusiastic back in July at the idea of his family starting a new life together in Madrid. He thought it would bond them all closer together, and that it would be great for his two little boys to learn Spanish. But things had not turned out the way he had hoped. After much searching in Madrid the Beckhams had found a home to rent that they considered to be up to their palatial standards – but once the home had been found Victoria lost practically all interest in living in it. She spent next to no time in Madrid, dividing her time between New York, where she endeavoured with more pluck than success to revive her career as a pop star, and London, where her parents lived and she was much more of a celebrity than she was in Spain. The older boy Brooklyn had been booked to go to what was reputed to be the best English-language school in Madrid, Runnymede, but his mother pulled him out and took the boys with her to London, where his grandparents could look after them when she was away. Beckham was upset to see his domestic dream go up in smoke but, worse from the point of view of Real, he seemed to spend half his life airborne, flying back and forth from Madrid to London on a private jet. Typically a game would end at ten or eleven at night and Beckham would be hot-tailing it to the airport, arriving in London in the early hours of the morning. He would spend the day, or in some cases just a few hours with his family, then dash back in time for training in Madrid. He kept up this draining routine once or twice a week every week, all the time becoming more depressed at his enforced absence from his little boys, whom he really did adore.

Pérez saw all this and grew unhappy. But not in the manner that the other big man, the one at Beckham's former club, had been. Alex Ferguson had found the lifestyle of Victoria 'Posh' Adams and everything she represented viscerally offensive. Pérez did not. He did not care very much either way, though if anything – from the point of view of developing the Real brand – he welcomed Beckham's off-field celebrity status. What he and others at Madrid feared was that the pull of the family, the one thing that mattered more to Beckham than his football, would see him end up in the clutches of Abramovich.

Others at the club were beginning to be concerned at Beckham's loss of form since the New Year. It might just have been a blip. Every player had periods of four or five weeks in which they played below their optimum level. And in fairness to Beckham he had spent the first four months of the season, the last four of 2003, playing at his very peak. Yet now, while his enthusiasm and energy remained high, he seemed to lack the poise and purposefulness he had shown in the early days when the onus was still on him to prove a point, to demonstrate he was up to playing alongside the best players in the world. Was this the consequence of not being happy at home and not getting enough sleep? Maybe, maybe not. But the one thing that was true was that the Beckham honeymoon at Real Madrid was over and relations between him and the club, while contented enough, had entered a less dreamy stage.

Neither had it been a great month for Florentino Pérez. It was not just that people everywhere were calling into question his revolutionary football project. Two days before the flight to la Coruña his mother died.

Pérez was not on the plane (his mother's death was just about the only eventuality that would have impeded him from going to a Real away game) and the three or four club directors who had made the trip seemed happier discussing looming construction projects, or plans to open new hotels, than talking football, a subject of conversation which no longer delivered much cheer. A large crowd of screaming fans awaited us at the airport exit, as usual, but this time you felt like saying to them, what are you doing here? Haven't you heard?

No matter. It was the same old story. They spotted Beckham's yellow mane and pandemonium ensued. As we emerged out of the terminal building I found myself pushed and shoved alongside Beckham, in other words to the epicentre of the general hysteria. It was shrill in there, claustrophobic and slightly frightening. TV and photo cameras in your face, your ribs, your back and, in a crush behind them a baying mob, faces expressing rapture, in some cases tears. Beckham kept walking, purposefully, unruffled, a thin smile on his lips, as if he hadn't just gone through the worst six weeks of his life.

Because while things had been really bad for him and the rest of the Galácticos in April, they had started to disintegrate in mid-March. Or, if you wanted to be precise about it, if you wanted to pin a date and time after which everything – but everything – started to go disastrously wrong, it would have to be 10.37 on the night of 10 March, nine hours before the terrorist bombs went off on the Madrid trains. It would be fanciful, as well as disrespectful, to make any cause and effect connection between one thing and the other but it nonetheless remains a curious fact that after the massacre Real were never quite the same again; that after that they fell apart.

Because the absolute high point in the season for the Florenteam and all its admirers around the world, the point from which the vertiginous drop began, was the moment when the final whistle blew in the last sixteen Champions League game against Bayern Munich at the Bernabéu. That they had managed to win that toughest of mentally tough games without Ronaldo and Roberto Carlos offered licence to dream, and dream large. No matter if there was a shambolically romantic quality to the team, if the central defence was a sieve, if there was not a defensive midfielder anywhere in sight, if Raúl was having a poor season (it felt in many games as if the team were giving their rivals a handicap and playing with ten men): the coaching manuals be damned; Florentino's Real were playing circus football, consigning all the old orthodoxies to the dustbin of history. They were like trapeze artists, as Valdano put it to me, trapeze artists so dazzlingly talented, so sure of their genius that they had no need of a safety net.

The *ilusión* level had reached, on the night of 10 March, its shrillest decibel pitch. The Galácticos were going to fulfill their glorious destiny. They were going to win everything. Some, like Zidane and Beckham, actually had the temerity to whisper the word 'treble' in front of the press. Most, afraid to tempt fate, kept quiet. But the magic thought was on everybody's mind. The Spanish Cup final was coming up in a week's time – a mere formality, every *madridista* agreed, against Zaragoza. The next rival in the Champions League, as was revealed in the draw thirty-six hours after the Bayern game, was Monaco. After the German adventure, a piece of cake. And as for the Spanish league, they were eight points clear and if anything was a formality, that was it. The all-singing, all-dancing, convention-flouting Florentino formula had proved itself to be a winner. Yes, indeed: if you bet on skill, if you had the wit to buy the world's most charismatic attackers, let the others worry about defence. Football was a simple game. Put the most talented players on the pitch and victory was yours.

The premise might have been called into question on the Saturday after the mid-week Bayern game, when Real put on a limp, listless performance to scrape a 1-1 home draw in the league against, as chance would have it, their cup final rivals Zaragoza. No alarm bells went off for the simple reason that everyone was in a state of shock after the bombings. It would almost have been indecent to invest too much energy in the effort to win with the massacre victims being buried that day all around the Spanish capital. Beckham, appearing before the press two days after that game, four days after the massacre, apologised on behalf of his teamamates but said that it had been very difficult to bring the usual focus to a game of foot-ball.

He spoke well on the horrors of 11 March. The England captain, for all his virtues on the field, is not a man one expects to perform oratorical miracles. But his comments on the horror that had afflicted his new home country conveyed sorrow and a sober assessment of the lessons to be drawn from the tragedy.

'When things like that happen it brings countries and people together whatever their nationality,' Beckham said. 'I'm English and living in Spain, but everyone has become united whatever their nationality, and that's a nice thing. What happened has shown solidarity among the people and I hope people can get over such a complicated time. It shows the strength of the people. It's been tough for everyone, but it's good to be part of the situation.'

Beckham was absolutely right. He never struck a shot more true. It was good to be part of the situation. It was a good time to be in Spain. 'You love life, we love death,' had said the man on the Al Qaeda video who, addressing himself to the Spanish people, had claimed responsibility for the train bombings. It was good to be in Spain when the Spanish people gave their response to that, when literally the whole country went out on the streets in a great national clamour against barbarism, a great cry for life and against death.

Beckham could have said what people usually say in these situations. Something along the lines of, 'These terrible events serve to put football in perspective.' But he was right not to. That's wrong. It is the other way around. It is what he does for a living that puts the horror in its place; it is football – with all the courage and generosity and talent and team spirit and all the other noble human attributes the game puts on display – that puts all that terrible brutish stuff into perspective; football – a game in which solidarity between teammates is all – that helps us see even more clearly what a load of shameful nonsense all these wretched slaughters are, perpetrated in the name of God, freedom or justice.

Bill Shankly was right. The great Liverpool manager's most quotable quote, repeated by football fans everywhere always, was that football was not about life and death, 'it is much more important than that'. There is a reason why everybody loves that quote so much, why people retell it every day the length and breadth of planet earth. It is because it resonates. It does strike a sincere chord. Football is the triumph of life over death; it is the joy that tempers the precariousness of everyday life for everyone, from the train commuters in Madrid to the poor of Africa.

There had been talk of cancelling that league game against Zaragoza out of respect for the dead. But precisely as a further affirmation of the value of life over death it was right that Beckham and Real Madrid should have been out there in the Bernabéu stadium again, barely forty-eight hours after the slaughter of 200 innocents, to play a game of football. Not as if nothing had happened. There were achingly empty seats at the Bernabéu. The Real players wore black armbands and observed a minute's silence before the game began. Spanish television showed a montage the next day of the same scene being replicated not only all over Spain, but all over Europe, players at Arsenal, Manchester United and Milan with bowed heads, arm in arm, their faces expressing genuine sorrow. That sequence of TV images was tremendously moving, a statement once again in favour of life by people who love life and who feel deeply what it means to lose it.

Amidst so much shock and emotion and depth of feeling it was in a peculiar mood that the Real team headed off the following Tuesday to Barcelona, at whose Olympic Stadium the *Copa del Rey* final was being played. There was a lingering sense of disbelief at what had happened that hardly encouraged the intense state of concentration required for a major final. That in turn encouraged a certain heedlessness in the attitude to the game, a lack of respect for the small-fry rivals from Zaragoza reminiscent of that infamous excursion to Munich three weeks earlier. This time there wasn't even the weather to worry about, which was perhaps why the club took the decision to let the players bring their wives and girlfriends along for the ride. It seemed like a fair reward. The difficult bit had been in January, the quarter-final against Valencia, the most solid team in Europe those last five years, the one with the most watertight defence, marshaled from central defence by the excellent Argentine captain Fabián Ayala, who Pérez had tried without success to buy in the summer. But Real won that quarter-final 5-1 on aggregate, 3-0 at the Bernabéu and, with a severely depleted team, 2-1 away. No one inflicted that kind of damage on Valencia. Only Real – only the Galácticos – could have done such a thing. So now, as for Zaragoza in the final, easy meat. Almost a bore, a yawn. The ninety minutes of running around that the game's laws required before the trophy could be taken home to Madrid were something of an irritating intrusion on an otherwise gentle interval on the sunny Mediterranean Sea. When barely twenty minutes into the game Beckham – seemingly redeeming what had been a pretty poor 2004 for him so far – scored one of those inch-perfect free kick goals that seemed almost to have lapsed from his repertoire at Real, that was just about that. It was a simple matter of keeping possession, letting the clock run down and part one of the Treble – the easy bit, admittedly – would be in the bag. This was fun. Pity Ronaldo hadn't recovered from injury in time to join in. It was just the sort of stroll in the park he'd have enjoyed.

Five minutes later Zaragoza equalised and on the forty-fifth minute Guti, with atrocious timing, gave away a penalty. The score going into half-time was 2-1 to Zaragoza: a setback, but not a calamity. And so it proved within three minutes of the restart when Roberto Carlos, in a spirit of anything-Beckham-can-do-I-can-do-better, smashed a free kick from thirty-five yards into the back of the Zaragoza net. When within twenty-three minutes, Cani – just another of the Zaragoza players that no one outside his home town had ever heard of – was sent off, it became clear that all the rather needless huffing and puffing Real had been reduced to was now at an end. Zaragoza, down to ten men, had no chance. But the minnows held on, led with courage and class by a centre half from Argentina Real Madrid had nearly bought in the summer – and Queiroz and Valdano had very much wanted to get at the start of the new year, but had been denied – by the name of Gabriel Milito. They held on long enough for Guti to be sent off six minutes into extra time, at which point – with numerical equality restored and the unbearably unprepared lightness of being with which Real had entered the game exacting its mental price – Zaragoza responded as if the game was theirs. They took the men in white by the scruff of the neck, scored from the one clear opportunity they had and won the cup. The mood in the Real dressing room afterwards was sepulchral. 'There was a big silence in there,' Beckham told the waiting press after the game. Real had failed their first decisive test of the season. Of course they were the better team. Collectively and man for man there was, on paper, no comparison. They had beaten themselves in the same way that they had nearly beaten themselves against Bayern in Munich. Complacency once again had been the enemy and complacency, this time, had won.

Still, as the reserve goalkeeper César said, last time Real had lost the final of the Spanish Cup – against Deportivo in 2002 – they had gone on to win the Champions League. And given a choice between one and the other, well, the *Copa del Rey* was, with the greatest respect to His Majesty, a trifling affair. So, yes, a defeat. A hard knock. But hardly a crisis. There was still all, or almost all, to play for.

With the league in the bag (despite a blip away to Athletic Bilbao – a 4-2 defeat – four days after the cup final), attention turned to Monaco. I watched the game at *La Amistad* bar, the *Madridista* enclave in the heart of Catalan land. Angel, Rafa and the boys were less buoyant, more wary, than I had seen them in previous visits. The dreadful run of the last couple of weeks had sapped their confidence. So it was almost in a spirit of vindication – sarcastic vindication – that they greeted the first goal of the game, by Monaco. Angel – in common with half the Bernabéu – was indignant with his heroes. '*No corren, caminan los cabrones!*' 'They don't run, these bastards, they walk!' The half-time whistle went with Monaco still 1-0 up. The Bernabéu jeered Real off the pitch. That is the way Real fans are, no quarter given; none of this 'we'll support you ever more', 'you'll never walk alone' business you hear from the more sentimental football folk of the north.

And then the transformation. The Real players emerged for the second half like Popeye after a tin of spinach. The Galácticos were galactic again. Stupefyingly, in one of those mad anomalies the game throws up sometimes, Monaco had beaten Deportivo la Coruña 8-3 in the first phase of the Champions League. But now, within no time at all, Real Madrid had restored order to the universe, reducing the oversized team of the little Principality to rabble. Ronaldo, back in the side after two weeks, was Ronaldo again and Real Madrid, showing how badly they had come to depend on him, were again Real Madrid. Four goals in half and hour. Bang, bang, bang, bang – and thank you very much: 4-1, the tie in the bag, semi-finals here we come.

The Madrid defence being what it was, and destiny liking to play its little jokes, Fernando Morientes scored a second for Monaco right at the end. Morientes, winner of three European Cups but seen as a second-rater at Real, had been loaned out to Monaco at the start of the season to save a bit of money – even though Real still paid more than half his salary. Never mind. The Bernabéu was pleased Morientes had scored. It might make the return leg in the Principality a bit more lively than it need be but that was all to the good. Morientes, a local Madrid boy, had been a good servant to the club, a scorer of lots of goals down the years, and good luck to him. He deserved his little moment of personal glory. As for the rest of the Monaco team, they hardly bothered to cheer the goal and went off at the end heads bowed, knowing that their plucky little European adventure was over. They'd have no chance against this lot back home, or anywhere else for that matter. Raúl had been quiet, again, but with the support of Zidane and especially on the night of Figo, Ronaldo was a simply unstoppable force, creator of one of the goals on the night, executor of the fourth. Beckham – at last putting in a performance that recalled his commanding start at the club – gave expression to the general certainty that the next Champions League game to worry about was not Monaco away but the semi-finals, against Arsenal, by getting himself deliberately yellow-carded right at the game's end. That way he avoided the risk of being suspended for the Arsenal game, a date which – especially given the ancient rivalry between his old club and the Gunners – he would have hated to have missed.

The Spanish sports press saluted Beckham's wisdom, and celebrated the glorious return to life of the Galácticos, noting that Ronaldo was all that had been missing to restore the glorious jigsaw to life. Juanma Trueba of *AS* spoke for the *Madridista* multitudes when he noted that Morientes's goal had been applauded by Bernabéu fans eager to warm their hands in preparation for the impending tie against Thierry Henry's Arsenal. 'There is nothing to fear in the return game [at Monaco],' Trueba wrote, 'nothing to worry about. Once Real Madrid started applying the pressure they discovered that Monaco was, in fact, Lilliput.'

Every other football columnist opined in the very same vein. I did too. Interviewed on Irish radio together with the former Liverpool player Mark Lawrenson and a Rome-based journalist called Paddy Agnew, I questioned their contention that there were only two teams left in the Champions League, that the trophy would be disputed between Arsenal and mighty Milan. I told them that to underestimate a team that contained players like Ronaldo, Zidane and Figo was plain foolish. What we all did agree on, though, was that Arsenal, having drawn away to Chelsea in the first leg, were hot favourites for the semis, and that Milan, who had thrashed Deportivo 4-1 in Milan, looked a dead cert to make it all the way to the final.

If anyone – anyone at all – harboured any lingering doubts as to Real's potent viability they were roundly dispelled in the next league match, the last in the month of March, at home to Sevilla. The lesson from the cup final defeat was now crystal clear: in the continued absence from battle of Raúl, Real depended on Ronaldo. But when the Brazilian was there, firing on all cylinders, there was nothing or no one that could stop this team. In fact, he – and he alone – provided the answer to all those who had maintained that Real lacked balance and strength in depth, that the failure to replace Makelele and Hierro had been a huge mistake. Ronaldo, with his goals, refuted the arguments of the *futbolero* naysayers, made the living, breathing case for the great Florentino argument that when you had the best players in the world on your team football was a simple game.

Real beat Sevilla 5-1 – nine goals now in two games against two far from contemptible teams, Sevilla having had until that point the fourth best defensive record in the Spanish league. Ronaldo scored two (one off a Beckham cross so pin-point perfect that even the notoriously header-challenged Brazilian could not miss) and set up the third for Salgado, scored by the right back on the rebound after Ronaldo had beaten three players and fired in a shot that the goalkeeper could only parry away. Ronaldo had now scored twenty-four goals in twenty-seven league games, thirty-one in all competitions. He was once again proving that point Queiroz had made about the Brazilian's contagiously glorious football. The journalist José Sámano, inspired by the 5-1 defeat of Sevilla, made the quite brilliant observation in *el País* that 'with Ronaldo in the side Real Madrid felt more protected than with the finest pedigree centre halves on the planet.'

And so to the month of April, described in the opening line of T. S. Eliot's *Wasteland* as the cruellest because it is neither one thing nor the other, neither winter nor quite summer, raising expectations that it disappoints. For David Beckham, though, the first Sunday of April – the fourth of the fourth month of 2004 – was far, far worse than that. That was the day when he experienced not so much disappointment, as crushing humiliation and pain when the biggest-selling national newspaper in the western world, the *News of the World*, broke the story that in the continued absence of his wife, who insisted on remaining in London, he had been having an affair with a certain Rebecca Loos. The paper, long known to British journalists as the 'News of the Screws', carried in breathlessly vivid detail the story of the alleged affair, carrying six pages of soft-porn narrative along the lines of 'then he swept her off to his suite at the Santa Mauro hotel – to the astonishment of his drivers and bodyguards – for a night of the kind of passion he has been missing with Posh'.

'As soon as they got in the room,' the *News of the World* continued, 'Rebecca said he seemed a little nervous. He realised he was taking a very big step . . . He held Rebecca's head in his hands and kissed her passionately and said, "I have wanted to be with you like this for so long." It was a very powerful moment. He dimmed the lights and started taking his clothes off. Rebecca stripped off too and they stood naked in the middle of the room, kissing passionately. David was a sensational lover – their sex was highly-charged and explosive. They made love for hours.'

The *News of the World* article spawned a feeding frenzy in the British press. Tabloids and broadsheets alike gorged themselves on fresh revelations, rumours, speculation and forests upon felled forests of opinion columns on what the bursting of the Beckham bubble – the seeming exposure of his goody two-shoes marital fidelity as a sham – meant for the Beckham marriage, for the Beckham children, for his footballing career, for the British people, for the institution of matrimony, for the future of the human race. Beckham himself, far from doing what any normal person would have done in the circumstances, namely have his face surgically reshaped and flee to Alice Springs, Australia, went out of his way to ensure he and his wife appeared on the covers of the following days' tabloid papers. Posing for the paparazzi on a ski trip to the Swiss Alps, Mr and Mrs Beckham denied the truth of the Loos woman's story and smiled and smiled for the cameras, a picture of unalloyed marital bliss. The general consensus in the tabloid punditocracy was that David was emerging rather better from all this than Victoria, whose smile – fixed as a clown's mask – seemed even less natural than usual. An article in the *Sun* by 'psychologist Mo Shapiro', alongside another one claiming Loos was bisexual, revealed less about what was going on in the marriage than about what a screamingly hilarious time *Sun* journalists had behind the scenes concocting these fables. Here, for posterity, is what the *Sun* published on the mighty question of what the body language in the pictures said about the state of the Beckham marriage: 'Mo Shapiro is not convinced by Posh and Becks' show of togetherness. She said: "On the surface these photos show a happy, loving couple. Go deeper and you see a great deal of distance. Victoria's apparently huge smile is actually a grimace. Her posture also belies her true feelings. She's very rigid and hunched, indicating there is a lot of tension between them. Yet she looks like she is hanging on to him, sometimes grasping. She seems desperate to keep him in a physical and emotional sense." The couple's eye contact was more telling, Mo added: "Victoria is making the running. While she looks adoringly at him, he is not looking at his wife in ANY of the photos".'

Another mighty question that these ruminations raised – and it was asked by every single tabloid commentator in Britain – was whether perhaps we might have in our sights the answer to the great question that had been agitating Middle England these last five or six years, 'who wore the trousers in the Beckham marriage, David or Posh?' The answer to this question would indeed be provided, but not until well into the month of May. Meanwhile, what we did discover was that Rebecca Loos had broken the world record for money to be made from a night of sex. The word in the British press was that her kiss-and-tell stories, sold not just to the news-papers but to Sky News who did a television interview with her, had reaped benefits in excess of one million pounds. As not a few women of my acquaintance proved unable to resist remarking, 'Nice work, if you can get it'.

Those kinds of sums were small potatoes for the good citizens of Monaco (pop. 32,000 – average wealth per inhabitant, roughly 100 million euros), half of whom were gathered at the one football stadium in the Principality (size: two sq. kms) on the night of 7 April 2004 for the privilege of going to their deaths able to boast they had seen the Galácticos with their own eyes. If you had told any member of the crowd before the game – or for that matter at half-time – that Monaco actually stood the remotest chance of winning and going through to the semi-finals, they would have found it hilarious. The one individual who perhaps did believe there was a glimmer of hope for the Monaguesques was Crown Prince Albert, the nearest thing to a hooligan at the Stade Louis II. If he'd had any hair left, he would have yanked it all out. Seeing the demented rage with which he reacted to the first goal of the game – by Raúl in the thirty-sixth minute of the first half – the only possible explanation for the failure of the police to come and take him away from the royal box, for fear that he might cause Florentino Pérez and his wife Pitina grievous bodily harm, was that in Monaco he enjoyed a less than democratic immunity from the law.

Once that Raúl goal went in, with Real Madrid pinging the ball around in that first half with a mastery reminiscent of the perform-ances in the previous year's quarter-finals against Manchester United, the outcome ceased to be in any doubt. Real were 5-2 up on aggre-gate and that was the end of that. But then, totally against the run of play, and deep in first-half injury time, Monaco equalised. Still, with the score at half-time 1-1, and Real leading 5-3 on aggregate, there was nothing at all to worry about. The evidence of the half, never mind the distorted scoreline, showed that Monaco were indeed Lilliputians next to the Gulliveresque Galácticos.

The evidence of the second half, by shocking contrast, revealed something quite different. Real were, in fact, Goliath to Monaco's David. Within seconds of the restart that man Morientes put Monaco 2-1 ahead with a tremendous header and in the sixty-fifth minute Monaco scored again for a 3-1 lead, 5-5 in aggregate but enough for Monaco to go through if the score stayed the same on the away goals rule. The score stayed that way to the end. It could so easily not have done. Raúl had a headed goal disallowed by the linesman in the seventy-third minute – one of those decisions that you could tell was right, by a matter of millimetres, only with the aid of a TV action replay; one of those decisions that five out of ten linesmen would have given the other way. And then, on the eighty-fifth minute, as conclusive evidence that this was categorically not Raúl's season, the Real captain missed a chance that in all his previous campaigns at the club he would have tucked comfortably into the back of the net. Receiving a perfect pass from Zidane on the Monaco penalty spot on his favoured left foot, with only the goalkeeper to beat, he shot wildly wide.

Raúl was normally the most phlegmatic of players. This time, though, it was different. When he missed that chance in the eighty-fifth minute his face was an image of anguish. It told you, far more eloquently than any words could, that he knew he had blown Real's season, that this moment captured more hideously than any other the loss of form he had inexplicably endured since taking over as team captain in the summer.

And that was that. Real Madrid out of Europe. Next morning, the very same journalists who had spent the previous six months crowing, celebrating the Galácticos' invincible charm, now turned vindictively on the Florentino project, blaming the Real president for his failure to heed the warnings of the *futboleros*, for his stubborn refusal to buy a new centre half and a new Makelele, for his insistence on sticking by the callow Pavones and – worst of all, of course, though this was a point that had occurred to no one until now –

for letting go of Fernando Morientes, who to the astonishment of just about everybody was now the season's top scorer in the Champions League.

As it happened, Arsenal and Milan swiftly followed Real out of the Champions League. Twenty-four hours after the Monaco fiasco, Arsenal were beaten 2-1 at home by nouveau riche Chelsea and – in the most implausible result anyone could remember in Europe – Milan failed to make good on their 4-1 home victory in the first leg to Deportivo, being thrashed 4-0 at la Coruña. Whereupon the argument, vehemently expressed the length and breadth of Europe until Deportivo's third goal went in, that Pérez's project was a mad delusion was once again called into question. Milan were the antithesis of the Florenteam. Packed with defensive midfielders, veteran centre halves and a substitutes' bench so talented and experienced, so far from the callow Pavones model, it could single-handedly – with a bit of luck and a following wind – win a World Cup, Milan had been dynamited out of the Champions League by tough, but tiny, Deportivo.

Didier Deschamps, the Monaco coach, got it right when he drew the conclusion that what happened in the quarter-finals of the Champions League merely offered further evidence of the great and deeply reassuring truth that 'in football anything can happen'.

Not that Deschamps' philosophising offered Real much comfort, any more than Milan's loss had done. What David Beckham made of that Monaco game, watching it as he did in his Swiss chalet with his less than happy wife, one can only wonder. He probably spent the night bashing his head against the wall, à la Basil Fawlty. The following Sunday (Resurrection Sunday, as the pro-Real press reminded everyone that morning) he had a chance at least to give vent to his energy on the football pitch, this time at home against Osasuna – a fairly manage-able rival at a time when it was important that Real buck up, get their heads up and focus, like the good pros that they all were, on the last prize left open to them this season, the Spanish league. That was not as grand a prize as the Champions, certainly, but neither was it all that far off. The Spanish league had acquired in recent years a reputation as not only the most skilful and entertaining league in

Europe (which no one disputed) but also the strongest in Europe (a claim only the Italians doubted). Evidence of that had been provided this season by the fact that Spain had been the only country to have four teams in the last sixteen of the Champions League (one of which, Celta, were later relegated to the Spanish second division) and two out of four semi-finalists in the other big European competition, the UEFA Cup.

Osasuna were one of those tough teams whose players no one outside their bull-running home town of Pamplona had heard of. One player whose identity the press drew attention to before the game began was a certain Valdo, who had risen through the Real youth ranks and been discarded. What happened with Zaragoza and the spurned Milito, and then Monaco and Morientes, had caused the press to detect a possible trend. Would Valdo be the latest Real reject to exact sweet revenge? As it happened, yes, Real did not so much resurrect as get well and truly buried. Osasuna won 3-0, in what was Real's first home defeat all season at the Bernabéu, and Valdo scored in the first minute, setting up his team's other two goals. The silence at the Bernabéu during the second half was deafening. There was the odd jeer, but most fans were too stunned even for that. Real, though, appeared to have fallen under a curse. Eight points clear at the top of the table forty days earlier, they had suddenly lost first place, for the first time in 2004, to that militarised machine of a team, Valencia. Beckham played as horribly as everyone else did, but probably slept less well than the others that night. The *News of the World* had dug up another woman who said she had had an affair with him. Someone of part Thai origin who lived in Australia, claimed to have loved him (unlike Loos, who claimed no such thing) and whose picture was all over the paper's front page. Not surprisingly, Beckham, the most amenable of players with the Spanish press, ceased talking to journalists altogether, uttered not a cheep, all the way through to the end of the season.

Florentino Pérez had something even more distressing to worry about. His mother had fallen gravely ill and had only days to live. That Sunday night after the Osasuna game he was in poor shape. Insults had been hurled his way by fans at the Bernabéu for the first time in his tenure of the club presidency and while rationally he remained convinced that the model he had invented – no more and no less than to have the world's best players in his team – had to be right, his heart had taken a beating. Doubts assailed him. His self-confidence, his most precious asset, was beginning ever so slightly to falter. Just as he had revelled in Real's triumphs, and rightly taken a lot of the credit for them, so now he was straining under the weight of defeat.

I went to watch Real in training the next day, curious to see what the mood would be like. I came across three or four hundred fans, some of whom had come to see their fallen heroes (adolescent cries of 'Beckham! Beckham!' filled the chilly morning air), some to express their displeasure. Along the back of the training pitch the players used, separated from onlookers by a high fence, a group of malcontents had strung a long banner that could be read by all the players. 'For you money and whores. For us indignation and depression' the banner read.

If Beckham felt specifically alluded to, he should not have done. Whores have long populated the Spanish male public's imagination of the world filthy rich football players inhabit. Partly true, partly wishful thinking – or wish-projection – in this case it conveyed fairly accurately the perception of lots of angry *madridistas* that the Galácticos had failed to give their all, as expected, to their club. These were the very same fans who barely a few weeks earlier would confess to all and sundry, but especially to fans of rival clubs, that never had there been a better time to be alive than now. You asked a sample of Real supporters back then, as I routinely had done all season, what their prevailing mood was and the response was always a variation on the same theme: euphoria.

As for the players at that first post-apocalyptic training session, they looked more subdued than usual at first as they trotted round the pitch, warming up, but once they started playing one of their little half-pitch practice games you would have been hard-pressed to guess they had just gone through one of the most horrible weeks in their lives. Queiroz, for his part, looked as inexplicably absorbed in the minutiae of these kickabouts, as he always was, which showed especially commendable discipline on his part given that by now it was taken for granted that he would be fired at the end of the season, that he would fulfill his scapegoat destiny, that he was a dead coach walking. But it was the attitude of the players that was more intriguing. These hardened pros loved the game, and had fun playing even a meaningless little encounter like this one. They shouted for the ball, they laughed like schoolboys, they cursed, they celebrated goals with genuine joy. Even Beckham, in a woolly hat, managed to raise a cheer, to get stuck into the game – the fun of doing what he enjoyed most in life obliterating for a brief while the recollection of the wretched domestic calamity he was staging for the benefit of news-paper readers back home, and buyers of gossip magazines – for the Spanish national newspapers virtually ignored the Loos story – in Spain. So appalled were the Real authorities, starting with Pérez, by the manner in which the British press had covered Beckham's love drama (the love drama itself Pérez simply did not have a view on) that English reporters who had come to the morning's training session were informed that, on orders from the top, they were being denied their habitual access to the players' area.

Whether it was the ban on the British press that did it, or some other equally inscrutable force that acts on footballing destiny, Real won their next game, away to Atlético Madrid, 2-1. The league cham-pionship was still on and victory the following weekend at the Bernabéu against Barcelona would go a long way towards keeping that last lingering dream of the season alive.

The players were packed off to the resort of La Manga, on the Mediterranean, to regroup and re-energise, but with the unintended consequence that they fetched up in a luxury hotel whose TV programming included Britain's Sky One, where on the Wednesday night of the team's stay they were broadcasting an interview with Rebecca Loos. Beckham was distraught at the news. 'He was in a terrible state. Very depressed, unable to speak, miserable one moment; then angry, fuming the next,' a member of the coaching staff told me. The club interceded and persuaded the hotel to block access to Sky One that night, which had the effect of reducing Beckham's embarrassment, if not his pain. Rumours inevitably started to circu-late in the British press that Beckham would be leaving Real at the end of the season; that he would succumb to Roman Abramovich's blandishments and leave for Chelsea. His wife had not made an effort to join him in Madrid, obliging him, first, to yo-yo back and forth on a private plane between Spain and England to see her and his children. She might have calculated, too, that, left alone, the world's favourite male pin-up might seek comfort in another woman's arms. It seemed not unreasonable to assume, as most British papers rapidly did, that the punishment Victoria would exact for his sins would be to insist that he return to England once and for all.

I met José Angel Sánchez and Jorge Valdano for lunch two days later, on the Friday before the Sunday of the *superclásico* against Barcelona. Two things became clear. That contrary to some of the stories appearing in the British press, Real had no desire, much less need, to sell Beckham. The club's finances had never been stronger, and the economic projections were sky-high – in part thanks to Beckham. Which was a large reason why the club was concerned that Beckham might leave for family reasons, though they knew perfectly well that on strict footballing grounds there was nowhere in the world – no matter the recent on-field calamities – that he would rather be. Real's ambitious plans for commercial expansion were ready for lift-off: we were just days away from the ceremony to mark the start of construction at *Ciudad Real Madrid*, the huge training complex that would include a theme park and a hotel; and a deal was about to be signed to clinch the necessary satellite access for Real Madrid Television to broadcast worldwide. Beckham was naturally considered an essential element in the sales package.

'If Chelsea want him they are going to have to tear him out of our hands,' Sánchez told me. 'It's the only way we'd let him go.' That meant Chelsea paying out the full amount of Beckham's contractually stipulated buy-out clause. And how much would that amount to, I asked Sánchez? '180 million euros. They'd have to smash – and I mean smash – the world transfer record that we set with Zidane, who cost us less than half that amount.' Was he serious? 'Not only am I serious, I still would rather keep him, even if Chelsea came up with that money.' Really? 'Really. Don't forget what I told you once. He's worth 500 million to us. He still is.'

In Spain the rumours that were sparking greater interest were those concerned with who Real might be buying in the summer, rather than who might go. I accompanied Sánchez after lunch to what he billed as a 'meeting' with Pérez. The venue was a bar on a street under the hospital where the Real president's mother was supposed to have died the night before, but was still clinging on, surrounded by her family. 'The people of that generation are of another race,' Pérez told me, repeating what he had said of his father almost a year earlier. 'They lived through war and privation and are tough in a way that we simply are not.'

So, I asked, was Beckham going to leave? 'No, no,' he said, dismissively, as if the question were not only unnecessary but boring. 'I've talked to him. He's staying.' And who was coming? Totti? 'He's the most likely option, the easiest operation to pull off,' Pérez replied. Totti would be a hell of a buy, I said. A fantastic player, a real Galáctico. Not only captain of Italy but the country's most talented player, an attacking midfielder who could shoot, head, scored lots of goals and was a big-hearted competitor. 'Yes, he's all of that. Galáctico material, all right. And as you say, we'd have yet another international captain,' Pérez said, not entirely commitaly. Anybody else in his sights? Ayala of Valencia, would he get him at last? 'The Argentina captain. Yes. Maybe.' Van Nistelrooy from Manchester United? Patrick Vieira of Arsenal? 'We've got a whole lot of hooks in the water,' Pérez replied. 'We're going to see which one of them pulls and then we'll decide what we do.'

Sánchez handed over to Sánchez a sheaf of documents from a leather bag. This was what the meeting was about. Pérez studying these documents, discussing them with Sánchez and another Real director who was sitting there with us on the street, Pedro López, the man who had gone to do the Beckham deal with Sánchez in Sardinia. We were sipping coffees and cokes, nibbling at potato chips and olives. A couple of bodyguards stood ten metres away, discreetly eyeing up the passers-by, doing their job of keeping Pérez alive, protecting him from ETA, who had not struck for some months but would very likely consider the Real Madrid president and construction magnate, pillar of the Spanish establishment, a worthwhile prize. The documents Pérez was leafing through showed the results of internal polls the club had done. Pérez's 'unconditional support' among Madrid fans had reached an all-time low, it turned out, following the Osasuna defeat. He had been down to sixty-six per cent (another fifteen per cent on top of that said they were merely 'satisfied' with him) from an average of ninety per cent plus during the totality of his presidency so far. Roberto Carlos, it turned out, was viewed as the most *simpático* member of the team, as he always had been. Yet there were plenty of reports Roberto Carlos was going to Chelsea in the summer. Pérez wouldn't do that to the fans, would he? 'Don't worry,' he said, 'Roberto Carlos stays.' And Queiroz? Pérez hardly looked up, but his reply was quite brutal. 'He's a good man, but he's a natural second – not a leader. We made a mistake signing him.'

As for the documents showing the club's income and projections, the graphs were a caricature of capitalist success, ever upward, on a steep curve, up from 137 million euros in Pérez's first year to 303 million for the financial year 2004/05. Profits after tax for the season just ending were 49.6 million euros. Pérez declared the meeting over and at 7.00 p.m. Sánchez and I were in his car driving to the airport. Those figures would keep rising over the next three or four years, he said. 'The income we're generating is showing that we're right: the best players are the cheapest.' The best players might be making money but they were not winning, I said. At what point did failure to win trophies translate into economic loss? 'Winning is not essential. The important thing is to remain always competitive, and if you achieve that you are going to win.'

How comforted the fans at the Bernabéu or the lads at the *La Amistad* bar might be by those words going into the big game against Barcelona that weekend – just how persuaded Sánchez himself, a Real Madrid nut when he was not working, might be – you had to wonder. So I went and found some fans to talk to about this. A group of fifteen members of the official Real Madrid Fan Club of Nippon, as they introduced themselves. We met in the club offices at the Bernabéu, in the boardroom, a couple of hours before the Barça game, for which the Japanese party had especially flown out.

The president of the fan club was called Shigeki Kubota and he spoke excellent Spanish. A young looking man in his mid-forties, he wore a suit and tie. The rest of the party, men and women mostly in their twenties, wore white Real Madrid shirts. They arrived before I did and were waiting for me seated at the long boardroom table, leaving empty the place at the head of the table for me. A more serious set of fans you would be hard pressed to find. Serious, that is, in their devotion to the cause. All fifteen of them in the room said they religiously watched all Real games live on TV, which meant they were staying up on Saturday and – more often – Sunday nights watching games that tended to begin at three or four in the morning. And how, I inquired, did they manage to work the next day? 'Oh, that's easy,' said Mr Kubota, who had formed his attachment to Real during a three-year spell he had spent in Madrid in the early Eighties. 'If Real Madrid win, we work happy and well. If they lose, we feel tired all day.'

I wanted to know how come they had become Real supporters in the first place. Some, Japanese soccer lovers well ahead of their time, had been fans for several years. Most, Mr Kubato said, had come to the game very recently. Because of Beckham, I asked, smiling expectantly? No. Not because of Beckham, they all – in one way or another – replied. But surely Beckham was huge in Japan. Yes, he was huge, Mr Kubota agreed. But among serious Real fans like them other players were more popular. I asked a lively, smiley young woman at the end of the table why she had become a Real fan. In halting Spanish, and to hysterical giggling all round, she replied, 'Because I am in love with Luis Figo.' Seiko Okano the translator lady tugged my shirtsleeve and whispered that this was the way most women got into football in Japan, by 'falling in love' with a player. I asked Keiko if she had liked football before coming across her Portuguese hero? 'Nothing,' she replied. Did this mean that she was only interested in Real games in which Figo played, that she lost interest when he was out injured or suspended? 'That's right,' Keiko said.

How many more, I asked the assembled company, were in love with or – in the case of the men – had formed a special attachment to Figo? Four hands went up. Raúl? Four more. And what about Zidane, who only two days earlier had been named the best European footballer of the past fifty years by fans in an online poll conducted by UEFA? Also four. Ronaldo? Three. And Beckham? Not one member of the Nipponese fan club lifted a finger. Some frowned at the very suggestion. It seemed to me like inverted snobbery, if such a thing existed in Japan. In Mr Kubato's case, the lack of excitement surrounding Beckham was serious enough. 'He is a good player, but one player more in the galaxy,' he said. What did he think of this Florentino project, I asked him? Things had not been going to well lately? Was it all too romantic for the harsh world of professional European football? 'I believe this team does need more balance between defence and attack,' Mr Kubato replied, very solemnly. 'It is maybe too attacking. But then look at Milan, which has that balance and also lost in the Champions League to a small team. So if you are going to lose anyway – as all teams must and do – it is far better to play the adventurous Madrid way, instead of that typical 0-0 or 1-0 Italian style.' At which point a young woman called Mimi who spoke strikingly good Spanish piped up: 'The truth is that Real Madrid is always Real Madrid. Madrid is the team of dreams. Now we have the best players in the world the best to watch for football fans everywhere, and that is enough in itself and that no one can dispute.'

What about today's game against Barcelona? How did they see it, especially in the absence of Ronaldo who yet again had injured himself? The Nipponese fan club all looked to Mr Kubato to answer these weighty questions. 'The absence of Ronaldo will be less of a factor that in normal games,' he replied. 'These games against Barça are always unique occasions in which form and logic counts for little.' Would anyone venture a forecast? It turned out there was a consensus on this one. 3-1. Real Madrid would win 3-1.

I thought of Mr Kubato's words often in the first half. Barcelona had come into the game on a great run of twelve games without defeat. They had been inching up the table, eating into an eighteen-point lead Real had had over them in December, after that historic defeat they had suffered against the old enemy at their own Camp Nou. If Barça won this game, they would be poised to do the unthinkable and beat Real to second place behind the now almost certain winners, Valencia. Sure enough the first half did not go according to form. Real were all over Barcelona whose goalkeeper, Victor Valdés, made one heroic save after another. Puyol, the Barça centre half, saved one shot off the line with his cheek. Zidane was playing well, Figo – as ever against Barcelona – was colossal. Somehow the score remained 0-0 at half-time but upon the restart Real went 1-0 up, the goal scored by the Argentine Solari, who rifled the ball in through a forest of legs in the penalty area. Then Kluivert scored for Barcelona and then Figo was sent off. Poor Keiko, I thought. And poor Real. Sure enough, the excellent Brazilian Ronaldinho – the Galáctico that got away – assumed control of the game, setting up the winner for Xavi. The final whistle blew and my first thoughts were, 'Poor Japanese!'

It had been one of those typically unfair games that football throws up. Real had played better than they had when they won at the Camp Nou by the same scoreline in December and a draw, at the very least, would have been fair. Figo's sending-off (rescinded by a Spanish football federation review panel four days later – four days too late) knocked the stuffing out of Real, who played the last fifteen minutes as if they were doomed, as if fate had decided against them tonight once again and there was nothing more to be done.

If one player had been specially marked out by fate, though, it had to be Beckham. His sunny life had entered a dark zone. Never since his infamous sending-off against Argentina in the 1998 World Cup had things looked so bleak. 'The football side of things', as he would have said, had failed abysmally to meet his high expectations, after that larger-than-life start he had made. The family side was in a worse mess by far than it had ever been. And he was not playing well. He was all over the place, no longer the commanding field marshal he had been in the first four months of the season. Perversely, the longer he was at the club, the tougher he was finding it to adapt. That was mainly because everyone else, with the exception of Figo, was playing below his best too. (In the case of Raúl, as Juanma Trueba of *AS* suggested, an exorcism seemed like the only possible solution.) But Beckham had seemed particularly out of sorts in this game. Valdano had said in the conversation we had just before Real's triumph at the Camp Nou in December that Beckham's great virtue was how he 'knit' the team together. But now he looked like the most unravelled player in the team. He was trying too hard to do too many things and nothing seemed to be coming off. The word Valdano used about the way he was playing now was 'disperse' – precisely what his mind had to have become with all those dawn flights back and forth between Madrid and London; with the tidal wave of tabloid tales about his private life; as well as the contagiously chaotic state of mind of the team as a whole, most of whom seemed to have fallen prey to a collective nervous breakdown since that cup final defeat to Zaragoza.

The thing about Beckham, as a member of the coaching staff at Real told me, is that he is a player who can do three or four things extremely well – and no more. He is a great striker of the ball; he has good vision, which means he has a quick football mind, a good eye for the right pass; and he has a good positional sense, a keen understanding of where he best serves the team's interests – in the case of Real he did best when, deploying his great stamina to maximum effect, he ranged behind the first line of attack in such a way as to be continually available to teammates under pressure, and to prompt new moves towards goal. In the second half of the season, after the New Year, he tried to do more. It was as if he had gone too far in believing his own propaganda, imagining that he had acquired by osmosis the wider breadth of talents possessed by the likes of Figo and Zidane. Instead of holding his position behind that first attacking wave he would start popping up all over the pitch, least usefully of all but with increasing frequency in and around the rival penalty area. He ceased to be what he had been at his best for Real, a re-assuring, commanding presence in deep midfield. At times he would even try what he was least equipped to do, to dribble, and had only ever done with any regularity once in his life: during the endless reshoots of a TV commercial for Adidas in February in which he slalomed down the middle of the pitch with the ball at his feet, bamboozling one tackler after another.

It did not mean that he did not have the occasional good game, sometimes a very good one. But overall from the start of 2004 he seemed to have suffered an identity crisis. His footballing identity seemed to have become as confused as his celebrity identity, the one that had been dealt such a blow by the allegations of marital infidelity.

Having portrayed himself all along as that most miraculously unlikely of figures, the famous and beautiful young man who never so much as looks at any woman who is not his wife, he had now lost that niche; he was not quite as unique as he used to be in the celebrity market. As a player too he had become more commonplace, less distinctly regal. The Spanish sports press, having salivated over him during the first four months of the season, almost ceased paying him any attention. As if, rather than acknowledge his melancholy decline, they preferred to ignore him altogether.

One moment in the game against Barça captured how lost he had become, how removed he seemed to be from the controlled, composed player who had dazzled the Bernabéu. With the score at 1-1 and Figo off he picked up the ball in space out on the right just inside his own half and started running and running in a straight line down the wing – as if he were Figo. One defender shadowed him; no teammate thought fit to accompany him forward. He ran and ran until he got to the Barça byline, at which point he stopped and, under pressure from the defender, lost the ball. The whole thing was such an exercise in vacuity, with such sad aptness did that gallop to nowhere sum up his contribution on the night, that he might as well have kept running up into the stands, out into the *Paseo de la Castellana* and home, for all the use he was being to his team.

Curiously the fans did not jeer him, the way they would have done if, say Ronaldo, had been guilty of an action so banal. I talked to Sebastián about this and he told me that the fans in the sector of the Bernabéu where he had his seat had formed a bond with Beckham curiously similar to the one they had with Raúl. 'Raúl has so much credit accumulated over his career that we'll always stand by him,' Sebastián said. 'Beckham has so much credit accumulated from his brilliant start to the season, mostly to do with our sense of him as a great warrior for the cause. During the Barcelona game I remember one moment when Beckham made a really poor pass. I could sense that the fans around me were about to start jeering and cursing the player, but that was until they realised who it had been. When they saw it was Beckham, they held back. They were more reverent than they would have been with someone like Ronaldo, who everyone knows is more brilliant than Beckham, but is always felt to be much less of a tryer.'

Sectors of the British press continued for their part to persist in the notion that Beckham was on his way out and that, what was more, Real Madrid actually wanted to get rid of him now. Where they got this information from, nobody quite knew – although the suspicion was that some journalists were making things up, purporting to have sources at the club they did not have, in order to keep the cash flowing in. The one thing I did hear was that Beckham was seething at what he was reading; that he was outraged to see people writing that, for example, he had gone to Pérez and asked him to let him go back home – which was pure fiction. It was all part of the spring prelude to the perennial summer transfer soap opera madness and, as such of course, par for the course. If Beckham was less amused by all the speculation than he might have been a year earlier it was because things had been tricky at home and were next to catastrophic on the field of play.

The following weekend's game against Deportivo in la Coruña did not offer much of a respite. Deportivo were a very strong side, not just victors of mighty Milan and Champions League semi-finalists, but among the most powerful teams in Europe for some years now. Amazing for a city so small (pop. 230,000), and an airport so innocuous. The game, though, would be make or break. The last chance for Real to salvage their season. If they did not win they could practically kiss the league goodbye. Which was why the mood on the flight up from Madrid was so ominous. Among Carlos Queiroz's coaching staff feelings were particularly bleak. They were in introspective mood, vindictive and reproachful. Chatting late into the night at the team hotel in la Coruña to people who asked not to have their names mentioned in print, I discovered that Queiroz had very nearly quit his job in December – and indeed would have done had other members of staff not threatened to quit with him in sympathy.

Why would he have wanted to do such a thing at precisely a time when everything was going the Galácticos's way, when everything was following the Hollywood script? Because, I was told, he felt betrayed. He felt the team's success was partly illusory. Or, rather, he feared that come the sharp end of the season, in March, the team's lack of strength in depth would be cruelly exposed. There was a limit to how many times you could count on Ronaldo's genius to win a game for you. And what if Ronaldo were injured or suspended? What kind of back-up did you have in the event that either he or one of the other geniuses ran short of inspiration at the wrong time? The reason he felt betrayed was that, as he saw it, he had been promised a review of the player situation in December, before the opening of the January transfer window. The loss of Makelele at the start of the season and the failure to bring in Gabriel Milito or someone of similar stature at centre half had been a heavy blow to Queiroz, but one he felt he could overcome if reinforcements were brought in at the New Year.

In the event, Pérez refused to contemplate discussion, even, of buying new players. Things were going so well that it seemed to Pérez – and for that matter, to the massed ranks of professional football commentators – that there was no need to disrupt team morale by needlessly bringing in outsiders.

Queiroz was exasperated but, worse than that, worried that he was going to end up presiding over a fiasco. He loved the core Pérez idea of building a team around attacking superstars, but he feared that without the necessary measure of defensive ballast the Galáctico ship was doomed to sink.

'We all love your Ronaldos and Zidanes more than any other kind of player but there is something that every football coach in the world knows that I am not sure Mr Pérez is even aware of,' he told me in a conversation we had on the night before the Deportivo game. 'One thing we often do in training is play defenders against attackers, six-a-side. In fact all coaches do it.' And what? I interrupted him. Did it turn out that defenders won more often that attackers? 'No,' Queiroz replied. 'The defenders always win. Always. And everywhere. Without exception. And you want to know why? Because defenders are by nature defensive and attackers are by nature attacking. Over the course of a game the attackers will leave far more gaps at the back, allow far more scoring opportunities than they are themselves able to create. This is true. It is fact. It is a law of football.'

Another law of football is that the best side does not always win. Once again, it was not going to be Real's night. Ronaldo and Raúl hit the woodwork three times. Each missed sitters early in the second half that they would ordinarily have put away with their eyes shut. Deportivo, in their first breakaway, scored. Goal number two was a screamer from thirty yards out by a defender, Capdevila, who had never scored or would ever score a goal like it in his life – a sure sign that the football gods had well and truly aligned themselves against Real, that there were forces at play too great for mere Galácticos to overcome. As if further evidence were needed that fate had indeed decisively intervened against Real, Zidane was sent off in the first half. Beckham was not playing too badly but for some reason, and to his displeasure, Queiroz decided to take him off fifteen minutes before the end. Queiroz need not have done that. It was Beckham's twenty-ninth birthday fifteen minutes after the final whistle went, at midnight on 2 May. I wished him happy birthday when he emerged showered out of the dressing room at 12.15. He said it was nice of me to have remembered. I told him things could only get better for him in his thirtieth year. He smiled, in wan agreement and walked on to the team bus.

A one-hour drive through the night lay ahead for us to Santiago de Compostela airport, la Coruña's being too small to function after eleven at night. Amazing. This small city tucked away here in the north-western tip of Spain had produced a team whose players, however unknown outside their country, however resonantless their brands, had gone further than Real in the Champions League, hammering Milan along the way. I sat next to Valdano on the ride to Santiago. He lamented, with Queiroz, the failure to buy a centre half. 'Football rules that people have found to have worked over fifty years cannot be dismissed just like that,' he said.

At Santiago airport the same questions formed themselves in my mind as had done upon arrival thirty-six hours earlier in la Coruña. What were they doing here? Hadn't they heard? It was nearly two in the morning and five hundred people had gathered at the terminal to see off the team. It might have been December, after the defeat of Barça; February after beating Bayern. It did not matter. The allure of the Galácticos was bigger than any football match, more enduring than the whimsy of the result. The fans screamed and begged for autographs and photos. Beckham, more than any other player, obliged. Most of his teammates were too crushed to play the film-star role. They were as upset, disappointed, bitter as the most hardened Bernabéu season-ticket holder. They weren't in it for the whores or even, when all was said, the money. They were in it because they loved the game and because they were winners who hated to lose.

No one had hated to lose that night against Deportivo, no one lamented the throwing away of the league title more than Queiroz. The others, the players, always had next season to revive their dreams, to redeem their failure. For Queiroz his one shot at glory had gone. He would never work at another club like Real Madrid; he would never coach another team like this one, whose players he admired so unreservedly. Perhaps he had admired them too unreservedly. Perhaps Pérez had been right when he told me that Queiroz was not a natural leader. Perhaps – notwithstanding the absence of the Makelele Factor – had Queiroz possessed something of the fire of his previous boss, Alex Ferguson, the catastrophic end-of-season slide might have been averted; the players' psychological collapse turned around.

Whatever the case, he was gone and he knew it. By the end of May he'd be looking for another, inevitably lesser job. On the flight home I sat along the same row of seats from him, across the other side of the aisle. Others on the plane closed their eyes and slept. Queiroz – I watched and watched him – did not blink. His eyes stared out of the window into the impenetrable darkness the whole flight home. He was a picture of desolation. Greatness had been in his grasp but, whether for reasons beyond his control or not, he had failed to seize it. And his chance – a chance like this one – would never, ever come his way again. I looked behind me at the players. Beckham was wide awake as usual. I caught his eye and we exchanged a rueful smile. Ronaldo slept. Roberto Carlos slept. Zidane slept. Figo slept. They were humans and they were tired. Tired of being Galácticos.

19: Fallen Angels

The Charge of the Light Brigade combines glory and catastrophe, beauty and despair, like no other episode in the history of war. 'Into the Valley of Death rode the six hundred,' wrote Lord Tennyson commemorating the heroic madness of British cavalrymen gorgeously attired in blue, gold and cherry-red as they galloped – sabres unsheathed and in splendid formation – into the waiting Russian artillery lines. Dozens of books, paintings and two Hollywood films have recreated the events of that day in 1854 in which the pride and joy of Britain's imperial army were cut to pieces by enemy shells. Of 673 men who charged down the valley into the canons' mouths, fewer than 200 returned.

'*C'est magnifique*,' said a French general, observing the action from a nearby height, '*mais ce n'est pas la guerre.*' It is magnificent, but it is not war.

The charge of Real Madrid's white cavalry was glorious while it lasted, unstoppable until the enemy guns opened fire. From then until it was all finally over, the plumed Galácticos lay writhing in the battle-field, eager to be put out of their misery. As Iker Casillas had said after defeat to Deportivo, 'We want this to be over now!' If only it could have been. After losing to Deportivo, Real lost at home to Mallorca, their executioner-in-chief yet another Real Madrid reject, the Cameroonian Samuel Eto'o; then they lost away to bottom of the table Murcia, who had already been relegated to divison two, who were playing only for pride, and Beckham got himself sent off for calling the linesman an *hijo de puta*, a son of a whore; and then the last game of the season, in which Beckham did not play because of the red card, when the chance remained at least to come runners-up in the league to champions Valencia, they ended up fourth – behind Barcelona – after losing at home to Real Sociedad, who had been struggling all season to avoid the drop, allowing them to end up up fifteenth out of twenty in the table. And Real didn't just lose to the small Basque team from San Sebastián, they got hammered 4-1, an appropriately humiliating conclusion to a sequence of successive league defeats – five – never before seen in the club's 102-year history. The Bernabéu was 'strewn', as a Victorian chronicler said of the Crimean plain where the Light Brigade fell, 'with the dead and dying'.

Someone who knew more than most about the dead and dying, a general in the Rwandan army, called me the morning after that final match of the season against Real Sociedad. 'What happened . . . ?' he asked, his voice faint. 'I just don't understand . . .' The general loved football and he loved this Real team because as he saw it they were the game at its best. He had watched Real's games live all season long with his two boys and the experience had gladdened his heart. 'How did it happen?' he repeated. 'You tell me,' I replied. 'You're the expert on catastrophes.' 'I could give you a list of reasons,' he said, 'but in the end I have to confess that I cannot understand.'

The general had called not to offer light relief, nor in the expectation that I could provide much myself. He had called to share his stupefaction. His solidarity in bafflement. The game was a mystery, we all knew that, but this was the most fathomless of all football mysteries that he – or I – could remember. There had never been a season like it in the history of the game. Never had a football team generated such enormous global expectations. Never had a team fallen so far, so fast and so hard from such a great height.

Individually, as well as collectively, they had fallen apart. Something in the players had died. Zidane could not even do the simple things right, misplacing one pass after another; Roberto Carlos had lost his zing; Ronaldo looked less like a buffalo than a cow; Beckham was a headless chicken; Raúl remained on Planet Zog. Only Figo kept battling away, attempting time and again to take on the entire rival team single-handed, correctly judging that the only possible hope lay in him trying to win the game on his own, everybody else having gone AWOL.

Valdano said he had never seen a collapse of such spectacular proportions. 'Homeric' was the word Sebastián, my friend the Real season-ticket holder, used to define the scale of the disaster. 'A historic and stupendous failure,' was the judgement of the sports editor of a national newspaper I spoke to in London. 'It will go down as football's classic case of the principle that the higher they rise, the harder they fall.'

The sports editor was right. Three-quarters of the way into the season they had been eight points clear at the top of the Spanish league, in the quarter-finals of the Champions League and in the final of the Spanish Cup. And then nothing. *Nada*. No Spanish Cup, no Champions League, and not second, or third but *fourth* in the Spanish league.

So what was it that went so suddenly and calamitously wrong? Or what, at any rate, were the arguments being put forward in the thousands upon thousands of conversations on the subject doing the rounds of planet earth?

The most obvious and most frequently heard explanation was that Florentino Pérez was to blame. That his ideas had been too dreamy, too romantic. He had let the spirit of the Light Brigade be his guide: we will defeat you by sheer *élan*. What Real had needed had been less gold brocade and more guns; fewer fancy horsemen, more honest footsoldiers. Thus went the conventional view, and the one to which almost everyone subscribed.

A variation on the same theme was this. Real had come to depend utterly on the genius and inspiration of the great players Pérez had bought. That, after all, was the idea. Who needed tactical systems, Pérez would scoff, when you had Ronaldo and Zidane? The problem with that, said the wise *futbolero* heads, was that genius and inspiration could not always be relied upon to do its stuff. Even the great ones had off days. Even the white angels had feet of clay. That was why it was important to have sound defenders and a solid system to fall back on, to ingrain machine-like habits in the players that, as Valencia had done, made the team more resistant to the vagaries of fortune and form.

Some of the players clearly agreed with this analysis, though they

were too loyal to say it in public. (Interestingly both Beckham and
Zidane said in interviews after the club season was over, speaking in
their capacity as captains of the England and France teams, that they
considered the presence of one specialist defensive midfielder to be
fundamental in a team.) One theory, and I heard it from insiders at
the club, was that part of the explanation for the collapse lay in a
sort of subconscious players' revolt – that they had played at the end
below their best, even if they had not realised it, as a way of sending
a message to Pérez and the rest of the Real board that they'd had
enough of these quixotic and dangerous experiments.

That image of Valdano's about the trapeze artists captured the idea
well. They were brilliant high-wire specialists, the best, these Real
players, but they had come to feel that it was too much to be asked
to perform game after game without a safety net.

I spoke to Valdano at the Bernabéu five days after the end of the
season, on the Friday after the Sunday of the defeat to Real Sociedad.
'Look,' he said, 'the Florentino model remains great. Brilliant. You do
want to have the best, the most exciting trapeze artists on your side.
But you do have off days and you do need that net. The thing is
that we have exaggerated on every front, we have carried things to
extremes, being Galácticos and being "*patéticos*".' Valdano did not say
it but, as a believer in football's traditional values, he did seem to
feel discreetly vindicated by what had happened. 'Now, I think it's
almost better that the disaster should have been so unalloyed because
that way we will learn and we will apply our lessons.' And how
would he summarise the lessons? 'I like the example of the mosaics
and the cement. The mosaics did not receive sufficient support from
the cement. The grip was not hard enough because the cement was
neither sufficiently solid nor sufficiently deep. There was, in other
words, a lack of depth and maturity in the squad.'

Did Florentino Pérez agree? He did, by and large. Humility was
not, as we have seen, a word you automatically associated with the
man but such had been the force of the fall Real had endured that
he had no choice but to admit that he had erred. 'We have been
given a lesson in humility, it is true,' he admitted, more than once,
to me along the course of a ninety-minute meeting we had at his

office in the ACS building a couple of hours after my encounter with Valdano. 'It is probably true that the squad was too thin, that we sinned from an excess of ambition, that we did not see things as clearly as we should have done.' I put it to him that this word he had used to describe Real Madrid the first time we met, the word *señorío* (that meant lordliness, nobility, class), perhaps carried with it a tinge of excessive superiority, of arrogance. Pérez did not dispute my point. 'Yes there has been arrogance. But it has been good for us to lose the way we did. I mean, spectacularly. We didn't just splutter. The whole machinery simply siezed up, stopped functioning. It is as if the pressure of generating so much excitement around the world, so much *ilusión*, just got too much for us and instead of energising us it stifled us. But look, let's be honest, if we had not been punished the way we have been we may not have learnt our lesson. We now have our feet on the ground.'

He showed he had his feet on the ground, he showed he was finally heeding the advice dispensed by the likes of the two teenage boys I had met in Medellín six months earlier, by acting immediately on his new-found wisdom in response to the end-of-season carnage. The very next day after the defeat to Real Sociedad he bought the Argentine central defender Walter Samuel, known in his former club Roma as *il muro* (the Wall), for 25 million euros. If you had told Pérez at the beginning of the season, or even two-thirds of the way through, that he'd be spending that much on a far-from-charismatic defender whose global brand value was less than zero he would have laughed in your face. (He would have laughed even harder had you told him that at the press conference where he announced the signing he would concede the need, as he in fact did, to have a 'balanced' team.) It was not a decision anyone could quarrel with, though, given Real had let in a staggering thirty goals in the last eleven games of the season. My friend from Manhiça in Mozambique, José Fajardo, wrote me a letter just before Samuel's signing making a point that pretty much every Real fan everywhere would have agreed with. 'Real Madrid at the moment remind me of a Ferrari with bicycle wheels at the back,' Fajardo wrote. 'I pray that the big boss of Real Madrid can see that and understand the needs of the team before it is too late.' Not only did the big boss understand that, he told me in our meeting that he had every intention of acting on the humbling lesson he had learnt by doing as the *futboleros* had advocated and buying later in the summer a defensive midfielder to complement Beckham. 'A Makelele type?', 'A Makelele type.'

Which was precisely the kind of player Queiroz had been asking for all season and Pérez had denied him. And now – less than twenty-four hours after defeat to Real Sociedad – Queiroz had been sacked. 'Look,' Pérez said, impatiently. 'I accept that we made mistakes but one of the biggest we made was to hire Queiroz. A big original error we made was to imagine that we did not really need a coach in the conventional sense of the word – I mean one capable of leading, of imposing discipline and authority. We thought we did not need a guy who slammed his fist on the table from time to time. But we did.' In Queiroz's place he had brought in José Antonio Camacho, the former Real Madrid defender and former Spain national coach, a man who was in almost every respect Queiroz's opposite: a blunt, loud, assertive, hyper-Spanish fist-slammer. Camacho's signing was, like Samuel's, an admission of failure.

Was it fair to say, though, that the quiet-spoken, philosophical Queiroz lacked the personality to be a leader of men? Maybe. (He did go straight back to his former job at Manchester United within days of the end of the season, apparently happy to find refuge once again under Alex Ferguson's wing.) But if it was true, that was precisely what Pérez had said he wanted. As he had told me at the start of the season what you needed with players like Real's was a coach who imparted a minimum of orders and gave a maximum of freedom. The premise was that the Galácticos were such consummate professionals that they knew how to administer their own tactics, their energies, their off-field exploits in such a way as to maximise the benefits for the team. 'This was a mistake too,' Pérez recognised. 'You do need a leader in the dressing room, galácticos or no galácticos – especially when morale slackens and things start to go wrong.'

Poor Queiroz. The players leapt to his defence. Figo said he had done everything he could given the means at his disposal. 'The responsibility is mine, Raúl's, Ronaldo's, Zidane's, as much as the coach's,' said Roberto Carlos. But the public, encouraged by the press, did the time-honoured thing – as old as the ancient Greeks – and savaged him. Only Santiago Segurola of *el País* sought to restore some balance. 'Queiroz ended the season the way he began: alone and with no credit,' Segurola wrote. 'No one praised him when the team won and everyone blamed him for the defeats. When Real Madrid enjoyed that period of crushing superiority that placed them at the top of the league it was common to hear that this team did not need a coach.'

Other than that, no one uttered a public word in defence of Queiroz, who the club ushered out of the back door as if he were an embarrassment, an aberration, best consigned to the rubbish heap of *madridista* history. In less than twenty-four hours Camacho was spouting forth with an energy and conviction Queiroz had never shown – had not been hired to show – about the need to have a stronger squad, to buy a replacement right back, for all practical purposes to ditch the notion that the youth team Pavones alone would supply the mechanical deficiencies in the team. Sounded like mutiny to me, I told Pérez. He smiled and said, 'I told you, we have sinned, we have learned our lesson, we have our feet on the ground.'

But if Pérez now had his feet on the ground it did not mean he was going to stop flying. Nor did it mean that he questioned his fundamental faith in the project in his new vision of the game of football. 'We'll be buying another Galáctico this summer, another world-famous attacking player, don't doubt that,' he said. 'We're going to keep generating more excitement than any other team on earth and we're going to keep applying the principle – for this has most definitely been shown to work – that the best and most expensive players are the cheapest.'

That was the core idea behind Real Madrid's new football philosophy and so long as Pérez remained in charge nothing was going to change it, he said. *El proyecto* was simply undergoing some adjustments, was succumbing to some of the ancient orthodoxies he had so unwisely disdained.

And yet, history's judgement could so easily have been so different. Had fate twisted ever so slightly this way instead of that, Pérez might never have been found out, the *futboleros* might have been obliged to accept, as they had done for three-quarters of the season, that Pérez's disdain for them was justified; that he was indeed privy to a superior wisdom. 'I have come round to the view that we do need a Samuel in central defence, we do need a defensive midfielder, we do need a more experienced bench,' Pérez said, 'but had things gone just a little differently we might never have reached the point of even having this conversation.'

That was right, because plausible and compelling as the argument was that some ballast was needed at the back, it did not explain why things had gone so sensationally well until 10 March as to convince practically every Spanish commentator, and many more beyond, to believe that the 'treble' was seriously on. When Real went 5-2 up on aggregate in the first half of that second leg quarter-final against Monaco on 6 April a lot of wise money would have bet on them going the whole way and lifting the European Cup in May at the Arena Aufschalke in Germany. This was the same team, after all, that in October had beaten Porto 3-1 away – Porto the team that had beaten Manchester United and Deportivo en route to the European Cup final, which they went on comprehensively to win against Monaco in the final.

Why had Real been so effective for so long with a team said to be so shockingly lacking in the defensive balance that tradition and orthodoxy required? Never mind their triumphs in cup competition, more random by definition than the evidence of the league, how on earth could you flout convention the way Pérez had, betting all on attack, and still manage to be eight points ahead of super-regimented Valencia twenty-six games into the season? And then, more baffling still, why the overnight collapse?

The absence of the Makelele factor was not in and of itself a convincing enough explanation.

So what other explanations were there. Raúl? What if Raúl, in the team but absent virtually all season, had played half as well as he had done during his previous eight seasons at the club? That alone might have been enough to change everything, especially if he had scored that easy chance in the eighty-fifth minute against Monaco. Real would then have gone through to the Champions League semi-finals, they would most definitely not have lost 0-3 at home to Osasuna four days later, they might quite easily have gone on and won the lot. Or what if Ronaldo, the season's top scorer in the Spanish league despite not scoring one goal in the last eight weeks of the season, had not started suffering a string of niggly injuries in early March? What if he had played in the Spanish Cup final against Zaragoza? Real would probably have won with him in the team and the rot, which began then, might never have set in.

What else? Looking at what happened at the end of the season in greater detail, one might wonder what would have happened if a different referee had taken charge of the decisive Real–Barcelona game, one who might have opted not to send off the team's best player in those dire final weeks, Luis Figo. Or what if Puyol had not saved that shot on goal, on the line, with his cheek? It would have been too late for the Champions League, but the destiny of the Spanish championship might have turned on that moment of strange luck. Or what about the suggestion of my friend Sebastián, who sent me a text message halfway through the game against Murcia suggesting there must be 'voodoo' at work. Someone was sticking pins into little dolls dressed in white. Why not? It seemed as valid a suggestion as any at this point.

I asked each of the Galácticos, except Beckham who refused to break his post-Loos silence, to give me their post-mortems on the end-of-season disaster. Like a detective at a crime scene I sat each one of them before me and asked them to confess what had gone wrong. Starting with Zidane, who pleaded guilty on all counts. 'The last month and a half of the season I have gone through a bad time. I mean I myself as an individual – the team is another matter,' said the man who during that month and a half had been voted by UEFA the best European player of the last fifty years. 'These are my worst times since I arrived at Real Madrid. I hadn't been like this since 1999, when I played for Juventus, after winning the World Cup.'

And his analysis? Was it too many games as some, including Queiroz, had said? For it was true that the Real Madrid players, competing in three competitions all season long, had played on average twenty per cent more games than, say, the players of Valencia. 'Look,' Zidane said, shaking his head. 'Over eight months we worked hard and played very well, often playing twice a week. Now, since Monaco, we've played just once a week, resting all week, and yet we have lost more games in these last weeks than in the whole of the rest of the season. You can't talk of physical exhaustion, as some people do. Something funny has happened. Something broke inside us, I think, after that defeat to Monaco. We were 4–2 up after the first leg; then 5–2 up and then we lose. It was a very hard blow. Very hard. And then we go and lose 0–3 to Osasuna. Something weird happened. We got into a really bad dynamic. In football when you win, you keep winning. When you lose, you keep losing. You fall into a rut that it is very hard to get out of. And then luck stops going your way, as happened to us against Barcelona and Deportivo. It's uncanny, but that is the way it is.'

So nothing to do with the physical strains they had had to endure over the season? 'I don't think so. I believe,' Zidane said, putting his index finger to his temple, 'it's something going on up here. But I don't know why or what.'

Ronaldo admitted that he was just as mystified. I asked him if he had any theories and he said, simply, no. Why not? 'People will say a thousand things but there is no explanation. Until two months ago everything was going very well. Eight points clear in the league, we expected to win everything. If we had carried on playing as we had done we would have. I don't know. Maybe it's true that there are too many games. That our squad was not very deep and the same players always played. Maybe. But really, there is no explanation I can honestly give you.'

As for Roberto Carlos, he too bowed before the inscrutable forces that shaped the great game. 'Look at some of the other teams. Look at Milan. They had a really big, powerful squad that allowed them to rest the players a lot more than we could. They have a fantastic team, so strong in all areas, and yet they lose 4–0 to Deportivo in

the Champions League and are out. They said Arsenal was maybe
the best team this year. They lose in the quarters like us. And we
were doing so well, poised to win the lot and then nothing. Yes, yes,
I know people say there are too many games but in the end I also
believe you cannot honestly explain what happened to us.'

I put it to Roberto Carlos that the outcome of a season can turn
on such tiny details as whether a linesman gives a narrow offside
decision or not, whether a shot hits the post and bounces in or
bounces out. He liked that. 'I always say I would hate to be a football journalist, I would hate to have to write match reports. Say a
game is going 1-1 in the eighty-ninth minute: you've got your article
written, you have explained in detail why a draw was the inevitable
result given what happened on the pitch etcetera. Then in the ninetieth
minute one team scores and the result is 2-1. You have to change
everything you've written, adapt your analysis to the result, explain
why the winning side deserved to win. Which is nonsense, of course.
And what it shows is the great truth that there is something about
football – a lot about football – that is just not amenable to logic.
You cannot reduce the game to these clear explanations . . . We may
have great players here at Real Madrid but the fact is that there is
no perfect player and no perfect team. God will never create either.'

I knew Figo would agree with that. He had been the one to
remind me way back when things were going brilliantly well that
the Galácticos were human, that while Real Madrid had the best
collection of individual players in the world, it remained to be seen
whether the results would prove them to be the most effective team.
'If we were robots our bodies would not tire, our minds would not
be affected by bad results,' said the ever-reflective captain of Portugal.
'If we were robots we wouldn't suffer ups and downs, our confidence would never ever lag. But over the course of a season there
are always ups and downs, individually and collectively. The way our
season went was this. Until December everything went great. After
Christmas we had a small dip, but then we recovered. But now in
this last month and a half, since the Spanish Cup final, we've been
on a permanent downer that's led us to lose everything. Not all the
players agree but I do believe it is partly physical. We do have a

tremendous rhythm of games, sometimes three a week. At first you don't notice it but in March, when a season is decided, it was almost always the same players playing and in some cases the effort was greater because people were playing in positions that were not theirs, playing roles in the team they were not accustomed to.' Like Beckham, I said, having to play like a sort of Roy Keane in defensive midfield? Like him, having to track back much more than usual in the absence of a Makelele? 'I don't want to name names,' Figo replied. 'But the important point is that when one player is obliged to exercise functions with which he is not naturally familiar then this has an effect on all the players, the whole team suffers a sort of domino effect. Suffice it to say that it all adds up over a season. But let's not forget also that, in the best of circumstances, there is always going to be a day when you're not going to play well. Sometimes you have the bad luck that those days when you are going to be below your best happen to be critical moments in the season, critical games. It's unfortunate, what can I say? We're human.'

But these mortal frailties of theirs, I put it to Figo, this physical exhaustion he spoke of: mightn't they have compensated for them if they'd had the injection of adrenaline that victory delivered? 'Absolutely. Yes. If we had won the Spanish Cup we'd have received an injection of energy, freshness and morale. But it was not to be and we carried the pain of that game inside us when we played in the Champions League against Monaco.'

The pain? How much did it hurt? Did the players feel it as keenly as the fans? 'I don't think anyone feels it more keenly than we do. Losing that game against Monaco was very, very hard for me. We scored five goals and lost. It was the thing that most hurt me all season and it took me a lot to get over it.' The second half of that game, said Figo, was one in which for whatever reason both the players and the team as a whole suffered one of those downs he spoke of. 'In football this is what can happen. Suddenly, for some reason, a week comes along when everything is difficult, when things don't work out. And after that when one thing doesn't work out, nothing works out. Goals that before would go in now hit the post. The other team has one shot on goal in a whole half and scores.

This is the stuff that you cannot understand or even try, in the end, to explain.' Like so much in life, I put it to him? 'Like so much in life,' he smiled. 'That's football. It is like life. It IS life.'

Raúl was in a similarly philosophical vein. 'Physically exhausted? Mentally drained? Paying the price of a squad that was too thin, in which the weight of the season was carried by twelve or thirteen players? Maybe,' said Raúl. 'But you know, everybody has their explanations, everybody tries to find arguments to justify their positions, to back up their preconceived views. The fact is that the coaching staff and the players have given their very best, maximum effort, since our tour of China in the summer. And as for how your game is affected by your state of mind, well, sure – but even there it is so hard to tell what is going on. I arrived for the game against Monaco full of optimism, in really good spirits. The very opposite of defeatist. And yet we lost. It's just that football is like that! Losing that game is one of those things that football has. The same against Barça and Deportivo: we played well and could and should have won both, but because Ronaldo's shot went three millimetres this way instead of three millimetres the other way it hits the post and instead of the ball going in it bounces out. On that moment the perception of success or failure over a whole season can turn. In the end there are so many justifications and explanations but one instant in which you lose your concentration, for whatever reason, one moment of carelessness precisely at the very point in the game when you cannot afford to be careless and what happens? You let in a goal, or you miss a goal that you should score, and the whole world changes. There are thousands of factors that decide final scores and results over the length of a season. That, anyway, is the way I see it. I mean, let me give you another example. At the Bernabéu I believe we played better against Barça than when we beat them at the Camp Nou. People attempt to explain and justify a game on the basis of a result, but football is not like that. On the other hand, there have been some games this season when we have won and people said it's because we have played well when in fact that has not been the case. Yet people still try and construct theories, provide explanations, on the basis purely of the final result. But the truth of the matter is that these are things that are determined by luck, by the nature of football and of life. Outcomes are unpredictable.'

Raúl, not known as the most loquacious of men, spoke with conviction and passion, as if unburdening himself of thoughts he had held inside his head for a long time but not had an opportunity so freely to unload before. He was only twenty-six years old yet, as top scorer in the history of the Champions League, top scorer in the history of the Spanish national team, he had accumulated several lifetimes of football experience – experience embellished by a great love and knowledge of the game. He was a fan, one of those trainspotter types obsessed with the details of the game (he was genuinely surprised and frustrated at his inability to recall the name of Manchester United's reserve goalkeeper in a game he played against them in 2000) yet he possessed that secret that was denied to ordinary fans: he knew and felt football from the inside; as a superstar player he had savoured every sorrow, every glory with an intensity no ordinary fan could approach. He was closer than we – the millions and milions of fans out there – were to the game's essence and mystery. He was football made flesh, Raúl. And the conclusion he had reached was precisely that the game we all loved was, in the end, inscrutable; unfathomable; resistant to 'explanations and justifications'.

Which was why predicting the outcome of games, a favourite sport of the fan, was a cast-iron recipe for failure. 'Put it this way,' Raúl said. 'On a given match-day I'm feeling well, confident, strong, convinced it's going to be my day. Or not: I feel bad, apprehensive, fearing the worst. And time and again what happens is the precise opposite of what I had expected. It's happened to me so many times. Take the case of my penalty against France.' He was referring, with some courage (for I had said nothing), to what had been the single most calamitous individual experience in his football life. It was a European nations' championships quarter-final against France in 2000. France were the World champions and, while Spain had played well enough to deserve to win, France were 2-1 up with one minute to go. Whereupon Spain got a penalty and Raúl stepped up to take it. If he scored they would almost certainly go through to extra time and Spain, with the morale boost of that equaliser behind them, would have gone in stronger. 'I remember the feeling so vividly as I placed the ball on the penalty spot,' Raúl continued. 'I was never so sure in my life that I was going to score. I would have bet anything – anything at all – on me scoring. And I missed . . . And it was terrible. I had a knife stuck in my guts for the next ten days, two weeks. And yet . . . and yet other times I have taken penalties when I have felt that, no, no way am I going to score. And I do. The same thing before a game. Or during a game. I am convinced we're going to win and no, we lose. So that's why, I insist, people look for explanations during a game for the final result but the truth is that there a thousand circumstances that can change the course of a game for you.' Like that header of his against Monaco that the linesman ruled offside? 'Exactly. Everybody makes their judgement but in the first half of that game we played very well, and nobody says anything about that because people want to explain, to justify why we lost. Well, we lost because that's the way the game is. That's football.'

Which, as Figo observed, is the same as to say 'that's life'. Valdano has arrived at the same conclusion. 'Football is democratic in the way that human life is ultimately democratic – we all reach the same end,' he said. 'The lesson football always teaches us, sooner or later, is that no one is indestructible, that the smallest and the weakest can teach the biggest and the strongest a lesson. It is the old story of David and Goliath, but in football I believe we see it played out more than in most other sports. In our case, look, we had this beautiful experiment going. A noble experiment. It seemed to be bubbling along very nicely and then suddenly it explodes in our faces. What the game showed was that it was as strong as life itself. You can try new experiments to defeat it but you cannot win. The game is stronger than you are. Always.'

I made my point to Valdano about how everything might have changed, every analysis of Real's season might have been different, had the linesman given Raúl's disallowed goal against Monaco. 'True,' said Valdano. 'But this is the way life is too. Everything is determined by little twists of fortune, by whether one day you happen to be in the particular place and particular time where you happen to come across the woman who is going to be your wife, with whom you

are going to have children, or whatever. It is these chance occur-
rences that determine everything. A game of football is, like life, a
chain of random happenings. And then these random happenings
exercise an influence over your way of thinking, your attitude, your
confidence, which generates a whole new chain of reactions. In the
case of Real Madrid's season the way we found to impose our will
on the game was by playing with these 'crack' players capable of
doing almost godlike things on the field of play. That worked so long
as the confidence remained high and opponents feared us. But a
football team, as I always say, is a state of mind and that state of mind
suddenly switched after a couple of things failed to go our way. And
then we suddenly stopped feeling indestructible and then luck stopped
going our way and the team's state of mind became filled with nega-
tivity.'

Could something have been done to turn the negative back to
positive? 'All of us endeavour, of course, to exercise some control
over these random happenings that shape our lives. It is the eternal
human impulse. The truth is that there is only so much you can do
but in the case of football I do believe that with a Samuel and a
Makelele in your side you do improve the odds for yourself.' What
would have happened if Pérez had acceded to buying a couple of
these at the start of the season, or even halfway through, as Queiroz
had wanted? 'Who can ever tell in football?' he replied. 'But I do
believe, in truth, that had we had one top-class centre half and one
specialist defensive midfielder we could have met all our objectives,
we could have won everything, we could have sealed the most
glorious season in Real Madrid's history.'

20: Beckham or the Bernabéu?

The one remaining member of the cast that I had to interrogate was José Angel Sánchez, the man regarded by some as the truly evil genius behind Real, the *éminence grise* to whose commercial requirements the entire operation – or so outraged traditionalists said – was being subordinated. So how was he getting along? How was the great marketing empire he had built? Surely this historic run of defeats had been bad for him.

Far from it. The Galácticos had been proving their worth. The Beckham factor had had a mightily beneficial influence on the club's accounts. He had been right in his estimation a year earlier. Beckham had been bought for a song. In business terms Beckham had been the best investment ever made by a football club. For, it turned out, Sánchez too had been making history. April had been the cruellest month for the team and the fans but even as they suffered, even as they were being mown down by Fortune's grim artillery, the club's Marketing Department had pulled off the mother of all results, won the king of all trophies. Sánchez had cut a deal with Adidas the likes of which had never been seen in the history of sports sponsorship. He was itching to tell me during a meeting we had in his office at the end of May exactly how much it was worth but he could not, out of loyalty to Adidas, who jealously protected this kind of information for fear of – precisely – making their other clients jealous. I told him I had seen in the Spanish press a figure of 168 million euros for eight years. 'Eight years is right,' Sánchez said. 'The sum the press mention is laughably below the real figure. What we are talking about here is the biggest sponsorship contract in the history of sport, one that has smashed all previous records.' OK, I said, so give me some clues. 'Well, how about this?' said Sánchez, very pleased with himself. 'Our deal with Adidas is worth double the deal Reebok have with the entire NBA [America's National Basketball Association].' And an analogy closer to home? 'OK. The deal is worth many times – in double figures – what Beckham cost us.' So that was at least 300 million euros, I calculated. But no, we were still far off the mark. 'Here. Take this. The benchmark until now in world sports has been Manchester United's deal with Nike. OK. Listen. Our deal with Adidas is worth double – *double* – what Manchester United got from Nike.'

I checked out what Manchester United got from Nike. It was a thirteen-year deal worth 450 million euros. That worked out at 34 million euros a year. Which meant Real Madrid had clinched a deal worth around 60 million euros; 480 million over the eight years of the contract. How come they had paid so much? 'Because football is the biggest leisure industry in the world. Do you know 1,100 million people watched our European Cup final against Bayer Leverkusen in 2002? And because we are the biggest club in the industry. And because we have Zidane, Ronaldo and – above all – Beckham. And Adidas, who know more about how to gauge these things than anyone else, understand this very well.'

On that point about football being the biggest leisure industry in the world, I put it to Sánchez that while the events of the season might have turned out more happily for Real what they had done was reinvigorate the industry, had they not? The season's lesson had been, after all, that football was endlessly surprising, as Raúl had said; that no hard-and-fast formulas existed (see Milan's defeat to Deportivo in the Champions League) that guaranteed victory; that little clubs like Porto and Monaco could, with a little luck and application, have their shot at reaching the stars; that to be big and rich like Real Madrid offered no guarantees of victory. 'I agree,' said Sánchez. 'The season has been a failure for Real Madrid in terms of trophies, at any rate, but a triumph for the game itself. And I would go further. For us to win five European Cups in a row the way the great Madrid team of the Fifties did would be counterproductive. It would undermine the game, it would in a certain sense kill the excitement and suspense and uncertainty that fuels the game's drama. In a way for

us to lose 3-0 at home to Osasuna is good for the game, if not necessarily for me personally, for us or our fans.'

Getting back to this Adidas deal, its success for Adidas being
contingent partly on the drama retaining its high pitch, Real would
have 60 million euros – a shade under Zidane's world record transfer
fee – guaranteed per year for eight years. This explained, I said to
Sánchez, a remark that Valdano had let slip a few weeks earlier. Valdano
had said that the economic health of the club was such that they
would be in a position to do 'what they liked' in the transfer market
over the coming years. Sánchez smiled, then said, 'What's more, we
have a lot more sources of income than Adidas.' But, I asked, could
he explain how this money-making formula of Real's – a formula
no other club seemed to have latched onto – actually worked? This
premise that the best players were the cheapest. Spell that out for
me in numbers, I said.

'A lot of factors go into it. It is hard to break down,' Sánchez
said. 'But the simplest thing is to look at the graph that shows the
increase in our regular income since Florentino arrived. We've been
spending all this money on the biggest names in the game and simul-
taneously there has been this steep upward curve in our income,
from 138 million euros in the year 2000/01 to our conservative esti-
mate for 2004/05, which is 304 million. This reflects growth in all
areas: ticketing, TV rights, friendly matches and, most of all, marketing.
So your question is, how much does this have to do with the policy
of buying Galácticos? Everything! Everything is the answer. We created
this model, one that generates masses of interest and focuses attention our way all over the world, and then the money comes in. That's
it: proof of the Galácticos self-financing right there.'

And Beckham? How unique was he? How unique a cash-generator?
Sánchez, during several encounters we'd had over the season, had
struggled to contain his wonder, bordering on dismay, at the power
of the Beckham brand. He had seen at first hand what the Beckham
effect meant but he could never quite believe it. He would always
just shake his head when I mentioned his name, repeating, 'amazing,
amazing,' over and over. 'It's not possible to put precise numbers to
it,' Sánchez said, 'but we do have a good indicator in shirt sales. The

sales of shirts do not in themselves constitute such a large slice of our cake but what they do is offer a faithful index of Beckham's commercial pull. Consider this. The season before this one we sold approximately 900,000 shirts. This season, following Beckham's arrival, we've sold three million. Draw your own conclusion.'

It didn't mean that the extra 2,100,000 were all Beckham shirts, but the figure was not far off, lending further credence to that point Rolf Beisswanger of Siemens had made about Manchester United losing half their brand value with Beckham's sale. Had Real not had Beckham aboard they would not have generated such spectacular over-the-odds income for playing friendly exhibition games. As the season was drawing to a close Sánchez closed a deal with the Japanese company Fujitsu whereby they would pay 14.5 million euros to Real for playing two games, in Tokyo and Osaka, in July 2004, just before the start of the new season. That was approximately seven times more than any other team in the world was being paid for taking part in similar pre-season extravaganzas.

It was true, and experience had confirmed it. Real had paid peanuts for Beckham. And yet, as far as the ordinary fan was concerned, the one who did not interest himself in all these matters of high finance, the Beckham purchase had failed to achieve its most elemental objective, namely help the club win more trophies. Might it be fair to conclude, I put it to Sánchez, that developing a brand and making money out of it was easier than creating a winning football team; that his job was a lot easier than the one held until recently by the hapless Queiroz? 'I agree completely,' Sánchez replied. 'Completely. And I will tell you why. In marketing there are certain constants that must always be applied, certain steps that you know you must take if you are going to succeed. There is a business discipline here that, if you observe it, will bring you the results you want. Not so in football. Everything there is up for debate. Everything is in the lap of the gods. The best-laid plans can be thwarted by the imponderables of fortune and the human factor.' Marketing, in other words, was a science and football was, as Raúl had said, inscrutable as life itself. 'Exactly right,' said Sánchez, acknowledging with a radiant smile that what he did for a living was all very well but small beer compared to the enormity and magnificence of the great game played at the greatest level. José Angel Sánchez might be a very clever chap, he might be channelling and administering Real's riches with great acumen and wit but he was only José Angel Sánchez. Next to Beckham, Zidane, Ronaldo, Figo, he was a mere bag-carrier. Pérez too understood what the balance of power was, deep down. He might have been the first celebrity football-club president but he knew that he was a nobody next to these guys. For one simple reason – that he worshipped them and they did not worship him.

Talking to Pérez continually over the season I could tell that he was as impressed and, almost, as overawed by the stars he had signed as the screaming teenagers who waited for a glimpse of them at airports. In Seville for a mid-season game I was staying at the same hotel as Pérez and the players. There was a young Japanese man, in his early twenties, who spent the first twenty-four hours we were there, day and night, waiting at the hotel door for players' autographs. By the twenty-fifth hour, as the team were having their final tactics talk in the hotel prior to catching the bus to the stadium for the game, the Japanese man had managed to infiltrate himself into the hotel lobby along with another forty or so eager onlookers. He was wearing a yellow Brazil shirt with the number nine and the name Ronaldo on it. He looked anxious, energised, a man on a mission. Spotting a Real Madrid security guy, he took off the yellow shirt and gave it to him, saying something at the same time. The security man nodded and went through some doors to the ballroom where the players were meeting. Five minutes later the security man re-emerged, with the shirt under his arm. He handed it to the Japanese man who looked at, registered that Ronaldo had signed his autograph on the front and let out a cry – a howl – of joy. For the next sixty seconds, or it might have been longer, he did not stop jumping up and down, disrupting the genteel calm of the five-star hotel lobby with his animal euphoria.

Florentino Pérez's response earlier that same day to achieving much what the Japanese fan had done was more measured, but no less heartfelt. What had happened was this. Pérez had a friend in

Sevilla, an art expert called Pepe Cobo, who had helped him build up his personal collection of modern art. Some months earlier Pérez had had a picture taken of himself on the Bernabéu grass posing alongside the four Galácticos he had signed, Figo and Beckham to one side of him, Ronaldo and Zidane on the other. Pérez was in regulation grey suit, blue shirt and tie. The players were in their white kits. Pérez had given the photograph to Cobo to blow up. Cobo had done a good job. The definition remained sharp despite the fact the photograph was now the size of half a double bed. I knew it was the size of half a double bed because Pérez took me up to his bedroom to show it off to me. Grinning like a little boy, he told me he would arrange for each of his four heroes to come to his bedroom and sign their names on the picture. We then discussed, together with his friend Cobo, which would be the most appropriate place for the autographs to go, on the shorts, the socks or the shirts. We agreed that the shirts would be best. Later that day Pérez found me sitting in the lobby bar and said, 'Come on! Come on up and see! They've signed the photo for me!' So up we went, and sure enough, there was Pérez's newest and quite possibly most treasured art work, each white shirt bearing the blue scribble of each of the four most famous football players on earth. Beckham had written, in game but incorrect Spanish, '*Con Mucho Simpatico*, David Beckham.'

Whether, once things began to fall apart for Beckham and Real, relations would continue to remain *simpatico*, or whether Beckham would be heading back home in the summer, was a question that generated almost as many column inches in Britain for a while as the transfer saga – 'the biggest sports story of the year' – that had played itself out twelve months earlier. As soon as the Rebecca Loos stories turned up on the front pages of the tabloids, stories started turning up in the sports pages at the back suggesting Beckham would be leaving Real for Chelsea. This particular tabloid drama, egged on at times by the more serious papers, ran for close on two months. The yarn that acquired the most credibility, that generated the most column inches in Britain, was this: Beckham was happy at Real Madrid and eager to stay but his wife was demanding he come home; his departure was all the more imminent because Real had fallen out of love with him and besides needed the money he would fetch, a sum the British press placed at around the same 35 million euro mark Real had paid for him.

Aside from the possibility that Victoria Beckham might indeed have insisted for a while that he return home, and then relented, the rest of the story was wildly off the mark. Real – meaning Pérez, Sánchez, Valdano and the entire Bernabéu – wanted him to stay. For footballing as well as commercial reasons. As for the notion that Real were in dire straits: this could not have been further from the truth. The club was in excellent financial shape, and had more than enough in the coffers to buy both another summer Galáctico and all the Makeleles that they needed. Beckham did not appear to know this, though, his lines of communication with the club not being as good as they might have been. He had failed to learn Spanish, a task at which he had not laboured as hard as he initially imagined he might. He spent much of his time back home in England and in Madrid moved everywhere in the company of a British retinue of advisers and bodyguards. Which meant that much of Beckham's information was coming from the British newspapers.

All of which explained why one day two weeks before the end of the season Beckham asked to see Pérez in order once and for all to clear up his future. Beckham, for his part, had already made up his own mind. After lengthy discussion of the matter with his wife, he had decided that he wished to continue after all to live in Spain, playing for Real. She had evolved in her own thinking too and was prepared to move lock, stock and barrel with the family to Madrid.

As for Beckham's own calculations on the matter, he understood that Chelsea would be a come-down in football and image terms. 'David Beckham: Chelsea and England' was one thing. 'David Beckham: Real Madrid and England' something else altogether. Were he to have left Real for Chelsea after just one year in Spain something told him that he would have a hard time one day explaining to his grandchildren why on earth he had done something so weak and so crass. But above all he had unfinished business in Spain. Despite the remarkable start he had made to his Real Madrid playing career, he still had that point of his to prove. Were he to return home from Madrid trophyless those critics of his whose judgement he took so much to heart would have a field day. (All the more so if Real were to go on to have a gloriously successful season without him.) Besides, there was another thing. He loved playing at the Bernabéu and he loved even more playing with Ronaldo and Zidane and there was nothing Roman Abramovich could pay him that would compensate for the loss of that.

Having come to these conclusions, having at last succeeded in persuading his wife to abandon England for Spain, it was understandable that Beckham should have started harbouring fears that it might all go terribly wrong; that perhaps the British newspaper stories might have been right, that perhaps Pérez did want to get rid of him. Thus it was that when he approached Pérez for that crunch meeting they had, in the second week of May, he was very apprehensive indeed. 'I want to be able to issue a statement, Mr President,' he said, 'saying that I am going to stay at Real, that my wife and family are going to come and live with me in Madrid. Can I say that, Mr President? Or is it true what they say that you want to sell me?'

Beckham wasn't trembling but his eyes were moist. This was the moment of truth. It had taken some courage to ask the question but, there was no getting away from it, it needed to be asked to put to rest once and for all the agony of uncertainty that had gripped him. Probably all would be well. Pérez had shown him nothing but affection and respect since he had arrived, but with these bigshot club presidents who knew? He had got rid of del Bosque and Hierro a year earlier. Queiroz was for the chop. Pérez was a ruthless bugger when it came to it. Inside the velvet glove there was an iron fist. Beckham knew this. He had forced the moment to its crisis aware that the terrible possibility existed of rejection – the most humiliating rejection of his professional life.

Pérez heard Beckham's question and smiled. Broadly. Warmly. Paternally. His reply could not have been more perfect, could not have provided a warmer, more luxuriant balm to the most famous man in the world's troubled soul. 'David, listen to me, David,' Pérez replied, 'I would sell the stadium – I would sell the Bernabéu – before I sold you.'

My informant on this story did not record what Beckham's reaction was, whether he wept for joy, whether he reached out and planted a large kiss on Pérez's cheek, or whether he merely beamed the biggest smile of his life. What I do know is what Beckham told Pérez next. 'Look, Mr President, I understand that a big offer is going to come in for me from an English club in the next few weeks. Take it from me, I don't want to know. I want to stay here. Please tell them you won't accept the offer.' 'Don't worry, David. So long as you want to stay at Real Madrid there is no chance of that.' Pérez reminded Beckham that the very first time they had talked (Beckham still did not know Pérez had been in a ladies' toilet at the time) he had told him that in joining Real Madrid he was joining a family. Well, Pérez said, the Real Madrid family stuck together and the idea that they would let go a favourite son was simply inconceivable. The newspapers might choose to dwell on his recent loss of form but Pérez had not forgotten the bravery and class he had displayed during the first half of the season, or how quickly he had won over the Bernabéu. Beckham had repaid Pérez's faith in him once and he had no doubt that, come next season, he would again.

Beckham was thrilled. He was still thrilled a week after that meeting with Pérez when I came across him at the Real Madrid training ground. He had just arrived in his four-by-four car for a morning practice session and when I asked him through the window of his car how he was, he gave me the widest of grins and said – Rebecca Loos and all that very clearly behind him now – 'Very well. Very well indeed!'

He was so much the better because, as I also discovered, Pérez had sorted out a couple of humdrum but unresolved practical problems for him. Where to live and where to send his older child to school. 'Leave it to me, David. I'll sort that out for you,' Pérez said. No sooner said than done. In no time at all Pérez found Beckham a place to live, a house which he would rent with an option to purchase; and, despite the fact that all the places at Beckham's school of choice for his son Brooklyn had been officially taken, Pérez used his charm and influence to ensure that the boy got in.

Thus it was that a week after my brief encounter with Beckham, three days after the sending off against Mallorca that had put an end to his season, he put paid to what had threatened to be a rerun of the previous year's summer soap opera by announcing that he had taken on a new lease on a Spanish property, that Brooklyn had been enrolled in a Madrid school, that he had every intention of fulfilling the three years remaining on his contract. In a joint statement with his wife, in case anyone thought he was imagining things, he declared, 'I have a long-term commitment to Real and to my life in Spain.' And Victoria Beckham was quoted separately as saying in the statement, 'The time is now right for the children to move to Madrid and we are all looking forward to it enormously.' Making it clear that at last she intended to do what she might helpfully have done a year earlier.

Pérez called me twenty-four hours before the Beckhams issued their statement and told me the news. 'Next season will be Beckham's great season at Real Madrid, you'll see,' he told me. 'It'll be like 1999 was for him, Manchester United's treble year, after he was sent off in the 1998 World Cup final. Well, he was sent off in his last game of the season here and next season he will win everything with Real Madrid. Just watch.'

Still, and amazingly, Chelsea persisted. Peter Kenyon, having sold Beckham to Real a year earlier on Manchester United's behalf, now wanted him back on Chelsea's. When I was sitting with Pérez in his office at ACS five days after the end of the season, on 29 May, calls kept coming into his mobile phone from people involved in one way or another with the buying and selling of players – the sport he was condemned to play until the end of summer. An Italian agent called to inform him of what he already knew, that Kenyon and his boss Abramovich were on the hunt for some Galácticos of their own and their first choice was Beckham. The agent apparently had a straight line to Kenyon, which was why Pérez made a point of spelling out precisely what his conditions would be before letting Beckham go. Pérez made, in fact, precisely the point Sánchez had made to me a month earlier. 'Tell Chelsea that the situation is this,' Pérez said down the phone. 'If they want Beckham they must pay his contractual buy-out clause in its entirety. That's 180 million euros. 180 million – not a euro less. Not 179 million. Not 179 million 999. 180 million. OK? That's the first thing. But second, what they must also do before I will even begin to consider letting him go is receive the consent of the player. He must want to leave Real Madrid. Only then would I agree to accept 180 million euros for him. Otherwise he stays.'

Pérez knew that he had to spell it out this way; that if he simply asserted that Beckham was staying and that was that Kenyon would only keep coming. He had absolutely no doubt of either his own or Beckham's intentions. He would never have said to Beckham that he'd sell the stadium before he sold him if he did not, metaphorically speaking, entirely mean it. He knew perfectly well that Beckham would not have issued a statement as categorical as the one he did unless he intended to stay. The funny thing was that Kenyon and Abramovich should have persisted in imagining he might still want to go to Chelsea and that Real might still want to let him go. The only explanation was that they had a blind faith in the power of money and that they were very poorly informed; that they were depending for their information on what they read in the papers.

Whether, in the event that Beckham had wished to leave, Roman Abramovich would indeed have paid 180 million euros for Beckham, who knows? He could certainly have afforded it. Much as he could have afforded to buy and pay a fortune in salaries to Michel Salgado, Ronaldo and Roberto Carlos – all of whom were approached by Chelsea, all of whom made it clear that Real Madrid was categorically their first choice of club, that honour and glory and their reputation in history counted for more than mere cash. Walter Samuel, Real's freshest acquisition, had made the very same calculation. Chelsea offered him nearly twice the salary, but he opted for Real. 'Real Madrid is the summit for me,' Samuel said two days after his new team's disastrous 4-1 home defeat to Real Sociedad. 'You cannot go any higher as a professional footballer.'

Things might have turned out badly last season but at Real, at this Real, the future was always bright – brighter than anywhere else in the football world. And in football it is the future that counts. That was why the club announced the signings of Samuel and Camacho within twenty-four hours of the last of the end-of-season fiascos, sending the message the fans wanted to hear: that it was time to start turning one's thoughts to the coming season. It was just the right thing to do because football fans – everywhere – have the memories of mosquitoes. They live for the future. They feed on *ilusión*, not nostalgia or sorrows past. Take my friends at the *La Amistad* bar in Roquetes, near Barcelona.

I watched the Real Sociedad game there with Angel and Rafa. It was a miserable night, lightened only by the occasional reminiscence about the great goals we had seen Ronaldo and Zidane score in months past. But as soon as the game was over, once we had digested the embarrassing implication of it – that Real had plummeted to fourth in the table – Angel and Rafa had only one thing on their minds. 'Please, talk to Florentino for us and find out how the two of us can become Real Madrid members,' Angel said. 'We've talked about it and we're dead serious. I know it takes money, but we're prepared to pay whatever it takes.' So, I said, we've just watched this calamity of a game, you've spent half the match cursing the players, and yet you say you're prepared to spend whatever it takes to become club members? Angel and Rafa nodded, as solemn as bridegrooms saying 'I will'. 'Whatever it takes, we'll pay it.' You'll sell your homes, if need be? 'For sure.' Your wives, your children . . . ? 'Absolutely. We're *Madridistas* for life. There is nothing bigger.'

Within a week all the stories in the press, the chatter in bars and buses from Madrid to Medellín was all about who the next Galáctico would be, with the odds strongly on Roma's Francesco Totti. There was talk of another centre half, and of maybe Patrick Vieira of Arsenal in central midfield to play alongside Beckham, liberating the Englishman to go forward, score more goals, improve on what in fact had been a decent tally of passes for goal, nine – one less than Figo, who had delivered the most. Already the talk was about how Zidane, also freed from defensive duties, would flourish once again in attack, how Totti would add another dimension to the team with his fine touch, and powerful all-round game; how great it would be to have, in someone like Totti, someone who was a good header of the ball, someone at last who could benefit from Real's possession of the two best crossers in the game, Beckham and Figo. Pérez would stand for re-election in July and no one had the slightest doubt that he would defeat all challengers, assuming any challengers were rash enough to make an appearance. And there was no doubt he would win because, for all the disappointment of the season just past, he had a plan – an ideology, as they liked to call it in Spain – that continued to deliver *ilusión* like no other project could. The dream machine had clattered to a halt at the end of the 2003/04 season, but in no time at all – football fans' memories being short, their dreams long – it had been re-oiled and reinvigorated, just as it had been twelve months earlier with the arrival of Beckham. Real Madrid remain, in Fajardo's words, a Ferrari; in Valdano's, a Rolls Royce. The back wheels had failed, the brakes needed readjusting, but these corrections were easily accomplished. The Rolls remained a Rolls.

Just as Zidane remained Zidane and Ronaldo remained Ronaldo. Real's temporary failure, and their own, had not for one instant undermined the admiration players or club elicited the world over. Whatever happened the next season, or the one after, Real Madrid would continue to dream big, to harbour the greatest ambitions of any football club in the world: namely to win with glory.

They might come unstuck again. Unlikely that lightning would strike twice, but it might. Never mind. It would take more than a run of spectacular defeats to dull the club's sheen. The failed Real Madrid team of David Beckham's continued to shine brighter than any other team in the world, even as they were being thrashed at home to Osasuna and Real Sociedad. The club's glamour and the heroic immoderateness of its ambition were unassailable. A hundred and fifty years after the Charge of the Light Brigade it was the Light Brigade that we remembered, that we celebrated, not the faceless Russian artillery officers. In the Hollywood films the British cavalrymen are played by Errol Flynn, Trevor Howard, John Gielgud; the parts of the Russians, by extras. The Russian canons were more efficient, they offered more solid results. Like Valencia Football Club in Spain. But, as Queiroz had the wisdom to observe a few weeks before he was fired, if Real Madrid played the militaristic brand of football played by Valencia – even if they won every competition in which they played – the fans would burn down the Bernabéu. The Real Madrid team that came fourth in the league, following the most dramatic exercise in self-destruction the game had ever seen, would be remembered long, long after Valencia's championship-winning team had been forgotten. At any rate, outside Valencia, whose triumphs –

however admirable – were of scarcely more than local interest. One crowded hour of glorious life is worth an age without a name, wrote Sir Walter Scott. The season in which Beckham, Ronaldo, Zidane, Figo, Raúl and Roberto Carlos played together was packed with hours of glorious life. They had generated more excitement and fun and dreams around the world than any other group of people engaged in any other activity anywhere. Thanks to the ubiquity of the television signal – this being one case of technology put to gloriously beneficial use – football's message had reached every corner of the earth. There were lots of things to be depressed about in the modern world, but amidst all the horrors and fears the appeal of the world game in our globalised age, the joy and shared passion it generated from Madrid to Gaza to Mozambique, did seem to mark an encouraging step forward in the evolution of the human species.

Real Madrid was doing its bit to goad evolution along. Already, with the season barely over, people everywhere were talking about the great feats Real Madrid would achieve, the magnificent goals they would score, the beautiful passages of play they would adorn our vision with next time they ran out on to a football pitch wearing the eternal white strip. As the new season approached Real Madrid was once again the team to beat; the names of Real Madrid's players were the ones on everybody's lips; all the excitement and expectation centred on watching them play – not Valencia, not Porto, not Chelsea, but Real Madrid. That was the triumph – the lasting, unassailable triumph – of Real's new football. The secret of it all, the great and brilliant secret, was the understanding that while Real Madrid was big, the biggest thing in world sports, there was one thing that was bigger – much bigger – than Real Madrid, and that was the game of football itself. Florentino Pérez's Real Madrid, while seeming arrogant, were in the end humble. They were acknowledging that the club's name, however resonant, needed the added value that came from the great players; and the greater the players, the greater the value. Because, as Gabriel Batistuta said of Ronaldo, the great players – the truly great ones – *were* football. That was the genius of the Real Madrid formula. You bet on the greatest talent in the world, you bet on what was enduring and universal, and then, even if you lost, you always won.

21: Welcome to the Sambadrome!

Summer 2005.

We could have been in Munich. We could have been in Seville. Or Mallorca. Or la Coruña, Los Angeles, Tokyo, Bangkok. It happened to be Beijing, but the scene, the mood as Real Madrid's team bus pulled up outside the hotel where the team were staying was identical. Waiting multitudes in white reacted with the same frenzied, taut commotion, heaving against a thin police line. The bus was empty, save for the driver, but its arrival was the signal that the players would be descending soon from their rooms. The fans had kept a patient vigil outside the hotel for hours in the drenching July heat but now the wait would yield its reward. They would snatch a glimpse of their idols; maybe steal a photograph. For a precious moment they would breathe the same air. Some happy soul would receive – or imagine he received, which would do just as well, for it would give meaning to his life for ever – the blessing of a careless smile.

Beijing's five-star Kunlun Hotel was base camp for the Real Madrid team on the China stage of their 'World Tour' 2005. That was what they called their pre-season summer mission (never shy, the Real PR people, never modest) taking them to the United States and Asia, lands of opportunity where football fever was still in its adolescent stage. Conflating the fever with the cash, making ever-larger profits out of the world's fastest growing religion; that was the purpose of the 'World Tour'. Everybody was doing it now, and not just Real's big rivals, like Manchester United or Barcelona. Even small teams like the Spanish league's Espanyol and England's Bolton Wanderers were getting in on the act, playing exhibition games in Asia, striving to build the beginnings of a global brand name. The gold rush – the scramble for Asia's emerging football market – was on. The old football establishment – so long on passion but so short on business acumen – was catching on to the philosophy of Florentino Pérez. They were finally figuring out that you could make money out of the game; that to be operating at a loss, as most of the famous clubs had done for years, was the pinnacle of ineptitude. Nothing was bigger than football, nothing elicited stronger or more far-flung passions among more people. Converting passion into profit; that was what the New Football was about. And at this game – irrespective of what happened on the football pitch – Real Madrid were the best in the world.

To witness the pull these passions exerted you needed to look no further than the crowds outside the Kunlun. Or, still more frighteningly intense, those inside – the hundred or so fanatics who had somehow made it into the inner sanctum of the hotel lobby, their eyes permanently fixed on the lift doors and ears hair-trigger tuned to every electronic 'ding', the sound that heralded the descent to earth of the visitors from on high. Never mind that they came from a city far away in a country none of the assembled faithful would ever have visited; never mind that the team they played for had not won anything in two years. Never mind logic and cold fact. Every 'ding' induced the same Pavlovian sequence of responses: first, a collective tremor, then gasps, then strangled shrieks, then a flurry and a push and loud screams and desperately craned necks. But first to emerge, before the players, was a ragged crew of wild-eyed youths in white bandannas and white Real shirts, the fundamentalist sector of Chinese football fandom. During the 72 hours that the team stayed at the hotel, half a dozen gangs – or rather, packs – of three or four autograph scavengers would spend day and night going up and down, up and down the elevators, pressing every single button, waiting and waiting till they struck lucky, till they achieved their holy grail, ambushing a player in a confined space. But now that the big moment had come they were being shooed out of the lifts into the lobby, to screams of teenage indignation, by large, humourless heavies. To be followed by the Galácticos' advance party, a retinue of bag-carriers, medics and assistant coaches and the head coach himself, the exuberantly named Brazilian Wanderley Luxemburgo – none of whom even registered on the Kunlun hysteria meter. Nor did half the players. The newly acquired Uruguayans Diogo and Pablo García, some of the members of the youth team – the promising defender Arbeola and the striker Soldado – might be considered worthy prey by the roaming elevator packs in the small hours of the morning, but not now. Not now that on the menu we had Zidane, Ronaldo, Roberto Carlos, Figo and Raúl – never mind the prize dish himself, the whitest of the white angels, David Beckham. The Chinese organisers of Real's visit had plastered Beijing with vast billboards displaying the faces, in heroic pose, of the six Galácticos. They did the same with the t-shirts. But in each case it was Beckham's face that dominated, like the leading man in an advertisement for a blockbuster film.

And that's what they had become here. Actors playing the role of superstar football players. The football, in this context, mattered not at all. No more than it mattered when Tom Cruise appeared at a Hollywood premiere whether in that particular film he was playing the part of a pilot, doctor or master spy. The scene in the Beijing hotel was pure show business, complete with red carpet and jostling crowds and ropes holding them back and straight-backed bodyguards escorting each of the superstars as they blurred past in a flash of cameras, dispensing the most absent of smiles, the most perfunctory of waves, before disappearing behind the blackened windows of the team bus. 'David! David! David!' one young woman cried, beside herself with pain and longing, as the blond apparition sailed by. And then they were gone, the bus chasing after its police escorts, hurtling off to one of the promotional events scheduled by the marketing department, this time in Tianjin, two hours away towards the East China Sea. But the emotional wreckage Typhoon David left behind in the hotel lobby was a sight to behold. It was not possible to tell whether it was in tragic response to the failure to get his autograph or in joyful reaction to the delusion that the thinnest of smiles had been aimed her way, but one girl aged about 16 – the most affected of a dozen who had been reduced to desperate sobs – collapsed to her knees and wailed and screamed and writhed. If you had been told she had just that moment received news of her mother's death in a plane crash you would have believed it. She was distraught beyond any possibility of consolation. Never, on stage or in real life, had grief more abject ever been portrayed. What Chairman Mao would have made of the spectacle, of the emotional torrent unleashed among the Chinese proletariat by this living icon of decadent Western capitalism, who knows? But it was most certainly not a picture the Great Helmsman had in mind back in the 60s when he hatched the plans for his Cultural Revolution, his great scheme to crush individualism once and for all and to sink all human aspirations into his dream of a classless society, devoid of greed and self-seeking.

Chairman Florentino's revolution had not exactly unfolded according to the script either. Or rather, in the economic aspect it had done, but on the football pitch his dreams had undergone a mauling. His fantasy football idea that in order to succeed in the game all you had to do was assemble the best attacking players and let them get on with it had not worked out the way he had anticipated. Scorning the orthodoxies of the *futboleros*, he had had no time for coaches – a necessary evil, he imagined – nor had he lain any store by the blackboard tacticians. And he had had even less time for those tedious – but so fashionable – notions of 'balance', a word which, as he saw it, was a euphemism employed by those who believed that a football team should be packed with defensive midfielders, players who only became relevant when the other team had the ball, who contributed nothing to the 'spectacle' that Real Madrid were honour-bound, above all things, to deliver. It had worked for six months. The team he had assembled in the glorious summer of 2003 – complete with his four Galáctico signings: Figo, Zidane, Ronaldo and now Beckham – had confounded all the conventional wisdoms and had threatened to sweep all before them, until the dream fell spectacularly to earth in that calamitous Madrid spring of 2004. To the joy of some of the *futboleros*, who drew righteous vindication from the team's collapse, 2004 ended up being the *annus horribilis* of Florentino's reign.

They accused Pérez of being everything from a Quixotic nincompoop to a Machiavellian fraud. Yet, more than 12 months on, no one had come up with a satisfactory explanation as to why, having had everything in their grasp, having lit up the Bernabéu like never before in 40 years, Real had ended the 2003/2004 season playing dull, hope-less, relegation football. A number of people within Real Madrid came privately to believe that there had been a half-mystical, half-psychological connection between the collapse and the Madrid train bombs of 11 March 2004, the precise date after which everything unravelled. Something unravelled inside Pérez's mind too. Famously cool under pressure during all of his enormously successful business life, he reacted to the Galácticos' implosion with what turned out to be a series of rashly short-term, panic buys. Part of the explana-tion was that he was coming up for re-election in July and, fearing a backlash from club members, responded to the clamour that arose for a coach to impose more discipline on the players, and for a greater emphasis on defence. His fears, as it happened, were misplaced. Such was the credit he had accumulated during his first four-year term in the presidency, that he could have hired a monkey to coach the team and still won. Pérez's manifestly populist signings of the sergeant-majorish José Antonio Camacho and the Argentine central defender Walter 'il Muro' Samuel undoubtedly boosted his numbers, though, seeing him to victory at the election with a Saddam Hussein-style share of the vote: 97 per cent.

Replacing Carlos Queiroz, who had been almost as much in awe of the Galácticos as the Kunlun celebrity hunters, with Camacho, who'd built a career out of pretending that he was in awe of no one, was an idea that did not last beyond the first month of the new season. The players, not displeased by the gentle manners of the Portuguese Mozambican, were bemused by Camacho's hectoring style. During training, as he barked orders and issued histrionic repri-mands, they would exchange sly glances and shake their heads, as if to say, 'What's WRONG with this guy?'

Camacho left, beaten by a combination of player power and a weight of expectation he proved unable to bear. His replacement was the ultimate interim appointment, a junior member of the coaching staff and forgotten former Real goalkeeper by the name of Mariano García Remón. Pérez and the rest of the hierarchy performed the usual ritual of publicly expressing their faith in him, declaring him to be a serious long-term appointment and so forth. To no one's

surprise, amidst a disastrous run of results grievously compounded
by defeat away to Barcelona (who were playing great football and
were rampant in the league), the Invisible Man was out of the door
by Christmas, never to be seen or heard of again.

Had Pérez injected some fresh animus into the project by signing
a Galáctico, the mood, at least, might have been different. But for
the first year since taking over as president he had not done so. The
best he had been able to come up with was Michael Owen from
Liverpool, a striker who had won the European Footballer of the
Year Award in 2001 but had been outgunned and outclassed since
then by a new generation of international strikers. He was a good
enough 'sniffer' in the box but lightweight in comparison to
Shevchenko at Milan, Henry at Arsenal, van Nistelrooy at Manchester
United and, worst of all, Barcelona's new signing, the electric
Cameroonian Samuel Eto'o. Owen, at 25, seemed doomed to remain
a player who had never quite lived up to the vast potential he had
shown when he was 18, the age at which the Englishman scored a
famous World Cup goal against Argentina. Real fans did not imagine
for one minute that the inexpressive Englishman ('the Sphinx', some
Spanish commentators came to call him) was the spark that would
kick the team back into life. But at least Owen came cheap, his
contract having been near completion at Liverpool. Real bought him
for 8 million pounds, comfortable in the knowledge that if they were
to resell him in a year's time they would, at the very least, recoup
their investment. As for the signing of Jonathan Woodgate from
Newcastle for 14 million pounds, that seemed even at the time like
the most badly informed business decision in the history of football.
Not because Woodgate was a bad player; Bobby Robson, his coach
at Newcastle, had said he was the best central defender in England.
What Robson did not say, though everyone who read a newspaper
in England knew it, was that Woodgate was also the most injury-
prone player in the Premiership. So injury-prone that within weeks
of his arrival it became clear that he would need at least six months
of intensive medical treatment before he was fit enough to play.

Woodgate's calamitous signing defined the cursed year of 2004.
Something had to be done. Drifting, the club was going to smash

itself against the rocks. Someone had to take charge at the wheel. Someone who knew what he was doing. Someone who had navigated a big ship like this before. Pérez found his man. He hired the bald, cerebral Arrigo Sacchi, coach of the famously brilliant Milan team that won the European Cup in 1989 and 1990, and gave him a clear brief: to analyse what had gone wrong and come up with the recipe to restore order. Sacchi's first decision, to which the somewhat demoralised Pérez instantly deferred, was to bring in Wanderley Luxemburgo as team coach, a former Brazil national coach who had just won the Brazilian championship with Pelé's old team Santos – Real's fourth coach in six months. Sacchi would be the general, the strategist observing from on high; Luxemburgo, the frontline tactician, the officer charged with stirring up the troops, building fitness and morale, preparing rigorously for each game. And some order was indeed restored. Under these two things did improve – though not necessarily in the way Pérez or other Real ideologues might have desired.

Zoran Vekic, Guti's agent, summed it up cruelly but not entirely unfairly when he said at the end of the season, 'It's true that Luxemburgo can boast some good results, but the football Real Madrid have been playing has been so dull that sheep would be bored watching it.' Vekic was peeved when he said that. Guti, a tremendously talented midfielder whose sad destiny it was always to fall out of favour with his coaches, rarely made it off the bench during Luxemburgo's first six months at the club. Nor, more dramatically, did Luis Figo. The Brazilian had decided that the time had come to call an end to Figo's brilliant career. While the former World Player of the Year remained a model professional, dourly serious in training, at 32 he had begun to lose pace and penetration. His talent for holding onto the ball was becoming a liability. Failing to race past his man the way he used to, his insistence on twisting this way and that, checking and turning, had the effect most of all of giving the rival defence precious time to regroup. Rather, Luxemburgo figured, get Beckham out there on the right. He'll never beat his man for speed, or through trickery, but he'll whip the ball into the penalty box more quickly than Figo, catching the defence off-balance, improving the chances of Ronaldo or Raúl or, for that matter, Michael Owen, scoring a goal.

Owen was the great beneficiary of Figo's indignity. He started more games under Luxemburgo than he had done with García Remón and ended up the season a favourite of the Bernabéu faithful, who admired his cool dedication to the Real cause and were grateful to him for his goals. No player in the Spanish league had a better ratio of goals scored per minutes played. Owen summed up the pragmatic philosophy of the Luxemburgo-Sacchi axis. Never a joy to watch, as Figo was, possessing none of the Portuguese winger's class in the first touch, Owen looked clumsy in Galáctico company when he received the ball outside the penalty box. In it, however, he was sharp and efficient. He rarely scored a goal that you'd want to savour in slow motion on your TV, but he helped Real rack up the points. So much so that at one stage it seemed they might catch up with Barcelona, who had been the runaway leaders at Christmas, 13 points ahead of Real. The high point of the season came in April when they beat Barça 4–2 at the Bernabéu. The second best Real player that day was Thomas Gravesen, a Danish pit-bull – a joker off the field, fearsome on it – who had been bought from Everton at Christmas in response to the first requirement that Sacchi had identified: adding some mettle in the midfield. But the best player of the *superclásico* was, by common consent, David Beckham. Even those critics in Spain who had developed (as some had done in England) a pyschologically intriguing Fergusonian prejudice against him struggled to disagree with the Bernabéu's judgement that in this biggest of all games, commanding possibly the greatest concentration of individual talent of any fixture in Europe, the England captain had been the decisive force.

Beckham the global celebrity is a fascinating phenomenon because it is so difficult to understand what it is that gets so many people in so many countries so exercised about him. But just as fascinating, because it is just as baffling, is people's reaction to the phenomenon of Beckham the footballer. Two years into his time at Real Madrid, at 30 years old, he was the most scrutinised player in the history of the game. Thanks to the global reach and technological virtuosity of TV, and thanks also to the cacophony of global chatter generated by the internet, Beckham's game had been studied, discussed, anatomised, debated from more angles and by more people than anyone's game ever had been before. Yet the jury was still out on whether he was a good player or not! In the same way that Beckham's celebrity status tells us more about the curiosities of human behaviour than anything else, the never-ending debate on Beckham's merits as a player offer further evidence of football's unfathomable quality. Fans around the world are split down the middle on Beckham. Football writers appear to be too. Two of the most eminent and veteran sports journalists in Spain, Santiago Segurola of *el País* and Alfredo Relaño of *AS* hold diametrically opposite views on the Englishman. Relaño, as we have seen, was in raptures about Beckham – 'the midfield marshall', 'the lion-hearted England captain' – from the start. Segurola, who had warned against signing him back in the spring of 2003, described him half-way through his second season at the club as a player who was 'discretísimo', best translated as 'extremely limited'. Another well-known Spanish football pundit used to say that 'if Beckham were bald, he would be playing for Alavés' – an unfashionable Spanish team whose natural place was hovering between the first and second divisions.

On the other hand, Segurola (the most talented football writer I have read anywhere) was an avid fan of Guti's. Part of Segurola's beef with Beckham was the insistence of one coach after another on putting him in the team instead of his own favourite blond angel. Segurola was not alone in considering this a gross injustice. You could see why. Guti was, on the face of it, a more complete midfielder than Beckham. For a start, the Spaniard was more comfortable on the ball. He had that quality you detect in the best players when they are still at school: with the ball at his feet he was very difficult to dispossess. Guti did not have Beckham's unique ability with the long ball but in the short, sharp pass, the one that put Ronaldo alone in front of goal, Guti was at least as incisive as Beckham. So, who was more like Zidane or Ronaldo? Who was closer to the Maradona ideal? Plainly, it was Guti. Yet the four coaches Beckham had at Real all had him as an automatic choice and all harboured grave doubts about Guti. You could say, as Beckham's detractors did, that the coaches feared incurring the wrath of Florentino Pérez if they dropped the club's great cash generator. Yet the coach that Pérez sacked immediately before Beckham joined the club, Vicente del Bosque, had always sung Beckham's praises, and he too had kept Guti on the bench. Guti's problem seemed to be that his concentration and self-belief were not of a piece with his talent. When you looked around the changing room before a game Guti was a player you could never rely on entirely to give his best for the team. Oscillating between petulant indolence and exuberant talent, he had too many demons inside his head, it seemed. As Queiroz had said of him, he is a great player but when you pick him you never know which Guti is going to appear on the field. Beckham, for all the siren songs that might have driven him mad off the pitch, was Mr Dependable on it. He might not always play well. He might have bad games. But if at the Bernabéu they never reproached him (whereas they often reproached Guti) it was because they always felt that he gave the best that he could. For some reason he was the captain of England; for some reason Guti rarely made it as first choice into the Spanish national team.

In the summer of 2005 Real were prepared to let Guti go but, while there was some interest from big clubs, the player chose to remain. With Beckham, by contrast, the offer Pérez had made a year earlier to sell the Bernabéu before selling him still stood. It was in similar terms, at any rate, that José Angel Sánchez responded to a Beckham emissary who came to see him in April 2005, a couple of weeks after the Barça match, to sound out the club's intentions with the England captain. Beckham, who still seemed to be getting his information about Real from the British tabloids, once again harboured genuine doubts as to Real's desire to keep him. The doubts distressed him because, as he told me – emphatically, repeatedly – in an interview I did with him in March, he was very settled at Real and his family were very happy in Madrid. Sánchez's response to, as it turned out, Beckham's charmingly misplaced anxieties, was as categorical as Pérez's had been. 'We would like David to extend his contract,' Sánchez told the emissary, 'until he's 85.'

Sánchez, who two years after negotiating Beckham's purchase still shook his head in wonder at how cheaply Manchester United had let him go for, remained a major power at the club, the artificer of the profit-making machine that Real had become. But he would have been less emphatic had he not known that he had the backing of Luxemburgo and Sacchi, Beckham's two biggest fans. Luxemburgo, who saw Beckham's natural position – as Beckham himself did – as right-centre midfield, was as impressed by Beckham's professionalism as Valdano had been. He told members of the club board after the victory against Barcelona that if he had had a Beckham on the left of midfield Real would have scored six. Sacchi described him to Real insiders as an 'all-terrain, all-pitches, all the time' player. In an interview with the Italian newspaper *il Giornale* in June 2005 Sacchi said that Beckham might not have 'the great brushstrokes of an artist' but 'with me, in my Milan, he would have played always'.

In so far as one could formulate a rule it seemed to be that people inside the game, coaches and players, admired him and that it was among the ranks of the passionate outsiders, the fans and football writers, that they doubted his worth. The only thing you knew for sure was that the Beckham debate would not end, and that it would rage on long after he had retired. Had he been a less high-profile player, had there been less of a ballyhoo around him off the pitch, his critics might have been less heated in their condemnation of him. In the same way that Real's critics might have been kinder with the team as a whole had the club been less celebrated, had the bar not been set so high. Real ended up the 2004/2005 season second in the Spanish league – only four points behind a Barça team widely reckoned to have been sensational, marvellous, the best in a decade – and ahead by 15 points of the third placed team, Villarreal. In the Champions League they were knocked out in extra time in one of those games that could have gone either way by a Juventus side that finished the season as champions of Italy. And yet, by just about every reckoning, Real's season had been an absolute, unmitigated disaster. By contrast, Manchester United, the only brand name in football to compete with Real's, had come third in the English league, 18 points behind champions Chelsea, and had been knocked out of the Champions League by Milan, who outclassed them ignominiously. And yet, while many described United's season as poor, no one said it had been disastrous.

All of which told us less about the quality of Real's play than it did about the mighty expectations the club generated in the era of Florentino Pérez. The worry, after two seasons without a trophy, was that those expectations would fall and the lustre would fade. That, to borrow Jorge Valdano's metaphor, the Rolls Royce would gather dust again. It was necessary, come the start of the 2005/2006 season, to build a team that would win a big trophy. Suddenly, winning became as important as 'spectacle', perhaps more so. The very thought was a betrayal of Real's ancient ideals and Pérez's dreams, but betrayal was what we saw. Or capitulation, at any rate. Come the summer of 2005, when Real set off on their 'World Tour', the revolutionary ideology set in place by Pérez had undergone what the Soviets had once called Perestroika and Fidel Castro called – when similarly obliged in the mid-80s to abandon some of his purer Marxist ideals – 'la Rectificación'. You could argue all day as to just how great a departure that represented from Pérez's founding philosophy, but the long and the short of it was that he had been obliged to cede much ground, that he had come to the regretful conclusion that the teenage boys I had spoken to while watching Real on TV in Medellín, Colombia, (and the millions who thought like them) may have been right all along. You needed 'balance' in a team. You need your Makeleles to mop up for your Zidanes. You needed a coach who imposed order and taught tactics, and to whose authority the men in suits would defer.

The very act of bringing Sacchi on board at the end of 2004, when the team's fortunes were at their lowest ebb, had been an acknowledgement of defeat, a tacit recognition that it was time to cede control to the *futbolero* traditionalists. Luxemburgo, a bossy Brazilian with a Teutonic sense of discipline, was a far cry from Pérez's previous vision of the coach as a cipher, as a ceremonial requirement in a football team of little more practical use than the nameless men in tracksuits who carried the bags of balls and cleaned the players' boots. Then came the muscular, all-action and singularly unstylish Thomas Gravesen, who the Pérez of a year earlier would never have contemplated buying. According to the old rules, you got your Gravesens from the youth squad; they rose from the ranks of the Pavons – or not at all. As for the first two signings Sacchi and

Luxemburgo made in the summer of 2005, they were even more shockingly out of tune with the Florentine symphony. Whatever else the two Uruguayan hard-nuts, Diogo and García, might have been, Galácticos they decidedly were not.

Yet there they were, the big summer signings, making up the numbers on the 'World Tour', on the bus to Tianjin. No one would have noticed if they had stayed at home. Riding along on the bus behind them, feeling like I was on a delegation of a visiting head of state (on the 80 kilometres to Tianjin our police escorts had turned every light to green, blocked every highway access, caused traffic jams that reached back miles so we would not suffer the inconvenience of having to brake at any point, let alone stop), it was hard to avoid the sensation that something was not quite right. That those hysterical fans at the Kunlun Hotel had missed a point; had arrived too late, after the party had ended. They chose to see the old magic in Real, but the truth was that it had faded. They were like a rock band that had been huge – the biggest thing in pop – one or two years ago but suddenly, with fearful abruptness, they had begun to look dated. The White Angels were still big, very big, but not as big as they were. Having been blown up to bursting point, the slow hissing sound you now heard was the balloon losing air. The only way left to go, it seemed, was down. Beckham still kept his shine, Ronaldo retained that charismatic bull-like presence, yet all of them were beginning to emanate the look, the feel and the smell of ageing rockers. None more so than Pérez's first two Galácticos, Figo and Zidane.

Figo was on his way out and he knew it. His behaviour throughout the 'World Tour', as various members of the Real delegation noted, had been irreverent, frivolous, demob happy. As if to say, you don't want me? Well I have no respect for you either. It was the behaviour of a man whose enormous pride had been grievously wounded, but who would do everything he could not to show it. I saw what the disapproving Real officials meant when we got off our buses at Tianjin. Even without Figo's antics, it was a bizarre scene. An example of the peculiar indignities (as if they were not footballers but politicians!) to which the Real players were obliged to succumb in the interests of promoting the club's name in Asia, of doing the fund-raising duties required by Sánchez's marketing department.

The bus had stopped outside a domed white building where hundreds of people gathered under a large banner that read 'Welcome to Real Madrid'. I had no idea where we were or what we were doing there. Nor did any club official (everything was in the hands of the trip's Chinese sponsors and organisers). As for the players, if you had told them we had crossed the border into North Korea and were about to meet Kim il Sung, they would have believed you. They did not have the slightest clue what was going on. They recognised the pandemonium as they stepped off the bus, though. They were familiar with the shrieks of the adolescent fans and the equally hysterical screams of policemen woefully unprepared to cope with such counter-revolutionary displays of emotion. The players entered the building one by one to shake the hand of a man in his sixties wearing a white shirt and a tie and a delighted smile on his face. Not one of the players knew his name or what he did for a living, nor – you could be sure of it – did they care. They then swept past a distinctly unimpressive buffet – dry biscuits and mini pizzas in a country with the world's richest culinary tradition after France (could it be that some subversive chef here in Tianjin had heard about the Galácticos' failures?) – and, ushered along by more screaming policemen and assorted officials exhibiting various degrees of rage, paused on some steps where, it unfolded, a group photograph was to be taken. The players positioned themselves in three ranks as, before them, a fourth rank lined up composed of a dozen grinning men in white shirts and ties, clones of the smiler who had received the players at the entrance. The players did as they were told with all the enthusiasm of automatons. Only Figo seemed determined to enjoy the moment. Clowning around, with a half-mad smile on his face, in a manner so at odds with the melancholic demeanour he wears on the pitch, he stood behind two of the men in shirts and ties, put his arms over their shoulders as if they were his best friends at a wedding and, smiling even more insanely for the artillery of cameras ranged before them, he grabbed each of the two Tianjin gents powerfully by their not insubstantial breasts. After a reproving glance from Roberto Carlos, who was playing a sober ambassadorial role also at odds with his on-field persona, Figo contained the urge to repeat the trick when half a dozen stout, giggling ladies barged into the shot. I asked an English-speaking Chinese photographer if he had any idea who all these people were. He shrugged, and said, 'They must be the mayor, his family and friends.'

And then it was back to the bus again, through the screams and the heaving crowds. Some of the new or younger players looked frightened. The veterans jostled their way through, grimly determined. Except Beckham, who was not grim, who never lost his smile, his otherworldly serenity. The newcomer Pablo García was to say later, in baffled but genuine admiration, 'I can smile for maybe 15 minutes at a time max. This guy just keeps smiling, smiling all day long . . .'

Zidane decidedly was not smiling. He does not smile much, not even when he scores goals. But these days he seemed to have even less to smile about than usual. His form over the previous season was one of the big reasons why many Real fans back home had entered a period of seemingly prolonged depression. Zidane was the beating heart of the White Angels, the lead singer in the band, and if he was on his last legs, then they all were. The Frenchman was the best player anywhere of the previous decade but over the last year he had been awful, contributing next to nothing even when the team started to achieve good results. His passing was woefully astray – a sad shadow of those amazing statistics he racked up in the memorable Champions League games barely two years earlier against Manchester United – and even his first touch had failed him embarrassingly on occasion. In the victory against Barcelona, a game in which he had to have wanted to excel, he was the most uninvolved player on the pitch. Everything indicated that the enthusiasm and the hunger had gone, that he was keeping his place more on reputation than on merit. The longer the season wore on, the more certain it seemed that we were witnessing the irreversible decline of a footballing genius. You began to think that the honourable thing for him to do would be to announce his retirement before the new season began.

With suggestions that Roberto Carlos was not quite the bullet he once was and Raúl non-existent for the second season running (my friend Angel at the Amistad bar used to console himself with the thought that if you considered Real had played two seasons with ten men, they had not done all that badly), all you had left was Ronaldo, whose facility for scoring goals out of nowhere, for going from languid to electric – from resting to stampeding buffalo – in the blink of an eye had not abated. And then there was Beckham, who was not in the same class, but on whom Luxemburgo and Sacchi pinned high hopes.

Not too many others did, though. Real looked like an old, tired team; magicians whose tricks had lost their zest, who had lost the gift to delight and amaze. If, on top of all that, Pérez was giving his blessing to the purchase of players like Diogo and García then, yes, it really seemed as if the game was up. The White Angels had worked wonders for Real's bank balance but in football terms it was a magnificent experiment that had had its day. It seemed a hell of a pity, for there had been something both heroic and romantic in the notion that you could flout footballing conventions the way Pérez had tried to do. Art had taken on science and, it seemed, had lost. Pérez's critics insisted on seeing him as a cynical money-grabber. They were wrong. There was a childlike quality to his relationship with football. He wished to rediscover, recreate, the fantasies of the singularly 'unbalanced', uncoached team of di Stefano and Puskas that he had watched with his parents in the Bernabéu when he was 12 years old. The money was at the service of the game, and not the other way around. Why, some wondered, if Real was a not-for-profit club, did Pérez (who received no salary from Real) feel this imperative to make so much money? The answer was simple: in order, precisely, to be able to keep Real a non-profit organisation, while competing at the highest level.

Pérez had told me two years earlier that he would no more think of selling Real Madrid, of converting it into a company with stocks and shares, than the Pope would think of doing the same with the Vatican. And yet in order to compete in football terms Real had to muster the same amounts of money as clubs owned by rich magnates, such as Chelsea, Milan, Inter and Manchester United. The irony was that Chelsea, a private company, were under far less pressure to operate as a commercially viable entity than Real. The chairman, Roman Abramovich, simply reached into his pocket and all problems were solved. That was why in the season 2004/2005 Chelsea operated at a loss of 80 million pounds and still spent more money than anyone else in England on new players the following summer. The reason why Real had to make pots of money was in order to compete with the spending power of Abramovich and all the other billionaires who could, upon a whim, take control of any other of the big clubs that were not clubs any more, but Plc's.

And yet in football terms Pérez appeared to have lost his nerve, or to have lost faith in his simple ideal. Sacchi made the point almost brutally – certainly patronisingly – in an interview in the summer of 2005 with *AS*. 'The president is an intelligent man,' said Sacchi. 'He has personality and when he has an idea in his head it is hard to get him to change. But now we have a team that is balanced.' In other words, said Sacchi, who very pointedly described himself as 'the president on the sporting side of things now', fantasy football had lost and the reality principle had triumphed. Alfredo Relaño, the editor of *AS*, bemoaned the end of the dream. 'I confess that I succumbed to the charms of that "Zidanes and Pavons" affair,' he wrote. 'I saw it as a flash of inspiration that had come to redeem football from the grip of the tacticians. And at the beginning it worked, and I shall never forget it.' It saddened him, Relaño continued, to see the model abandoned, because he believed it deserved more faith, 'because had it worked, it would have been such a wonderful counterpoint to the football of the blackboard'.

As an example of why it might have worked just as well to stick with glamour and ignore the gloomy warnings of the wise old football men, Relaño cited the examples of Beckham and Samuel. The *futboleros* said that buying Beckham had been an act of unpardonable frivolity, while buying Samuel had represented mature footballing sense. And what happened? 'Beckham plays football well, centres the ball better than anyone, scores from free kicks . . . and sells shirts. Samuel only commits fouls, if he has the ball he passes it back to Casillas or to a rival player and, of course, he does not sell shirts.' Yet Samuel had been the player judged by the *futboleros* to be of greater value to the Real team. And yet, amidst no complaints from anybody, Samuel was sold to Inter Milan after just one season

(Figo ended up there too, as did the Argentine midfielder Santiago Solari), while if Beckham were to be sold not only would there be a mutiny at the Bernabéu but Sacchi and Luxemburgo would in all probability resign.

My own answer to the *futboleros*, and the reason why I agreed with Relaño that it was a pity not to have kept more faith with the wild romanticism of the original Pérez model was the same I always gave. Given that the great truth about football is that it is inscrutable, that everybody gets it wrong and that when they get it right it is more often by chance than due to any great wisdom or insight, you might as well opt for the one constant, which is spectacle, or excitement, or that wonderfully rich Spanish noun *ilusión* that means excitement, thrill, hope and expectation all combined. As an example, let us look again at Milan. An admirable team, wonderfully balanced, they had lost to Deportivo de la Coruña in the Champions League quarter finals of 2004 in a manner even more unlikely and unpredictable than Real's loss at the same stage to Monaco. The same team, only stronger, made it to the final of the Champions League in 2005. You would not have bet a prayer on their rivals, Liverpool, before the game and you would have bet your house, your mother and everything else on them lifting the European Cup when they went 3-0 up – entirely deservedly – at half-time. Liverpool had a team that was utterly unbalanced (the difference with Real being that it was top-heavy in defence and had next to nothing in attack) and unable to keep possession for more than three passes at a time. They played passionate, courageous, defensive, horrible, rebound football. And yet they equalised in the second half and then won on penalties. At which point the best thing any honourable, self-respecting *futbolero* could have done would have been to rip up his diagrams, tear down his blackboards and acknowledge that the game was simply not susceptible to theory, any more than life was.

Or, for that matter, the genius of Zidane. That was my other lament, as we raced along on the bus to our next stop, Tianjin's space-age stadium – a vision of the future, one more symbol among many we saw on our Chinese travels of the country's economic boom, of the leap in barely 20 years from North Korean-style poverty to something approaching American-style skyscraper affluence. The future belonged to China, but not, it seemed, to Zidane. His glories were behind him now. Or so I, and practically everybody I knew, had concluded, to our regret and distress. But then something happened. Then I saw him on the perfect grass of the Tianjin stadium, packed with 30,000 people who had paid between 10 and 50 Euros per head – fortunes for the average Chinese worker – to watch Real train. And I saw the way he played in a muck-about practice game that lasted 10 minutes each half, 11 against 11, and I began to wonder whether he might have been serious when he had said, in a press conference a few weeks back, that he knew he still had it in him to play at his best level, that he was determined to show it in the coming season. For suddenly he was raging against the dying of the light, in a passion to prove the obituary writers wrong. In the first two games of Real's 'World Tour', convincing victories in Chicago and Los Angeles, he was by far the best player on the field. In the sweltering heat of that practice game in Tianjin he played like a man possessed, fighting for the ball with more vigour and pace – and skill and effectiveness – than any other member of the squad, as if he were a youngster desperate to win a place in the team. After the training session was over, as the rest of the players lay in a heap, he did a high-speed sequence of stomach crunches, followed by 20 piston-sharp push-ups.

After witnessing that, after becoming suddenly convinced in my mind that Zidane was determined to go out of football not with a whimper but with a bang and that he had a vision of a glorious last year ahead of him, it was not a surprise to hear him announce two weeks later that he was returning to the French national team, having said a year earlier that he had retired from international football for ever. Nor was it such a great surprise to learn, through an interview later with *France Football*, that he had had an epiphany, that he had woken up at three in the morning and understood he still had greatness in him. 'It was something mystical,' he said, 'something irrational and because of that only I can really feel it.' Less irrationally, he said he knew he had 'lost' his football in recent months and even lost at times his sense of who he was. 'Now,' he said, 'I want to dedicate myself completely to my football and I want to have a season that is sensational.'

Sacchi confirmed the suspicion that Zidane was for real, that he was not kidding himself, when he said that while the previous season Zidane had lacked 'desire and enthusiasm' now he was brimming with both. 'Zidane,' Sacchi said, 'is a new player.'

Upon returning late at night to the Kunlun Hotel from Tianjin I came across Florentino Pérez in a dark corner of the lounge bar talking on his mobile phone to José Angel Sánchez in Madrid, who was on another line to Brazil, talking to the agent of the player who was said to be Brazil's latest sensation and was Luxemburgo's former player at Santos, Robson de Souza, better known as Robinho. Zidane was not the only new player for the coming season, and neither were García and Diogo. There had been all manner of complications. (I had talked to Sánchez about the Robinho negotiation a number of times over the previous months and the poor man, veteran of the endless Beckham and Ronaldo transfer sagas, was on the verge of despair at the frustrating predictability of it all.) The whole business lasted more than six months. For most of that time it seemed that the deal was on. Then it seemed that it was off. Then all the signals suggested he would join Real in time to take part in the 'World Tour'. When he did not make it, though the player himself was aching to move to Madrid, it seemed the deal was definitely off. But now, hearing Pérez on the phone, it was clear that it was on again. The most exciting player since Pelé (they said in Brazil) seemed finally to be in the bag. The mood at Real underwent a sea change at the idea of the hungry, talented, goal-scoring 21-year-old Robinho in partnership up front with Ronaldo, completing a magic triangle with Zidane. In football you lurch from hope to despair to hope in the blink of an eye. (If you doubt it, ask a Liverpool fan what he thinks.) And here was yet another case in point. Suddenly, having been convinced barely eight hours earlier on the empty road to Tianjin that Real were doomed to have another depressing season, I said good night to the most cheerful Pérez I had seen in months and went to bed convinced there was life in Real Madrid yet.

Two weeks later the Robinho deal was made official as was the signing – utterly out of the blue – of another Brazilian, Julio Cesar 'the Beast' Baptista. Baptista, a formidable physical specimen signed from Sevilla, was a goal-scorer and excellent with his head. At last Beckham was going to have a target for his 'half-goal' crosses, and maybe even someone new to share the crossing duties with on the right, for then Real announced they had signed a deal for a 'first option' to buy yet another Brazilian sensation, the right back Cicinho from Sao Paulo. They'd have to rename the club Real Brazil, someone said; rename the Bernabéu the 'Sambadrome'. For you suddenly had the prospect of five Brazilians in the starting line-up, in addition to the Brazilian coach. An entirely natural fusion had been achieved between the world's most charismatic footballing nation and the world's most charismatic club. But there was also room for Old England in the mix, for the signs were encouraging that Jonathan Woodgate would re-emerge from the doctor's table, as the fifth new 'signing' of the summer, having not played for one minute in the whole of his first season at the club. If it was true, there were suddenly plenty of able bodies in defence. The purchase a few weeks later of the 19-year-old Sergio Ramos, an unusually skilful defender, for the vast sum of 30 million Euros showed how far Sacchi-sense had prevailed over the old devil-may-care Pérez model. The Italian, typically blunt, said on the morning after Ramos had been signed, 'This year the president has changed a lot'. He had not changed so much, on the other hand, as to convert Real into a defensive machine, into a team like Juventus whose raison d'etre was to stop the other team from playing football. In the positions where Real had Beckham, Baptista and Zidane, Juventus, and a majority of Serie A teams, put players whose chief talent was robbing the ball. There was ample consolation for Pérez and like-minded *Madridistas* in the knowledge that the artillery up front looked once again as if it could be the most awesome of any team anywhere. And that was without including Owen, who soon left – for double the money Real paid for him – to join Newcastle United.

And then Robinho arrived, landing at Madrid's Barajas Airport at 5.45 in the morning of Friday 26 August 2005. He had never been to Spain before in his life. Within seven hours he was being officially presented as a Real player, before 8,000 fans at the Bernabéu who had convinced themselves – who had needed to convince themselves – that the saviour had arrived, the man to breathe new spirit into the old Galácticos. Pérez, setting the bar dangerously high in his welcoming speech, declared that Robinho was 'fantasy football' made flesh, that he would conquer Europe, that he marked the beginning of a new *Madridista* dream. Robinho trained with the team for the first time, at ease and smiling as if he had played for Real all his life, and then the next day he got on a plane with his new team mates south to Cádiz, the city from which Columbus set off on his second voyage of discovery to America and – happily – Brazil. He slept with his new team mates in a Cádiz hotel, the fourth bed he had slept in on four successive nights. And the next day, the Sunday, was the first game of the 2005/2006 season, against the local team, freshly ascended from the second division, raring to bloody the Galácticos' noses. Ronaldo scored within four minutes. Not from a half chance, but from a quarter chance. One that maybe two or three other players in the world would have seen as a clear shot of goal, but that only he could put away with such careless ease. It was the loudest and clearest of signals that the world's greatest centre forward of the previous ten years was back in business. It seemed a rout was on, but no. The rest of the team toiled prettily in midfield but to little effect. Beckham tried hard, as usual, and Zidane showed some of his thrilling flashes of skill, but something was still missing and it was no great surprise when Cádiz equalised. What did come as a surprise was Luxemburgo's reaction. Throwing caution to the winds – as if suddenly renouncing his mechanical habits of mind and letting the rash White Angel spirit suffuse him – he took off a defensive player, Gravesen, and replaced him with an out-and-out forward. The mother of all out-and-out forwards, as it turned out. The young man who had flown for 12 hours across the Atlantic Ocean two days earlier.

Robinho came on and everything changed. 'And then,' as a Spanish newspaper would write the next day, 'God created Robinho.' From his first touch the whole of Spain and the watching millions around the world could see that here was a player with a supreme gift for the game, genetically programmed for football. It was the second-nature simplicity with which he controlled the most awkward pass, the ease with which he got the ball to obey his every desire. It was his speed on the ball, his Fred Astaire grace, his eel-like feints and wriggles. It was – the biggest surprise of all – his selflessness, his eye for the timely, well-weighed pass, his creativity in the cause of the team. For the 27 minutes he was on the pitch the game became a one-man show. Real won, the decisive goal coming from a blunderbuss of a 50-yard Beckham ball that Robinho controlled on his chest as if it were a pillow, and slipped it to Ronaldo who thundered three steps into the penalty area and slid the ball inside to Raúl, who prodded it into an empty net.

It was one of the most sensational debuts in football history. It made nonsense of the old saw about players needing time to adapt to a new team. Or maybe not. Maybe ordinary players, even ordinarily great players, need time. But if you had talent as exceptional as this, talent imposed itself. The team had to adapt to Robinho; to this small, thin waif who, were he to lose ten more pounds, might figure in an advertisement to raise money for malnourished children. And adapt the team did. He galvanised them, made them hard and shining again. He contaged them with his enthusiasm and inventiveness. They raised their game, recovered their confidence, rediscovered the genius they had forgotten they had. It might all change again in yet another blink of an eye. That's football. But, for now, and in football it is only *now* that matters, the zest and the belief were back. The White Angels had wings again – the finest quality wings, Made in Brazil. The new Galáctico, the child among them, had done the trick. He had restored, in one magical stroke, that most elemental, most innocent, most powerful of all football emotions, *la ilusión*. Pérez had not exaggerated. Robinho *was* football fantasy made flesh. Paco Gento, veteran of the mighty di Stefano team on which the Real legend was built, was beaming the day after Robinho's debut. 'Now again we will be giving people something to talk about,' he said. It was true. The whole footballing world – from Mozambique to Medellín, from Barcelona to Beijing – would be hanging, once again, on the feats of the men in white. It was late summer, a new season was beginning and the Real Madrid dream machine was back.

Epilogue

Halfway through the 2002 World Cup I found myself in Fukuoka, a breezy seaside city on the southern Japanese island of Kyushu. There I came across a man called Hiroaki Kitano who reckoned that by the year 2050 robots would be playing football better than humans. Kitano, a boffin at Sony, was already working to make his dream come true. He'd developed a Star Wars-type humanoid contraption that was still some way short of performing a Zidane pirouette but had mastered the art of prodding a stationary ball in more or less the intended direction. Mr Kitano said he was confident that the finished product – blessed with 'real-time reasoning' and the capacity to engage in 'multi-agent collaboration' – would eventually make monkeys out of the most organised *homo sapiens* defences.

The reason his creations would eventually defeat the mid-century Ronaldos, Beckhams and Raúls, according to Mr Kitano, was that they would be programmed never to commit fouls, to put all penalties in the back of the net and never, ever to tire. The flesh-and-blood mortals who performed in your Real Madrids and Manchester Uniteds would arrive for a World Cup exhausted by the rigours of the European season. These little beauties would play every day of the week and still turn up for the 2050 World Cup fresh as daisies, ready to roll. But there did remain a problem. A problem that Mr Kitano, for all his mechanical wizardry, had failed sufficiently to factor into his calculations. An eternal problem in football.

How did you programme the software?

And the answer, as the experience of the 2002 World Cup – and two years later the experience of Real Madrid – served to demonstrate, was that no one had a clue. Because, try as you might with

your 4-4-2 and 4-3-3's, there was no science to the game whatsoever. Because football is not susceptible to reason. Because, as the
zanily enigmatic goings-on in that first Far Eastern World Cup revealed
beyond doubt, football was baffling, enigmatic, unfathomable. Those
who should have known the most, who thought they knew the
most, knew, if anything, the least. Socrates – the Greek philosopher,
not the Brazilian captain in the 1982 World Cup – said all he knew
was that he did not know. And that went for everybody. From your
Sven-Goran Erikssons to your Johan Cruyffs, to the planetary Babel
of pundits and football writers, to the hundreds of millions who
shared their lust for the greatest game of all. There was only one
thing to be done: bow our heads, all of us, before the football gods
and humbly acknowledge that we are in the face of a mystery that
surpasses human understanding.

As my plane flew back home from Japan over the frozen wastes
of Siberia I whiled away the time trying to think of one person, just
one, who had predicted that France would lose to Senegal in the
first game of the tournament and would come last in their group,
exiting the competition at the same time as Saudi Arabia; that the
other pre-tournament co-favourite, Argentina, would not make it
past the preliminary phase either; that the United States would go
3-0 up against Portugal inside half an hour; that South Korea would
beat Italy and Spain; that Germany, the weakest Germany in living
memory we all thought, would cruise to the World Cup final; that
Brazil, who struggled like hell to qualify for the Japan and Korea
finals should emerge once again as glorious winners. The truth was
that this World Cup had made fools out of everybody – from Cruyff
(Argentina, were strong, he said, but 'above all' he fancied France),
to Pelé, to Beckenbauer, to Bobby Charlton, to the world's greatest
sports writer, to you, dear reader, to me.

The 2003/04 season in Europe made fools out of all of us all
over again. Who on earth would have predicted – no, who would
have imagined – that the final of the European Cup would be
disputed between Porto and Monaco? No one at all. What everybody was saying at the beginning of the season, when Real Madrid
thrashed Porto in Porto, was that Real were the greatest team in

living memory. Mario Zagallo said it. Beckenbauer said it. Capello said it. Marcello Lippi said it. Sven-Goran Eriksson said it. Even the Porto coach, the celebrated José Mourinho said it.

And then what happens? In the three critical games of the season they get beaten by Zaragoza, Monaco and Osasuna, three teams that few people outside their home countries knew to be teams, the identity of whose players was not known to anyone beyond their home towns – not until they beat Real Madrid, at any rate, at which point they became for the first time in their history fleetingly famous. And then after the world's greatest team lose those three games they lose every other game, being especially soundly thrashed the weaker the quality of the opposition. There came a point in April and May when the Galácticos could not have beaten a team of grannies. And why this unbelievable state of affairs should have come to pass, nobody knew. Then, just in case there might have been some lingering belief that the game was amenable to reason, there came Euro 2004. A month or so after the end of the league season the great nations of Europe battled it out in Portugal for continental supremacy. Of the six teams that surely *had* to provide the eventual winner, three – Italy, Germany and Spain – fell at the first hurdle, and two – France and England – at the second. The sixth, Figo's Portugal, made it to the final, only to be defeated by Greece, on whose chances of ending up champions of Europe no one outside Greece – and probably no one inside either – would have bet one penny before the tournament began.

There were a million theories on how to succeed in football but no answers. No one had the software, no one knew the programme. Valdano cheerfully admitted as much in one his football books, *Stage Fright*. 'Knowing about football,' he wrote, 'and what's that? Nothing. Football admits too many truths to allow anyone to pretend that they have the right answer.' The only thing you could say with any certainty, Valdano concluded after lengthy reflection on the subject, was that football was a game. A much blunter fellow than Valdano, the West German national coach in the 1954 World Cup Sepp Herberger, once allowed himself the luxury of expanding a little on the game's nature. '*Ball ist rund*,' he once famously (famously in

Germany at any rate) said, '*Spiel dauert neunzig Minuten. Soviel ist schon mal klar. Alles andere ist Theorie.*' The ball is round. The game lasts ninety minutes. That much is crystal clear. All the rest is theory.

The same brutal simplicity of approach made Herberger's team world champions. Few people outside West Germany remember that West Germany won the World Cup in 1954. Everywhere else the national team associated with the Fifties was Hungary. They were to international football then what Real Madrid were to club football, except that the Hungarians never won the trophy they most desired. They put on magnificently memorable cameo performances, notably the 6-3 victory against England in 1953, and in players like Ferenc Puskas and Sandor Kocsis – 'the Magical Magyars', a marvelling English press called them – they had names that posterity would treasure. But they lost in the 1954 World Cup final to the Germans. They lost 3-2, having been 2-0 up, and having beaten them 8-3 in an earlier stage of the competition. No one could explain how it happened. In terms of World Cup surprises it was right up there with North Korea beating Italy in 1966.

And yet the German team was forgotten almost as soon as the final whistle blew, while the Hungarians are remembered lyrically by people who never saw them play, such is the stamp they left, the force of their legend. That German team was simply forgotten by the football world just as the identity of the 2004 European Cup and Spanish league champions would be. Some will think that is unfair, especially in Porto and Valencia, but there it is. The gloriously failed Real Madrid of 2004, in contrast, would resound down the ages.

Why is that? Because, beyond all the theories, there is one great truth. That scores are short but art is long. As Johan Cruyff once said in a conversation with Valdano that, while results were a mere circumstance 'if you have the best players, you've already won'. We forget results, we lose count of the numbers, but we remember great dramas that occur on the football field, magnificent passages of play and we remember – above all – the great players. We preserve images of them in our minds, indelibly till the day we die, because what makes them great is that they are unique, that they have a style, a way of playing the old, old game that is entirely and memorably their own. So you say the word 'Maradona' to a football fan and a clear, sharp mental image – as well as an atmosphere that was special to Maradona – immediately comes to mind. You say 'Pelé', for those old enough to have seen him, and the same thing. 'Cruyff', the same again.

That was why Florentino Pérez was on to something quite brilliant when he decided what he had to do was bring the greatest available talent to Real Madrid. That was why, when Pérez stood for re-election to the Real presidency in July 2004, barely six weeks after that calamitous 4-1 defeat at home to Real Sociedad, he won with nearly ninety-five per cent of the vote – the biggest margin of victory in the history of the club. Pérez's genius was to understand that, no matter the vagaries of the results, the great ones captured the imagination like no one else, allowing people everywhere – himself not excluded – to dream, to feel *ilusión*, while by the happiest of coincidence also enabling his club to make money, and keep the dream going by adding still more great players year after year to his team. Let's go through the players of the white Light Brigade, the magnificent six whose memory people will still be savouring 500 years from now.

Beckham: who made up for his lack of all-round talent by striking the ball with unmatched sweetness and elegance, creating an image that all who saw him would never quite be able to eliminate from their minds. Roberto Carlos: the electric pace, the power in the shot, the quintessentially Brazilian joy of living in the way he played. Raúl: a dour Castillian on the field of play, so hunched, so remorselessly driven, so intelligent, so clinically cold. Figo: a man of iron who possessed all the skills – all of them. Ronaldo: power and grace, a buffalo and a panther, combined. Zidane: Zinedine Zidane, an unforgettably melodious name for an unforgettably melodious football player.

To have seen Zidane play is one of the joys or, depending on your circumstances, consolations that life has offered at the end of the twentieth century and start of the twenty-first. Other people, those who do not respond to football the way so many hundreds of millions of us do, will derive their joys and consolations – if they are as lucky as we are – from other art forms. One day towards Christmas 2003 I was in Rome walking down the *Via Torino* past the *Teatro dell'Opera*. High up on an old grey wall, on one side of the theatre building, I saw a stone plaque with the following words engraved on it:

RUDOLF NUREYEV
IN QUESTO TEATRO HA ESPRESSO
LA SUA ARTE SUBLIME.
IL TEATRO DELL'OPERA
LO RICORDA.

'Rudolf Nureyev in this theatre has expressed his sublime art. The Teatro dell'Opera remembers him.'

Nureyev did not need to score goals, to win trophies, to get 'results'. He just was what he was, a talent for the ages. Zidane, like Nureyev, will one day have to stop dancing. He will leave a huge vacuum, he will be missed terribly. When that day comes they must put on a wall of the Bernabéu a plaque in his honour. It must say that here, on this stage, Zidane expressed his sublime art. The world of football remembers him.

Acknowledgements

There are two categories of people that I must thank. Those who helped me with this book knowingly and those who had no idea they were being used.

In the latter group first mention must go to Spain's two great sports newspapers, *Marca* and *AS*, and the terrific reporters each has. Daily immersion in their pages has contributed greatly to the fun I have had working on this book.

My morning ritual has not been complete without scouring the sports pages of the British press on the internet. I can say with my hand on my heart that this book is not 'a clippings job' – or, to borrow a Mexican phrase, a mish-mash of 'refried' newspaper articles – but the journalists that have become my unwitting breakfast companions these past months have instructed and entertained me in equal measure.

Of those journalists who have knowingly helped, special thanks are due to my colleagues on *el País*, Santiago Segurola, José Sámano and Diego Torres, all in their different ways quite brilliant sports writers. Reading them I have learnt so much about football; lunching with them I have learnt even more.

The borderline lunatic enthusiasm for the game of my good friend and e-mail pal Matt Tench – sports editor of the *Independent*, last time I looked – has egged my own madness along. If I get a bit too over-excited at times in these pages, blame him.

On the subject of friends, big thanks to Stephen Robinson who read the book when it was in its early stages and did me the immeasurable service of setting me straight, when I was heading in the wrong direction. Richard Askwith, with a love that surpasseth understanding, read the whole thing twice. His comments and suggestions were as sharp and valuable as I expected from a newspaper editor who has been improving my work unfailingly for over a decade.

James Lemoyne not only thought of the book in the first place and helped me hugely with the original proposal, he then read the first draft of the manuscript and submitted copious suggestions on how to make it better. If any credit is due this book, he deserves a lot of it.

Anne McDermid, my agent, did a spectacularly efficient job getting my proposal out there. Within ten days of my writing it − surely some kind of a record − we had clinched a deal with Bloomsbury. Mike Jones, my editor at Bloomsbury, must be saluted for his rashness in buying the book in the first place, and for the steady wisdom he has shown in guiding it through to completion. My copy editor at Bloomsbury, Nicola Barr, improved every single sentence she touched.

The editors of the Spanish version of my book, Adolfo García Ortega and Elena Ramirez of *Seix Barral*, were each in their way extraordinary. Adolfo's eye for the big picture, his cool philosophy, sustained me at a stage in the writing of the book when I was beginning to go perilously wobbly. Elena's relentless hard work and passion for the project was a source of constant inspiration.

At Real Madrid, thanks are due all over the place. To Jorge Valdano, Carlos Queiroz and Ignacio Frauca, each of whom has moved on to other things. To Paco Navacerrada, Marta Santiesteban and Javi Coll, who were as helpful as they were kind. And to the big men, Carlos Martinez de Albornoz, José Angel Sánchez and Florentino Pérez, who opened the doors of the club to me.

As for the players, well, I saw every single game of the 2003/2004 season and while they did not always achieve the results they sought, watching them perform has been its own reward. No matter whether this book turns out to be a success or a disaster, or something in between, seeing the *Galácticos* in action week in, week out over a year has been a privilege and a joy that I shall treasure for the rest of my days.

Index

a note on the author

John Carlin, currently living in Spain, has been a foreign correspondent for many British newspapers. A football fanatic, he covered
the World Cup in 2002 for the *Observer* and *el País*. In the writing
of this book he has had unprecedented access to the Real Madrid
team, travelling with them to matches, conducting extensive interviews with the players, the coaching staff, the directors and the
charismatic and driven chairman Florentino Pérez.

a note on the type

The text of this book is set in Bembo. This type was first used in 1495 by the Venetian printer Aldus Manutius for Cardinal Bembo's *De Aetna*, and was cut for Manutius by Francesco Griffo. It was one of the types used by Claude Garamond (1480–1561) as a model for his Romain de L'Université, and so it was the forerunner of what became standard European type for the following two centuries. Its modern form follows the original types and was designed for Monotype in 1929.